ANDREW JACKSON

First printing: February 2011

Copyright © 2011 by Attic Books. All rights reserved. No part of this book may be used or reproduced in any manner whatsoever without written permission of the publisher, except in the case of brief quotations in articles and reviews.

For information write:
New Leaf Publishing Group, P.O. Box 726, Green Forest, AR 72638.
Attic Books is a division of the New Leaf Publishing Group, Inc.

ISBN-13: 978-0-89051-603-4

Library of Congress Number: 2010919215

Printed in the United States of America

Please visit our website for other great titles: www.nlpg.com

Originally published in 1850

Entered according to Act of Congress, in the year 1850, by
GEO. H. DERBY & CO.,
In the Clerk's Office for the Northern District of New York.

JEWETT, THOMAS, & CO.,
STEREOTYPERS AND PRINTERS,
Buffalo, N. Y.

LIFE

AND

PUBLIC SERVICES

OF

GEN. ANDREW JACKSON

SEVENTH PRESIDENT OF THE UNITED STATES;

INCLUDING

THE MOST IMPORTANT OF HIS STATE PAPERS.

EDITED BY JOHN S. JENKINS, A. M.

WITH

THE EULOGY,

DELIVERED AT WASHINGTON CITY, JUNE 21, 1845.

BY HON. GEORGE BANCROFT.

ORIGINALLY PUBLISHED BY:
GEO. H. DERBY AND CO
BUFFALO

1850.

PREFACE.

THE following Memoirs hardly require an introduction to the American reader. The life of ANDREW JACKSON is so intimately connected with the history of the country, that the careful student of the one, will not rest satisfied, until he is able fully to understand and appreciate the other. Whatever may be the views entertained in regard to his merits as a warrior, or his abilities as a statesman, his conduct in both capacities was such as must necessarily command attention. His admirers will always be eager to discover some new object for their remembrance and regard; while those who are unwilling to approve his course, either in the camp or the cabinet, will feel impelled, from curiosity, if from no other motive, to examine the incidents of his memorable life. There are many features in his character, and those by no means of the least importance, which all will deem worthy of commendation; and none can be so much influenced by the prejudices which have survived the termination of his earthly career, as to withhold the appropriate tribute of their respect.

A large portion of the matter to be found in these pages has been heretofore published, in different shapes. While the writer has not hesitated to make free and liberal use of such materials as were within his reach, both the language and the arrangement have, in all cases, been so modified and changed, as to harmonize with his desire of giving to the public, a fair, candid, and impartial life, of the distinguished citizen and soldier whose name appears on the title-page of the volume. But little merit, therefore, is claimed on the score of originality; and if those for whom it has been prepared, are in any degree gratified by its appearance, the labor bestowed upon it will be amply rewarded.

An attempt has been made, which it is hoped may not be regarded as altogether unsuccessful, to present a full and complete account of the early history of General Jackson, his campaigns against the

Indians, his brilliant achievements during the war of 1812, and his official acts as governor of Florida. A general outline of his administration of the national government is also given; but for reasons which must be obvious, the space devoted to this purpose is comparatively brief. Less could not have been said, without marring the completeness of the work; and, on the other hand, had the text been more full and explicit, political sympathies and affinities might have been manifested, which ought to be carefully concealed.

CONTENTS.

CHAPTER I.

                                                                                  PAGE

1767. Introductory remarks—Birth and parentage of Andrew Jackson—His early life—Influence of his mother—War of the Revolution—Colonel Buford surprised and defeated—Martial spirit of the colonists—Andrew Jackson joins the American army—Heroic conduct in defending Captain Lands—Surprise of the Waxhaw settlers at their rendezvous—Escape and capture of Jackson—His stratagem to prevent the seizure of Thompson—Imprisonment at Camden—His release, and death of his brother and mother—Pecuniary difficulties—Commences the study of the law—Is licensed to practice—Appointed Solicitor for the western district of North Carolina—Arrival at Nashville. 1789 12

CHAPTER II.

1789. Early settlements on the Cumberland—Hardships endured by Jackson, in the discharge of his official duties—Escape from the Indians—His presence of mind—Adventures in the wilderness—Locates at Nashville—Fruitless attempts to intimidate him—Indian depredations—Becomes acquainted with Mrs. Robards—His marriage—A member of the Tennessee convention—Chosen a senator in Congress—His resignation, and appointment as a judge of the Supreme Court—Firmness and decision of character as a judge—Difficulty with Governor Sevier—Resigns his office, and devotes himself to agricultural pursuits. 1804 24

CHAPTER III.

1804. Fondness of General Jackson for horses—Duel with Dickinson—Forms a mercantile partnership—Pecuniary difficulties—Adventure with the Choctaw agent—Affray with Colonel Benton—Their subsequent friendship for each other—Hostilities with Great Britain—Declaration of war in 1812—Jackson raises a volunteer force—Their services accepted by government—Ordered to embark for Natchez—Arrival of the troops, and order to disband them—His disobedience of orders—Attempt of General Wilkinson to prevent the return of the volunteers—Object of the order—Jackson's decision exhibited—Shares the privations of the soldiers on their homeward march—Return, and disbandment of his force. 1813 . 37

CHAPTER IV.

1813. Depredations committed by the Creeks on the borders of Tennessee and Kentucky—Attack on Fort Mimms—Preparations for war—Jackson calls out the volunteers and militia—Address to the troops—Takes the field—Enforces strict military discipline—Rapid march to Huntsville—Delay in forwarding supplies—Thwarted in his movements by General Cocke—Jealousy of the latter—Scarcity of provisions—Efforts of Jackson to procure supplies—Address to the soldiers on entering the enemy's country—Arrival at the Ten Islands—Difficulty with the contractors—Destitute condition of the army—Battle of Tallushatchee—Humanity of Jackson—His adoption of an Indian boy. 1813 50

CHAPTER V.

1813. Erection of Fort Strother, and establishment of a depot on the Coosa—Continued difficulties growing out of the movements of General Cocke—Battle of Talladega—Gallant conduct of Colonel Carroll and Lieutenant-Colonel Dyer—Destitution of the army—Generosity and benevolence of Jackson—His example in submitting to privations—Anecdote of the acorns—Discontent among the troops—Mutiny suppressed by his firmness and resolution—His appeal to the contractors to furnish supplies—Answer to the overtures of peace made by the Hillabee tribes—Efforts to raise additional troops—Letter to his friend in Tennessee—Demand of the volunteers to be discharged, on the ground that their term of service had expired—Reply of Jackson—His unflinching determination—Suppression of the mutiny, and return of the volunteers. 1813 63

CHAPTER VI.

PAGE

1814. Arrival of recruits—Battle of Emuckfaw—Return of the army—Ambuscade of the enemy—Battle of Enotochopco—Bravery of General Carroll and Lieutenant Armstrong—Return to Fort Strother—The army reinforced—Battle of Tohopeka—Kindness of Jackson to a prisoner—Preparations to attack Hoithlewalle—Address to the troops—The Indians abandon their towns at Jackson's approach—Termination of the campaign—Operations of the British at Pensacola—Conduct of the Spanish governor—Proclamation of Colonel Nicholls—Unsuccessful attack on Fort Bowyer—Jackson marches to Pensacola and demolishes it. 1814 82

CHAPTER VII.

1814. Jackson marches to New Orleans—Preparations to defend the city—Surrounded by traitors and spies—Situation of the country—Strength of the British expedition—Firmness of Jackson—The city placed under martial law—Vigorous measures rendered absolutely necessary—Landing of the British—Alarm in the city—Jackson determines to attack them—Disposition of his forces—Battle on the night of the twenty-third of December—Gallant conduct of the American troops—Repulse of the British—The complete triumph of the Americans prevented by the darkness of the night—Adventure of Colonels Dyer and Gibson—The Americans fall back to a new position, and prepare to fortify it—Effect of the battle. 1814 94

CHAPTER VIII.

1814. The Americans fortify their position—Jackson's peremptory orders to Major Lacoste—Defence of the Pass Barrataria—Captain Lafitte—Attack made by the British on the 28th of December—Defensive preparations hastened—Death of Colonel Henderson—Disaffection in New Orleans—Information communicated to the British fleet—Stratagem of Mr. Shields—Conduct of the Louisiana legislature—Patriotic reply of Jackson to the committee—Attempt to supply his troops with arms—Gallantry of Colonel Hinds—Cannonade on the 1st of January—Position of the American army—Jackson's orders to the Frenchman to defend his property—Defences on the right bank of the river—Caution of Jackson in concealing the number of his troops. 1815 113

CONTENTS

CHAPTER IX.

1815. Arrival of fresh troops from Kentucky—Preparations of both armies for an attack—The disposition of Jackson's force made known to the British by a deserter—Success of Colonel Thornton on the right bank of the river—Eagerness of the American soldiers for an engagement—Activity and energy of Jackson—The eighth of January—Advance of the British towards the American intrenchments—Destructive fire from the fortifications—Repulse of the British—Death of Sir Edward Packenham—Terrible havoc made in the ranks of the enemy—Bravery of Colonel Rennie—Number of killed and wounded in the battle—Watchword of the British army—Generous benevolence of the American soldiers—An armistice proposed by General Lambert and accepted, with modifications—Brave conduct of the American troops—Want of arms prevents Jackson from capturing the whole British army—English version of the battle. 1815 138

CHAPTER X.

1815. Gratitude of the citizens of New Orleans to their deliverer—Jackson strengthens his position—Anonymous publications inciting his troops to revolt—The author placed in arrest—Judge Hall ordered into custody for his interference—The British retire to their shipping—Treaty of peace signed—Cessation of hostilities—Jackson submits to the fine imposed by the judge—Farewell address to his troops—Return to Nashville—Depredations committed by the Seminole Indians—Jackson ordered to take command of the southern army—Enters Florida with his army—Execution of Arbuthnot and Ambrister—Capture of St. Marks and Pensacola—Termination of hostilities—Jackson's conduct approved—Appointed governor of Florida—Administration of his judicial duties—Difficulty with the Ex-governor, Callava—Jackson's ill health compels him to return home. 1821 155

CHAPTER XI.

1821. Jackson resigns his office in the army—Testimonials of public respect—A candidate for the Presidency—Defeated in the House of Representatives—Election of Mr. Adams—Course of Jackson's friends—His renomination—Warmth of the contest—Elected president—Death of his wife—Kindness to her relatives—His first message—Veto of the Maysville road bill—Dissolution of the Cabinet—Opposition to the United States Bank—Veto message—Re-elected president—Difficulty with the nullifiers—Assaulted by Lieutenant Randolph—Removal of the deposits—Public excitement—Controversy with France—Retirement to private life. 1837 . . 170

CHAPTER XII.

PAGE

1837. Ill health of General Jackson—Arrival at the Hermitage—Influence with his party—Friendly to the annexation of Texas—His occupations—Embarrassed in his pecuniary affairs—Refunding of the fine imposed by Judge Hall—Failure of his health—His last illness—His Christian resignation and death—Honors paid to his memory—Remarks of Reverdy Johnson—Speech of Daniel Webster—Character of Jackson—His qualifications as a soldier and statesman—Attachment to his friends—His personal appearance—His patriotism. 1845 184

CHAPTER XIII.

Bancroft's Eulogy 194
Inaugural Address 219
Maysville Road Veto 223
Message to the United States Senate on returning the Bank Bill 239
Proclamation on the Nullification Question 261
Extracts from the Protest 285
Sixth Annual Message 304
Message in relation to Texas 342
Farewell Address 348
Letter to Commodore Elliott, declining a Sarcophagus . . . 371
Last Will and Testament 373
Dr. Bethune's Discourse 379

LIFE

OF

ANDREW JACKSON.

CHAPTER I.

1767. Introductory remarks—Birth and parentage of Andrew Jackson—His early life—Influence of his mother—War of the Revolution—Colonel Buford surprised and defeated—Martial spirit of the colonists—Andrew Jackson joins the American army—Heroic conduct in defending Captain Lands—Surprise of the Waxhaw settlers at their rendezvous—Escape and capture of Jackson—His stratagem to prevent the seizure of Thompson—Imprisonment at Camden—His release, and death of his brother and mother—Pecuniary difficulties—Commences the study of the law—Is licensed to practice—Appointed Solicitor for the western district of North Carolina—Arrival at Nashville. 1789.

IN seasons of high party excitement, it is not to be expected, that full and impartial justice will at all times be rendered to the statesman or politician. There is an ancient French maxim, which cautions the legislator to "think of the rising generation, rather than of that which is passed." It is not amid the prejudices and jealousies of the present, but in the enlightened judgment of the far-off future that he must look for his reward. Cotemporaneous history is always hasty, and often unjust, in its conclusions; but "the sober second thought" of posterity is ever prompt to repair the wrong. It was the fortune of the subject of these memoirs to occupy, for a series of years, a prominent place in the public estimation, as the leader of the political party to which he was attached. During that time, much was said, both for and against him, which it would scarcely become the dignity of history

HIS YOUTH

to record; nor would his most devoted admirer ask, at this day, that any thing should be written concerning him, except what was conceived in the same spirit that prompted the memorable remark of the iron-hearted Cromwell to young Lely, "Paint me as I am!" His death has hushed the embittered passions of the hour, and public opinion has already settled down upon a conviction highly favorable to his memory. Few men have ever lived, who exhibited, in a more remarkable degree, those salient points of character, calculated to enforce attention and respect, or possessed those peculiar traits of disposition, which are sure to inspire the warm and devoted attachment of personal friends. His life and his character, both as a public and private citizen, the storied incidents of his military career, and the important services rendered to the country, are now regarded, by general consent, as the common property of the nation. Like truly great men, he has left the impress of his mind upon the age in which he lived; and there is not a single American, whose heart is alive to the emotions of patriotism, but feels it beat with a quicker and warmer glow, at the mention of his honored name.

Andrew Jackson was descended from a Scotch family, who emigrated to the north of Ireland, at a very remote period. His ancestors suffered many hardships, on account of the cruel and arbitrary exactions of the English government. The continuance of these grievances, which at times almost passed the limits of human endurance, induced his father, Andrew Jackson, after whom he was named, to emigrate to this country, with his wife and two sons, Hugh and Robert, in the year 1765. He landed at Charleston, in South Carolina, and shortly afterwards purchased a tract of land, in what was then called the "Waxhaw settlement," about forty-five miles above Camden, and near the boundary line of North Carolina, where he settled with his family. His son, Andrew, was born on the 15th day of March, 1767, about two years subsequent to the arrival of his parents in this country.

Soon after the birth of young Andrew, his father died: leaving him, and his two brothers, to the sole care and guardianship of their mother, who appears to have been a most exemplary woman. She possessed many excellent qualities, both of head and heart; and her children were, early in life, deeply imbued with the straight forward resoluteness of purpose, and Spartan heroism of character, for which she was distinguished. Among the many noble mothers, whose sons have reaped the rich harvest of renown springing from the seed planted by their hands, none deserve higher praise or commendation. To the lessons she inculcated on the youthful minds of her sons, may, in a great measure, be attributed that fixed opposition to British tyranny and oppression, which they afterwards manifested. Often would she spend the winter evenings, in recounting to them the sufferings of their grandfather at the siege of Carrickfergus, and the oppressions exercised by the nobility of Ireland over the laboring poor; impressing it upon them as a first duty, to expend their lives, if it should become necessary, in defending and supporting the natural rights of man.

As they inherited but a small patrimony from their father, it was impossible that all the sons could receive an expensive education. The two eldest, therefore, were only taught the rudiments of their mother tongue, at a common country school. But Andrew, being intended by his mother for the ministry, was sent to a flourishing academy at the Waxhaw meeting-house, superintended by Mr. Humphries. Here he was placed on the study of the dead languages, and continued until the revolutionary war, extending its ravages into that section of South Carolina where he then was, rendered it necessary that every one should either betake himself to the American standard, seek protection with the enemy, or flee his country.

When the revolutionary war first broke out, in 1775, Andrew Jackson was but eight years old, and it was a long time before its horrors were felt in the immediate vicinity of his residence. But from his youth up, he was familiar with the story of the repeated aggressions and insults, which forced the American colonists to resort to the last remedy of an injured people. He eagerly listened

HIS YOUTH

to the thrilling accounts that reached his quiet neighborhood, of the heroic deeds performed by his brave countrymen, at Lexington and Bunker-hill, Saratoga and Monmouth; and while he listened, his heart burned with the fire of an incipient patriotism, to avenge the wrongs of his native land. The young and middle-aged men around him were constantly training themselves for any emergency, and his mother encouraged, rather than checked, his growing passion for a soldier's life, instead of the peaceful profession for which he was designed. It was a critical time in the destinies of the infant republic, and she required the aid of every stout hand and strong heart, whether it beat beneath the surplice of the priest, or the rough habiliments of the back-woodsman.

An opportunity was soon afforded, for him to gratify his ardent desire of mingling in the deadly strife which had imbrued the American soil with blood. South Carolina was invaded by the British, under General Prevost, in 1779, and in the month of May of the following year, Colonel Buford and about four hundred men under his command were overtaken by Colonel Tarleton, who had been despatched to cut off the party by Lord Cornwallis, with a force of seven hundred men, and an indiscriminate slaughter ensued, although little or no resistance was offered. Many begged for quarter in vain. The only answer was a stroke of the sabre, or a thrust of the bayonet. This act of atrocious barbarity was followed by others of a similar character. Men could not sleep in their own houses unguarded, without danger of surprise and murder. Even boys, who were stout enough to carry muskets, were induced, by a regard for their own safety, as well as from inclination, to incur the dangers of men. Young Jackson and his brothers had their guns and horses, and were almost always in company with some armed party of their kindred or neighbors. Hugh, who was the eldest of the three, was present at the battle of Stono, and lost his life, from the excessive heat of the weather and the fatigue of the day. Shortly after this event, Mrs. Jackson retired before the invading army, with her two remaining sons, Robert and Andrew, into North Carolina. She remained there but a short time, and, on returning to the Waxhaws, both Robert and Andrew joined the American army, and were present at the battle of Hanging Rock, on the sixth of August, 1780, in which the corps to which they belonged particularly distinguished itself. In the month of September, Mrs. Jackson and her sons, with most of the Waxhaw settlers, were again compelled to retire into North Carolina; from which they returned in February, 1781, as soon as they heard that Lord Cornwallis had crossed the Yadkin.

It was during the trying scenes of this period of the revolutionary struggle, that Andrew Jackson gave the first illustration of that quickness of thought, and promptitude of action, which afterwards placed him in the front rank of military commanders. A Whig captain, named Lands, who had been absent from home for some time, desired to spend a night with his family. Robert and Andrew Jackson, with one of the Crawfords, and five others, constituted his guard. There were nine men and seven muskets. Having no special apprehensions of an attack, they lay down on their arms, and, with the exception of a British deserter, who was one of the party, went to sleep. Lands' house was in the centre of an enclosed yard, and had two doors, facing east and west. Before the east door stood a forked apple-tree. In the southwest corner of the yard were a corncrib and stable under one roof, ranging east and west. On the south was a wood, and through it passed the road by which the house was approached.

A party of Tories became apprized of Lands' return, and determined to surprise and kill him. Approaching through the wood, and tying their horses behind the stable, they divided into two parties, one advancing round the east end of the stable towards the east door of the house, and the other round the west end towards the west door. At this moment, the wakeful soldier, hearing a noise in the direction of the stable, went out to see what was the matter, and perceived the party which were entering the yard at the east end of the building. Running back in terror, he seized Andrew Jackson, who was nearest the door, by the hair, exclaiming, "The Tories are upon us." Our young hero ran out, and, putting his gun through the fork of the apple-tree, hailed the approaching band. Having repeated his hail without an answer, and perceiving the party rapidly advancing and but a few rods distant, he fired. A volley was returned, which killed the soldier, who, having aroused the inmates of the house, had followed young Jackson, and was standing near him. The other band of Tories had now emerged from the west end of the stable, and mistaking the discharge of the advance party, then nearly on a line between them and the apple-tree, for the fire of a sallying party from the house, commenced a sharp fire upon their own friends. Thus both parties were brought to a stand. Young Andrew, after discharging his gun, returned into the house; and, with two others, commenced a fire from the west door, where both of his companions were shot down, one of them with a mortal wound. The Tories still kept up the fire upon each other, as well as upon the house, until, startled by the sound of a cavalry bugle in the distance, they betook themselves to their horses, and fled. The charge was sounded by a Major Isbel, who had not a man with him, but, hearing the firing, and knowing that Lands was attacked, he gave the blast upon his trumpet to alarm the assailants.

The British commander, having been advised of the return of the Waxhaw settlers, despatched Major Coffin, with a corps of light dragoons, a company of infantry, and a considerable number of Tories, for their capture and destruction. Hearing of their approach, the settlers appointed the Waxhaw meeting-house as a place of rendezvous, and about forty of them, among whom were the two Jacksons, had assembled there on the day appointed, and were waiting for a friendly company under Captain Nisbett. When the enemy approached, their commanding officer placed the Tories in front, in order to conceal the dragoons; and the little band of settlers were completely deceived by the stratagem. Supposing the reinforcement for which they had been waiting was approaching, they were prepared to welcome them as friends, but the moment after they discovered their unfortunate mistake. Eleven of the number were taken prisoners, and the rest sought for safety in flight. The two Jacksons were among those who escaped, and temporarily eluded pursuit. They remained together during the ensuing night, and on the approach of morning concealed themselves in a thicket on the bank of a small creek, not far from the house of Lieutenant Crawford, who had been wounded and made prisoner. Becoming very hungry, they left their horses in the wood, and ventured out to Crawford's for food. But a party of Tories, who were well acquainted with the country, and the passes through the forest, unfortunately passed the creek, in the mean time, at the very point where the horses and baggage had been left; and, guided by one of their number, whose name was Johnson, they approached the house, in company with a small body of dragoons, and presented themselves at the door, before the young Jacksons were aware of their approach.

Resistance and flight were alike hopeless, and neither was attempted. Mrs. Crawford, with several children, one of whom was at the breast, were the inmates of the house. A scene of destruction immediately took place. All the glass, crockery, and other furniture, were dashed in pieces. The beds were ripped open, and the feathers scattered to the winds. The clothing of the whole family, men, women, and children, was cut and torn into fragments. Even the children's clothes shared the fate of the rest. Mercy for the wife and little ones of a husband and father, who was already wounded and in their hands, and doomed to imprisonment, if not death, touched not the hearts of these remorseless men, and nothing was left to the terrified and wretched family, but the clothes they had on, and a desolate habitation. No attempt was made, by the British officer commanding, to arrest this destruction. While it was in progress, he ordered Andrew Jackson to clean his muddy boots. The young soldier refused, claiming to be treated with the respect due to a prisoner of war. Instead of admiring this manly spirit in one so young, the cowardly ruffian struck at his

TAKEN PRISONER BY THE BRITISH 19

head with his sword; but, throwing up his left hand, the intended victim received a gash upon it, the scar of which he carried to the grave. Turning to Robert Jackson, the officer ordered him to perform the menial task, and, receiving a like refusal, aimed a furious blow at his head also, and inflicted a wound from which he never recovered.

After these exhibitions of ferocity, the party set Andrew Jackson upon a horse, and ordered him, on pain of instant death, to lead them to the house of a well-known Whig, by the name of Thompson. Apprehending that Thompson was at home, it occurred to his young friend that he might save him by a stratagem. At that time, when men were at home, they generally kept a look-out to avoid surprise, and had a horse ready for flight. Instead of leading the party by the usual route, young Andrew took them through woods and fields, which brought them over an eminence in sight of the house, at the distance of half a mile. On reaching the summit, he beheld Thompson's horse tied to his rack, a sure sign that his owner was at home. The British dragoons darted forward, and, in breathless apprehension, Andrew Jackson kept his eye upon Thompson's horse. With inexpressible joy, he saw Thompson, while the dragoons were still a few hundred yards distant, rush out, mount his horse, dash into the creek which ran foaming by, and in a minute ascend the opposite bank. He was then out of pistol shot, and as his pursuers dared not swim the rapid stream, he stopped long enough to shout execration and defiance, and then rode leisurely off.

Andrew Jackson and his brother, with about twenty other prisoners, were mounted on captured horses, and started for Camden, over forty miles distant. Not a mouthful of food, or drop of water, was given them on the route. The streams which they forded had been swollen by recent rains; but when they stooped to take up a little water in the palms of their hands, to assuage their burning thirst, they were ordered to desist by the brutal guard.

Arrived at Camden, they were confined, with about two hundred and fifty other prisoners, in a redoubt surrounding the jail, and overlooking the country to the north. No attention was paid to their wounds or their wants. They had no beds, nor any substitute; and their only food was a scanty supply of bad bread. They were robbed of a portion of their clothing, taunted by Tories with being rebels, and assured that they would be hanged. Andrew Jackson himself was stripped of his jacket and shoes. With a refinement of cruelty, the Jacksons and their cousin, Thomas Crawford, two of them severely wounded, were separated as soon as their relationship was known, and kept in perfect ignorance of each other's condition or fate. In aggravation of their sufferings, the small-pox made its appearance among them. Not a step was taken to stay its progress or mitigate its afflictions. Without physicians or nurses, denied even the kind attentions and sympathy of relatives who were fellow-prisoners, their keepers left them to perish, not only without compassion, but with apparent satisfaction.

One day Andrew Jackson was sunning himself in the entrance of his prison, when the officer of the guard, apparently struck with his youthful appearance, entered into conversation with him. With characteristic energy, the fearless lad described to him the condition of the prisoners; and among the rest, their sufferings from the scantiness and bad quality of their food. Immediately meat was added to their bread, and there was otherwise a decided improvement. The Provost was a Tory from New York; and it was afterwards alleged that he withheld the meat he had contracted to supply for the support of the prisoners, to feed a gang of negroes, which he had collected from the plantations of the Whigs, with intent to convert them to his own use.

During the confinement of the Waxhaw prisoners at Camden, General Greene made his unsuccessful attack on the British forces at that post under Lord Rawdon. The American army was encamped on Hobkirk's Hill, about a mile distant, and in full view of the redoubt in which the prisoners were confined. On the morning of the 24th of April, Andrew Jackson became convinced, from what he saw and heard, that a battle was soon to take place. He was exceedingly anxious to witness the conflict, but the thick plank fence that extended around the redoubt, completely shut out the view of the surrounding country. Determined that he would not be foiled in his wish, he set himself at work with an old razor-blade, which had been given to the prisoners to eat their rations with, and by working the greater part of the night, he contrived to cut one of the knots out of a plank, and through this obtained a view of Greene's encampment, and of the sanguinary struggle which took place on the following day.

In a few days after the battle before Camden, the two Jacksons were released, in pursuance of a partial exchange effected by the intercessions and exertions of their mother, and Captain Walker of the militia. While he was confined in prison, Robert had suffered greatly from the wound in his head which had never been dressed. Inflammation of the brain soon after ensued, which brought him to his grave, in a few days after his liberation. The mother also, worn out with anxiety and solicitude for her children, and her incessant efforts to relieve the sufferings of the prisoners who had been brought from her own neighborhood, was taken sick, and expired in a few weeks, near the lines of the enemy in the vicinity of Charleston. These repeated afflictions were keenly felt by young Jackson, and it was some time before he entirely recovered from the shock occasioned by so sudden a bereavement. He was tenderly attached to his mother and brother, and as they were his only relatives, their death must have been a severe blow to him. The buoyancy of youth, however, enabled him to bear up manfully against misfortune, and he soon after entered into the enjoyment of his estate, which, though small, was sufficient to have given him a liberal education. Unfortunately he had become quite intimate with a number of the most polished citizens of Charleston, who had retired to the Waxhaw settlement, during the occupation of that city by the British, and had contracted habits, and imbibed tastes, which it was unwise in him to indulge. He accompanied his friends on their return to Charleston; and, as he determined not to be outdone by his associates, his money was expended so profusely that his whole patrimony was soon exhausted, and he was left with nothing but a fine horse which he had taken from the Waxhaws. The animal itself was at length staked against a sum of money, in a game of "rattle and snap." Jackson won the game; and, forming a sudden resolution, he pocketed the money, bade adieu to his friends, and returned home.

This occurrence took place in the winter of 1784, and immediately after his return to the Waxhaws, Jackson collected the remains of his little property, with the intention of acquiring a profession, and preparing himself to enter on the busy scenes of life. After pursuing the study of the languages, and other desultory branches of education, under Mr. McCulloch, in that part of Carolina which was then called the New Acquisition, near Hill's Iron Works, for several months, he concluded to abandon the pulpit for which he had been designed by his mother, and embraced the legal profession. In pursuance of this determination, he repaired to Salisbury, in North Carolina, and commenced the study of the law, under Spruce McCay, Esq., afterwards one of the judges of that state, and subsequently continued it under Colonel John Stokes. Having remained at Salisbury until the winter of 1786, he obtained a license from the judges to practice law, and continued in the state until the spring of 1788. As an evidence of the estimation in which his talents were at that time held by the influential men of North Carolina, he soon after received from the governor the appointment of Solicitor for the western district of that state, of which the present state of Tennessee then formed a part.

The observations he was enabled to make while engaged in the study of his profession, had convinced him that North Carolina presented few inducements to a young attorney; and recollecting that he stood solitary in life, without relations to aid him in the outset, when innumerable difficulties arise and retard success, he determined to seek a new country. But for this he might have again returned to his native state. The death, however, of every relation he had, had wiped away all those endearing recollections and circumstances which attach the mind to the place of its nativity. The western district of the state was often spoken of, as presenting flattering prospects to adventurers, and his official appointment in that quarter happened quite opportunely to enable him to carry out his intention of visiting that section of the country. In the year 1788, at the age of twenty-one years, he accompanied Judge McNairy, who was going out to hold the first Supreme Court that had ever sat in the district. Having reached the Holston, they ascertained that it would be impossible to arrive at the time appointed for the session of the court; and therefore took up their residence, for some time, at Jonesborough, then the principal seat of justice in the western district. They recommenced their journey, in October, 1789, and passing through an extensive uninhabited country, reached Nashville in the same month.

CHAPTER II.

1789. Early settlements on the Cumberland—Hardships endured by Jackson, in the discharge of his official duties—Escape from the Indians—His presence of mind—Adventures in the wilderness—Locates at Nashville—Fruitless attempts to intimidate him—Indian depredations—Becomes acquainted with Mrs. Robards—His marriage—A member of the Tennessee convention—Chosen a senator in Congress—His resignation, and appointment as a judge of the Supreme Court—Firmness and decision of character as a judge—Difficulty with Governor Sevier—Resigns his office, and devotes himself to agricultural pursuits. 1804.

AT the time of the first visit made by Andrew Jackson, to the infant settlements on the Cumberland river, including that at French creek, near the present site of Nashville, almost all the settlers were residing in stations, and it was several years before it was entirely safe for them to spread over the country, and live in separate cabins. While the Shawanese from the north were carrying on perpetual war with the settlers in Kentucky, the Cherokees and Choctaws from the south were wreaking their vengeance on the intruders upon their hunting-grounds in Tennessee. Twenty-two times during this period of danger and blood, did General Jackson, in the performance of his public and private duties, cross the wilderness of two hundred miles, then intervening between Jonesborough and the settlements on the Cumberland. The hardships and perils of those journeys it is difficult for travellers at the present day duly to appreciate.

In addition to his rider, with a loaded rifle on his shoulder, the patient horse carried upon his back his master's blankets, provisions, and equipments. His food was the foliage of the bushes and the native grass. At a fire kindled from a tinder-box, or the flash of his rifle, the traveller roasted his bacon or wild meat on a stick, and cut it with his hunter's knife, while his fingers served him instead of forks. Wrapped in his blanket, with his rifle for a bed-fellow, and his horse standing by, he slept, with no roof to protect him but the boughs of the forest. Without a water-proof hat or India-rubber coat, he was drenched to the skin by the falling rain. Often when he was hungry with fasting, and a delicious pheasant, or plump deer was before him, he dared not kill it, lest the report of his rifle should give notice of his presence to a lurking savage.

At one time when Jackson was traversing the wilderness alone, he came, after night, and amid torrents of rain, to a creek, the noise of whose tumbling waters, already swollen to a great depth, warned him not to attempt crossing the ford. Dismounting from his horse, and turning his saddle bottom upward, at the root of a tree, he wrapped his blanket around him, and with his rifle in one hand and his bridle in the other, sat upon it, with his horse standing before him, listening to the roaring stream and the pattering of the raindrops on the leaves of the forest, until the return of day enabled him to proceed.

On another occasion, he was in company with three companions, on his way from Jonesborough to the Cumberland. They arrived, just after dark, at the east side of the Emory, where it issues from the mountains, and discovered the fires of a large party of hostile Indians on the opposite bank. The moment the discovery was made, Andrew Jackson, as if by instinct, assumed the direction of the party. He enjoined silence and instant retreat, and having retired some distance into the mountains, directed his companions to quit the road cautiously and at different points, so as to leave no distinct trace behind them, and to reunite, and proceed up the stream, for the purpose of crossing at some ford above and eluding the Indians. Guided by the noise of the waters, they progressed upward among the mountains during the night, and, as soon as it was day, approached the stream. They found it too much swollen to be forded, and too rapid to be swam. Still apprehensive of pursuit, they resumed their march, and about two o'clock in the afternoon reached a place where the stream, after dashing over a rough precipice, spread out with a lake-like surface, broken at a short distance below by another cataract. Here the party, not feeling safe until their trail was broken by the intervening stream, determined to attempt a passage. Binding logs and bushes together with hickory withes, they soon constructed a small raft sufficient to convey three or four men, and affixed two rude oars to the bows, and one as a steering-oar or rudder to the stern. It was cold, March weather, and very important to keep their clothes, blankets, and saddles, as well as their rifles and powder, from getting wet. To that end, it was concluded that Jackson and one of his companions should first cross with every thing but the horses, and that on a second trip, they should be swam over alongside the raft. The craft was freighted accordingly, and pushed off from shore; but in an instant, an irresistible under-current seized the rude flotilla, and hurled it down the stream. For a few moments, Jackson, who was at the oars, regardless of the shouts of his companions, who followed him downward on the bank, struggled with the flood; but, perceiving that farther effort could only end in destruction, he reversed the direction of the raft, in the hope of reaching the shore he had left. Notwithstanding he exerted all his strength, he was unable to bring it to land; and although within a few feet, the suck of the cataract had already seized it. A moment more, and the raft, with its passengers, would have been dashed in pieces, when Jackson, wrenching one of his oars from its fastenings, sprung to the stern, and bracing himself there, held it out to his companions on shore, who seized it, and brought them safe to land. Being reproached for not heeding their first warnings, Jackson coolly replied: "A miss is as good as a mile; you see how near I can graze danger. Come on, and I will save you yet." Re-equipping themselves and horses, they resumed their march up the stream; and after spending another night, supperless, in the woods, found a ford the next day, and, by a circuitous route, reached a log cabin on the road, about forty miles in the rear of the Indian encampment.

At another time, he reached Bean's station, the rendezvous of a party with whom he was to cross the wilderness·

on the evening after they had left. Determined to overtake them, he employed a guide well acquainted with Indian signs and stratagems, and travelled all night. Just before day, they came to the fires where the party had encamped the first part of the night. Following on, they soon discovered, by the trail in the road, that a party of Indians, about twenty-two in number, were in pursuit of their friends ahead. They hastened forward rapidly, until they approached so near the Indians that the water, which the weight of their tread had pressed out of the rotten logs, was not yet dry. The guide now refused to proceed; but Jackson resolved to save his friends, or, at least, hazard his life in the attempt. Dividing provisions, he and his guide proceeded in opposite directions, Jackson cautiously advancing, and watching the tracks of the Indians. At length he saw where they had turned off to the right, probably for the purpose of getting ahead of the party, and attacking them from ambush, or falling upon them in the night. The danger was imminent, and pressing on with increased speed, he overtook his friends before dark. Having crossed a stream which was very deep and partly frozen over, they had halted and kindled fires, at which they were drying their clothes and baggage. Warned of their danger, they immediately resumed their march, and continued it without intermission, during the whole night and the next day. The sky was overcast with clouds, and in the evening it began to snow. While upon the route, they arrived at the log cabins of a party of hunters, and requested shelter and protection; but, contrary to their expectations, for such churlishness was unusual among men of their class, they were rudely refused. The party were therefore compelled to bivouac in the forest. Jackson was wearied with his fatiguing march, and as he had not closed his eyes for two nights, he wrapped himself in his blanket, and laid down upon the ground, where he slept soundly. When he awoke in the morning, he found himself covered with six inches of snow.

The party resumed their march, and reached their destination in safety; but they afterwards learned that the hunters, who had refused them the hospitality of their cabins, had been murdered by the Indians.

In the course of his frequent professional visits made from Jonesborough to the settlement on the Cumberland, the advantages of Nashville as a suitable locality in which to establish himself, attracted Jackson's notice, and he concluded to make it his future place of residence. It had not been his original intention to locate permanently in Tennessee. His visit was merely experimental, and his stay remained to be determined by the prospect that might be disclosed: but finding, soon after his arrival, that a considerable opening was offered for the success of a young attorney, he decided to remain. To a person of refined feelings, the condition of things was far from encouraging. As must be the case in all newly settled countries, society was loosely formed, and united by but few of those ties which have a tendency to enforce the performance of moral duty, and the execution of strict and impartial justice. The young men of the place, who were adventurers from different sections of the union, had become deeply indebted to the merchants. There was but one lawyer in the country, and they had so contrived as to retain him in their business; the consequence was, that the merchants were entirely deprived of the means of enforcing against those gentlemen the execution of their contracts. In this state of things, Jackson made his appearance at Nashville, and, while the creditor class looked to it with great satisfaction, the debtors were sorely displeased. Applications were immediately made to him for his professional services, and on the morning after his arival, he issued seventy writs. To those prodigal gentlemen it was an alarming circumstance; their former security was impaired; but that it might not wholly depart, they determined to force him, in some way or other, to leave the country; and to effect this, broils and quarrels with him were resorted to.

In the state of society then existing in Tennessee, there was a grade of men who prided themselves on their courage and prowess, as mere bullies, and were always ready, like the brute beast, to decide the question of su-

ESTABLISHES HIMSELF AT NASHVILLE 29

periority, by a fight. Equals in standing, who hated, but dared not encounter the fearless Jackson, stimulated this class of men to attack, in the hope of degrading, if they could not destroy him. The first man set upon him, with scarcely a pretence of provocation, was a flax-breaker of great strength and courage, whom he soon reduced to submission with his own winding-blades, the only weapon within his reach. His next encounter was at a court in Sumner county, with a noted bully whom he did not know. While he was conversing with a gentleman, on business, the bully approached, and without saying a word, placed his heels on Jackson's feet. Pushing him off, Jackson seized a slab, and with a forward thrust upon the breast, brought him to the ground. The interference of the crowd put an end to the conflict; but the baffled bully, snatching a stake from the fence, again approached with dreadful imprecations. At the earnest entreaty of Jackson, the crowd retired from between them. Poising his slab, he then advanced, with a firm step and steady eye, upon his antagonist, who dropped his stake at his approach, jumped over the fence, and ran into the woods.

These attempts to intimidate Jackson in the performance of what he conceived to be his duty to his clients, were found wholly unavailing, and were soon abandoned. His enemies were convinced by the first controversy in which they had involved him, that his decision and firmness were such as to leave no hope of effecting any thing through this channel. Disregarding the opposition manifested towards him, he continued, with care and industry, to press forward in his professional course; and his attention soon brought him forward, and introduced him to a profitable practice. The western district of North Carolina having been ceded to the national government, an erected into a territory, in 1790, Jackson was appointed, by president Washington, the United States attorney for the new judicial district, in which capacity he continued to act for several years.

The depredations committed by the Indians, in the vicinity of the Cumberland river, about this time, compelled every man, of necessity, to become a soldier. Unassisted by the government, the settlers were forced to rely, for security, on their own bravery and exertions. Although young, no person was more distinguished than Andrew Jackson, in defending the country against these predatory incursions of the Indians, who continually harassed the frontiers, and not unfrequently approached the heart of the settlements, which were thin, but not widely extended. Frequent expeditions were undertaken from Nashville against them, in most of which he took part. This state of things continued until 1794, when a large party, among whom was Jackson, attacked and destroyed the Indian town of Nickajak, near the Tennessee river. In these affairs, his courage and gallantry were so conspicuous, that the red warriors gave him the appellation of "Sharp Knife," and the hardy hunters who accompanied him were proud of his friendship and esteem.

When Jackson first located himself in Nashville, he boarded, in company with the late Judge Overton, in the family of Mrs. Donelson, a widow lady who had emigrated from Virginia, first to Kentucky, and afterwards to Nashville. Mrs. Robards, her daughter, who afterwards became the wife of Jackson, was then living in the family with her mother, whom she had followed to Tennessee, on account of the ill treatment which she had received at the hands of her husband, who was dissipated in his habits and of a morose and jealous disposition, while she, on the contrary, was celebrated for her gayety, sweetness, and affability. A short time before Jackson became an inmate of the family, a reconciliation had taken place between Robards and his wife; but a second rupture afterwards occurred, and Robards went to Kentucky. His wife soon learned that he intended to compel her to accompany him, and, in the spring of 1791, with the advice of her friends, she determined to descend the river as far as Natchez, in company with Colonel Stark, who was then making preparations for the voyage. At the earnest request of Colonel Stark, Jackson piloted his family through the Indian country. After his return, Judge Overton communicated to him the astounding intelligence, that he was the unconscious cause of the last separation; that it arose from Robards' jealousy of him; and that the circumstance of his accompanying Colonel Stark, who was an elderly man, and apprehensive of danger, had been seized upon by Robards as a ground of divorce, in a petition to the Virginia legislature.

The thought that an innocent woman was suffering so unjustly on his account, made Jackson's sensitive mind most uneasy and unhappy. He immediately sought out Robards and expostulated with him, on the injustice and cruelty of his causeless suspicion; but the interview ended in mutual defiances. At length news came that the Virginia legislature had actually granted the divorce in accordance with Robards' petition. Forthwith Jackson hastened to Natchez, and offered his hand and his heart to the innocent and amiable woman, who had been made so unhappy by false and unfounded accusations, in order that he might give the world the highest evidence in his power of her entire innocence.

Although free to form a new connection, Mrs. Robards declined the proffered offer. But her suitor was not to be denied. His feelings were warmly enlisted in her favor. His attachment for her was ardent and sincere, and when he addressed her in the language of Ruth to Naomi: " Entreat me not to leave thee or to return from following after thee, for where thou goest I will go, where thou lodgest I will lodge, thy people shall be my people, and thy God my God; where thou diest I will die, and there will I be buried," she found herself unable to resist his importunities, and they were soon after married and returned to Tennessee. On arriving there, it was discovered that all the necessary forms to complete the divorce in Virginia had not been finished at the time of the marriage; consequently the ceremony was again performed after their arrival at Nashville. The attachment thus consummated was a source of unfailing pleasure to Andrew Jackson. He was devotedly fond of his wife; after her decease he cherished her memory with an almost holy reverence; and he refused the sarcophagus of the Emperor Severus, that he might not be denied the privilege of being buried by her side.

In the year 1796, measures were taken by the people of Tennessee to form a state government. The acknowledged talents, patriotism, and decision of character, of Andrew Jackson were not to be overlooked on such an occasion, and without solicitation on his part, he was elected one of the members of the convention to frame a state constitution. His good conduct and zeal for the public interest, and the republican feelings and sentiments which were conspicuously manifested in the formation and arrangement of this instrument, brought him more prominently to view; and, without proposing or soliciting the office, he was in the same year elected a member of the House of Representatives in Congress, for the state of Tennessee. The following year, his reputation continuing to increase, and his constituents generally concurring in the wish to elevate him to still higher honors, he was chosen a senator in Congress, and took his seat on the 22d day of November, 1797. About the middle of April, 1798, business of an important and private nature imposed on him the necessity of asking leave of absence, and returning home. Leave was granted, and before the next session he resigned his seat. He was but little more than thirty years of age; and hence scarcely eligible by the constitution, at the time he was elected. The sedition law, about which so much concern and feeling had been manifested through the country, was introduced into the senate by Mr. Lloyd, of Maryland, in June, 1798, and passed that body on the 4th of July following; hence the name of Jackson, owing to his absence from his seat, does not appear on the journals. At the time of the passage of the alien law, and the effort to repeal the stamp act, he was present, and voted with the minority, in accordance with his well-known republican sentiments.

Shortly after his resignation of the office of senator, the legislature of Tennessee, most unexpectedly to himself, conferred upon him the appointment of judge of the Supreme Court, a station which he accepted with reluctance, and from which he withdrew at an early day. His first court was held at Jonesborough, where an incident occurred, illustrative alike of the rudeness of the times and the firmness of the new judge:

A man named Russell Bean was indicted for cutting off the ears of his infant child in a drunken frolic. He was in the courtyard; but such was his strength and ferocity, that the sheriff, not daring to approach him, made a return to the court that "Russell Bean will not be taken." Judge Jackson, with his peculiar emphasis, said that such a return was an absurdity, and could not be received. "He must be taken," said the judge, "and, if necessary, you must summon the *posse comitatus.*" The mortified sheriff retired, and waiting until the court adjourned for dinner, summoned the judges themselves, as part of the *posse.* Conceiving that the object of the sheriff was to avoid a dangerous service, under cover of the judges' refusal to obey the summons, Judge Jackson instantly replied, "Yes, sir, I will attend you, and see that you do *your* duty." Learning that Bean was armed, he requested a loaded pistol, which was put into his hand. He then said to the sheriff: "Advance and arrest him; I will protect you from harm." Bean, armed with a dirk and brace of pistols, assumed an attitude of defiance and desperation. But when the judge drew near, he began to retreat. "Stop and submit to the law," cried the judge. The culprit stopped, threw down his pistols, and replied, "I will surrender to you, sir, but to no one else." This exemplary firmness and decision of Judge Jackson, in maintaining the supremacy of the law, produced a happy change in the conduct of the turbulent spirits of the vicinity.

General Jackson was distinguished throughout his whole life for a remarkable fidelity to his friends. This trait in his character was strikingly exhibited in the progress of a serious difficulty between Governor Sevier and himself, which took place in 1803. A misunderstanding arose between Jackson and his former friend, Judge McNairy, growing out of the agency of the latter in the removal of

General Robertson, one of the oldest and most respected citizens of the state, from the office of agent for the Chickasaw Indians. One of the consequences of that removal was, that a Mr. Searcy, who had emigrated to the country with them, and continued their steadfast friend, lost his office as clerk to the agency, on which he depended for support. Not perceiving any public reasons requiring this removal, Jackson remonstrated with McNairy on the course he had pursued. An altercation ensued, which produced an alienation never entirely obliterated. This incident added the weight of a respectable and powerful family to the hostile interests already arrayed against him.

Among others who became inimical towards him on this account, was John Sevier, governor of the state. Sevier was very popular, and being a candidate for reelection, in 1803, his exasperation against General Jackson was imbibed, in the course of the canvass, by the powerful party which supported him. In East Tennessee it had arisen to a high pitch; and while on his way to Jonesborough to hold his court, in the fall of 1803, he was informed that a combination had been organized to mob him on his arrival. It had no effect but to increase his anxiety to reach his destination. Having been sick on the road, he pushed forward while scarcely able to sit on his horse, and on his arrival at Jonesborough could not dismount without assistance. Having a high fever upon him, he retired immediately to his room, and lay down upon the bed. In a short time a friend called, and informed him that a regiment of men, headed by Colonel Harrison, had assembled to tar and feather him, and begged him to lock his door. He immediately rose, threw the door wide open, and said to his friend, "Give my compliments to Colonel Harrison, and tell him my door is open to receive him and his regiment whenever they choose to wait upon me; and I hope the colonel's chivalry will induce him to lead his men, and not follow them." Upon the delivery of his message, the mob dispersed; and having apologized for the inconsiderate violence of his conduct, Harrison remained ever after on good terms with General Jackson.

FIRMNESS AND DECISION AS A JUDGE 35

His next court was at Knoxville, where the legislature was then in session. They had entered into an investigation of certain land frauds which Jackson had done much to defeat, and there was some evidence tending to implicate the governor, who consequently became still more highly exasperated, and determined to revenge himself. As Judge Jackson left the court-house on the first day of his court, he found a crowd in front, in the midst of which stood Governor Sevier, with his sword in his hand, haranguing them in a loud voice. As Jackson advanced, the governor turned upon him; and an altercation ensued, in which insults were given and retorted. Being repeatedly defied by the governor to meet him in single combat, the general sent him a challenge, which was accepted. But in consequence of difficulties on the part of the challenged party, as to the time and place of meeting, the general published him in the usual form. It was then understood, without any formal arrangement, that they would meet at a place called Southwest Point, within the Indian boundary. Thither the general repaired with a single friend. Having waited a couple of days, without seeing or hearing of the governor, he resolved to return to Knoxville, and bring the quarrel to a close. He had not proceeded a mile, however, when he saw the governor approaching, escorted by about twenty men. He had already prepared another note to the governor, setting forth his manifold grievances, and halting in the road, he sent his friend forward to deliver it. The governor refused to receive it. Out of patience with what he conceived to be an aggravation of former indignities, the general resolved to end the matter on the spot. He was armed with a brace of pistols at his saddle-bow, and a cane; the governor with a brace of pistols and a sword. Advancing slowly until within one hundred yards of the governor, he levelled his cane as ancient knights did their spears, put spurs to his horse, and charged upon his antagonist. Astounded at this bold and unexpected movement, the governor's friends had not presence of mind enough to interpose; and the governor himself, dismounting to avoid the shock, trod on the scabbard of his sword, and was rendered incapable of resistance. A rally of his attendants prevented any very serious mischief. In the governor's party were gentlemen who were as much the friends of General Jackson as of himself; and through their intercession, all further hostile intentions were abandoned, and the parties rode on some miles together.

On the admission of Tennessee into the union, it comprised one military division. The death of Major-general Conway, which occurred about this time, created a vacancy in the office, which was filled by the election of Jackson. This was the only public station he filled for a number of years, as, in 1804, he sent in his resignation of the judgeship to the legislature, which was accepted in July, about six years after his original appointment. He always distrusted his own abilities as a judge, and was quite willing that others should discharge its intricate and responsible duties. Unambitious of obtaining those distinctions and honors, which young men are usually proud to possess, and finding too that his circumstances and condition in life were not such as to permit his time and attention to be devoted to public matters, he determined to yield them into other hands, and to devote himself to agricultural pursuits. He accordingly settled himself on an excellent farm, ten miles from Nashville, on the Cumberland river, where for several years he enjoyed all the comforts of domestic and social intercourse. Abstracted from the busy scenes of public life, pleased with retirement, surrounded by friends whom he loved, and who entertained for him the highest veneration and respect, and blessed with an amiable and affectionate wife, nothing seemed wanting to the completion of that happiness which he so anxiously desired while in office.

CHAPTER III.

1804. Fondness of General Jackson for horses—Duel with Dickinson—Forms a mercantile partnership—Pecuniary difficulties—Adventure with the Choctaw agent—Affray with Colonel Benton—Their subsequent friendship for each other—Hostilities with Great Britain—Declaration of war in 1812—Jackson raises a volunteer force—Their services accepted by government—Ordered to embark for Natchez—Arrival of the troops, and order to disband them—His disobedience of orders—Attempt of General Wilkinson to prevent the return of the volunteers—Object of the order—Jackson's decision exhibited—Shares the privations of the soldiers on their homeward march—Return, and disbandment of his force. 1813.

GENERAL JACKSON had a strong passion for fine horses, and it became a principal branch of his farming business, to raise them from the best blooded stock imported from Virginia and North Carolina. The enthusiasm of his character displayed itself in his attachment to favorite animals he had raised, and perhaps no man in the western country was equally successful in that branch of agricultural pursuits. More for the purpose of exhibiting his stock and recommending it to purchasers, than to indulge in the practices common at such places, he brought out his favorite horses upon the race-courses of the day, and, though not a sportsman, in the technical sense of the term, he lost and won in many a well-contested field. An occasion of this sort, however, led to one of the most unfortunate incidents of his life.

He owned a favorite horse, named Truxton, which he was challenged to run against a horse owned by a Mr. Erwin and his son-in-law, Charles Dickinson. The stakes were to be two thousand dollars on a side, in cash notes, with a forfeiture of eight hundred dollars. The bet was accepted, and a list of notes made out; but when the time for running arrived, Erwin and Dickinson chose to pay the forfeit. Erwin offered sundry notes not due, withholding the list which was in the hands of Dickinson. Jackson refused to receive them, and demanded the list, claiming the right to select from the notes described upon it. The list was produced, a selection made, and the affair satisfactorily adjusted. Afterwards a rumor reached Dickinson, that General Jackson charged Erwin with producing a list of notes different from the true one. In an interview between Jackson and Dickinson, the former denied the statement, and the latter gave his author. Jackson instantly proposed to call him in; but Dickinson declined. Meeting with the author shortly after, Jackson had an altercation with him, which ended in blows. Here the affair ought to have ended. But there were those who desired to produce a duel between Jackson and Dickinson. The latter was brave and reckless, a trader in slaves and blooded horses, and reputed to be the best shot in the country. A quarrel with such a man as General Jackson was flattering to his pride, and officious friends were not wanting to take advantage of the weakness of the one party, and the inflexibility of the other, in order to push matters to extremities. Exasperation was produced; publication followed publication; insults were given and retorted; until, at length, General Jackson was informed that a paper, more severe than its predecessors, was in the hands of the printer, and that Dickinson was about to leave the state. He flew to Nashville, and demanded a sight of it in the printer's hands. It was insulting in the highest degree, contained a direct imputation of cowardice, and concluded with a notice that the author would leave for Maryland, within the coming week. A stern challenge, demanding immediate satisfaction, was the consequence. The challenge was given on the 23d of May, and Dickinson's publication appeared the next morning. Jackson pressed for an instant meeting; but it was postponed, at the request of the other party, until the 30th, at which time it was to take place, at Harrison's Mills, on Red River, within the limits of Kentucky. Dickinson occupied the intermediate time in practicing; and his ferocious boasts, how often he had hit the general chalked out on a tree, and his unfeeling offers to bet that he would kill him at the approaching meeting, being duly communicated, had an effect upon his antagonist which can be better conceived than described. Jackson went upon the ground firmly impressed with the conviction that his life was eagerly sought, and in the expectation of losing it, but with a determination which such a conviction naturally inspired in a bosom that never knew fear. At the word, Dickinson fired, and the dust was seen to fly from Jackson's clothes; the next instant, the latter fired, and Dickinson fell. Jackson, with his friend and surgeon, left the ground, and had travelled about twenty miles towards home, when his attendant first discovered that the general was wounded, by seeing the blood oozing through his clothes. On examination, it was found that Dickinson's ball had buried itself in his breast, and shattered two of his ribs near their articulation with the breastbone. It was some weeks before he was able to attend to business. Dickinson was taken to a neighbouring house, where he survived but a few hours.

The friends of Dickinson, and the enemies of Jackson, circulated charges of unfairness in the fight, but these were soon put down, in the estimation of candid and impartial judges, by the certificates of the seconds, that all had been done according to the previous understanding between the parties, and proof that Dickinson himself, though able to converse, never uttered a single word of complaint before his death.

The firmness and steadiness of nerve exhibited by General Jackson on this occasion, have often been the subject of commendation, even among those who do not hesitate to condemn, in decided terms, the inexcusable practice, which was then not only tolerated, but actually encouraged, in that section of the country. There are many brave men who can look danger in the face, without the change of a muscle; but there are few who can take a sure aim, at the moment when they are conscious of being severely wounded. Not a man on the ground, except General Jackson himself, knew that he had received a wound; and every muscle was as quiet, and his hand as steady, as if he had not known it himself. The stern purpose which might in part have nerved him, was best described by himself, when a friend expressed astonishment at his self-command: "Sir," said he, "I should have killed him, if he had shot me through the brain."

Not long after this occurrence, General Jackson entered into partnership with a merchant in Nashville. He took no active part in the business himself, and their affairs were conducted for some time, without his having any more than a general knowledge of what was going on. Circumstances, however, soon attracted his attention, which led him to suspect that all was not right. He promptly demanded a full investigation, which resulted in the discovery that his partner, in whose fidelity and capacity he had reposed the most implicit confidence, had involved him for many thousand dollars, over and above what could be satisfied out of the partnership property. With a promptitude which did him great honor, he sold his fine plantation, paid off his debts with the proceeds of the sale, and retired into a log-cabin to begin the world anew. His extraordinary energy and perseverance, and the rigid system of economy he adopted, enabled him in a few years to recover from his embarrassments, and to be once more comfortable in the world.

In the year 1811, General Jackson had occasion to visit Natchez, in the territory of Mississippi, for the purpose of bringing up a number of slaves, a part of whom had become his property in consequence of having been security for a friend, and the remainder were hands which had been employed by a nephew, in the neighborhood of that place. The road led through the country inhabited by the Chickasaw and Choctaw Indians, and the station of the agent for the Choctaws was upon it. On reaching the agency, he found seven or eight families of emigrants, and two members of the Mississippi legislative council, detained there, under the pretence that it was necessary for them to have passports from the governor of Mississippi. One of their number had been sent forward to procure them. In the mean time, the emigrants were buying corn from the agent, at an extravagant price, and splitting rails for

ADVENTURE WITH THE CHOCTAW AGENT

him at a very moderate one. Indignant at the wrong inflicted on the emigrants, he reproached the members of the council for submitting to the detention, and asked the agent how he dared to demand a pass from a free American, travelling on a public road. The agent replied, by inquiring, with much temper, whether he had a pass. "Yes, sir," rejoined the general, "I always carry mine with me: I am a free-born American citizen; and that is a passport all over the world." He then directed the emigrants to gear up their wagons, and if any one attempted to obstruct them, to shoot him down as a highway robber. Setting them the example, he continued his journey, regardless of the threats of the agent.

After concluding his business, he was informed that the agent had collected about fifty white men and one hundred Indians, to stop him on his return, unless he produced a passport. Though advised by his friends to procure one, he refused to do so; stating that no American citizen should ever be subjected to the insult and indignity of procuring a pass, to enable him to travel a public highway in his own country. Like all travellers among the Indians, at that time, he was armed with a brace of pistols; and having added a rifle, and another pistol, he commenced his return journey. When within a few miles of the agency, he was informed by a friend who had gone forward to reconnoitre, that the agent had his force in readiness to stop him. He directed his friend to advance again, and tell the agent, that if he attempted to stop him, it would be at the peril of his life. He then put his slaves in order, and armed them with axes and clubs; at the same time telling them not to stop unless directed by him, and if any one offered to oppose them, to cut him down. Riding by their side, he approached the station, when the agent appeared, and asked him whether he meant to stop and show his passport. Jackson replied: "That depends on circumstances. I am told that you mean to stop me by force; whoever attempts such a thing will not have long to live;" and with a look that was not to be mistaken, he grasped his bridle with a firmer grip. His determined manner had such an effect, that the agent declared he had no intention of stopping him, and he and his party were suffered to pass on, without further molestation or interruption. He afterwards reported the conduct of the agent to the government, and he was dismissed from his agency.

After the return of General Jackson from Natchez, he was called upon by his friend, the late Governor Carroll, to act as his second, in an affair of honor with a brother of Colonel Thomas H. Benton, for so many years the distinguished representative of the state of Missouri, in the senate of the United States. In the duel, Mr. Benton was severely wounded. The colonel, who had long been on terms of friendly intimacy with Jackson, thought that the latter acted ungenerously, in taking such a part against his kinsman, and expressed himself accordingly in a letter addressed to him. General Jackson, however, felt himself bound by the relations which had existed between Governor Carroll and himself, to perform the act of friendship which he required, and replied to that effect, in very pointed terms. The angry correspondence that ensued only widened the breach, and it ended in a fight at a public-house in Nashville, in which Jackson's left arm was shattered by a pistol shot. For several years afterwards, both gentlemen appeared to cherish feelings of animosity towards each other, but the political associations of a later day united them together in the bonds of a sincere and constant friendship. The many noble traits in the character of Andrew Jackson elicited the warmest admiration and respect of Colonel Benton, while the former was proud to manifest his attachment to one of the firmest and ablest supporters of his administration.

The repose of Jackson, and the pleasures he had enjoyed in his quiet home, were now destined to be terminated by the public exigencies, which compelled him to abandon the peaceful pursuits of agriculture for the harassing cares and anxieties of a military career. The difficulties between the United States and Great Britain, which had originated with the adoption of the Orders in Council, and the passage of the Embargo Act, in 1807, had long threatened to disturb the peace of the two countries. In the spring of 1811, affairs began to assume a most threatening aspect. On the first of March, the American minister, Mr. Pinckney, took a formal leave of the Prince Regent, in obedience to the instructions of his government. Active preparations were at once made for the commencement of hostilities. Privateers were fitted out in every harbor, and throughout the whole extent of the Union, there prevailed a strong feeling of indignation at the repeated wrongs and injuries which our countrymen had endured from the English government. The war-spirit was aroused, and, from the Atlantic to the Mississippi, there glowed a strong and manly enthusiasm which bounded to defend the honor of the nation, and maintain, at any sacrifice, the "searchless shelter" of their flag. In accordance with the decided expressions of public sentiment, the American Congress passed an act, in the month of February, 1812, authorizing the president to accept the services of a large volunteer force. On the 20th day of June war was declared against Great Britain, and in July following, a second act was passed, making further provisions for calling out fifty thousand volunteers.

At this time, General Jackson was living happily on his farm, and, though only forty-five years of age, he had retired, as he thought, for ever, from all participation in public affairs. But the fire of that true and devoted patriotism which never ceased to glow in his bosom, needed but the quickening spark, to cause it to revive with all the fervor of youth. He was roused by the insults that had been so repeatedly offered to his country, by the wrongs inflicted upon her citizens, and by the bitter recollections connected with the death of his mother and his two brothers. He could recall the many horrid tales, to which he had listened, of English cruelty and oppression in the birth-place of his ancestors. There was also that scar on his hand, inflicted by a British officer, who had aimed a blow at his life because he had refused to clean the dirt from his boots; that scar remained to keep his virtuous resentment alive, even if he could otherwise have forgotten the injuries of his native land, the wrongs of Ireland, and the extermination of every relative in the world.

Jackson did not seek a command in the regular army, but immediately issued a spirited address to the citizens of his division, calling upon them to unite with him in protecting the rights and the honor of the republic. In a few days twenty-five hundred volunteers flocked to his standard, ready to follow wheresoever he might see fit to lead them. A tender of their services having been made to the general government, and the offer accepted, he received orders in November, 1812, to place himself at their head and to descend the Mississippi, for the defence of the lower country, which was then supposed to be in danger. Accordingly, on the 10th of December, 1812, the men under his command rendezvoused at Nashville, prepared to advance to the place of their destination; and although the weather was then excessively severe, and the ground covered with snow, no troops could have displayed greater firmness. The general was everywhere with them, inspiring them with the ardor that animated his own bosom. The cheerful spirit with which they submitted to hardships and bore privations, at the very outset of their military life, as well as the order and subordination they so readily observed, were happy presages of what was to be expected when they should be directed to face an enemy.

Having procured supplies, and made the necessary arrangements for an active campaign, the volunteers commenced their journey on the 7th of January, 1813, and descending the Ohio and Mississippi through cold and ice, arrived and halted at Natchez. Here Jackson had been instructed to remain until he should receive further orders. Having chosen a healthy site for the encampment of his troops, he devoted his time with the utmost industry, to training and preparing them for active service. The clouds of war in that quarter having temporarily blown over, an order was received, soon after his arrival, from the Secretary of War, dated the 5th of January, 1813, directing him, on the receipt thereof, to dismiss the men under his command from service, and to take measures for delivering over every article of public property in his possession to Brigadier-General Wilkinson.

When this order reached the camp of General Jackson, there were one hundred and fifty men on the sick report, fifty-six of whom were unable to rise from their beds, and almost the whole number were without the means of defraying the expenses of their return. The consequence of a strict compliance with the Secretary's order, would inevitably have been, that many of the sick must have perished, while most of the others, from their destitute condition, would, of necessity, have been compelled to enlist in the regular army, under General Wilkinson. Such alternatives were neither congenial with their general's wishes, nor such as they had expected, on adventuring with him in the service of their country. He had taken them from home, and he regarded it as a solemn duty to bring them back. Whether an expectation that, by this plan, many of them would be forced into the regular ranks, had formed any part of the motive that occasioned the order for their discharge, at so great a distance from home, cannot be known; and it would be uncharitable to insinuate against the government so serious an accusation, without the strongest evidence to support it. Be this as it may, General Jackson could not think of sacrificing, or injuring, an army that had shown such devotedness to their country; and he determined to disregard the order, and march them again to their homes, where they had been embodied, rather than to discharge them where they would be exposed to the greatest hardships and dangers. To this measure he was prompted, not only by the reasons already mentioned, but by the consideration that many of them were young men, the children of his neighbors and acquaintances, who had delivered them into his hands, as to a guardian, with the expectation that he would watch over and protect them. To have abandoned them, therefore, at such a time, and under such circumstances, would have drawn on him the merited censure of the most deserving part of his fellow-citizens, and deeply wounded his own generous feelings. In addition to this, the young men who were confined by sickness, learning the nature of the order he had received, implored him, with tears in their eyes, not to abandon them in so great an extremity, and reminded him, at the same time, of his assurance that he would be to them as a father, and of the implicit confidence they had placed in his word. This was an appeal which it would have been difficult for Jackson to have resisted, had he been inclined to disregard other considerations; but influenced by them all, he had no hesitation in coming to a determination.

Having made known his resolution to the field-officers of his division, it apparently met their approbation; but after retiring from his presence, they assembled late at night, in secret caucus, and proceeded to recommend to him an abandonment of his purpose, and an immediate discharge of the troops. Great as was the astonishment which this movement excited in the general, it produced a still stronger feeling of indignation. In reply, he urged the duplicity of their conduct, and reminded them that although to those who possessed money and health, such a course could produce no inconvenience, yet to the unfortunate soldier, who was alike destitute of both, no measure could be more calamitous. He concluded, by telling them, that his resolution, not having been hastily concluded on, nor founded on light considerations, was unalterably fixed; and that immediate preparations must be made for carrying into execution the determination he had formed.

He lost no time in making known to the Secretary of War the resolution he had adopted, to disregard the order he had received, and to return his army to the place where he had received it. He painted, in strong terms, the evils which the course pursued by the government was calculated to produce, and expressed the astonishment he felt, that it should ever have been seriously determined on.

General Wilkinson, to whom the public stores were directed to be delivered, learning the determination which had been taken by Jackson to march his troops back, and to take with them such articles as might be necessary for their return, in a letter of solemn and mysterious import admonished him of the consequences which were before him, and of the awful and dangerous responsibility he was taking on himself by so bold a measure. General Jack-

DISOBEDIENCE OF ORDERS

son replied, that his conduct, and the consequences to which it might lead, had been deliberately weighed, and well considered, and that he was prepared to abide the result, whatever it might be. Wilkinson had previously given orders to his officers, to recruit from Jackson's army: but they were advised, on their first appearance, that those troops were already in the service of the United States, and that, thus situated, they should not be enlisted; and that General Jackson would arrest, and confine, the first officer who dared to enter his encampment with any such object in view.

The quarter-master, having been ordered to furnish the necessary transportation for the conveyance of the sick and the baggage to Tennessee, immediately set about the performance of the task; but, as the event proved, without any intention to execute it. Still he continued to keep up the semblance of exertion; and, on the very day before that which had been appointed for breaking up the encampment and commencing the return march, eleven wagons arrived there by his order. But early the next morning, when every thing was about to be packed up, he entered the encampment, and discharged the whole. He was grossly mistaken, however, in the man he had to deal with, and had now played his tricks too far to be able to accomplish the object, which, without doubt, he had been intrusted to effect. Disregarding their dismissal, so evidently designed to prevent marching back his men, General Jackson seized upon the wagons, yet within his lines, and compelled them to proceed in the transportation of his sick. Among them was a young man, reported by the surgeon to be in a dying condition, whom it was useless to remove. "Not a man shall be left who has life in him," said the general. The young man was lifted into a wagon, in a state of torpor, and wholly insensible. The melancholy march commenced; and the general, with parental solicitude, passed along the train, taking special care that the invalids, in position and appliances, should have every comfort of which their situation was susceptible. With peculiar anxiety, he watched the apparently dying youth, as he was jostled by the movements of the wagon. At length the young man opened his eyes, and the next instant exclaimed, "Where am I?"

"On your way home, my good fellow," replied the general, in a cheering tone. The effect was electric; he improved from that moment, and in a few weeks the general had the pleasure of restoring him, in good health, to his family and friends. It deserves to be mentioned, that the quarter-master, as soon as he received directions for furnishing transportation, had despatched an express to General Wilkinson; and there can be little question, that the course of duplicity he afterwards pursued, was a concerted plan between him and that general, to defeat the design of Jackson, compel him to abandon the determination he had formed, and, in this way, draw to the regular army many of the soldiers, who would be driven to enlist. In this attempt they were fortunately disappointed. Adhering to his original purpose, General Jackson successfully resisted every stratagem of Wilkinson, and marched the whole of his division to the section of country whence they had been drawn, and dismissed them from service, in the spring of 1813.

In addition to the philanthropic act we have just detailed, General Jackson gave up his own horses to the sick, and, trudging along on foot, submitted to all the privations that were endured by the soldiers. It was at a time of the year when the roads were extremely bad; and the swamps along their route were deep and full; yet, under these circumstances, he gave his troops an example of patience and endurance of hardship that lulled to silence all complaints, and won for him additional respect and esteem. On arriving at Nashville, he communicated to the president of the United States the course he had pursued, and the reasons that had induced it. If it had become necessary, he had sufficient grounds on which he could have justified his conduct. Had he suffered General Wilkinson to have accomplished what was clearly his intention, although it was an event which might, at the moment, have benefited the service, by adding an increased strength to the army, yet the example would have been of so serious and exceptionable a character, that in-

SUFFERINGS ON THE MARCH HOME 49

jury would have been the final and unavoidable result. Whether the intention of thus forcing these men to enlist into the regular ranks, had its existence under the direction of the government or not, such would have been the universal belief; and all would have felt a deep abhorrence, at beholding the citizens of the country drawn off from their homes under pretence of danger; while the concealed design was, to reduce them to such necessity, at a distance from their residence, as to compel them to an act which they would have avoided under different circumstances. His conduct, exceptionable as it might at first appear, was, in the end, approved, and the expenses incurred were directed to be paid by the government. General Armstrong, the secretary of war, by whom the cruel and unfeeling order was issued, was soon after severely censured, and forced to resign his seat in the cabinet, on account of his culpable neglect to provide suitable means of defence for the city of Washington. The reputation of General Wilkinson, who had been appointed to supplant Jackson, was also tarnished, by his unfortunate operations in Canada, during the campaign of 1814.

CHAPTER IV.

1813. Depredations committed by the Creeks on the borders of Tennessee and Kentucky—Attack on Fort Mimms—Preparations for war—Jackson calls out the volunteers and militia—Address to the troops—Takes the field—Enforces strict military discipline—Rapid march to Huntsville—Delay in forwarding supplies—Thwarted in his movements by General Cocke—Jealousy of the latter—Scarcity of provisions—Efforts of Jackson to procure supplies—Address to the soldiers on entering the enemy's country—Arrival at the Ten Islands—Difficulty with the contractors—Destitute condition of the army—Battle of Tallushatchee—Humanity of Jackson—His adoption of an Indian boy. 1813.

THE repose of General Jackson and his volunteers was of short duration. They had scarcely reached their homes, when the Indian nations scattered over the territory composing the states of Alabama and Mississippi, made incursions into Tennessee and Kentucky, and committed the most savage murders and cruelties. The frontier settlements were constantly harassed by their depredations, and one atrocious act of barbarity followed so closely on another, that the inhabitants began to fear the worst from the revengeful spirit which Tecumseh, and his brother, the prophet, who were secretly aided and encouraged by the English government, had aroused in the breasts of their followers. The Creek Indians, residing in the vicinity of the Coosa and Tallapoosa rivers, were the most hostile and vindictive of all the tribes. Having collected a supply of ammunition, from the Spaniards at Pensacola, a party of their warriors, numbering about seven hundred men, commanded by Weatherford, a distinguished chief of the nation, made an attack on Fort Mimms, situated in the Tensaw settlement, in the territory of Mississippi. The fort was occupied by Major Beasley, with a force of one hundred and fifty men, and a large number of women and children who had sought shelter and protection. The assault was commenced on the 30th of August, 1813, and proved to be successful. A most dreadful slaughter took place. Mercy was shown to none; neither age nor sex were respected; and the same stroke of the tomahawk often cleft mother and child. But seventeen of the whole number of persons in the fort made their escape.

As soon as the intelligence of this monstrous outrage reached Tennessee, the authorities of that state took immediate measures to chastise the perpetrators. All eyes were instinctively turned towards General Jackson, who, though suffering severely from a fractured arm, promptly responded to the orders of his government by calling out the militia and volunteers. In his proclamation, he made a special appeal to those who had accompanied him to Natchez, to join him on this occasion. He pointed out the imperious necessity that demanded their services, and urged them to be punctual. "Already," said he, "are large bodies of the hostile Creeks marching to your borders, with their scalping-knives unsheathed, to butcher your women and children: time is not to be lost. We must hasten to the frontier, or we shall find it drenched in the blood of our citizens. The health of your general is restored—he will command in person." In the mean time, until these troops could be collected and organized, Colonel Coffee, with the force then under his command, and such additional mounted riflemen as could be attached at a short notice, was directed to hasten forward to the neighborhood of Huntsville, and occupy some eligible position for the defence of the frontier.

The 4th of October, which was the day appointed for the rendezvous, having arrived, and the general not being sufficiently recovered to attend in person, he forwarded by his aid-de-camp, Major Reid, an address, to be read to the troops, in which he pointed out the unprovoked injuries they were called upon to redress, in the following eloquent and stirring appeal:

"We are about to furnish these savages a lesson of admonition; we are about to teach them that our long forbearance has not proceeded from an insensibility to wrongs, or an inability to redress them. They stand in need of such warning. In proportion as we have borne with their insults, and submitted to their outrages, they have multiplied in number, and increased in atrocity. But the measure of their offences is at length filled. The blood of our women and children, recently spilt at Fort Mimms, calls for our vengeance; it must not call in vain. Our borders must no longer be disturbed by the war-whoop of these savages, and the cries of their suffering victims. The torch that has been lighted up must be made to blaze in the heart of their own country. It is time they should be made to feel the weight of a power, which, because it was merciful, they believed to be impotent. But how shall a war so long forborne, and so loudly called for by retributive justice, be waged? Shall we imitate the example of our enemies, in the disorder of their movements and the savageness of their dispositions? Is it worthy the character of American soldiers, who take up arms to redress the wrongs of an injured country, to assume no better models than those furnished them by barbarians? No, fellow-soldiers; great as are the grievances that have called us from our homes, we must not permit disorderly passions to tarnish the reputation we shall carry along with us. We must and will be victorious; but we must conquer as men who owe nothing to chance, and who, in the midst of victory, can still be mindful of what is due to humanity!

" We will commence the campaign by an inviolable attention to discipline and subordination. Without a strict observance of these, victory must ever be uncertain, and ought hardly to be exulted in, even when gained. To what but the entire disregard of order and subordination, are we to ascribe the disasters which have attended our arms in the north during the present war? How glorious will it be to remove the blots which have tarnished the fair character bequeathed us by the fathers of our revolution! The bosom of your general is full of hope. He knows the ardor which animates you, and already exults in the triumph which your strict observance of discipline and good order will render certain."

Accompanying this address, was the following order for

the establishment of the police of the camp, which strikingly illustrates his promptitude and decision as a military commander:

"The chain of sentinels will be marked, and the sentries posted, precisely at ten o'clock to-day.

"No sutler will be suffered to sell spirituous liquors to any soldier, without permission in writing, from a commissioned officer, under the penalties prescribed by the rules and articles of war.

"No citizen will be permitted to pass the chain of sentinels after retreat-beat in the evening, until reveille in the morning. Drunkenness, the bane of all orderly encampments, is positively forbidden, both in officers and privates: officers, under the penalty of immediate arrest; and privates, of being placed under guard, there to remain until liberated by a court-martial.

"At reveille-beat, all officers and soldiers are to appear on parade, with their arms and accoutrements in proper order.

"On parade, silence, the duty of a soldier, is positively commanded.

"No officer or soldier is to sleep out of camp, but by permission obtained."

However harsh it may at first blush appear, to attempt the enforcement of such rules, in the very first stage of military discipline, yet the conduct of General Jackson was dictated by the most praiseworthy motives. The expedition on which he was about to march was certain to be both difficult and dangerous. He was aware that hardships must of necessity be endured, which would appal and dispirit his troops, if they were not early taught the lesson of strict compliance with the orders of their commander; and he considered it much safer, therefore, to lay before them at once the rules of conduct to which they would be required to conform.

Impatient to join his division, although his health was far from being restored, the general, in a few days afterwards, set out for the encampment, which he reached on the 7th of October. On the evening of the following day, a letter was received from Colonel Coffee, who had proceeded with his mounted volunteers to Huntsville, dated two days before, and informing the general that two friendly Indians had just arrived at the Tennessee river, from Chinnaby's fort, on the Coosa, from whom he learned that a party of eight hundred or a thousand Creeks had been despatched to attack the frontiers of Georgia, and that the remainder of their warriors were marching against Huntsville, or Fort Hampton. On the 9th instant, another express arrived, confirming the former statement, and representing the enemy, in great force, to be rapidly approaching the Tennessee. Orders were now given for preparing the line of march, and by nine o'clock on the 10th, the whole division was in motion. They had not proceeded many miles, when they were met with the intelligence that Colonel Gibson, who had been sent out by Coffee to reconnoitre the movements of the enemy, had been killed by their advance. A strong desire had been previously manifested to be led forward; that desire was now strengthened by the information just received; and it was with difficulty that the troops could be restrained. They hastened their march, and before eight o'clock at night arrived at Huntsville, a distance of thirty-two miles. Learning here that the information was erroneous which had occasioned so hasty a movement, the general encamped his troops; having intended to reach the Tennessee river that night had it been confirmed. The next day the line of march was resumed. The influence of the late excitement was now visible in the lassitude which followed its removal. Proceeding slowly, the division crossed the Tennessee at Ditto's landing, and united in the evening with Colonel Coffee's regiment, which had previously occupied a commanding bluff on the south bank of the river. From this place, a few days afterwards, Jackson detached Colonel Coffee, with seven hundred men, to scour the Black Warrior, a stream running from the northeast, and emptying into the Tombigbee; on which were supposed to be situated several populous villages of the enemy. He himself remained at the encampment a week, busily occupied in drilling his troops, and in endeavouring to procure the necessary supplies for a campaign, which he

MARCH INTO THE CREEK COUNTRY 55

had determined to carry into the heart of the enemy's country.

At the same time that General Jackson took up his line of march for the Creek country, General Cocke had been ordered with an equal force from East Tennessee; while another was despatched from Georgia, under Major Floyd, to enter the Indian territory on the east; and a regiment of United States troops, with the Mississippi volunteers, under General Claiborne, were to attack the hostile tribes on the west. An arrangement had been made in the preceding month, with General Cocke, to furnish large quantities of bread-stuff at Ditto's landing, for the troops under Jackson. The facility of procuring it in that quarter, and the convenient transportation afforded by the river, left no doubt on the mind of the latter that the engagement would be punctually complied with. To provide, however, against the bare possibility of a failure, and to be guarded against all contingencies that might happen, he addressed letters to the governor of Georgia, Colonel Meigs, the Cherokee agent, and General White, who commanded the advance of the East Tennessee troops, urging them to send forward supplies with all possible haste. General Cocke, who had been ordered to join him with the forces under his command, not only failed to come up in season, but neglected to furnish the provisions he had engaged to procure. The conduct of this officer was severely censured at the time, and it is quite evident that most of his movements during the campaign were prompted by a desire to thwart the operations of Jackson.

On his arrival at Ditto's landing, General Jackson found that the contractors were utterly unable to fulfil their engagements, and he was therefore compelled to wait patiently for the supplies which had so long been promised, and were hourly expected. While he was encamped there, a son of Chinnaby, one of the principal chiefs among the friendly Creeks, a large body of whom had refused to unite with their countrymen in making war against the Americans, arrived at the landing, and requested a movement to be made for the relief of his father's fort, which was threatened by a considerable body of the war party. Influenced by his representations, the general gave orders for resuming the march on the 19th of October, and notified the contractors of this arrangement, that they might be prepared to issue immediately such supplies as they had on hand ; but to his great astonishment, he was then, for the first time, apprised of their entire inability to supply him while on his march. Having drawn what they had it in their power to furnish, amounting to only a few days' rations, he immediately vacated their offices, and selected others on whose industry and fidelity he thought he could more safely rely. The scarcity of his provisions, however, was not sufficient to waive the determination he had already made. The route to the fort lay for a considerable distance up the river, and he hoped to meet with the boats expected from Hiwassee on the way. He accordingly determined to proceed, and having safely crossed a range of mountains, thought to be almost impassable on foot, with his army and baggage wagons, he arrived on the 22d of October, at Thompson's creek, which empties into the Tennessee, twenty-four miles above Ditto's. At this place he proposed the establishment of a permanent depot, for the reception of supplies, to be sent either up or down the river. Disappointed in the hopes with which he had ventured on his march, he remained here several days anxiously looking for the arrival of provisions. Fearing that this culpable neglect might involve him in still further embarrassments, he informed Governor Blount, of Tennessee, of the condition of things, and made a pressing application to General Flournoy, who commanded at Mobile, and Colonel McKee, the Choctaw agent, who was then on the Tombigbee, to procure bread-stuff and forward it to him without delay. He also despatched expresses to General White, who had arrived at the Look-out mountain, in the Cherokee nation, urging him by all means to hasten on the supplies.

While these measures were in progress, two runners, despatched from Turkeytown by Path-killer, a chief of the Cherokees, arrived at the camp. They brought information that the enemy, from nine of the hostile towns, were assembling in great force near the Ten Islands ; and

FAILURE OF THE SUPPLIES

solicited that immediate assistance should be afforded the friendly Creeks and Cherokees in their neighborhood, who were exposed to imminent danger. His want of provisions was not yet remedied; but distributing the partial supply that was on hand, he resolved to proceed, in expectation that the relief he had so earnestly looked for, would in a little while arrive, and be forwarded. In order to prepare his troops for the engagement he anticipated, he addressed them as follows, in his usual nervous and spirited style:

"You have, fellow-soldiers, at length penetrated the country of your enemies. It is not to be believed that they will abandon the soil that imbosoms the bones of their forefathers, without furnishing you an opportunity of signalizing your valor. Wise men do not expect; brave men will not desire it. It was not to travel unmolested through a barren wilderness, that you quitted your families and homes, and submitted to so many privations; it was to avenge the cruelties committed upon our defenceless frontiers by the inhuman Creeks, instigated by their no less inhuman allies. You shall not be disappointed. If the enemy flee before us, we will overtake and chastise him: we will teach him how dreadful, when once aroused, is the resentment of freemen. But it is not by boasting that punishment is to be inflicted, or victory obtained. The same resolution that prompted us to take up arms, must inspire us in battle. Men thus animated, and thus resolved, barbarians can never conquer; and it is an enemy barbarous in the extreme that we have now to face. Their reliance will be on the damage they can do you while you are asleep, and unprepared for action: their hopes shall fail them in the hour of experiment. Soldiers who know their duty, and are ambitious to perform it, are not to be taken by surprise. Our sentinels will never sleep, nor our soldiers be unprepared for action; yet, while it is enjoined upon the sentinels vigilantly to watch the approach of the foe, they are at the same time commanded not to fire at shadows. Imaginary dangers must not deprive them of entire self-possession. Our soldiers will lie with their arms in their hands; and the moment an alarm is given, they will move to their respective positions, without noise and without confusion. They will be thus enabled to hear the orders of their officers, and to obey them with promptitude.

"Great reliance will be placed, by the enemy, on the consternation they may be able to spread through our ranks, by the hideous yells with which they commence their battles; but brave men will laugh at such efforts to alarm them. It is not by bellowings and screams, that the wounds of death are inflicted. You will teach these noisy assailants how weak are their weapons of warfare, by opposing them with the bayonet. What Indian ever withstood its charge? what army, of any nation, ever withstood it long?

"Yes, soldiers, the order for a charge will be the signal for victory. In that moment, your enemy will be seen fleeing in every direction before you. But in the moment of action, coolness and deliberation must be regarded; your fires made with precision and aim; and when ordered to charge with the bayonet, you must proceed to the assault, with a quick and firm step, without trepidation or alarm. Then shall you behold the completion of your hopes, in the discomfiture of your enemy. Your general, whose duty, as well as inclination, is to watch over your safety, will not, to gratify any wishes of his own, urge you unnecessarily into danger. He knows, however, that it is not in assailing an enemy that men are destroyed; it is when retreating, and in confusion. Aware of this, he will be prompted as much by a regard for your lives as your honor. He laments that he has been compelled, even incidentally, to hint at a retreat, when speaking to freemen and to soldiers. Never, until you forget all that is due to yourselves and your country, will you have any practical understanding of that word. Shall an enemy wholly unacquainted with military evolutions, and who rely more for victory on their grim visages and hideous yells, than upon their bravery or their weapons; shall such an enemy ever drive before them the well-trained youths of our country, whose bosoms pant for glory, and a desire to avenge the wrongs they have received? Your general will not live to behold such a spectacle; rather would he rush into the thickest of the enemy, and submit himself to their scalping-knives: but he has no fears of such a result. He knows the valor of the men he commands; and how certainly that valor, regulated as it will be, will lead to victory. With his soldiers, he will face all dangers, and with them participate in the glory of conquest."

Having issued this address, and again instructed General White to form a junction with him, and send on all the supplies he could command, General Jackson resumed his march, with about six days' rations of meat, and less than two of meal. The army had advanced but a short distance, when unexpected embarrassments were again presented. Information was received, by which it was clearly ascertained that the present contractors, who had been so much and so certainly relied on, could not, with all their exertions, procure the necessary supplies. Major Rose, of the quarter-master's department, who had been sent into Madison county to aid them in their endeavors, having satisfied himself, as well from their own admissions as from evidence derived from other sources, that their want of funds, and consequent want of credit, rendered them a very unsafe dependence, returned, and disclosed the facts to the general. He stated that there were persons of fortune and industry in that county, who might be confided in, and who would be willing to contract for the army if it were necessary. Jackson lost no time in embracing this plan, and gave the contract to Mr. Pope, in whose means and exertions he believed every reliance might be reposed. At the same time, he wrote to the other contractors, stating, that although he might manage with generosity or indulgence, whatever concerned himself as a private citizen, in his public capacity he had no such discretion; and that he therefore felt compelled to give the contract to one who was able to execute it, on condition that they were indemnified for their trouble.

This arrangement being made, the army continued its march, and having arrived within a few miles of the Ten Islands, was met by the Indian chief, Chinnaby. He brought with him, and surrendered up, two of the hostile Creeks, who had lately been made prisoners by his party. At this place it was represented that they were within sixteen miles of the enemy, who were collected, to the number of a thousand, to oppose their passage. This information was little relied on, and afterwards proved untrue. Jackson continued his route, and in a few days reached the islands of the Coosa, having been detained a day, on the way, for the purpose of obtaining small supplies of corn from the neighboring Indians. This acquisition to the scanty stock on hand, while it afforded subsistence for the present, encouraged his hopes for the future, as a means of temporary resort, should his other resources fail.

In a letter to Governor Blount from this place, speaking of the difficulties with which he had to contend, he observed: "Indeed, sir, we have been very wretchedly supplied—scarcely two rations in succession have been regularly drawn; yet we are not despondent. While we can procure an ear of corn apiece, or any thing that will answer as a substitute for it, we shall continue our exertions to accomplish the object for which we were sent. The cheerfulness with which my men submit to privations, and are ready to encounter danger, does honor to them, and to the government whose rights they are defending."

On the 28th of October, Colonel Dyer, who had been detached from the main body, on the march to the Ten Islands, with a body of two hundred cavalry, returned to camp. He had destroyed the Indian village of Littafutchee-town, at the head of Canoe creek, and brought with him twenty-nine prisoners. On the 31st, Jackson despatched another express to General White, repeating his former orders. Soon after, he received information that a considerable body of the enemy had posted themselves at Tallushatchee, on the south side of the Coosa, about thirteen miles distant; whereupon, he ordered General Coffee, with nine hundred men, to attack and disperse them. With this force that officer was enabled, under the direction of an Indian pilot, to ford the Coosa at the Fish-dams, about four miles above the Islands; and, having encamped beyond it, he proceeded, early on the morning of the 3d of November, to execute the order. Having arrived within a mile and a half, he formed his detachment into two divisions, and directed them to march so as to encircle the town, by uniting their fronts beyond it. The enemy, hearing of his approach, began to prepare for action, which was announced by the beating of drums, mingled with savage yells and war-whoops. An hour after sunrise, the battle was commenced by Captain Hammond's and Lieutenant Patterson's companies of spies, who had gone within the circle of alignment, for the purpose of drawing the Indians from their buildings. No sooner had these companies exhibited their front in view of the town, and given a few scattering shots, than the enemy formed, and made a violent charge. Being compelled to give way, the advance-guard were pursued until they reached the main body of the army, which immediately opened a general fire, and charged in their turn. The Indians retreated, but continued firing, until they reached their buildings, where an obstinate conflict ensued. Those who maintained their ground, persisted in fighting as long as they could stand or sit, without manifesting fear or soliciting quarter. Their loss was a hundred and eighty-six killed; among whom, unfortunately, and through accident, were a few women and children. Eighty-four women and children were taken prisoners, towards whom the utmost humanity was shown. Of the Americans, five were killed and forty-one wounded. Two were killed with arrows, which on this occasion formed a principal part of the arms of the Indians; each one having a bow and quiver, which he used after the first fire of his gun, until an opportunity occurred for reloading.

Having buried his dead and provided for his wounded General Coffee united with the main army, late in the evening of the same day, bringing with him about forty prisoners. Of the residue, a part were too badly wounded to be removed, and were therefore left, with a sufficient number to take care of them. Those whom he brought in, received every comfort their situation demanded, and were immediately sent into the settlements for security.

Among the slain at the battle of Tallushatchee, there was found an Indian woman, with an infant boy, unhurt, sucking her lifeless breast. The little orphan was carried to camp with the other prisoners, and General Jackson attempted to hire some of the captive women to take care of him. They refused, saying, "All his relations are dead; kill him too." The general had a little brown sugar left, and he directed his attendants to feed the child with it until he reached Huntsville, where he sent him to be nursed at his expense. Upon his return from the campaign, he took the child home, named him Lincoyer, and with the cordial aid of Mrs. Jackson, raised him as tenderly as if he had been his own son. He grew to be a beautiful and robust young man, as well educated as the white boys of the most respectable families. Yet his tastes were unchanged. He delighted in rambling over the fields and through the woods, and sticking into his hair and clothes every gay feather he could find. He was always anxious to return to the Creek nation with the chiefs, who, for many years after the war, continued to visit General Jackson at the Hermitage, as his residence was called. Desiring that he should follow some mechanical employment, his benefactor took him into the various shops in Nashville, that he might make his selection. He was best pleased with the saddler's business, and was accordingly bound out as an apprentice to that trade. Regularly every other Saturday he visited the Hermitage, and was generally sent to Nashville on horseback the next Monday morning. His health beginning to decline, the general took him home to the Hermitage, where he was nursed with a father's and mother's tenderness; but in vain. He sunk rapidly into a consumption, and died ere he had arrived at the age of manhood. He was mourned as a favorite son by the general and Mrs. Jackson, and they always spoke of him with parental affection.

CHAPTER V.

1813. Erection of Fort Strother, and establishment of a depot on the Coosa—Continued difficulties growing out of the movements of General Cocke—Battle of Talladega—Gallant conduct of Colonel Carroll and Lieutenant-Colonel Dyer—Destitution of the army—Generosity and benevolence of Jackson—His example in submitting to privations—Anecdote of the acorns—Discontent among the troops—Mutiny suppressed by his firmness and resolution—His appeal to the contractors to furnish supplies—Answer to the overtures of peace made by the Hillabee tribes—Efforts to raise additional troops—Letter to his friend in Tennessee—Demand of the volunteers to be discharged, on the ground that their term of service had expired—Reply of Jackson—His unflinching determination—Suppression of the mutiny, and return of the volunteers. 1813.

In consequence of his not receiving the necessary supplies of provisions, without which it was utterly impossible to proceed, General Jackson was detained for nearly a month, in the neighbourhood of the Tennessee river, without being able to penetrate the hostile territory, and strike a decisive blow. During this time, he erected a fort and depot, at the Ten Islands, which was called Fort Strother. It was his intention, after completing the works, to proceed along the Coosa to its junction with the Tallapoosa, near which, it was expected, from information he had received, that the main force of the enemy was collected. In order to accomplish this in safety, he desired to unite as soon as possible with the troops from East Tennessee. The advance under General White had arrived at Turkey-town, twenty-five miles above, and on the 4th of November an express was despatched to him to hasten forward immediately. A similar message was sent on the 7th of the same month, but failed to produce any effect. General White chose rather to obey the orders of the immediate commander of his division, General Cocke, who persisted in his singular efforts to thwart the movements of Jackson and the forces under his command. Although he endeavoured to shelter himself from the consequences of his unsoldierlike conduct, beneath the decision of a council of officers which he had formed, his jealousy of General Jackson was so apparent, that the public were not slow in forming a most unfavorable opinion of his character.

As yet, no certain intelligence had been received, in regard to the position of the enemy. Late, however, on the evening of the 7th of November, a runner arrived from Talladega, a fort of the friendly Indians, distant about thirty miles below, with information that the enemy had that morning encamped before it in great numbers, and would certainly destroy it, unless immediate assistance could be afforded. Confiding in the statement, Jackson determined to lose no time in extending the relief which was solicited. Understanding that General White, agreeably to his order, was on his way to join him, he despatched a messenger to meet him, directing him to reach his encampment in the course of the ensuing night, and to protect it in his absence. He now gave orders for taking up the line of march, with twelve hundred infantry, and eight hundred cavalry and mounted gun-men; leaving behind the sick, the wounded, and all his baggage, with a force which was deemed sufficient for their protection, until the reinforcement from Turkey-town should arrive.

The friendly Indians who had taken refuge in this besieged fort, had involved themselves in their present perilous situation from a disposition to preserve their amicable relations with the United States. To suffer them to fall a sacrifice from any tardiness of movement, would have been unpardonable; and unless relief should be immediately extended, it might arrive too late. Acting under these impressions, the general concluded to move instantly forward to their assistance. At twelve o'clock at night, every thing was in readiness; and in an hour afterwards the army commenced crossing the river, about a mile above the camp; each of the mounted men carrying one of the infantry behind him. The river at this place was six hundred yards wide, and it being necessary to send back the horses for the remainder of the infantry, several hours were consumed before a passage of all the troops could be effected. Nevertheless, though greatly fatigued and deprived of sleep, they continued the march with animation, and by evening had arrived within six miles of the enemy. In this march, Jackson used the utmost precaution to prevent surprise: marching his army, as was his constant custom, in three columns, so that, by a speedy manœuvre, they might be thrown into such a situation as to be capable of resisting an attack from any quarter. Having judiciously encamped his men on an eligible piece of ground, he sent forward two of the friendly Indians and a white man, who had for many years been detained a captive in the nation, and was now acting as interpreter, to reconnoitre the position of the enemy. About eleven o'clock at night they returned, with information that the savages were posted within a quarter of a mile of the fort, and appeared to be in great force; but that they had not been able to approach near enough to ascertain either their numbers or precise situation. About an hour later, a runner arrived from Turkeytown, with a letter from General White, stating that after having taken up the line of march to unite at Fort Strother, he had received orders from General Cocke to change his course, and proceed to the mouth of Chatauga creek. Intelligence so disagreeable, and withal so unexpected, filled the mind of Jackson with apprehensions of a serious and alarming character; and dreading lest the enemy, by taking a different route, should attack his encampment in his absence, he determined to lose no time in bringing them to battle. Orders were accordingly given to the adjutant-general to prepare the line, and by four o'clock on the morning of the 9th, the army was again in motion. The infantry proceeded in three columns; the cavalry in the same order, in the rear, with flankers on each wing. The advance, consisting of a company of artillerists with muskets, two companies of riflemen, and one of spies, marched about four hundred yards in front, under the command of Colonel Carroll, inspector-general, with orders, after commencing the action, to fall back on the centre, so as to draw the enemy after them. At seven o'clock, having arrived within a mile of the position they occupied, the columns were displayed in order of battle. Two hundred and fifty of the cavalry, under Lieut. Colonel Dyer, were placed in the rear of the centre, as a corps-de-reserve. The remainder of the mounted troops were directed to advance on the right and left, and after encircling the enemy, by uniting the fronts of their columns, and keeping their rear rested on the infantry, to face and press towards the centre, so as to leave them no possibility of escape. The remaining part of the army was ordered to move up by heads of companies; General Hall's brigade occupying the right, and General Roberts' the left.

About eight o'clock, the advance having arrived within eighty yards of the enemy, who were concealed in a thick shrubbery that covered the margin of a small rivulet, received a heavy fire, which they instantly returned with much spirit. Falling in with the enemy, agreeably to their instructions, they retired towards the centre, but not before they had dislodged them from their position. The Indians rushed forward, screaming and yelling hideously, in the direction of General Roberts' brigade, a few companies of which, alarmed by their numbers and yells, gave way at the first fire. To fill the chasm which was thus created, Jackson directed the regiment commanded by Colonel Bradley to be moved up, which, from some unaccountable cause, had failed to advance in a line with the others, and now occupied a position in the rear of the centre. Bradley, however, to whom this order was given by one of the staff, omitted to execute it in time, alleging that he was determined to remain on the eminence which he then possessed, until he should be approached and attacked by the enemy. Owing to this failure in the volunteer regiment, it became necessary to dismount the reserve, which, with great firmness, met the approach of the enemy, who were rapidly moving in this direction. The retreating militia, somewhat mortified at seeing their places so promptly supplied, rallied, and recovering their former position in the line, aided in checking the advance of the savages.

The action now became general, and in fifteen minutes the Indians were seen flying in every direction. On the left they were met and repulsed by the mounted riflemen; but on the right, owing to the halt of Bradley's regiment, which was intended to occupy the extreme right, and to the circumstance that Colonel Alcorn, who commanded one of the wings of the cavalry, had taken too large a circuit, a considerable space was left between the infantry and the cavalry, through which numbers escaped. The fight was maintained with great spirit and effect on both sides, as well before as after the retreat commenced; nor did the pursuit and slaughter terminate until the mountains were reached, at the distance of three miles.

Jackson, in his report of this action, bestowed high commendation on the officers and soldiers. "Too much praise," he said, at the close, "cannot be bestowed on the advance led by Colonel Carroll, for the spirited manner in which they commenced and sustained the attack; nor upon the reserve, commanded by Lieut. Colonel Dyer, for the gallantry with which they met and repulsed the enemy. In a word, officers of every grade, as well as privates, realized the high expectations I had formed of them, and merit the gratitude of their country."

In this battle, the force of the enemy was one thousand and eighty, of whom two hundred and ninety-nine were left dead on the ground; and it is believed that many were killed in the flight, who were not found when the estimate was made. Probably few escaped unhurt. Their loss on this occasion, as since stated by themselves, was not less than six hundred: that of the Americans was fifteen killed, and eighty wounded, several of whom afterwards died. Jackson, after collecting his dead and wounded, advanced his army beyond the fort, and encamped for the night. The Indians who had been for several days shut up by the besiegers, thus fortunately liberated from the most dreadful apprehensions and severest privations, having for some days been entirely without water, received the army with all the demonstrations of gratitude that Indians could give. Their manifestations of joy for their deliverance, presented an interesting and affecting spectacle. Their fears had been already greatly excited, for it was the very day when they were to have been assaulted, and when every soul within the fort must have perished. All the provisions they could spare from their scanty stock they sold to the general, who purchased them with his own money, and generously distributed them among his almost destitute soldiers.

It was with great regret that Jackson now found he was without the means of availing himself fully of the advantages of his victory; but the condition of his posts in the rear, and the want of provisions, (having left his encampment at Fort Strother with little more than one day's rations,) compelled him to return; thus giving the enemy time to recover from the consternation of their first defeat, and to re-assemble their forces. On returning to Fort Strother, he found that through the wilful mismanagement of General Cocke, no supplies had reached that post, and the soldiers were beginning to exhibit symptoms of discontent. Even his private stores, brought on at his own expense, and upon which he and his staff had hitherto wholly subsisted, had been in his absence distributed among the sick by the hospital surgeon, who had been previously instructed to do so if their wants should require it. A few dozen biscuits, which remained on his return, were given to hungry applicants, without being tasted by himself or family, who were probably not less hungry than those who were thus relieved. A scanty supply of indifferent beef, taken from the enemy or purchased of the Cherokees, was the only support afforded. Left thus destitute, Jackson, with the utmost cheerfulness of temper, repaired to the bullock pen, and of the offal there thrown away, provided for himself and staff what he was pleased to call, and seemed really to think, a very comfortable repast. Tripes, however, hastily provided in a camp, without bread or seasoning, can only be palatable to an appetite very highly whetted. Yet this constituted for several days the only diet at head quarters, during which time the general seemed entirely satisfied with his fare. Neither this, nor the liberal donations which he made to relieve the suffering soldier, deserve to be ascribed to ostentation or design: the one flowed from benevolence, the other from necessity, and a desire to place before his men an example of patience and suffering, which he felt might be necessary, and hoped might be serviceable. Charity in him was a warm and active propensity of the heart, urging him, by an instantaneous impulse, to minister to the wants of the distressed, without regarding, or even thinking of the consequences. Many of those to whom aid was extended, had no conception of the source that supplied them, and believed the comforts they received were, indeed, drawn from stores provided for the hospital department.

On one occasion, during these difficulties, a soldier, with a wo-begone countenance, approached the general, stating that he was nearly starved, that he had nothing to eat, and that he did not know what he should do. He was the more encouraged to complain, from perceiving that the general, who had seated himself at the root of a tree, was busily engaged in eating something, and confidently expected to be relieved. Jackson replied to him, that it had always been a rule with him, never to turn away a hungry man when it was in his power to relieve him. "I will most cheerfully," said he, "divide with you what I have;" and putting his hand in his pocket, he drew forth a few acorns, from which he had been feasting, at the same time remarking, in addition, that this was the only fare he had. The soldier seemed much surprised, and forthwith circulated the intelligence among his comrades, that their general was feeding on acorns, and urged them not to complain.

But while General Jackson remained wholly unmoved by his own privations, he was filled with solicitude and concern for his army. His utmost exertions, unceasingly applied were insufficient to remove the sufferings to which he saw they were exposed; and although they were by no means so great as were represented, yet were they undoubtedly such as to be sensibly and severely felt. Discontents, and a desire to return home, arose, and presently spread through the camp; and these were still further imbittered and augmented by the arts of a few designing officers, who, believing that the campaign would break up, hoped to make themselves popular on their return, by encouraging and taking part in the complaints of the soldiery. It is a singular fact, that those officers who pretended on this occasion to feel most sensibly for the wants of the army, and who contrived most effectually to instigate it to revolt, had never themselves been without provisions; and were, at that very moment, enjoying in abundance what would have relieved the distresses of many, had it been as generously and freely distributed as were their words of advice and condolence.

During this period of scarcity and discontent, small quantities of supplies were occasionally forwarded by the contractors, but not a sufficiency for present want, and still less to remove the apprehensions that were entertained for the future. At length, revolt began to show itself openly. The officers and soldiers of the militia, collecting in their tents and talking over their grievances, determined to yield up their patriotism and to abandon the camp. Several of the officers of the old volunteer corps exerted themselves clandestinely, to produce disaffection. Looking upon themselves somewhat in the light of veterans, from the discipline they had acquired in the expedition to Natchez, they were unwilling to be seen foremost in setting an example of mutiny, but wished to make the defection of others a pretext for their own.

It was almost unreasonable to expect men to be patient, while starvation was staring them in the face. Overlooking the fact that their difficulties were mainly occasioned by the malicious feelings of a single officer, they began to feel that they were neglected by their country, whose battles they had fought, and resentment and discontent took possession of their bosoms. Increasing from day to day, and extending from individuals to companies, and from companies to regiments, they soon threatened an entire dissolution of the army. The volunteers, though deeply imbued with this feeling, were at first restrained from any public exhibition of it, by their soldierly pride; but the militia regiments determined to leave the camp, and return to Tennessee. Apprised of their intention,

General Jackson resolved to defeat it; and as they drew out in the morning to commence their march, they found the volunteers drawn up across their path, with orders to require them, under penalty of instant military execution, to return to their position. They at once obeyed, admiring the firmness which baffled their design.

In this operation the volunteers had been unwilling instruments in the hands of their general, and, chagrined at their own success, resolved themselves the next day to abandon the camp in a body. What was their surprise, on making a movement to accomplish that object, to find the very militia whose mutiny they had the day before repressed, drawn up in the same position to resist them! So determined was their look, that the volunteers deemed it prudent to carry out the parallel, and returned quietly to their quarters. This process, by which nearly a whole army, anxious to desert, was kept in service by arraying one species of force against another, though effectual for the moment, would not bear repetition, and the general was sensible how feeble was the thread by which he held them together. The cavalry, who not only shared in the general privation, but had no forage, petitioned for permission to retire to the vicinity of Huntsville, pledging themselves to return when called on, after recruiting their horses and receiving their winter clothing. Their petition was granted, and they immediately left the camp.

Having received letters from Colonel Pope, assuring him that abundant supplies were on the way, General Jackson resolved to make an effort to produce good feeling throughout the army, in order that they might be able to act with promptitude when an opportunity offered for striking a decisive blow. He accordingly invited the field and platoon officers to his quarters, on the 14th of November, and communicated to them the information he had received, and the wishes and expectations which he had based upon it. "To be sure," said he, "we do not live sumptuously; but no one has died of hunger, or is likely to die; and then how animating are our prospects! Large supplies are at Deposit, and already are officers despatched to hasten them on. Wagons are on the way; a large number of beeves are in the neighborhood; and detachments are out to bring them in. All these resources surely cannot fail. I have no wish to starve you—none to deceive you. Stay contentedly; and if supplies do not arrive within two days, we will all march back together, and throw the blame of our failure where it should properly lie: until then we certainly have the means of subsisting; and if we are compelled to bear privations, let us remember that they are borne for our country, and are not greater than many—perhaps most armies have been compelled to endure. I have called you together to tell you my feelings and my wishes; this evening think on them seriously, and let me know yours in the morning."

After addressing them in such kind and generous terms, notwithstanding many of them had secretly encouraged the disaffection, how great must have been his grief and mortification in the morning, when he received from the officers of the volunteer regiments the annunciation that, in their opinion, "Nothing short of marching the army immediately back to the settlements, could prevent those difficulties and that disgrace which must attend a forcible desertion of the camp by his soldiers."

The officers of the militia, however, reported their willingness to wait a few days longer for a supply of provisions, and, if it should be received, to proceed with the campaign; otherwise, they insisted on being marched back where supplies could be procured. To preserve the volunteers for farther service, if possible, the general determined to gratify their wishes, and ordered General Hall to lead them back to Fort Deposit, there to obtain relief for themselves, and then to return as an escort to the provisions. But the second regiment of volunteers were ashamed to be found less loyal than the militia, and begged permission to remain with their general, and the first regiment marched alone. It is impossible to describe the emotions of General Jackson, when he saw a regiment of brave men, whom he had refused to abandon at Natchez even at the command of his government, for the preservation of whose well-earned fame he would have hazarded his life, deserting him in the wilderness, reckless of honor, of patriotism, of gratitude, and humanity. He could not avoid giving expression to his feelings in strong and decided terms. "I was prepared," he said, "to endure every evil but disgrace; and this, as I can never submit to myself, I can give no encouragement to in others."

On the 16th of November, General Jackson addressed a letter to Colonel Pope, the contractor, in which he said:

"My men are all starving. More than half of there left me yesterday for Fort Deposit, in consequence of the scarcity, and the whole will do so in a few days if plentiful supplies do not arrive. Again and again I must entreat you to spare neither labor nor expense to furnish me, and furnish me without delay. We have already struck the blow which would, if followed up, put an end to Creek hostility. I cannot express the torture of my feelings when I reflect that a campaign so auspiciously begun, and which might be so soon and so gloriously terminated, is likely to be rendered abortive for the want of supplies. For God's sake, prevent so great an evil."

In his address to the officers on the 14th, the general had told them that in case supplies did not reach them within two days, he would lead the army back where provisions could be had. Two days had elapsed after the departure of the volunteers, and no supplies had come. The declaration had been made in the confident expectation that provisions, then known to be on the way, would reach them before the expiration of that period; but the general felt bound to comply with his word. He immediately proceeded to make arrangements for the abandonment of Fort Strother; but, contemplating the new courage with which it would inspire the enemy, the calamities it was likely to bring on the frontiers, and the disgrace upon his army, if not on himself, he exclaimed, "If only two men will remain with me, I will never abandon this post." "You have one, general," promptly replied Captain Gordon, of the spies; "let us look if we cannot find another." The captain immediately beat up for volunteers, and, with the aid of some of the general staff, soon raised one hundred and nine, who agreed to stand by their general to the last extremity.

Confident that supplies were at hand, the general marched with the militia, announcing that they would be ordered back if provisions should be met at no great distance from the fort. Within ten or twelve miles they met a drove of a hundred and fifty beeves. They halted, butchered, and ate; but the courage inspired by satiety was that of mutineers. Upon receiving an order to return, with the exception of a small party to convey the sick and wounded, they resolved to disobey it. One company resumed its march homeward, before General Jackson was apprised of their design. Informed of this movement, he hastened to a spot about a quarter of a mile ahead, where General Coffee, with a part of the staff and a few soldiers, had halted, and ordered them instantly to form across the road, and fire on the mutineers if they should attempt to pass. Rather than encounter the bold faces before them, the mutinous company thought it expedient to return to the main body, and it was hoped that no farther opposition would be exhibited.

Going alone for the purpose of mixing among his men, and appeasing them by argument and remonstrance, the general found a spirit of mutiny pervading the whole brigade. They had formed, and were on the point of moving off, knowing that no force was at hand powerful enough to resist them; but they had to deal with a man who was a host in himself. He seized a musket, threw it across his horse's neck, placed himself in front of the brigade drawn up in column, and declared he would shoot the first man who took a step in advance. Struck with awe, the men gazed at him in sullen silence. In this position, General Coffee and some of the members of his staff rode up, and placed themselves at his side. The faithful officers and soldiers, amounting to about two companies, formed in his rear, under orders to fire when he did. For some minutes not a word was uttered. A murmur then arose among the mutineers, and at length they signified their willingness to return. The matter was amicably arranged, and the troops marched back to Fort Strother, though not in the best spirits.

This incident derives additional interest from the fact,

that the general's left arm was not so far healed as to enable him to aim a musket, and the weapon he had was too much out of order to be fired.

Shortly after the battle of Talladega, the Hillabee tribes, who had been the principal sufferers on that occasion, applied to General Jackson for peace ; declaring their willingness to receive it on such terms as he might be pleased to dictate. He promptly replied, that his government had taken up arms to bring to a proper sense of duty a people to whom she had ever shown the utmost kindness, but who, nevertheless, had committed against her citizens the most unprovoked depredations ; and that she would lay them down only when certain that this object was attained. "Upon those," continued he, "who are friendly, I neither wish nor intend to make war ; but they must afford evidences of the sincerity of their professions ; the prisoners and property they have taken from us and the friendly Creeks, must be restored ; the instigators of the war, and the murderers of our citizens, must be surrendered ; the latter must and will be made to feel the force of our resentment. Long shall they remember Fort Mimms, in bitterness and tears."

Having communicated to General Cocke, whose division was acting in this section of the nation, the propositions that had been made by the Hillabee tribes, with the answer returned, and urged him to detach to Fort Strother six hundred of his men to aid in the defence of that place during his absence, and in the operations he intended to resume on his return, Jackson proceeded to Deposit and Ditto's landing, where the most effectual means in his power were taken for obtaining regular supplies in future. The contractors were required to furnish immediately thirty days' rations at Fort Strother, forty at Talladega, and as many at the junction of the Coosa and Tallapoosa two hundred packhorses and forty wagons were also put in requisition to facilitate their transportation. Understanding now that the whole detachment from Tennessee had been received into the service of the United States, he persuaded himself that the difficulties previously encountered would not again recur, and looked forward, with sanguine expectations, to the speedy accomplishment of the objects of the expedition. But the satisfaction he felt, and the hopes he began to cherish, were of short continuance.

The volunteers who had formerly been enrolled in the expedition to Natchez, began to look anxiously for the 10th of December, at which time they supposed their enlistments would expire. Anticipating difficulty from this cause, General Jackson was exceedingly anxious to fill up the deficiencies in his ranks. General Roberts was accordingly ordered to return and complete his brigade, and Colonel Carroll and Major Searcy were despatched to Tennessee, to raise volunteers for six months, or during the campaign. At the same time, the general wrote to several patriotic citizens of that state, urging them to contribute their aid and assistance. In one of his letters, he expressed himself in the following touching language, which shows how deeply his heart was enlisted in the enterprise he had undertaken to accomplish:

"I left Tennessee with an army, brave, I believe, as any general ever commanded. I have seen them in battle, and my opinion of their bravery is not changed. But their fortitude—on this too I relied—has been too severely tested. Perhaps I was wrong in believing that nothing but death could conquer the spirits of brave men. I am sure I was; for my men I know are brave, yet privations have rendered them discontented—that is enough. The expedition must nevertheless be prosecuted to a successful termination. New volunteers must be raised to conclude what has been so auspiciously begun by the old ones. Gladly would I save these men from themselves, and insure them a harvest which they have sown; but if they will abandon it to others, it must be so. * * * * * * So far as my exertions can contribute, the purposes both of the savage and his instigator shall be defeated; and so far as yours can, I hope—I know they will be employed. I have said enough—I want men, and want them immediately."

Anxious to prosecute the campaign as soon as possible, that by employing his troops actively he might dispel from their minds that discontent so frequently manifested, Jackson wrote to General Cocke, early in December, earnestly desiring him to hasten to the Ten Islands, with fifteen hundred men. He assured him that the mounted men, who had returned to the settlements for subsistence, and to recruit their horses, would arrive by the 12th of the month. He wished to commence his operations directly, " knowing they would be prepared for it, and well knowing they would require it. 1 am astonished," he continued, "to hear that your supplies continue deficient. In the name of God, what are the contractors doing, and about what are they engaged? Every letter I receive from Governor Blount, assures me I am to receive plentiful supplies from them, and seems to take for granted, notwithstanding all I have said to the contrary, that they have been hitherto regularly furnished. Considering the generous loan the state has made for this purpose, and the facility of procuring bread-stuffs in East Tennessee, and the transporting them by water to Fort Deposit, it is to me wholly unaccountable that not a pound has ever arrived at that place. This evil must continue no longer—it must be remedied. I expect, therefore, and through you must require, that in twenty days they furnish at Deposit every necessary supply."

While these preparations for the vigorous prosecution of hostilities were being made, the volunteers were congratulating themselves upon their anticipated discharge from the service. They had originally enlisted on the 10th of December, 1812, to serve for twelve months. A portion of this time, however, after their return from Natchez, they had not been actually engaged in service. This fact was entirely overlooked in their calculations, and they commenced pressing their officers on the subject of their discharge.

General Jackson received a letter from the colonel who commanded the second regiment, dated the 4th of December, 1813, in which was attempted to be detailed their whole ground of complaint. He began by stating, that, painful as it was, he nevertheless felt himself bound to disclose an important and unpleasant truth: that, on the

10th instant, the service would be deprived of the regiment he commanded. He seemed to deplore, with great sensibility, the scene that would be exhibited on that day, should opposition be made to their departure; and still more sensibly, the consequences that would result from a disorderly abandonment of the camp. He stated that they had all considered themselves finally discharged, on the 20th of April, 1813, and never knew to the contrary, until they saw his order of the 24th of September, 1813, requiring them to rendezvous on the 4th of October. "Thus situated," proceeded the colonel, "there was considerable opposition to the order; on which the officers generally, as I am advised, and I know myself in particular, gave it as an unequivocal opinion, that their term of service would terminate on the 10th of December, 1813. They therefore look to their general, who has their confidence, for an honorable discharge on that day; and that, in every respect, he will see that justice be done them. They regret that their particular situations and circumstances require them to leave their general, at a time when their services are important to the common cause.

"It would be desirable," he continued, "that those men who have served with honor, should be honorably discharged, and that they should return to their families and friends without even the semblance of disgrace; with their general they leave it to place them in that situation. They have received him as an affectionate father, while they have honored, revered, and obeyed him; but having devoted a considerable portion of their time to the service of their country, by which their domestic concerns are greatly deranged, they wish to return, and attend to their own affairs."

Although this communication announced the determination of only a part of the volunteer brigade, the commander in chief had abundant evidence that the defection was but too general. The difficulty which he had heretofore been compelled to encounter, from the discontent of his troops, might well induce him to regret that a spirit of insubordination should again threaten to appear in his camp. That he might prevent it, if possible, he hastened

DIFFICULTY WITH THE VOLUNTEERS 79

to lay before them the error and impropriety of their views, and the consequences involved, should they persist in their purpose.

To the foregoing letter he returned a reply which, for unshrinking firmness of resolution, and patriotic devotion to the interests of his country, was never surpassed. He declared his determination to prevent their return, at the hazard of his life, and called upon God to witness, that the scenes of blood which might be exhibited on the 10th of December should not be laid to his charge. He reminded the volunteers that they had been enlisted for twelve months' actual service; that but a portion of that time had expired; and that at the time of their dismissal, after their return from Natchez, a certificate was given to each man, setting forth the number of months he had served, and they were expressly told that they were liable to be again called out to complete the full term. He also stated that he was ready and willing to discharge them, provided he received orders to that effect from the President of the United States, or the Governor of the State, but otherwise, they must remain with him. The letter concluded with the following remarkable words: "I cannot, must not believe, that 'the volunteers of Tennessee,' a name ever dear to fame, will disgrace themselves, and a country which they have honored, by abandoning her standard, as mutineers and deserters; but should I be disappointed, and compelled to resign this pleasing hope, one thing I will not resign—my duty. Mutiny and sedition, so long as I possess the power of quelling them, shall be put down; and even when left destitute of this, I will still be found, in the last extremity, endeavoring to discharge the duty I owe my country and myself."

To the platoon officers, who addressed him on the same subject, he replied with nearly the same spirited feeling; but discontent was too deeply fastened, and had been too artfully fomented, to be removed by any thing like argument or entreaty. At length, on the evening of the 9th of December, 1813, General Hall hastened to the tent of Jackson, with information that his whole brigade was in a state of mutiny, and making preparations to move forcibly off. This was a measure which every consideration of policy, duty, and honor, required Jackson to oppose ; and to this purpose he instantly applied all the means he possessed. He immediately issued the following general order : "The commanding general being informed that an actual mutiny exists in his camp, all officers and soldiers are commanded to put it down. The officers and soldiers of the first brigade will, without delay, parade on the west side of the fort, and await further orders." The artillery company, with two small field-pieces, being posted in the front and rear, and the militia, under the command of Colonel Wynne, on the eminences, in advance, were ordered to prevent any forcible departure of the volunteers.

The general rode along the line, which had been previously formed agreeably to his orders, and addressed them, by companies, in a strain of impassioned eloquence. He feelingly expatiated on their former good conduct, and the esteem and applause it had secured them ; and pointed to the disgrace which they must heap upon themselves, their families, and country, by persisting, even if they could succeed, in their present mutiny. He told them, however, that they should not succeed but by passing over his body ; that even in opposing their mutinous spirit, he should perish honorably—by perishing at his post, and in the discharge of his duty. "Reinforcements," he continued, "are preparing to hasten to my assistance ; it cannot be long before they will arrive. I am, too, in daily expectation of receiving information, whether you may be discharged or not—until then you must not, and shall not, retire. I have done with entreaty,—it has been used long enough. I will attempt it no more. You must now determine whether you will go, or peaceably remain ; if you still persist in your determination to move forcibly off, the point between us shall soon be decided." At first they hesitated ; he demanded an explicit and positive answer. They still hesitated, and he commanded the artillerist to prepare the match ; he himself remaining in front of the volunteers, and within the line of fire, which he intended soon to order. Alarmed at his apparent determination,

SUPPRESSION OF THE MUTINY

and dreading the consequences involved in such a contest, "Let us return," was presently lisped along the line, and soon after determined upon. The officers came forward and pledged themselves for their men, who either nodded assent, or openly expressed a willingness to retire to their quarters, and remain without further tumult, until information was received, or the expected aid should arrive. Thus passed away a moment of the greatest peril, and pregnant with important consequences.

Notwithstanding all General Jackson's firmness, the want of supplies and the actual necessities of his army, at length compelled him reluctantly to allow them to return home, while he himself remained, with about one hundred faithful soldiers, in the garrison at Fort Strother, there to await the arrival of reinforcements.

CHAPTER VI.

1814. Arrival of recruits—Battle of Emuckfaw—Return of the army—Ambuscade of the enemy—Battle of Enotochopco—Bravery of General Carroll and Lieutenant Armstrong—Return to Fort Strother—The army reinforced—Battle of Tohopeka—Kindness of Jackson to a prisoner—Preparations to attack Hoithlewalle—Address to the troops—The Indians abandon their towns at Jackson's approach—Termination of the campaign—Operations of the British at Pensacola—Conduct of the Spanish governor—Proclamation of Colonel Nicholls—Unsuccessful attack on Fort Bowyer—Jackson marches to Pensacola and demolishes it. 1814.

THE difficulties and embarrassments which had thus far in the campaign attended the operations of General Jackson, might well have appalled a braver spirit; but his was not a nature to sink beneath the frowns of adverse fortune. His intrepidity of spirit, and resoluteness of purpose, were never more signally manifested, than at the very moment when the return of the volunteers left him without the means to pursue the advantages he had already gained. He again urged the governor of Tennessee to expedite the enlistment of troops, and provide means for furnishing supplies at such points as they might be needed. About the middle of January, 1814, eight hundred new recruits reached his camp at Fort Strother. Considering it utterly impracticable to penetrate the Creek country with so meagre a force, he determined to make a diversion in favor of Major Floyd, who, it was feared, might be closely pressed by the enemy, in consequence of his failure to co-operate with the troops from Tennessee.

Having received authentic intelligence, that a large body of the "red-sticks," or hostile Indians, were collected on the Emuckfaw creek, in a bend of the Tallapoosa river, Jackson directed his march thither; and on the evening of the 21st of January, he encamped within a short distance

ARRIVAL OF RECRUITS

of the enemy. A friendly Indian spy, who had reconnoitred the enemy's camp, brought in word that the Indians were removing their women and children—a sure indication that they meditated an attack. Before daylight, on the morning of the 22d, a brisk firing was heard upon the right, and in a few moments the action became general. The enemy were soon repulsed, with the loss of many of their best and bravest warriors; but their undoubted strength, and the fact that they were constantly receiving reinforcements, determined the general to return to Fort Strother. The object he had in view was fortunately accomplished, as it was afterwards known that the battle of Emuckfaw was, in all probability, the means of saving Major Floyd's troops, who was hotly engaged with the enemy on the 27th, and would have been destroyed if their force had not been so seriously diminished.

General Jackson buried the dead on the field of battle, and on the 23d of January commenced a retrograde march. During the night of the 23d there came on a violent storm, which was known to be always favorable to the Indian mode of fighting, and as his troops were not attacked on the night of the 22d, or while on their march the following day, he rightly conjectured that the enemy were lying in ambush for him at the ford of Enotochopco, about twelve miles from Emuckfaw. The stream, at this point, ran through a narrow defile; the ford was deep; and the banks were covered with underwood and reeds. The eagle eye of Jackson had discovered the natural advantages of the place for an ambush, on his previous march to Emuckfaw, and he resolved to cross the stream at a ford six hundred yards lower down. In order to guard against an attack from the enemy, if they saw fit to follow him after discovering the change in his course, he formed his rear to receive them. This movement was wisely made. Part of the army had crossed the creek, and the artillery were on the point of entering it, when an alarm gun was heard in the rear, and the next instant the whooping and yelling of the savages told plainly enough that they were coming on in fearful numbers. The militia, on the right and left, being struck with a sudden panic, instantly retreated down the bank, with their colonels at their head, leaving the brave General Carroll, and about twenty-five men, to check the advance of the enemy. As Colonel Stump came plunging towards the creek where General Jackson was superintending the crossing of the troops, the latter made an unsuccessful attempt to draw his sword and cut him down. He was afterwards tried by a court-martial, on a charge of cowardice, and cashiered.

In the mean time, Lieutenant Armstrong ordered his company of artillery to form on the hill, and with the assistance of one or two others, he drew up the cannon, a six-pounder, and pointed it towards the enemy. The ramrod and picker had been lost, but Jackson supplied the deficiency by using muskets and their ramrods to load the piece. It was fired twice, and did fearful execution. The Indians began to waver, and when the general had succeeded in rallying a number of the fugitives, and formed them for a charge, they fled with precipitation, throwing away their packs, and leaving twenty-six of their warriors dead on the field.

After this repulse, the army resumed their march, and reached Fort Strother in safety, on the 27th of January, where they were dismissed by their general, until he received further orders from government, which he desired to provide him with a competent force to enter the Creek country, and put a termination to the war. Through the patriotic exertions of Governor Blount, General Jackson was again at the head of a fine army, early in March, and ready to recommence the campaign. His force at this time consisted of four thousand Tennessee militia and volunteers, and a regiment of United States regulars. In the month of February, he had received information that the hostile Indians, about one thousand in number, were fortifying themselves in a bend of the Tallapoosa river, fifty miles from Emuckfaw, where they had determined to make a last stand. The country between the Coosa and Tallapoosa rivers, known to the whites as the "Hickory Ground," had always been held sacred by the Indians, and they were taught, by their prophets, to believe that no white man could ever enter this territory to conquer it. Gene-

BATTLE OF ENOTOCHOPCO 85

ral Jackson saw at once that the conquest of this tract of ground would compel them to sue for peace, and he determined on forcing them to a general engagement. He accordingly marched his army down the Coosa, and, having established a fort at the mouth of Cedar Creek, called Fort Williams, he crossed over to the Tallapoosa. He was three days in crossing the Hickory Ground, as the road had to be cut from one river to the other. On the morning of the 27th of March, he arrived near Tohopeka with a force of over two thousand men.

The bend of the river in which the enemy were fortified, as its name imports, resembles a horse-shoe in shape. Across the neck of land by which the peninsula was entered from the north, the Indians had thrown up a rude breastwork of logs, seven or eight feet high, but so constructed that assailants would be exposed to a double and cross-fire. About a hundred acres lay within the bend, and at the bottom of it there was an Indian village, around which were a great number of canoes fastened to the bank of the river. After reconnoitering the position, General Jackson detached General Coffee to surround the bend opposite to where the canoes were secured, while he himself advanced to assault the breastwork. As soon as General Coffee had reported, by signals, the fulfilment of the order, the two pieces of artillery, a six and three pounder, began to play upon the breastwork. The firing had continued for about two hours, when some of the friendly Cherokees who were with General Coffee, swam the river, and brought over the canoes. A number of Coffee's troops immediately crossed over, set fire to the village, and attacked the Indians in the rear. On discovering this movement, General Jackson ordered a push to be made at the breastwork, and carried it by storm. The battle now commenced in earnest, and a most bloody and desperate hand to hand conflict ensued, in which the Indians were finally overpowered, and compelled to give way. A number of them attempted to escape across the river, but were shot by the spies and mounted men under General Coffee. Some took refuge among the brush and fallen timber on the cliffs overhanging the river, from which they fired upon the victors. Jackson was desirous to prevent the further loss of life, and sent an interpreter within call to offer them terms, but he was also fired upon and severely wounded. The cannon were then brought to bear on the place of their concealment, yet they still refused to surrender. After losing several men in an ineffectual charge, the general, as a last resort, commanded the brush and timber to be fired, and such of them as were driven from their hiding-places were shot as they ran. Night at length put an end to the battle, and a few of the miserable survivors escaped in the darkness. Five hundred and fifty-seven of their number were found dead on the field, and three hundred women and children were taken prisoners. The American loss was fifty-five killed and one hundred and forty-six wounded; nearly one-third of which fell upon the friendly Creeks and Cherokees. Among the Indians slain were three of their prophets, who had been the most active in exciting them to war. Up to the last moment, they maintained their influence over their deluded countrymen, and continued their wild and unseemly dances amid the thunder of battle. One of them was struck dead, with a grape shot, in the midst of his incantations.

An incident occurred after the battle highly characteristic of the American general. A young Indian was brought before him who had received a severe wound in the leg. A surgeon was sent for to dress it, and the savage quietly submitted to the operation; but while it was going on, he looked inquiringly at the general, and said, "Cure 'im, kill 'im again?" Jackson assured him, in a friendly manner, that he need not apprehend any further injury, and he soon recovered. The general was struck with his manly bearing, and having ascertained that all his relations had perished in the battle, he sent him to his own house in Tennessee. After the conclusion of the war, he bound him out to a trade in Nashville, where he married, and established himself in business.

As his men had taken but seven days' rations with them when they left Fort Williams, Jackson was compelled to return to that post. Before doing so, he took the precau-

KINDNESS TO AN INDIAN PRISONER 87

tion to sink the dead bodies of his soldiers in the river, that they might be beyond the reach of the savages who had disinterred those buried at Emuckfaw and Enotochopco, for the purpose of obtaining their scalps.

The original plan of the expedition against the Creek nation, formed by General Pinckney, the commander in chief, contemplated the junction of the different divisions sent from Georgia, Tennessee, and Mississippi, at the bend of the Coosa and Tallapoosa; but the failure to furnish provisions to the Tennessee troops, in the early part of the campaign, prevented the accomplishment of this design. General Jackson, however, after his return to Tohopeka, resolved upon the complete conquest of the Hickory Ground. He immediately made preparations to attack Hoithlewalle, an Indian town in this territory, where a large body of the enemy were said to be concentrated. On the 7th of April, just five days after his return from Tohopeka, he commenced his march. Each of his men carried eight days' provisions on his back. This supply was thought to be abundantly sufficient, as he expected soon to meet the eastern army under Colonel Milton, who had orders from General Pinckney to furnish him with supplies. Most of the friendly Indians were dismissed, on account of the difficulty in obtaining provisions. Before setting out, Jackson issued an animated address to his troops, in the following terms:

" Soldiers,—You have entitled yourselves to the gratitude of your country and your general. The expedition from which you have returned, has, by your good conduct, been rendered prosperous beyond any example in the history of our warfare; it has redeemed the character of your state, and of that description of troops of which the greater part of you are.

" The fiends of the Tallapoosa will no longer murder our women and children, or disturb the quiet of our borders. Their midnight flambeaux will no more illumine their council-house, or shine upon the victims of their infernal orgies. In their places a new generation will arise, who will know their duty better. The weapons of warfare will be exchanged for the utensils of husbandry;

and the wilderness, which now withers in sterility, and mourns the desolation which overspreads her, will blossom as the rose, and become the nursery of the arts. But, before this happy day can arrive, other chastisements remain to be inflicted. It is indeed lamentable, that the path to peace should lead through blood, and over the bodies of the slain; but it is a dispensation of Providence, and perhaps a wise one, to inflict partial evils that ultimate good may follow."

It was Jackson's intention to reach Hoithlewalle on the 11th of April; but the roads had been rendered almost impassable by the heavy rains, and he found himself unable to do so. When within ten or twelve miles of the town, he ascertained that the inhabitants had deserted it. He then directed his march for Fooshatchie, three miles lower down the river, where he took several prisoners. The Indians generally, on his approach, fled across the Tallapoosa. He had anticipated this, and his orders to Colonel Milton, to co-operate with him from the east, were intended to prevent the escape of the enemy in that direction. That officer, however, not only disregarded the orders he had received, but suffered the Indians to pass him unmolested, when he was preparing to cross the river and attack them. The rapid rising of the Tallapoosa, and the want of provisions, compelled Jackson temporarily to desist from the pursuit. Soon after, he made application to Colonel Milton, who was advancing to attack Hoithlewalle, which he had already destroyed, for provisions to supply his troops. The colonel replied that he did not feel himself under obligation to furnish any to the Tennessee troops, but he would lend them some if it were absolutely necessary. Jackson instantly sent him a peremptory order, by Captain Gordon of the spies, requiring him to furnish the provisions which he had previously requested, and to form a junction with him the next day. On reading the order, Colonel Milton inquired of Captain Gordon, what sort of a man General Jackson was. "He is a man," replied the captain, "who intends when he gives an order that it shall be obeyed!" Colonel Milton then said he would furnish provisions, not because they were ordered, but because the men were suffering for want of them; nevertheless he afterwards obeyed the order in full, and joined the army under Jackson with his force.

In order to intercept the Indians who had fled across the river, Jackson detached a body of mounted men to scour the left bank of the Tallapoosa, while he himself, with the main army, prepared to march down the Coosa as far as their junction. Just as the army was about to commence its march, word was brought to the general that Colonel Milton's brigade could not move, as the wagon-horses had strayed away in the night and could not be found. Jackson sent back word that he had discovered an effectual remedy in such cases, which was to detail twenty men to each wagon. Milton took the hint, and having dismounted a few of his dragoons, attached their horses to the wagons, and soon put his brigade in motion.

The army did not encounter the least opposition on their march, and it was now evident that the battle of Tohopeka had ended the Creek war. No effort was made by the surviving warriors to rally, after that fatal day, and as General Jackson advanced, they either fled before him, or came in and offered submission. In a few months peace and quiet were restored; whereupon the Tennessee soldiers returned home, and were honorably discharged.

Upon the resignation of General Harrison, in the spring of 1814, Jackson was appointed a major-general in the army of the United States. The protection of the coast near the mouths of the Mississippi was intrusted to him; and his first attention was turned to the encouragement and protection which the savages received, from the Spanish governor and Spanish authorities in the fortress of Pensacola, which is situated on the Gulf of Mexico, at about a hundred miles' distance from the main fastness of the Creek Indians. His opinion was, that the savages were constantly receiving assistance from the Spanish garrison, and from the British, through the means of the garrison; and he was persuaded that the latter would finally attack New Orleans after having prepared themselves at Pensacola. On his way to the south, he learned that about three hundred British troops had landed, and were fortifying themselves at no great distance from that post. In this state of things, he endeavored to prevail upon the Spanish governor to desist from all acts injurious to the United States. That officer at first prevaricated, but afterwards boldly falsified the truth. The news had already been received, of the fall of Napoleon, and his banishment to Elba; and this event inspired new villany, and new courage, everywhere, inasmuch as it greatly increased the ability of Great Britain to prosecute her hostile operations against the United States. The Spanish garrison at Pensacola was, in fact, a rendezvous for the British, and their Indian allies. Captain Gordon was sent by General Jackson, in the month of August, 1814, to reconnoitre the post, and, on his return, he reported that he had seen from fifty to two hundred officers and soldiers, a park of artillery, and about five hundred savages drilling under British officers, and dressed in British uniform. These facts were duly communicated to the government, and an order was issued on the 18th of July, by General Armstrong, then secretary of war, authorizing General Jackson to attack Pensacola. By some strange and unaccountable delay, the letter containing this order did not reach him until the 17th of January, 1815.

General Jackson regarded the operations of the British at Pensacola, with considerable anxiety; and on the appearance of the following proclamation, addressed to the inhabitants of the southern and western states, and dated at Pensacola, the "head-quarters" of the officer whose name was attached, he decided to act on his own responsibility:

"Natives of Louisiana! on you the first call is made, to assist in liberating from a faithless, imbecile government, your paternal soil: Spaniards, Frenchmen, Italians, and British, whether settled, or residing for a time, in Louisiana, on you, also, I call to aid me in this just cause. The American usurpation in this country must be abolished, and the lawful owners of the soil put in possession. I am at the head of a large body of Indians, well armed, disciplined, and commanded by British officers—a good train of artillery, with every requisite, seconded by the powerful aid of a numerous British and Spanish squadron of ships and vessels of war. Be not alarmed, inhabitants of the country, at our approach; the same good faith and disinterestedness, which have distinguished the conduct of Britons in Europe, accompany them here; you will have no fear of litigious taxes imposed on you for the purpose of carrying on an unnatural and unjust war; your property, your laws, the peace and tranquillity of your country, will be guarantied to you by men who will suffer no infringement of theirs; rest assured that these brave red men only burn with an ardent desire of satisfaction for the wrongs they have suffered from the Americans, and to join you in liberating these southern provinces from their yoke, and drive them into those limits formerly prescribed by my sovereign. The Indians have pledged themselves in the most solemn manner, not to injure, in the slightest degree, the persons or property of any but enemies. A flag over any door, whether Spanish, French, or British, will be a certain protection; nor dare any Indian put his foot on the threshold thereof, under penalty of death from his own countrymen; not even an enemy will an Indian put to death, except resisting in arms; and as for injuring helpless women and children, the red men, by their good conduct and treatment to them, will (if it be possible) make the Americans blush for their more inhuman conduct, lately, on the Escambia, and within a neutral territory.

"Inhabitants of Kentucky, you have too long borne with grievous impositions—the whole brunt of the war has fallen on your brave sons: be imposed on no longer; but either range yourselves under the standard of your forefathers, or observe a strict neutrality. If you comply with either of these offers, whatever provisions you send down will be paid for in dollars, and the safety of the persons bringing them, as well as the free navigation of the Mississippi, guarantied to you. Men of Kentucky, let me call to your view, (and I trust to your abhorrence,) the conduct of those factions which hurried you into this civil, unjust, and unnatural war, at a time when Great Britain was straining every nerve in defence of her own and the liberties of the world—when the bravest of her sons were fighting and bleeding in so sacred a cause—when she was spending millions of her treasure in endeavoring to pull down one of the most formidable and dangerous tyrants that ever disgraced the form of man—when groaning Europe was almost in her last gasp—when Britons alone showed an undaunted front—basely did those assassins endeavor to stab her from the rear; she has turned on them, renovated from the bloody but successful struggle—Europe is happy and free, and she now hastens justly to avenge the unprovoked insult. Show them that you are not collectively unjust; leave that contemptible few to shift for themselves; let those slaves of the tyrant send an embassy to Elba, and implore his aid; but let every honest, upright American, spurn them with united contempt. After the experience of twenty-one years, can you longer support those brawlers for liberty who call it freedom when themselves are free? Be no longer their dupes—accept of my offers—every thing I have promised in this paper I guaranty to you on the sacred honor of a British officer.

"Given under my hand, at my head-quarters, Pensacola, this 29th day of August, 1814.

EDWARD NICHOLLS."

The mere fact of allowing this document to go forth to the world, unaccompanied as it was by any disavowal on the part of the Spanish governor, constituted a sufficient justification for the subsequent conduct of General Jackson. Troops had been drilled, savages supplied with weapons, and munitions of war prepared, under the immediate observation of the Spanish authorities; and, as if to leave no room for doubt, their implied consent, at least, was given to the waiver of their rights of neutrality, by suffering a British commander, unrebuked, to establish his "head-quarters" in their midst. The attack on Pensacola, by General Jackson, was afterwards made the subject of an investigation in Congress, and has frequently been referred to, in other quarters, in terms of censure. His conduct was approved by his government, and the facts certainly present a complete justification.

ATTACK ON PENSACOLA

While General Jackson was making preparation, for his contemplated attack on Pensacola, an assault was made by the British troops from that post, upon Fort Bowyer, which was situated on the Mobile river. On the 15th of September, 1814, Colonel Nicholls attacked the fort by land, while several vessels, mounting altogether about ninety guns, approached by sea. The expedition ended in blowing up one of the English ships, greatly damaging another and sending off Colonel Nicholls with the loss of one of his ships, and, as it was said, one of his eyes. Major Lawrence commanded the American fort. His brave band consisted of only one hundred and thirty men; while the force of the British was ninety guns by sea, and Nicholls assaulted the fort by land, with a twelve-pound howitzer, and several hundred marines, sailors, and savages. This affair was highly creditable to Major Lawrence and his men. The disparity of force was very great; and this disgraceful beating at the outset must have had a considerable effect upon the enemy. Jackson was still more firmly resolved, after this attack, to break up the rendezvous at Pensacola; and on the 6th of November, 1814, he marched against it, demolished all its defences and protections, drove out the British and the savages, and taught Nicholls and the Spanish governor, that there was still one country left which was not to be insulted with impunity by the satellites of despotism.

CHAPTER VII.

1814. Jackson marches to New Orleans—Preparations to defend the city—Surrounded by traitors and spies—Situation of the country—Strength of the British expedition—Firmness of Jackson—The city placed under martial law—Vigorous measures rendered absolutely necessary—Landing of the British—Alarm in the city—Jackson determines to attack them—Disposition of his forces—Battle on the night of the twenty-third of December—Gallant conduct of the American troops—Repulse of the British—The complete triumph of the Americans prevented by the darkness of the night—Adventure of Colonels Dyer and Gibson—The Americans fall back to a new position, and prepare to fortify it—Effect of the battle. 1814.

AFTER administering this severe, but deserved rebuke, to the Spanish governor, General Jackson immediately repaired, with a small portion of his army, to the city of New Orleans, at that time the most vulnerable point on the southern frontier. He arrived there on the 1st day of December, 1814, and on the 4th it was rumored that a British fleet was approaching the coast. Two days after, the report was confirmed, and it was positively known that Admiral Cochrane and Sir George Cockburn, who had been compelled to retreat down the Chesapeake after the burning of Washington city, had sailed for the Gulf of Mexico with the forces under their command. Jackson did not lose a single moment, but at once applied himself vigorously to the work of preparation. Previous to his arrival, the inhabitants had become desponding and indifferent. The influence of a master-mind soon aroused every thing into activity. Confidence was speedily restored. Resources that none had ever dreamed of sprang up at his bidding. His genius and perseverance soon found means for the crisis, desperate as it appeared, while his determined energy and resolute will, manifested on all occasions, in the midst of danger and alarm, excited the hopes of the timid, and infused new courage into the breasts of the wavering and faint-hearted.

The city of New Orleans, at this time, contained a population of about 30,000 inhabitants, most of whom, as the territory of Louisiana had but recently been purchased, were of French and Spanish descent. As a very natural consequence, their attachment to their new government was any thing but ardent or sincere. Jackson had no only prejudices and jealousies to contend against, but treason lurked everywhere around him. Spies were constantly engaged in observing his motions, and the very men whose firesides he came to protect from outrage and molestation, corresponded with the enemy at Pensacola. In addition to these difficulties, the American general was seriously embarrassed from the want of arms, ammunition, and troops. The Tennessee militia under General Carroll, and the mounted riflemen, commanded by General Coffee, arrived soon after Jackson reached the city. In order to conceal his real weakness from the enemy, these troops were encamped a few miles out of town, and their number intentionally represented to be much larger than it really was. He did not wish his detachments to be counted; and it was a part of his policy to exaggerate his force, to deceive the spies and impose upon the enemy. Besides this, the appearance and accoutrements of the western volunteers, though exactly suited to their mode of warfare, were not particularly calculated to inspire confidence or courage in those who would have been more highly gratified at beholding all "the pride, pomp, and circumstance of glorious war." In distributing his forces, Jackson took especial care to place them in such a manner, that they could be readily assembled in a single mass upon New Orleans.

The city itself was the point really menaced. It is situated around a bend of the Mississippi river, on the eastern bank. It is generally approached by vessels, from the river, although small craft, such as schooners and sloops, navigate lakes Pontchartrain and Borgne. A narrow strip of land, varying from a few hundred yards to two or three miles, borders the river, gradually tapering off into a swamp, as it recedes, until it reaches the lakes. This strip of land is covered with plantations, and is protected from the inundations of the river by an embankment of earth, called the "levee," which extends far above the city, on both sides of the river.

The expedition fitted out by the British against New Orleans was truly a formidable one. The fleet under Admiral Cochrane numbered more than eighty sail, previous to the arrival of the reinforcements. On board the transports were eleven thousand "heroes of the Peninsula," fresh from the blood-stained field of Vittoria, commanded by four able and experienced generals; two admirals, and twelve thousand seamen and marines, with fire-ships, rockets, ammunition, and artillery in abundance. This array of strength, which lost nothing of its terrors in the rumors circulated by the agents of the British government, was not by any means to be despised. General Jackson foresaw the danger, and determined to avert it. He felt that it was one of those rare occasions which will sometimes occur, when it was absolutely necessary for the will of one man to guide and control every thing. The press itself had been, in part, suborned by the enemy, and the legislature was too much under British influence to listen to his wise suggestion in favor of the repeal of the Habeas Corpus Act. He accordingly resolved, without a moment's hesitation, to assume the power which cowardice dared not exercise. The city was placed under martial law, and in one instance, where a traitor whom he had imprisoned had been set at liberty by Judge Hall, he ordered the judge himself into confinement for interfering with his authority. The sequel conclusively showed that these vigorous measures were absolutely necessary for the safety and protection of the city, and a grateful country did not fail to appreciate the patriotic motives which prompted him in the exercise of this supreme power.

The English armament, instead of coming up the river, entered the lakes which connect with the gulf, and on the 23d of December commenced landing their forces on the narrow strip of land bordering the river. They reached this point by means of the Bayou Bienvenu and Villere's canal, through which they passed in their boats. They were at this time ignorant of the extent of the preparations made by Jackson to receive them, and instead of marching directly upon the city, which would have been the safest course, their commander encamped where he had landed, on the plantations of two or three French settlers. When Jackson received the intelligence that the British had effected a landing, he determined to attack them on the night of the 23d. Generals Coffee and Carroll were ordered to proceed immediately from their encampment, and join him with all haste. Although four miles above, they arrived in the city in less than two hours after the order had been issued. These forces, with the seventh and forty-fourth regiments, the Louisiana troops, and Colonel Hinds' dragoons, from Mississippi, constituted the strength of his army, which could be brought into action against the enemy. It was thought advisable that General Carroll and his division should be disposed in the rear, for the reason that there was no correct information of the force landed through Villere's canal, and because Jackson feared that this probably might be merely a feint intended to divert his attention, while a much stronger and more numerous division, having already gained some point higher on the lake, might, by advancing in his absence, gain his rear, and succeed in their design. Being thus ignorant of their movements, it was essential that he should be prepared for the worst, and by different dispositions of his troops be ready to offer an effectual resistance in whatever quarter he might be assailed. General Carroll, therefore, at the head of his division, and Governor Claiborne, with the state militia, were directed to take post on the Gentilly road, which leads from Chef Menteur another landing-place, to New Orleans, and to defend it to the last extremity. With the remainder of his troops, about two thousand in number, Jackson hastened down the river, towards the point where it had been reported the British had effected a landing.

Alarm pervaded the city. The marching and countermarching of the troops, the proximity of the enemy, with the approaching contest, and uncertainty of the issue, had excited a general apprehension. It was feared that the British might be already on their way, before the necessary arrangements could be made to oppose them. To prevent this, Colonel Hayne, with two companies of riflemen, and the Mississippi dragoons, was sent forward to reconnoitre their camp, and learn their position and numbers, and if they should be found advancing, to harass and oppose them at every step, until the main body should arrive.

An inconsiderable circumstance at this moment evinced what unlimited confidence was reposed in Jackson's skill and bravery. As his troops were marching through the city, his ears were assailed with the screams and cries of innumerable females, who had collected on the way, and seemed to apprehend the worst of consequences. Feeling for their distresses, and anxious to quiet them, he directed Mr. Livingston, one of his aids-de-camp, to address them in the French language. "Say to them," said he, "not to be alarmed: the enemy shall never reach the city!" It operated like an electric shock. To know that he himself was not apprehensive of a fatal result, inspired them with altered feelings; sorrow was ended, and their grief converted into hope and confidence.

The general arrived in view of the enemy a little before dark. Having previously ascertained from Colonel Hayne, who had been sent in advance, their position, and that their strength was about two thousand, though it afterwards proved to be three thousand, he immediately concerted the mode of attack, and hastened to execute it.

General Coffee, with his brigade, Colonel Hinds' dragoons, and Captain Beal's company of riflemen, was directed to march to the left, keeping near the swamp, and, if possible, to turn the enemy's right, and drive them towards the river, where the Caroline, a schooner of war commanded by Commodore Patterson, would drop down and open upon them. The firing of the vessel was the appointed signal for a simultaneous attack on all sides. The rest of the troops, consisting of the regulars, and Planche's city volunteers, Daquin's colored troops, and the artillery under

Lieutenant Spotts, supported by a company of marines commanded by Colonel McKee, advanced on the road along the bank of the Mississippi, and were commanded by Jackson in person.

On approaching the enemy's position, their encampment was discovered, by the light of their camp-fires, to be formed with the left resting on the river, and extending into the open field. General Coffee had advanced, with caution and silence, beyond their pickets, next the swamp and nearly reached the point to which he was ordered, when a broadside from the Caroline announced that the battle had begun. Patterson had proceeded slowly, giving time, as he believed, for the execution of the arrangements contemplated on shore. So sanguine had the British been in the belief that they would be kindly received, and little opposition attempted, that the Caroline floated by the sentinels, and anchored before their camp, without the least molestation. On passing the front picket, she was hailed in a low tone of voice, but not returning an answer, no further question was made. This, added to some other attendant circumstances, confirmed the opinion that they believed her to be a vessel laden with provisions, which had been sent out from New Orleans, and was intended for them. Having reached what appeared, from their fires, to be the centre of their encampment, her anchors were cast, and her character and business disclosed by her guns. So unexpected an attack produced a momentary confusion; but recovering from their surprise, the enemy answered the fire with a discharge of musketry and flight of Congreve rockets, which passed without injury, while the grape and cannister from her guns were pouring destruction upon them. They then extinguished their fires, by the light of which the vessel had directed her guns with remarkable precision, and retired two or three hundred yards into the open field. They were still within range of the cannon, but the darkness of the night afforded them considerable protection.

General Coffee, having dismounted his men, and turned his horses loose, at a large ditch in the rear of Laronde's plantation, had gained, as he thought, the centre of the enemy's line, when the signal from the Caroline reached him. He directly wheeled his column in, and forming his line parallel with the river, moved towards their camp. He had scarcely advanced more than a hundred yards, when he received a heavy fire from the enemy in his front; this was an unexpected circumstance to him, because he supposed them to be lying principally at a distance, and that the only opposition he should meet, until he approached towards the levee, would be from their advanced pickets. The circumstance of his coming in contact with them so soon, was owing to the severe attack of the schooner, which had compelled the enemy to abandon their camp, and form without the reach of her deadly fire. The moon was shining, but reflected her light too feebly to discover objects at a distance. The only means, therefore, of producing any positive effect, with the kind of force engaged, which consisted chiefly of riflemen, was not to venture at random, but to discharge their pieces only when there should be a certainty of hitting the object aimed at. This order being given, the line pressed on, and having gained a position near enough to distinguish the enemy, a general fire was given; it was well directed, and too severe and destructive to be withstood; the British gave way and retreated; they rallied again, however, but were again attacked and forced to retire. The gallant yeomanry, led by their brave commander, pressed fearlessly on, and drove the invaders from every position they attempted to maintain. It was unnecessary for their general to encourage and allure them to deeds of valor: his own example was sufficient to excite them. Always in their midst, he was cool and collected. Unmindful of danger, he continued to remind his troops that they had often said they could fight, and now was the time to prove it.

The British, driven back by the resolute firmness and intrepidity of their assailants, reached a grove of orange trees, with a ditch running past it, protected by a fence on the margin, where they were halted and formed for battle. It was a favorable position, promising entire security, and it was occupied with a confidence that they could not be forced to yield it. Coffee's brave troops, strengthened in their hopes of success, moved on, nor discovered the advantages against them, until a fire from the entire British line showed their position and defence. A sudden check was given; but it was only momentary, for gathering fresh ardor, they charged across the ditch, gave a deadly and destructive fire, and compelled the enemy to retire. The retreat continued, until gaining a similar position, the British made another stand, and were again driven from it with considerable loss.

Thus the battle was carried on, upon the left wing, until the British reached the bank of the river; here a determined stand was made, and further encroachments resisted: for half an hour the conflict was extremely violent on both sides. The American troops could not be driven from their purpose, nor the British made to yield their ground; but at length, having suffered greatly, the latter were under the necessity of taking refuge behind the levee, which afforded a breastwork, and protected them from the fatal fire of our riflemen. General Coffee, though unacquainted with their position, for the darkness had greatly increased, contemplated another charge; but one of his officers, who had discovered the advantage their situation gave them, assured him it was too hazardous; that they could be driven no farther, and would, from the point they occupied, resist with the bayonet, and repel, with considerable loss, any attempt that might be made to dislodge them. The place of their retirement was covered in front by a strong bank, which had been extended into the field, to keep out the river, in consequence of the first bank having been encroached upon and undermined in several places: the latter, however, was still entire in many parts, and, interposing between them and the Mississippi, it afforded security from the broadsides of the schooner which lay off at some distance. A further apprehension, lest, by moving still nearer to the river, he might greatly expose himself to the fire of the Caroline, which was yet spiritedly maintaining the conflict, induced Coffee to retire until he could hear from the commanding general, and receive his further orders.

During this time, the right wing, under Jackson, had been no less prompt and active. The advance, consisting of a detachment of artillery under Lieutenant Spotts, supported by sixty marines, moved down the road next the levee. On their left was the seventh regiment of infantry, led by Major Piere. The forty-fourth, commanded by Major Baker, was formed on the extreme left; while Planche's and Daquin's battalions of city guards were directed to be posted in the centre, between the seventh and forty-fourth. The general had ordered Colonel Ross, (who acted in the capacity of brigadier-general,) on hearing the signal from the Caroline, to move off by heads of companies, and, on reaching the enemy's line, to deploy, and unite the left wing of his command with the right of General Coffee's. This order was omitted to be executed; and the consequence was, an early introduction of confusion in the ranks, which prevented the important design of uniting the two divisions.

Instead of moving in column from the first position, the troops, with the exception of the seventh regiment, next the person of the general, which advanced agreeably to the instructions that had been given, were formed and marched in extended line. Having sufficient ground to form on at first, no inconvenience was at the moment sustained; but this advantage presently failing, the centre became compressed, and was forced in the rear. The river gradually inclined to the left from the place where they were formed, and diminished the space originally possessed. Farther in, stood Laronde's house, surrounded by a grove of clustered orange-trees: this pressing the left, and the river the right wing, to the centre, formed a curve, which presently threw the principal part of Planche's and Daquin's battalions without the line. This inconvenience might have been remedied, but for the briskness of the advance, and the darkness of the night. A heavy fire from behind a fence, immediately before them, brought the enemy to view. Acting in obedience to their orders, not to waste their ammunition at random, our troops pressed forward against the opposition in their front, and thereby threw those battalions in the rear.

A fog rising from the river, and mingling with the smoke from the guns, covered the plain, and gradually diminished the little light shed by the moon, at the same time greatly increasing the darkness of the night: no clue was left, therefore, to ascertain how or where the enemy were situated. There was no alternative but to move on in the direction of their fire, which subjected the assailants to material disadvantages. The British, driven from their first position, had retired and occupied another, behind a deep ditch that ran out of the Mississippi towards the swamp, on the margin of which was a wood-railed fence. Here, strengthened by increased numbers, they again opposed the advance of our troops. Having waited until they had approached sufficiently near their fastnesses to be discovered, they discharged a fire upon the advancing army. Instantly the American battery was formed, and began to play briskly upon them; while the infantry, pressing forward, aided in the conflict, which at this point was for some time spiritedly maintained. At this moment a brisk sally was made upon our advance, when the marines, unequal to the assault, were already giving way. The adjutant-general, and Colonels Platt and Chotard, hastening to their support, with a part of the seventh, drove the enemy, and saved the artillery from capture. General Jackson, perceiving the decided advantages which were derived from the position they occupied, ordered their line to be charged. It was obeyed with cheerfulness, and executed with promptness. Pressing on, our troops gained the ditch; and pouring across it a well-aimed fire, compelled them to retreat, and to abandon their intrenchment. The plain on which they were contending was cut to pieces by races from the river, to convey the water to the swamp. The enemy were therefore very soon enabled to occupy another position, equally favourable with the one whence they had been just driven, where they formed for battle, and for some time gallantly maintained themselves; but they were at length, after a stubborn resistance, forced to yield their ground.

The enemy discovering the firm and obstinate advance made by the right wing of the American army, and presuming, perhaps, that its principal strength was posted on the road, formed the intention of attacking the left. Obliquing for this purpose, an attempt was made to turn it. At this moment, Daquin's battalion and the city guards, being marched up and formed on the left of the fortyfourth regiment, met and repulsed them.

The nature of the contest prevented securing those benefits which might have been derived from the artillery. The darkness of the night was such, that the blaze of the enemy's musketry was the only light afforded by which to determine their position, or be capable of taking that of the Americans to advantage; yet, notwithstanding, it greatly annoyed them, whenever it could be brought to bear. Directed by Lieutenant Spotts, a vigilant and skilful officer, with men to aid him who looked to nothing but a zealous discharge of their duty, the most essential and important services were rendered.

The enemy had been thrice assailed and beaten, and compelled to retreat for nearly a mile. They had now retired, and if found, were to be sought for amid the darkness of the night. The general, therefore, determined to halt, and ascertain Coffee's position and success, before proceeding farther, for as yet no communication had passed between them. He entertained no doubt, from the brisk firing in that direction, that he had been warmly engaged; but this had now nearly subsided: the Caroline, too, had almost ceased her operations; it being only occasionally that the noise of her guns disclosed the little opportunity she possessed of acting efficiently.

The express despatched to General Jackson from the left wing, having reached him, he determined not to prosecute the successes he had gained. The darkness of the night, the confusion into which his own division had been thrown, and a similar disaster produced in Coffee's ranks, all pointed to the necessity of retiring from the field, and abandoning the contest for the time. The bravery and firmness already displayed by his troops, had impressed him with the belief, that by pushing forward he might capture the whole British army: at any rate, he considered it but a game of venture and hazard, which, if unsuccessful, could not occasion his own defeat. If incompetent to its execution, and superior numbers or superior discipline should compel him to retire in his turn, he well knew that the enemy would not have temerity enough to attempt pursuit, on account of the extreme darkness, and their ignorance of the situation of the country. But on the arrival of the express from General Coffee, and having been informed of the strength of the position to which the enemy had retired, and that a part of the left wing had been detached, and were in all probability captured, he determined to retire from the field. General Coffee was accordingly directed to withdraw, and take up his position at Laronde's plantation, where the line had been first formed; the troops on the right were also ordered to the same point.

The last charge made by the left wing had separated Colonel Dyer from the main body, with two hundred men, and Captain Beal's company of riflemen. What might be their fate, whether they were captured or had effected their retreat, was, at this time, altogether uncertain.

Colonel Dyer, who commanded the extreme left, on clearing the grove, after the enemy had retired, was marching in the direction in which he expected to find General Coffee; he very soon discovered a force in front, and halting his men, hastened towards it; arriving within a short distance, he was hailed, ordered to stop, and report to whom he belonged: Dyer, and Gibson, his lieutenant-colonel, who had accompanied him, advanced and stated that they were of Coffee's brigade; by this time, they had nearly reached the line, and perceiving that the name of the brigade they had stated was not understood, their apprehensions were awakened, lest it might be a detachment of the enemy; in this opinion they were immediately confirmed, and having wheeled about to return, they were fired on and pursued. Gibson had scarcely started, when he fell; before he could recover, a soldier, quicker than the rest, had reached him, and pinned him to the ground with his bayonet; fortunately he was but slightly wounded and only held by his clothes; thus pinioned, and perceiving others to be briskly advancing, but a moment was left for deliberation ; making a violent exertion, and springing to his feet, he threw his assailant to the ground, and made good his escape. Colonel Dyer had retreated about fifty yards, when his horse dropped dead. Being entangled in the fall, and receiving a wound in the thigh, there was little prospect of relief, for the enemy were briskly advancing. He therefore ordered his men, who were close at hand, to advance and fire, which checked the approach of the enemy, and enabled him to escape. Having thus discovered an enemy in a direction he had not expected, and uncertain how or where he might find General Coffee, he determined to seek him to the right, and moving on with his little band, forced his way through the enemy's lines, with the loss of sixty-three of his men, who were killed and taken. Captain Beal, with equal bravery, charged through their ranks, carrying off some prisoners, and losing several of his own company.

This body of the enemy proved to be a reinforcement which had arrived from Bayou Bienvenu after night. The boats that landed the first detachment had proceeded back to the shipping, and having returned, were on their way up the Bayou, when they heard the guns of the Caroline: moving hastily on to the assistance of those who had debarked before them, they reached the shore, and knowing nothing of the situation of the two armies, during the engagement, advanced in the rear of General Coffee's brigade. Coming in contact with Colonel Dyer and Captain Beal, they filed off to the left, and reached the British lines.

This detached part of Coffee's brigade, unable to unite with or find him, retired to the place where they had first formed, and joined Colonel Hinds' dragoons, who had remained on the ground that they might cover the retreat of the troops if it became necessary.

Jackson went into this battle confident of success; and his arrangements were such as would have insured it even to a much greater extent, but for the intervention of circumstances that were not and could not have been foreseen. The Caroline gave her signals, and commenced the battle a little too early, before Coffee had reached and taken his position, and before every thing was fully in readiness to attain the objects desired; but it was chiefly owing to the confusion in the ranks at first which checked the rapidity of Jackson's advance, gave the enemy time for preparation, and prevented his division from uniting with the right wing of General Coffee's brigade.

Colonel Hinds, and his dragoons, were not brought into action during the night. Interspersed as the plain was with innumerable ditches, diverging in different directions it was impossible that cavalry could act to any kind of advantage. After the battle was over, they were formed in advance to watch the movements of the enemy until morning.

From the experiment just made, Jackson believed it would be in his power to capture the British army; he concluded, therefore, to order General Carroll, with his division, down to his assistance, and to attack them again at the dawn of day. Directing Governor Claiborne to remain at his post, with the Louisiana militia, for the defence of the Gentilly road, an important pass to the city, he despatched an express to Carroll, stating to him, that if there had been no appearance of a force during the night, in the direction of Chef Menteur, to hasten and join him with the troops under his command; this order was executed by one o'clock in the morning. Previously, however, to his arrival, a different determination was made. It was ascertained from prisoners who had been brought in, and through deserters, that the strength of the enemy during the battle was four thousand, and, with the reinforcements which had reached them after its commencement, and during the action, their force could not be less than six; at any rate, it would greatly exceed that of the Americans, even with the addition of the Tennessee division. Although very decided advantages had been obtained, yet they had been procured under circumstances that might be wholly lost in a contest waged in open day, between forces so disproportionate, and by undisciplined troops against veteran soldiers. Jackson well knew it was incumbent upon him to act a part entirely defensive: should the attempt to gain and destroy the city succeed, numerous difficulties would present themselves, which might be avoided so long as he could hold the enemy in check, and foil their designs.

Being firmly persuaded that it was important to pursue a course calculated to insure safety, and believing it attainable in no way so effectually, as in occupying some point, and by the strength he might give it, compensate for the inferiority of his numbers and their want of discipline, Jackson determined to make no further offensive efforts until he could more certainly discover the views of the enemy, and until the Kentucky troops, which had not yet arrived, should reach him. In pursuance of this idea, after having ordered Colonel Hinds to occupy the ground he was then abandoning, and to observe the enemy closely, he fell back in the morning, and formed his line behind a deep ditch that extended to the swamp, at right angles from the river. There were two circumstances strongly recommending the importance of this place :—the swamp, which, from the highlands at Baton Rouge, skirted the river at irregular distances, and in many places was almost impervious, at this point, approached within four hundred yards of the Mississippi, and hence, from the narrowness of the pass, was more easily to be defended ; in addition to this, there was a deep canal, the dirt from which having been thrown on the upper side, already formed a tolerable work of defence. Behind this his troops were formed, and proper measures adopted for increasing the strength of the position, with the determination never to abandon it.

The soldier who is familiar with the scenes of the battle-field, and understands what slight circumstances frequently counteract the operations of a whole campaign, and produce the most decided advantages, where a different issue might not unreasonably have been expected, will be able properly to appreciate the effect of the attack made by General Jackson on the advance of the enemy, upon the night of the 23d of December. Although the dreadful carnage of the 8th of January was, in point of fact, the finishing blow that struck down the towering hopes of the invaders, and put an end to the contest, yet in

EFFECT OF THE BATTLE

the previous engagement there was much to excite their fears and apprehensions. They had reached the Mississippi without the fire of a gun, and encamped upon its banks as composedly as if they had been seated on their own soil, and at a distance from all danger. These were circumstances which impressed them with the belief that they need expect but little opposition; that success was certain; and that the troops with whom they were to contend would scarcely venture to resist them. So confident were they in their expectations, that they intended to move forward the next day, and attack the city. But Jackson well knew how essential an early impression was to ultimate success, and resolved to assail them at the moment of their landing, and "attack them in their first position." With a force inferior by one-half to that of the enemy, at an unexpected moment he had broken into their camp, and with his undisciplined yeomanry driven before him the pride of England and the conquerors of Europe. It was an event that could not fail to destroy all previous theories, and establish a conclusion which the British had not before formed, that they were contending against valor inferior to none they had seen, and before which their own bravery and skill availed nothing. It had the effect of satisfying them, that the quantity and kind of troops it was in our power to bring into action, were very different from any thing that had been represented to them; for much as they had heard of the courage of the man with whom they were contending, they could not suppose that a general, having a country to defend, and a reputation to preserve, would venture to attack a force greatly superior to his own, on ground they had chosen, and one too, which, by the numerous victories it had achieved, had already acquired the highest distinction. All these circumstances tended to convince them that his force must far surpass their expectations, and be composed of materials very different from what they had imagined.

The American troops which were actually engaged in the action, did not amount to two thousand men, as appears by the following statement:

Part of Coffee's brigade and Captain Beal's company,
  amounting to   -   -   -   -   -   -   648
The 7th and 44th regiments,   -   -   -   -   763
Company of marines and artillery,   -   -   -   82
Planche's and Daquin's battalions,   -   -   - 488

                                          Total   1981

This small body of men, for more than an hour, maintained a severe conflict with a force of four or five thousand, and retired in safety from the field, with the loss of but twenty-four killed, and one hundred and fifteen wounded, and seventy-four made prisoners; while the killed, wounded, and prisoners of the enemy, were not less than four hundred. The officers and soldiers under Jackson executed every order with promptitude, and nobly sustained the honour of their country. Lieutenant-Colonel Lauderdale, of Coffee's brigade, an officer of great promise, and on whom every reliance was placed, fell manfully fighting at his post. He entered the service, and descended the river with the volunteers under General Jackson, in the winter of 1812; passed through all the hardships and difficulties of the Creek war; and ever manifested a commendable alacrity in the discharge of his duty. Young, brave, and skilful, he had already afforded evidences of a capacity which promised to be exceedingly useful in the career he had embraced. His exemplary conduct, both in civil and military life, had acquired for him a respect that rendered his death a subject of general regret. Lieutenant McLelland, a valuable young officer of the 7th, was also among the slain. General Coffee's brigade imitated the example of their commander during the action, and bravely and ably supported the character they had previously established. The unequal contest in which they were engaged never occurred to their minds, nor checked, for a moment, the rapidity of their advance. Had the British known that they were merely riflemen, and without bayonets, a firm stand would have arrested their progress, and destruction or capture would have been the inevitable consequence; but this circumstance being unknown, every charge they made was crowned with

DEATH OF COLONEL LAUDERDALE 111

success, producing discomfiture in the opposing ranks, and routing and driving superior numbers before them. Officers, from the highest to the inferior grades, were alike prompt and efficient. Ensign Leach, of the 7th regiment, being wounded through the body, still remained at his post, in the performance of his duty. Colonel Kemper, amid the confusion introduced on the left wing, found himself at the head of a handful of men, detached from the main body, and in the midst of a party of the enemy: never did any man better exemplify the truth of the assertion, that discretion is sometimes the better part of valor; to attempt resistance was idle, and could only end in certain destruction. Calling to a group of soldiers who were near him, in a positive tone, he demanded of them where their regiment was. Being themselves at fault, they were unable to answer; but supposing him to be one of their officers, they obeyed his orders, and followed him to his own line, where they were made prisoners.

The 7th regiment, commanded by Major Piere, and the 44th, under Major Baker, aided by Major Butler, gallantly maintained the conflict; forced the enemy from every position they attempted to occupy; and drove them some distance from the first point of attack. Confiding in themselves, and in their general, who was constantly with them, exposed to danger and in the midst of the fight, inspiring them by his ardor and encouraging them by his example, the American soldiers bravely advanced to the conflict, nor evinced a disposition to retire, until the prudence of their commander dictated the necessary order.

BATTLE OF NEW ORLEANS

CHAPTER VIII.

1814. The Americans fortify their position—Jackson's peremptory orders to Major Lacoste—Defence of the Pass Barrataria—Captain Lafitte—Attack made by the British on the 28th of December—Defensive preparations hastened—Death of Colonel Henderson—Disaffection in New Orleans—Information communicated to the British fleet—Stratagem of Mr. Shields—Conduct of the Louisiana legislature—Patriotic reply of Jackson to the committee—Attempt to supply his troops with arms—Gallantry of Colonel Hinds—Cannonade on the 1st of January—Position of the American army—Jackson's orders to the Frenchman to defend his property—Defences on the right bank of the river—Caution of Jackson in concealing the number of his troops. 1815.

THE distinguishing traits in the character of General Jackson, as a military commander, were clear-headed sagacity, promptness of decision, and rapidity of execution. He had no sooner resolved on the course which he thought necessary to be pursued, than he hastened with all possible dispatch, to secure its completion. After the engagement with the British on the night of the 23d of December, it was evident to his mind that it would be exceedingly unwise to risk an encounter with the enemy, in an open field, at the head of an inferior, undisciplined, and unarmed force. He conceived, therefore, that a defensive policy was the most judicious, and that by prudence and caution he would be able to preserve what might be endangered by any offensive movement. Hence, he determined to fortify himself as effectually as the peril and exigencies of the moment would permit. When to expect an attack, he could not tell; preparation and readiness to meet it, were for him to determine upon; all else was for the enemy. He proceeded promptly with his system of defence, and such was his thoughtfulness and anxiety, that, until the night of the 27th, when his lines were completed, he never slept, or closed his eyes for a moment. Resting his hopes of safety and security to the city, on his ability to check the advance of the enemy, he was everywhere present, encouraging his troops, and hastening a completion of the work. The concern and excitement produced by the important object before him, were so great, that for five days and four nights he was constantly employed. His line of defence, the celebrated cotton embankment, being completed on the night of the 27th, for the first time since the arrival of the enemy, he sought that rest and repose he so much needed.

The violence of the attack made on the night of the 23d of December, naturally excited the fears of the British troops, and it was considered important to keep their apprehensions alive, with a view to destroy the overweening confidence with which they had arrived on our shores, and to compel them to act for a time upon the defensive. To effect this, General Coffee, with his brigade, was ordered down on the morning of the 24th, to unite with Colonel Hinds, and make a show in the rear of Lacoste's plantation. The enemy being not yet recovered from the panic produced by the assault of the preceding evening, believed it was in contemplation to urge another attack, and immediately formed themselves to repel it; but Coffee, having succeeded in recovering some of his horses, which were wandering along the margin of the swamp, and in regaining part of the clothing that his troops had lost the night before, returned to the line, leaving them to conjecture the object of his movement.

The scanty supply of clothes and blankets that remained to the soldiers, from their long and exposed marches, had been left where they dismounted to meet the enemy. Their numbers were too limited, and the strength of their opponents too well ascertained, for any part of their forces to remain and take care of what was left behind; it was so essential to hasten on and reach their destination, that they might be ready to act when the signal was given from the Caroline, that no time was afforded them to secure their horses, which were turned loose, and their recovery trusted entirely to chance. Although many were regained, many were lost; while most of the men remained with but a single suit, to encounter in the open field, and in swamps covered with water, the hardships of a camp, and the severity of winter. It is a circumstance which entitles them to much credit, that under privations so severely oppressive, complaints or murmurs were never heard. This state of things fortunately was not of long continuance. The story of their sufferings and misfortunes was no sooner known, than the legislature appropriated a sum of money for their relief, which was greatly increased by subscriptions in the city and neighborhood. Materials having been purchased, the ladies, with that Christian charity and warmth of heart characteristic of their sex, at once exerted themselves in supplying their wants; all their industry was called into action, and in a little time the suffering soldiers were relieved. Such generous conduct, in extending assistance, at a moment when it was so much needed, while it conferred on those females the highest honor, could not fail to nerve the arm of the brave soldier with new zeal for the defence of his fair benefactors. This distinguished mark of their patriotism and benevolence is still remembered; and often, as these valiant men are heard to recount the dangers they have passed, and with peculiar pride to dwell on the mingled honors and hardships of the campaign, they breathe a sentiment of gratitude for those who conferred upon them such distinguished marks of their kindness, and who by their timely interference alleviated their misfortunes and their sufferings.

In order to prevent the advance of the enemy, and keep up a show of resistance, detachments of light troops were occasionally kept in front of their line, assailing and harassing their advanced posts, whenever an opportunity was offered for acting to advantage. Every moment that could be gained, and every delay that could hinder or retard the enemy's attempts to reach the city, was of the utmost importance. The works were rapidly progressing, and hourly increasing in strength. The militia of the state were every day arriving, and every day the prospect of successful opposition became brighter and more auspicious.

The enemy still remained at their first encampment; but that every thing might be in readiness to repel an assault, when attempted, the most active preparations were made in the American camp. The canal covering the front of the line was deepened and widened, and a strong mud wall formed of the earth that had been originally thrown out. To prevent any approach until his system of defence should be in a state of greater forwardness, Jackson ordered the levee to be cut about a hundred yards below the point he had occupied. The river being very high, a broad stream of water passed rapidly through the plain, and covered it to the depth of thirty or forty inches which prevented the march of troops on foot. Embrasures were formed, and two pieces of artillery, under the command of Lieutenant Spotts, were placed in a position to rake the road leading up the levee, early on the morning of the 24th of December.

General Jackson was under the constant apprehension lest, in spite of his exertions below, the city might be reached and destroyed through some other route. His fears were increased on the 24th, by a report that a strong force had arrived; debarked at the head of Lake Borgne; and compelled an abandonment of the defence at Chef Menteur. This, however, proved to be unfounded: the enemy had not appeared in that direction, nor had the officer to whom the command of this important fort was intrusted, forgotten his duty or forsaken his post. Acting upon the statement that Major Lacoste had retired from the fort, and fallen back on Bayou St. John, and incensed that orders, which, from their importance, should have been faithfully executed, had been thus lightly regarded, Jackson hastened to inform him what he had understood, and to forbid his leaving his position. "The battery I have placed under your command," said the general, "must be defended at all hazards. In you, and the valor of your troops, I repose every confidence—let me not be deceived. With us every thing goes on well; the enemy has not yet advanced. Our troops have covered themselves with glory: it is a noble example, and worthy to be followed by all. Maintain your post, nor ever think

ORDERS TO MAJOR LACOSTE

of retreating." To give additional strength to a place deemed so important, and to inspire confidence and insure safety, Colonel Dyer, with two hundred men, was ordered there, to assist in its defence, and act as videttes, in advance of the occupied points.

General Morgan, who commanded the fort on the east bank of the river, was instructed to proceed as near the enemy's camp as prudence and safety would permit, and by destroying the levee, to let in the waters of the Mississippi between them. The execution of this order, and a similar one previously made below the line of defence, entirely insulated the enemy, and prevented his march against either place. On the 26th, the commanding general, fearing for the situation of Morgan, who, as the British occupied the intermediate ground, was entirely detached from his camp, directed him to abandon the post, carry off such of the cannon as might be wanted, and throw the remainder into the river, where they could be again recovered when the waters receded; and after doing this, to retire across the river, and assume a position on the right bank, nearly opposite to his line, and fortify it. This movement was rendered necessary by the relative disposition of the two armies.

From the intelligence obtained through deserters and prisoners, it was evident that the British fleet would make an effort to ascend the river, and co-operate with the troops already landed. Lest this, or a diversion in a different quarter, might be attempted, exertions were made to offer resistance at all points, and to interpose such defences on the Mississippi as might secure protection. The forts on the river, being well supported with brave men and heavy pieces of artillery, might, it was thought, have the effect to deter their shipping from venturing in that direction, and dispose them to seek some safer route, if any could be discovered. Pass Barrataria was best calculated for this purpose, and it was expected that the effort would, in all probability, be made in that quarter. The difficulty of ascending the Mississippi, from the rapidity of the current, its winding course, and the ample protection already given at forts St. Philip and Bourbon, were circumstances to which the British were not strangers : nor was it to be expected that, with a knowledge of them, they would venture the success of an enterprise on which so much depended. It was a more rational conjecture that they would seek a passage through Barrataria, proceed up on the right bank of the river, and gain a position from which, by co-operating with the forces on the east side, they might drive the Americans from the line they had formed, and succeed in the accomplishment of their designs. Major Reynolds was accordingly ordered thither, with instructions to place the bayous emptying through this pass in the best possible state of defence—to occupy and strengthen the island—to mount sufficient ordnance, and draw a chain within cannon-shot across the channel. Lafitte, who had previously been promised a pardon for the outrages committed against the laws of the United States, and who had already shown a lively zeal on behalf of his adopted country, was also despatched with Reynolds. He was selected, because no doubt was entertained of his fidelity, and because his knowledge of the topography and precise situation of this section of the state was remarkably correct: it was the point where he had constantly rendezvoused, while cruising against the merchant vessels of Spain, under a commission obtained at Carthagena, and where he had become perfectly acquainted with every inlet and entrance to the gulf, through which a passage could be effected.

With these arrangements, all being anxiously alive to the interests of the country, and disposed to protect it, there was little room to apprehend or fear disaster. To use the general's own expression on another occasion : " the surest defence, and one which seldom failed of success, was a rampart of high-minded and brave men." That there were some of this description with him, on whom he could safely rely in moments of extreme peril, he well knew ; but that there were many strangers to him and to danger, who had never been called to act in situations where the horrors of the field of battle appal and unnerve even the most resolute, was equally certain; whether they would support the cause in which they had embarked, with manly firmness, and realize his anxious wishes on the subject, could be known only in the hour of conflict and trial.

As yet, the enemy were not informed of the position of Jackson. What was his situation—what was intended—whether offensive or defensive operations would be pursued, were matters in regard to which they possessed no correct knowledge, nor could it be obtained; still their exertions were unremitting to have all things prepared, and in readiness to urge their designs, whenever the moment for action should arrive. They had been constantly engaged since their landing, in procuring from their shipping every thing necessary to ulterior operations. A complete command on the lakes, and possession of a point on the margin, presented an uninterrupted ingress and egress, and afforded the opportunity of conveying whatever was wanted, in perfect safety, to their camp. The height of the Mississippi, and the discharge of water through the openings made in the levee, had given an increased depth to the canal, from which they had first debarked; they were enabled to advance their boats much farther in the direction of their encampment, and to bring up, with greater convenience, their artillery, bombs, and munitions. They were thus engaged during the first three days after their arrival, and early on the morning of the 27th a battery was discovered on the bank of the river, which had been erected during the preceding night, and on which were mounted several pieces of heavy ordnance; from this position a fire was opened on the Caroline schooner, lying under the opposite shore.

After the battle of the 23d, in which this vessel rendered such effectual assistance, she passed to the opposite side of the river, where she had since lain. Her services were too highly appreciated not to be again desired, should the enemy endeavor to advance. Her present situation was considered an unsafe one, but several vain attempts had been made to advance her higher up the stream. No favorable breeze had yet arisen to aid her in stemming the current; and towing, and other remedies, had been already resorted to, but without success. Her safety might have been ensured by floating her down the river, and placing her under cover of the guns of the fort; but it was preferred, as a matter of policy, to risk her where she was. Commodore Patterson left her on the 26th, by the order of the commanding general, when Captain Henly made a further but ineffectual effort to force her up the current, near to the line, for the double purpose of its defence and for her own safety.

This attempt being discovered at daylight on the morning of the 27th, a battery, mounting five guns, opened upon her, discharging bombs and red-hot shot; it was spiritedly answered, but without affecting the battery; there being but a long twelve-pounder that was of service. The second fire lodged a hot shot in the hold, directly under her cables, whence it could not be removed, and where it immediately communicated fire to the schooner. The shot from the battery were constantly taking effect, firing her in different places, and otherwise producing material injury; while the blaze, already kindled under her cables, was rapidly extending its ravages. A well grounded apprehension of her commander, that she could be no longer defended,—the flames bursting forth in different parts, and fast increasing—induced a fear lest the magazine should be soon reached, and every thing destroyed. One of his crew being killed, and six wounded, and not a glimmering of hope entertained that she could be preserved, orders were given to abandon her. The crew reached the shore in safety, and in a short time afterwards she blew up.

Although thus unexpectedly deprived of so material a dependence for successful defence, an opportunity was soon presented of using her brave crew to advantage. Gathering confidence from what had just been effected, the enemy left their encampment, and moved in the direction of the American line. Their numbers had been increased, and Major-General Sir Edward Packenham now commanded in person. Early on the 28th, his columns commenced their advance to storm the works. At the distance of half a mile, their heavy artillery opened, and quantities of bombs, balls, and Congreve rockets were discharged. It was a scene of terror and alarm, which they had probably calculated would excite a panic in the minds of the raw troops of our army, and compel them to surrender at discretion, or abandon their strong-hold. But our soldiers had afforded abundant proof, that, whether disciplined or not, they well knew how to defend the honor and interests of their country; and had sufficient valor not to be alarmed at the reality—still less at the semblance of danger. Far from exciting their apprehensions, and driving them from their ground, their firmness remained unchanged; and they still manifested a determination not to tarnish a reputation they had hardly earned, and which had become too dear, from the difficulties and dangers they had passed to acquire it, to be tamely surrendered. The Congreve rockets, though an instrument of destruction to which the American troops had been hitherto strangers, excited no other feeling than that which novelty inspires. At the moment, therefore, that the British, in different columns, were moving up, in all the pomp and parade of battle, preceded by the insignia of terror more than danger, and expecting to behold their " Yankee foes" retire and flee before them, the batteries opened, and checked their advance.

In addition to the two pieces of cannon mounted on the works on the 24th, three others, of heavy calibre, obtained from the navy department, had been formed along the line; these opening on the enemy, checked their progress, and disclosed to them the hazard of their project. Lieutenants Crawley and Norris volunteered, and with the crew of the Caroline rendered important services, and maintained at the guns they commanded that firmness and decision for which, on previous occasions, they had been so highly distinguished. They had been selected by the general because of their superior knowledge in gunnery; and on this occasion gave a further evidence of their skill and judgment, and of a disposition to act in any situation where they could be serviceable. The line, which, from the labors bestowed on it, was daily strengthening, was not yet in a situation to offer effectual resistance; this deficiency, however, was remedied by the brave men who were formed in its rear.

The greatest injury was effected from the river. Lieutenant Thompson, who commanded the Louisiana sloop, which lay nearly opposite the line of defence, no sooner discovered the columns approaching, than, warping her around, he brought her starboard guns to bear, and produced such an effect as forced them to retreat; but from their heavy artillery, the enemy maintained the conflict with great spirit, constantly discharging their bombs and rockets for seven hours, when, unable to make a breach, or silence the fire from the sloop, they abandoned a contest where few advantages seemed to be presented. The crew of this vessel was composed of new recruits, and of discordant materials—of soldiers, citizens, and seamen; yet, by the activity of their commander, they were so well perfected in their duty, that they already managed their guns with the greatest precision and certainty of effect; and by three o'clock in the evening, with the aid of the land batteries, had completely silenced and driven back the enemy. Emboldened by the effect produced the day before, on the Caroline, the furnaces of the enemy were put in operation, and numbers of hot shot thrown from a heavy piece which was placed behind and protected by the levee. An attempt was now made to carry it off, when their former protection being taken away, those in the direction of it were fairly exposed to the American fire, and suffered greatly. In their endeavors to remove it, "I saw," says Commodore Patterson, "distinctly, with the aid of a glass, several balls strike in the midst of the men who were employed in dragging it away." In this engagement little or no injury was received. The Louisiana sloop, against which the most violent exertions were made, had but a single man wounded, by the fragments of a shell which burst over her deck. Her entire loss did not exceed nine killed, and eight or ten wounded. The enemy being more exposed, acting in the open field, and in range of her guns, suffered, from information afterwards procured, considerable injury; at least one hundred and twenty were killed and wounded.

DEATH OF COLONEL HENDERSON 123

Among the Americans killed was Colonel James Henderson, of the Tennessee militia. An advance party of the British had taken post, during the action, behind a fence that ran obliquely to, and not very remote from our line. Henderson, with a detachment of two hundred men, was sent out by General Carroll to drive them from a position whence they were effecting some injury, and greatly annoying his troops. Had he advanced in the manner directed, he would have been less exposed, and enabled more effectually to have secured the object intended : but misunderstanding the order, he proceeded in a different route, and fell a victim to his error. Instead of marching in the direction of the wood, and turning the enemy, which might have cut off their retreat, he proceeded in front, towards the river, leaving them in rear of the fence, and himself and his detachment open and exposed. His mistake being perceived from the line, he was called by the adjutant-general, and directed to return ; but the noise of the water, through which they were wading, prevented any communication. Having reached a knoll of dry ground, he formed, and attempted the execution of his order; but soon fell from a wound in the head. Deprived of their commander, and perceiving their situation hazardous and untenable, the detachment retreated to the line, with the loss of their colonel and five men.

While this advance was made, a column of the enemy was threatening an attack on the extreme left. To frustrate the attempt, General Coffee was ordered with his riflemen to hasten through the woods and check their approach. The enemy, although greatly superior to him in numbers, no sooner discovered his movement, than they retired, and abandoned the attack they had previously meditated.

The evident disaffection in New Orleans, and the presence of an enemy in front, were circumstances well calculated to excite unpleasant forebodings. General Jackson believed it necessary and essential to his security, while contending with avowed foes, not to be wholly inattentive to dangers lurking at home ; but, by guarding vigilantly, to be able to suppress any treasonable purpose the moment it should be developed, and before it should have time to mature. Previously, therefore, to departing from the city, on the evening of the 23d, he had ordered Major Butler, his aid, to remain with the guards, and be careful that nothing transpired in his absence calculated to operate injuriously. His fears that there were many of the inhabitants who felt no attachment to the government, and would not scruple to surrender it whenever it should become necessary to their interest, has been already noticed.

Subsequent circumstances evinced that there was no mistake in this belief, and showed that to his assiduity and energy it is to be ascribed that the country was protected and saved. It is a fact, which was disclosed on making an exchange of prisoners, that, despite all the efforts made to prevent it, the enemy were daily and constantly apprised of every thing that transpired in the camp. Every arrangement, and every change of position, was immediately communicated. On the day subsequent to a contest on the lakes on the 14th of December, Mr. Shields, a purser in the navy, was despatched with a flag, to Cat island, accompanied by Dr. Murrell, for the purpose of alleviating the situation of the wounded, and to effect a negotiation, by which they should be liberated on parol. We are not aware that such an application militated against the usages and customs of war: if not, the flag of truce should have been respected; nor ought its bearer to have been detained as a prisoner. Admiral Cochrane pretended to be fearful that it was a trick designed to ascertain his strength and situation, but this was very far from presenting any sufficient excuse for so wanton an outrage on propriety and the rules of war. If, indeed, such a result was apprehended, could not the messengers have been met at a distance from the fleet, and ordered back without a near approach? Had this been done, no information could have been gained, and the object designed to be secured by the detention would have been answered, without infringing that amicable intercourse between contending armies, which, when violated or disregarded, opens a door to brutal and savage warfare. When it was found in the American camp, that they did not return, the cause of it was at once correctly divined.

The British admiral was very solicitous, and resorted to various means, to obtain from these gentlemen information of the strength, condition, and disposition of the American army; but so cautious a reserve was maintained, that nothing could be elicited. Shields was perceived to be quite deaf, and calculating on some advantage to be derived from this circumstance, he and the doctor were placed at night in the green-room, where any conversation which occurred between them could readily be heard. Suspecting, perhaps, something of the kind, after having retired, they began to speak of their situation—the circumstance of their being detained, and of the prudent caution with which they had guarded themselves against communicating any information to the British admiral. But, continued Shields, how greatly these gentlemen will be disappointed in their expectations, for Jackson, with the twenty thousand troops he now has, and the reinforcements from Kentucky, which must speedily reach him, will be able to destroy any force that can be landed from these ships. Every word was heard and treasured, and not supposing there was any design, or that he presumed himself overheard, they were beguiled by it, and at once concluded our force to be as great as it was represented; and hence, no doubt, arose the reason of that prudent care and caution with which the enemy afterwards proceeded; for "nothing," remarked a British officer, at the close of the invasion, "was kept a secret from us, except your numbers; this, although diligently sought after, could never be procured."

Between the 23d, and the attempt on the 28th, to carry the line, Major Butler, who remained at his post in the city, was applied to by Mr. Skipwith, at that time Speaker of the Senate, to ascertain the commanding general's views, provided he should be driven from his line of encampment, and compelled to retreat through the city; and the question was asked, whether, in that event, he would destroy it? It was, indeed, a curious inquiry from one who, having spent his life in serving his country in different capacities, might better have understood the duty of a subordinate officer; and that even, if, from his situation, Major Butler had so far acquired the confidence of his general as to have become acquainted with his views and designs, he was not at liberty to divulge them, without destroying confidence and acting criminally. Upon asking the cause of the inquiry, Mr. Skipwith replied, it was rumored, and so understood, that if driven from his position, and made to retreat upon the city, General Jackson had it in contemplation to lay it in ruins; the legislature, he said, desired information on this subject, that if such were his intentions, they might, by offering terms of capitulation to the enemy, avert so serious a calamity. That a sentiment having for its object a surrender of the city, should be entertained by this body, was scarcely credible; yet a few days made it still more apparent, and showed that they were already devising plans to insure the safety of themselves and property, even at any sacrifice. While the general was hastening along the line, he was hailed by Mr. Duncan, one of his volunteer aids, and informed that it was already agitated in secret, by the members of the legislature, to offer terms of capitulation to the enemy, and proffer a surrender, and that Governor Claiborne awaited his orders on the subject. Critical as the time was, the safety or fall of the city being still uncertain, it was plainly to be perceived, that, although with a strong army before them, no such resolution could be carried into effect, yet it might be productive of evil, and in the end bring about the most fatal consequences. Even the disclosure of such a wish on the part of the legislature might create parties, excite opposition in the army, and inspire the enemy with renewed confidence. The Tennessee forces, and Mississippi volunteers, could not be affected by the measure; but it might detach the Louisiana militia, and even extend itself to the ranks of the regular troops. Jackson was greatly incensed, that those whose safety he had so much at heart should be seeking, under the authority of office, to mar his best exertions. He was too warmly pressed at the moment to give it the attention its importance merited; but availing himself of the first leisure moment, he apprized Governor Claiborne of what he had heard;—ordered him to watch the conduct of the legislature closely, and the moment a project of offering a capitulation to the enemy should be fully disclosed, to place a guard at the door and confine them to their chamber. The governor, in his zeal to execute the command, and from a fear of the consequences involved in such conduct, construed the order to be imperative, and placing an armed force at the door of the capitol, prevented the members from convening, and their schemes from maturing.

The purport of this order was either essentially misconceived by the governor; or, with a view to avoid subsequent inconveniences and complaints, was designedly mistaken. Jackson's object was not to restrain the legislature in the discharge of their official duties; for although he thought that such a moment, when the sound of the cannon was constantly pealing in their ears, was inauspicious to wholesome legislation, and that it would have better comported with the state of the times for them to abandon their civil duties and appear in the field, yet it was a matter indelicate to be proposed: and it was hence preferred, that they should adopt whatever course might be suggested by their own notions of propriety. This opinion would have been still adhered to; but when, through the communication of Mr. Duncan, they were represented as entertaining opinions and schemes adverse to the general interest and safety of the country, the necessity of a new and different course of conduct was at once obvious. But he did not order Governor Claiborne to interfere with or prevent them from proceeding with their duties; on the contrary, he was instructed, as soon as any thing hostile to the general cause should be ascertained, to place a guard at the door, and keep the members to their post and to their duty. "My object in this," remarked the general, "was, that they would then be able to proceed with their business without producing the slightest injury: whatever schemes they might entertain would have remained with themselves, without the power of circulating them to the prejudice of any other interest than their own. I had intended to have had them well treated and kindly dealt by; and thus abstracted from every thing passing without doors, a better opportunity would have been afforded them to enact good and wholesome laws; but Governor Claiborne mistook my order, and instead of shutting them in doors, contrary to my wishes and expectations turned them out."

Previous to this occurrence, Jackson had been waited on by a special committee of the legislature, to know what his course would be, should necessity compel him to abandon his position. "If," replied the general, "I thought the hair of my head could divine what I should do, I would cut it off forthwith; go back with this answer; say to your honorable body, that if disaster does overtake me, and the fate of war drives me from my line to the city, they may expect to have a very warm session." " And what did you design to do," asked a friend, " provided you had been forced to retreat?" "I should," he replied, "have retreated to the city, fired it, and fought the enemy amid the surrounding flames. There were with me men of wealth, owners of considerable property, who, in such an event, would have been among the foremost to have applied the torch to their own buildings; and what they had left undone, I should have completed. Nothing for the comfortable maintenance of the enemy would have been left in the rear. I would have destroyed New Orleans—occupied a position above on the river— cut off all supplies, and in this way compelled them to depart from the country."

We shall not pretend to ascribe this conduct of the legislature to disaffection, or to treasonable motives. No doubt the impulse that produced it was interest—a principle of the human mind which strongly sways, and often destroys its best conclusions. The disparity of the two armies, in numbers, preparation, and discipline, had excited apprehension, and destroyed hope. If Jackson were driven back, and little else was looked for, rumor announced his determination of devoting the city to destruction: but even if such were not his intention, the wrath and vengeance of the enemy might be fairly calculated to be in proportion to the opposition they should receive. Although these considerations may somewhat palliate, they do not justify. The government was represented in the person of the commanding general, on whom rested all responsibility, and whose voice on the subject of resistance or capitulation should alone have been heard. In the field were persons who were enduring hardships and straining every nerve for the general safety. A few of the members of their own body, too, were there who did not despond. Might not patriotism, then, have admonished these men, honored as they were with the confidence of the people, rather to have pursued a course having for its object to keep up the excitement, than to have endeavored to introduce fear and paralyze exertion? Such conduct, if productive of nothing worse, was well calculated to excite alarm. If the militia, who had been hastily drawn to the camp, and who were yet trembling for the safety of their families, had been told that a few private men of standing in society had expressed their opinions, and declared resistance useless, it would without doubt have occasioned serious apprehensions; but in a much greater degree would they be likely to arise, when told that the members of the legislature, chosen to preside over the safety and destinies of the state, after due deliberation, had pronounced all attempts at successful opposition vain and ineffectual.

Here was an additional reason why expedients should be devised, and every precaution adopted, to prevent any communication by which the slightest intelligence should be had of their situation, already indeed sufficiently deplorable. Additional guards were posted along the swamp, on both sides of the Mississippi, to arrest all intercourse; while on the river, the common highway, watch boats were constantly plying during the night, in different directions, so that a log could scarcely float down the stream unperceived. Two flat-bottomed boats, on a dark night, were turned adrift above, to ascertain if vigilance were preserved, and whether there would be any possibility of escaping the guards, and passing in safety to the British lines. The light boats discovered them on their passage, and on the alarm being given, they were opened upon by the Louisiana sloop, and the batteries on the shore, and in a few minutes were sunk. In spite, however, of every precaution, treason still discovered avenues through which to project and execute her nefarious plans, and information was constantly afforded to the enemy.

As an evidence of the extent of the information imparted to the officers of the British army, Charles K. Blanchard, who was on board the fleet, addressed a letter to General Jackson, in which he gave the substance of a conversation with a quarter-master of one of the vessels, and said that he was told, "that the commanding officers of the British forces were daily in the receipt of every information from the city of New Orleans which they might require, in aid of their operations, for the completion of the objects of the expedition: that they were perfectly acquainted with the situation of every part of our forces, the manner in which the same was situated, the number of our fortifications, their strength, position, &c. As to the battery on the left bank of the Mississippi, he described its situation, its distance from the main post, and promptly offered me a plan of the works. He furthermore stated, that the above information was received from seven or eight persons, in the city of New Orleans, from whom he could, at any hour, procure every information necessary to promote His Majesty's interest."

Great inconvenience was sustained for the want of arms, and much anxiety felt, lest the enemy, through their faithful adherents, might on this subject also obtain information. To prevent it as far as possible, General Jackson endeavored to conceal the strength and situation of his army, by suffering his reports to be seen by none but himself and the adjutant-general. Many of the troops in the field were supplied with common guns, which were of little service. The Kentucky troops, who were daily expected, were also understood to be badly provided with arms Believing that the city might yet contain many article that would be serviceable, orders were issued to the mayor of New Orleans, directing him diligently to inquire through every store and house, and take possession of all the muskets, bayonets, spades, and axes, he could find. He was also instructed to obtain a register of every man in the city under the age of fifty, that measures might be concerted for drawing forth those who had hitherto appeared backward in engaging in the pending contest.

Frequent light skirmishes by advanced parties, without material loss on either side, were the only incidents that took place for several days. Colonel Hinds, at the head of the Mississippi dragoons, on the 30th of December, was ordered to dislodge a party of the enemy who, under cover of a ditch that ran across the plain, were annoying the American fatigue parties. In advancing, he was unexpectedly thrown into an ambuscade, and became exposed to the fire of a line which had hitherto been concealed and unobserved. His collected conduct and gallant deportment extricated him from the danger in which he was placed, and gained for him and his corps the approbation of the commanding general. The enemy, being forced from their position, retired, and the colonel returned to the line with the loss of five of his men.

The British were encamped two miles below the American army, on a perfect plain, and in full view. Although foiled in their attempt to carry the works by the force of their batteries on the 28th, they resolved upon another attack, which they believed would be more successful Presuming their failure to have arisen from not having sufficiently strong batteries and heavy ordnance, a more enlarged arrangement was resorted to, with a confidence of silencing opposition, and effecting such breaches in the intrenchment as would enable their columns to pass, without being exposed to any considerable hazard. The interim between the 28th of December and the 1st of January was accordingly spent in preparing to execute their designs. Their boats were despatched to the shipping, and an additional supply of heavy cannon landed through Bayou Bienvenu, where they had first debarked.

During the night of the 31st of December they were busily engaged. An impenetrable fog, which was not dispelled until nine o'clock the next morning, aided them in the plans they were projecting, and gave time to complete their works. When the mist disappeared, several heavy batteries, at the distance of six hundred yards, mounting eighteen and twenty-four pound carronades, were presented to view. No sooner was it sufficiently clear to distinguish objects at a distance, than these were opened, and a tremendous burst of artillery commenced, accompanied with Congreve rockets, that filled the air in all directions. Our troops, being protected by a defence, which they believed to be impregnable, were unmoved and undisturbed. The British, through the friendly interference of some disaffected citizens, having been apprised of the fact that the general occupied a house at a small distance in the rear of his line of defence, directed against it their first and principal efforts. So great was the number of balls thrown, that in a little while its porticoes were beaten down, and the building made a complete wreck. This dishonorable attempt to destroy Jackson was unsuccessful; as it was a constant practice with him, on the first appearance of danger, not to wait in his quarters watching events, but instantly to proceed to the line, and be ready to form his arrangements as circumstances might require. Constantly in expectation of an attack, he was never absent from the post of duty; and he had repaired, at the first sound of the cannon, to aid in the defence, and inspire his troops with firmness. The guns along the American line were opened to repel the assault, and a constant roar of cannon, on both sides, continued until nearly noon; when, by the superior skill of Jackson's engineers, the two batteries formed on the right, next the woods, were nearly beaten down, and many of the guns dismounted, broken, and rendered useless. That next the river still continued its fire until three o'clock; when, perceiving all attempts to force a breach ineffectual, the enemy gave up the contest and retired. Every act of theirs discovered a strange delusion, and showed upon what wild and fanciful grounds all their expectations were founded. That the American troops were well posted, and strongly defended by pieces of heavy ordnance, mounted along their line, was a fact well known; yet a belief was constantly indulged that the undisciplined collection which constituted the strength of our army, would be able to derive little benefit from such a circumstance; and that artillery could produce but slight advantages in the hands

FAILURE OF THE ATTACK

of persons who were strangers to the manner of using it. That many who, from necessity, were called to the direction of the guns, were at first entirely unacquainted with their management, is indeed true; yet the accuracy and precision with which they threw their shot, afforded convincing proof, either that they possessed the capacity of becoming in a short time well acquainted with the art of gunnery, or that it was a science the acquisition of which was not attended with insurmountable difficulties.

That they would be able to effect an opening, and march through the strong defence in their front, was an idea so fondly cherished by the British, that an apprehension of failure had scarcely been conceived. So sanguine were they in this belief, that early in the morning their soldiers were arranged along the ditches, in rear of their batteries, prepared to advance to the charge the moment a breach could be made.

Perceiving that their attempts must fail, and that such an effect could not be produced as would warrant their advance, another expedient was resorted to, but with no better success. It occurred to the British commander that an attack might be made with advantage, next to the woods, and a force was accordingly ordered to penetrate in this direction, and turn the left of our line, which was supposed not to extend farther than to the margin of the swamp. In this way it was expected a diversion could be made, while the reserve columns, being in readiness and waiting, were to press forward the moment this object could be effected. Here, too, disappointment resulted. General Coffee's brigade, being already extended into the swamp, as far as it was possible for an advancing party to penetrate, brought unexpected dangers into view, and occasioned an abandonment of the project. The genius and foresight of Jackson had provided against this emergency. Although cutting the levee had raised the waters in the swamp, and increased the difficulties of keeping troops there, yet a fear lest this pass might be sought by the enemy, and the rear of the line thereby gained, had determined the general to extend his defences in that direction. This had been intrusted to General Coffee, and a more arduous duty could scarcely be imagined. To form a breastwork in such a place was attended with many difficulties and considerable exposure. A slight defence, however, had been thrown up, and the underwood, for thirty or forty yards in front, cut down, that the riflemen stationed for its protection might have a complete view of any force that might attempt a passage through this route. When it is recollected that this position was to be maintained night and day, and that the only opportunity afforded our troops for rest was on logs and brush thrown together, by which they were raised above the surrounding water, it may be truly said, that it has seldom fallen to the lot of men to encounter greater hardships; but accustomed to privation, and alive to those feelings which a love of country enkindles, they obeyed without complaining, and cheerfully kept their position until all danger had ceased. Sensible of the importance of the point they defended, and that it was necessary to be maintained, be the sacrifice what it might, they looked to nothing but a zealous and faithful discharge of the trust confided to them.

Our loss in this affair was eleven killed and twenty-three wounded; that of the enemy was never correctly known. The only certain information is contained in a communication of the 28th of January, from General Lambert to Earl Bathurst, in which the casualties and losses, from the 1st to the 5th, are stated at seventy-eight. Many allowances are to be made for this report. It was written at a time when, from the numerous disasters encountered, it was not to be presumed the general's mind was in a situation patiently to remember the facts, or minutely to detail them. From the great precision of the American fire, and the injury visibly sustained by their batteries, their loss was no doubt considerable. The enemy's heavy shot having penetrated Jackson's intrenchment in many places, it was discovered not to be as strong as had at first been imagined. Fatigue parties were again employed, and its strength daily increased; an additional number of bales of cotton were taken to be applied to strengthening and defending the embrasures along the line. A Frenchman, whose property had been seized, without his consent, fearful of the injury it might sustain, proceeded in person to General Jackson to reclaim it, and to demand its delivery. The general, having heard his complaint, and ascertained from him that he was unemployed in any military service, directed a musket to be brought to him, and placing it in his hand, ordered him on the line, remarking, at the same time, that as he seemed to be a man possessed of property, he knew of none who had a better right to fight and to defend it.

The British again retired to their encampment. It was well understood by Jackson that they were in daily expectation of considerable reinforcements; though he rested with confidence in the belief that a few more days would also bring to his assistance the troops from Kentucky. Each party, therefore, was busily and constantly engaged in preparation, the one to wage a vigorous attack, the other bravely to defend, and resolutely to oppose it.

The position of the American army was in the rear of an intrenchment formed of earth, and which extended in a straight line from the river to a considerable distance in the swamp. In front was a deep ditch, which had been formerly used as a mill-race. The Mississippi had receded and left the ditch dry, next the river, though in many places the water still remained. Along the line, and at unequal distances, to the centre of General Carroll's command, were guns mounted, of different calibre, from six to thirty-two pounders. Near the river, and in advance of the intrenchment, was erected a redoubt, with embrasures, commanding the road along the levee, and calculated to rake the ditch in front.

We have heretofore stated, that General Morgan was ordered, on the 24th of December, to cross to the west bank of the Mississippi. From an apprehension entertained that an attempt might be made through Barrataria, and the city reached from the right bank of the river, the general had extended his defences there likewise: in fact, unacquainted with the enemy's views, not knowing the number of their troops, nor but that they might have sufficient strength to make an assault in different quarters, and anxiously solicitous to be prepared at all points, he carefully divided his forces. His greatest fear was for the Chef Menteur road, and hence his strongest defence, aside from the principal encampment, was in that quarter, where Governor Claiborne, at the head of the Louisiana militia, was posted. The position on the right was formed on the same plan with the line on the left, but lower down than the latter, and extending to the swamp at right angles to the river. At this point General Morgan was stationed.

To be prepared against every possible contingency that might arise, Jackson had established another line of defence, about two miles in the rear of the one at present occupied, which was intended as a rallying point if he should be driven from his first position. With the aid of his cavalry, to give a momentary check to the advance of the enemy, he expected to be enabled to reach it without much injury, and be again in a situation to dispute a further passage to the city, and arrest the progress of the enemy. To inspirit his own soldiers, and to exhibit to the enemy as great a show as possible of strength and intended resistance, his unarmed troops, which constituted no inconsiderable number, were stationed here. All intercourse between the lines, except by confidential officers, was prohibited; and every precaution and vigilance employed, not only to keep this want of preparation concealed from the enemy, but even from being known in his own ranks.

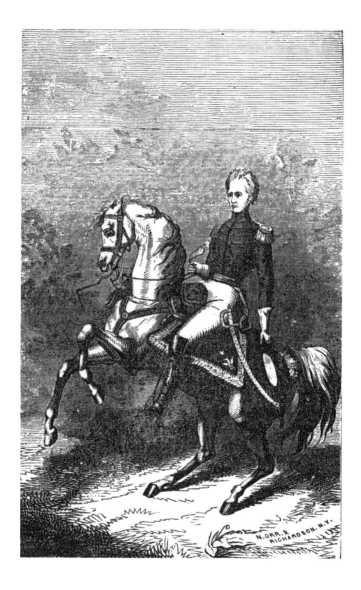

CHAPTER IX.

1815. Arrival of fresh troops from Kentucky—Preparations of both armies for an attack—The disposition of Jackson's force made known to the British by a deserter—Success of Colonel Thornton on the right bank of the river—Eagerness of the American soldiers for an engagement—Activity and energy of Jackson—The eighth of January—Advance of the British towards the American intrenchments—Destructive fire from the fortifications—Repulse of the British—Death of Sir Edward Packenham—Terrible havoc made in the ranks of the enemy—Bravery of Colonel Rennie—Number of killed and wounded in the battle—Watchword of the British army—Generous benevolence of the American soldiers—An armistice proposed by General Lambert and accepted, with modifications—Brave conduct of the American troops—Want of arms prevents Jackson from capturing the whole British army—English version of the battle. 1815.

AFTER the cannonade on the 1st of January, nothing of interest occurred in the movements of either army, prior to the memorable day which, while it placed the reputation of General Jackson for military genius and skill, on a level with that of the ablest commanders of the age, shed an unfading lustre on the American arms. A straggling fire was kept up, but it produced little or no effect. Both parties were actively engaged in watching the movements of each other, and in making preparations; the one for a contemplated attack, and the other for an effectual resistance. On the 4th day of the month, the long-expected reinforcement from Kentucky, of twenty-two hundred and fifty men, under the command of Major-general Thomas, arrived at the American head-quarters; but they were so ill provided with arms as to be incapable of rendering any efficient service. The alacrity with which the citizens of that state had proceeded to the frontiers, and aided in the north-western campaigns, added to the disasters which ill-timed policy or misfortune had produced, had created such a scarcity of arms that they were not to be procured. The force under General Thomas had confidently expected to be supplied on their arrival. About five hundred of them had muskets; the rest were provided with guns, which were more or less unserviceable. The mayor of New Orleans, at the request of General Jackson, had already examined and drawn from the city every weapon that could be found; while the arrival of the Louisiana militia, in an equally unprepared situation, rendered it impossible for the evil to be effectually remedied. A boat laden with arms intended for the use and defence of the lower country, was somewhere on the river; but where it was, or when it might arrive, rested entirely on hope and conjecture. Expresses had been despatched up the river, for three hundred miles, to seek and hasten it on; still there were no tidings of its approach. That so many brave men, at a moment of such anxious peril, should be compelled to stand with folded arms, unable, from their situation, to render the least possible service to their country, was an event greatly to be deplored, and did not fail to excite the feelings of the commanding general. His active mind could discover no means by which their services might be made available, and no alternative was presented, but to place them at his intrenchment in the rear, conceal their actual condition, and by the show they might make, add to his appearance and numbers, without at all increasing his effective strength.

Information was now received, that Major-general Lambert had joined the British commander in chief, with a considerable reinforcement. It had been previously announced in the American camp that additional forces were expected, and something decisive might be looked for as soon as they should arrive. This circumstance, in connection with others no less favoring the idea, led to the conclusion that a few days more would, in all probability, bring on the struggle which was to decide the fate of the city. It was more than ever necessary to keep the situation of the American army concealed, and General Jackson determined at once to restrict all communication, even with his own lines. None were permitted to leave the line, and none from without to pass into his camp, but such as were to be implicitly confided in. The chain of sentinels was strengthened in front, to prevent a passage to the enemy, should desertion be attempted; yet, notwithstanding his caution and vigilance, the condition of his army, and its disposition in the intrenchments, were made known to the enemy, by a soldier who eluded the sentinels, and made his escape, on the night of the 6th of January. His desertion was discovered early next morning, and it was rightly conjectured that he had gone to the British camp, and would afford them all the information in his power to communicate. This opinion, as subsequent circumstances disclosed, was well founded; and dearly did he atone his crime. He unfolded to the British the situation of the American line, the number of the reinforcements lately arrived, and the unarmed condition of many of the troops; and pointing to the centre of General Carroll's division, as a place occupied by militia alone, he recommended it as the point where an attack might be most safely and prudently made.

The information obtained by the commanding general on the 7th, confirmed him in the belief that an attack was in contemplation. It was ascertained from some prisoners taken on the lake, that the enemy were busily engaged in deepening Villere's canal, with the intention of passing their boats and ordnance into the Mississippi. During the day a constant bustle was perceived in their camp. Their soldiers were continually in motion along the borders of the canal, marching and manœuvring, for no other purpose except that of concealing the men who were busily engaged at work in the rear. In order to ascertain the cause and object of this uncommon movement, as far as was practicable, Commodore Patterson proceeded down the river, on the opposite side, and having gained a favorable position in front of their encampment, discovered them to be actually engaged in deepening the passage to the river. It was no difficult matter to divine their purpose. It was clearly evident that an assault was intended to be made on the line of defence commanded by General

PREPARATIONS FOR AN ATTACK

Morgan; which, if successful, would expose the Americans on the left bank to the fire of the redoubt erected on the right, and in this way compel them to an abandonment of their position. It was important to counteract this design; and measures were immediately taken to prevent its execution. The force on the right bank was increased The second regiment of Louisiana militia, and four hundred Kentucky troops, were ordered to reinforce the troops occupying that side of the river. Owing to some delay and difficulty in arming them, the latter, amounting, instead of four hundred, to but one hundred and eighty, did not arrive until the morning of the 8th. A little before day they were despatched to the aid of an advanced party, under the command of Major Arnaut, who had been sent to watch the movements of the enemy, and oppose their landing. The hopes indulged from their opposition were not realized; and the enemy reached the shore unmolested.

The position of General Morgan, besides being strengthened by several brass twelves, was defended by a strong battery, mounting twenty-four pounders, under the direction of Commodore Patterson, which was an important addition to its strength and security. The line itself was not strong; yet, if properly maintained by the troops selected for its defence, it was believed to be fully adequate to the purpose of successful resistance. Late at night, Patterson ascertained that the enemy had succeeded in passing their boats through the canal, and immediately communicated his information to the general. The commodore had already formed the idea of dropping the Louisiana schooner down, to attack and sink them. This thought, though well conceived, was abandoned, on account of the danger involved, and from an apprehension lest the batteries erected on the river, with which she would come in collision, might, by the aid of hot shot succeed in blowing her up. It was preferred patiently to await the arrival of the enemy, in the belief that it would be practicable, with the bravery of more than fifteen hundred men, and the advantages possessed from their line of defence, to maintain their position, and repel the assailants. In this expectation they were disappointed, as

Morgan was compelled to abandon his position by the detachment under Colonel Thornton.

On the left bank, where the general commanded in person, every thing was in readiness to meet the assault when it should be made. The redoubt on the levee was defended by a company of the seventh regiment, under the command of Lieutenant Ross. The regular troops occupied that part of the intrenchment next the river. General Carroll's division was in the centre, supported by the Kentucky troops, under General John Adair; while the extreme left, extending for a considerable distance into the swamp, was protected by the brigade of General Coffee. How soon the attack would be made, was a matter of uncertainty; but the brave soldiers whom Jackson had gathered around him, calmly awaited the approach of the enemy, behind the breastwork of cotton bags which the sagacity of their commander had provided, not as a shelter for cowardice, but as a protection against the onset of a superior force. Sharing the same high hopes and the same lofty enthusiasm that swelled in his bosom, they snuffed the breeze that bore to their ears the sounds of an approaching conflict, with as much eagerness as the war-worn veteran inured to the scenes of the battle-field. The general himself was not dismayed, either by the condition of his troops, or the great disparity of numbers when compared with the enemy, but, unmoved by appearances, he anxiously desired a contest, which he believed would give a triumph to his arms, and terminate the hardships of his suffering soldiers. Unremitting in his exertions, and constantly vigilant, his precaution kept pace with the zeal and preparation of the British commander. He seldom slept: he was always at his post, performing the duties of both general and soldier. His sentinels were doubled, and extended as far as possible in the direction of the British camp: while a considerable portion of the troops were constantly at the lines, with arms in their hands, ready to act when the first alarm should be given.

For eight days had the two armies lain upon the same field, in view of each other, without any thing decisive having been effected on either side. Twice since their

PREPARATIONS FOR AN ATTACK 143

landing had the British columns attempted to carry out their plans by storm, and twice had they been compelled to relinquish the attempt, and retire from the contest. It was not to be expected that matters would continue to remain in such a doubtful state. The pride of the English soldiery, the boasted conquerors of Europe, were there, with distinguished generals for their leaders, who earnestly desired to announce their signal achievements to the country and to the world. The high expectations which had been indulged in regard to the success of this expedition, were to be realized at every peril, or disgrace would follow the failure.

The 8th of January at length arrived. At the dawn of day, the signals intended to produce concert in the enemy's movements were discovered. A skyrocket was perceived rising in the air, on the left of their line, near the swamp, which was answered by another on the right, next the river. The British columns were instantly put in motion, and advanced with such rapidity, that the American outposts had barely time to reach the lines. The sky was lighted with blazing Congreve rockets, and an incessant shower of shells and bombs was poured from the British batteries, which, though demolished on the first of the month, had been re-established and remounted with heavy pieces of cannon, during the preceding night.

The enemy's force advanced in two divisions, commanded by Sir Edward Packenham in person, supported by Generals Keane and Gibbs; the right pressing forward against the centre of General Carroll's command, and the left against the redoubt on the levee. The dense fog which spread over the river and the adjacent country, enabled them to approach within a short distance of the American intrenchment before they were perceived. They were then discovered advancing with a firm, quick, and steady pace, in columns, with a front of sixty or seventy deep. The Americans had been in readiness for some time, waiting their appearance, and as they approached they gave three hearty cheers, when, upon the instant, their whole line was lighted with the blaze of their fire. A burst of artillery and small arms, pouring with destructive aim upon them, mowed down their front, and arrested their advance. In the musketry, there was not a moment's intermission: as one party discharged their pieces, another succeeded; alternately loading and appearing, no pause could be perceived—it was one continued volley. The columns already perceived their dangerous and exposed situation. Battery No. 7, on the left, was ably served by Lieutenant Spotts, and galled them with an incessant and destructive fire. Batteries Nos. 6 and 8 were no less actively employed, and no less successful in felling them to the ground. Notwithstanding the severity of the fire, which few troops could for a moment have withstood, some brave men pressed on, and succeeded in gaining the ditch in front of the works, where they remained during the action, and were afterwards made prisoners. The horrors before them were too great to be withstood, and the British columns soon began to waver in their determination, and retire from the conflict. At this moment, Sir Edward Packenham hastened to the front, and endeavored to encourage and inspire them with renewed zeal. His example was of short duration; he soon fell, mortally wounded, in the arms of his aid-de-camp, not far from the American line. Generals Gibbs and Keane also fell, and were borne from the field dangerously wounded. At this moment, General Lambert, who was advancing at a small distance in the rear, with the reserve, met the columns precipitately retreating, and in great confusion. His efforts to stop them were unavailing; they continued their retreat until they reached a ditch at the distance of four hundred yards, where they were rallied and halted.

The field before them, over which they had advanced, was strewed with the dead and dying. Danger still hovered around them; but the importunities of their officers finally prevailed so far as to induce them to advance once more to the charge. They were already near enough to deploy, and were endeavoring to do so; but the same constant and unremitting fire that caused their first retreat, continued without abatement. The American batteries had never ceased their fire; their constant discharges of grape and canister, and the fatal aim of the musketry, mowed down the front of the columns as fast as they could be formed. Satisfied that nothing could be done, and that certain destruction awaited all further attempts, they forsook the contest and the field, in disorder, leaving it almost entirely covered with the dead and wounded. It was in vain their officers endeavored to animate them to further perseverance, and equally vain to attempt coercion. The panic produced by the dreadful repulse they had experienced, and the terrible havoc made in their ranks, while with their most zealous exertions they had been unable to obtain the slightest advantage, were circumstances well calculated to make even the most submissive soldier rebel against the authority that would control him.

The light companies of fusileers, the forty-third and ninety-third regiments, and one hundred men from the West India regiment, forming the left of General Keane's command, led by Colonel Rennie, were ordered to proceed under cover of some chimneys standing in the field, until they had cleared them, when they were directed to oblique to the river, and availing themselves of the protection afforded by the levee, to advance against the redoubt on the right of the American line. This work had been but recently commenced, and was in an unfinished state. It was only on the fourth of the month that General Jackson, much against his own opinion, yielded to the suggestions of the other officers, and permitted the work to be commenced. The plan of its projection was such, that it was impossible to defend it against an attack, in its incomplete condition. Rennie executed his orders with great bravery, and pressing forward rapidly, soon reached the ditch. His advance was greatly annoyed by Commodore Patterson's battery on the left bank of the river, and the cannon mounted on the redoubt; but having reached the works, he gallantly passed the ditch, sword in hand. He instantly leaped on the wall, and calling to his troops, bade them follow him. The words had scarcely left his lips, when he fell by the fatal aim of a rifleman. Overpowered by the impetuosity of the superior numbers who were mounting the wall and entering at the embrasures, the Americans retired to the line, in rear of the redoubt.

A momentary pause ensued, but only to be interrupted by increased horrors. Captain Beal, with the city riflemen, perceiving the enemy in his front, opened upon them, and at every discharge brought numbers of them to the ground. To advance, or maintain the point gained, was equally impracticable for the enemy: to retreat or surrender was the only alternative; for they already perceived that the division on the right was thrown into confusion, and hastily leaving the field.

General Jackson being informed of the partial success of the enemy on the right, and of their having obtained temporary possession of the redoubt, sent a detachment to retake it; but previous to its arrival, the enemy had abandoned the work, and commenced retiring. They were severely galled in their retreat by such of the guns as could be brought to bear. The levee afforded them considerable protection; yet they suffered greatly from Commodore Patterson's redoubt on the right bank. Being enfiladed by this on their advance, they had sustained considerable injury, and now in their retreat were no less severely assailed. Numbers found a grave in the ditch before the line; and of those who originally gained the redoubt, it is believed that not one escaped: they were shot down as fast as they entered. The route along which they advanced and retired was strewed with bodies. Affrighted at the carnage, the surviving members of the detachment fled from the scene hastily and in confusion. The American batteries still continued to pour forth their deadly fire, cutting them down at every step: safety seemed only to be attainable by retiring beyond the range of the shot; which, to troops galled so severely as they were, was too remote a relief. Influenced by this consideration, they fled to the ditch, whither the right division had retreated, and there remained until night permitted them to retire.

The loss of the British in the main attack on the left bank, has been variously stated. The killed, wounded and prisoners, as ascertained on the day after the battle, by Colonel Hayne, the inspector-general, was twenty-six hundred General Lambert's report to Lord Bathurst, stated it to be but two thousand and seventy. Judging from the accounts given by the prisoners, and information derived through other sources, it must have been even greater than was represented in either account. Among the killed, were the commander in chief, and Major-general Gibbs, who died of his wounds the next day, besides many other valuable and distinguished officers. The loss of the Americans, in killed and wounded, was but thirteen. Their effective force at the line on the left bank, was three thousand seven hundred; that of the enemy was, at least, nine thousand. The whole number of troops landed has been differently reported; but the best information places it at about fourteen thousand. A part of this force was with Colonel Thornton; the climate had rendered many unfit for the duties of the field; while a considerable number were killed and wounded, in the different contests previous to that on the 8th. Their real strength, therefore, may be fairly estimated at the number we have stated; at any rate, it could hardly be less.

It is very evident that the assault on the American intrenchments was considered by the British commander in chief, an undertaking of greater magnitude than was openly admitted. The officer who leads his troops on a forlorn attempt, not unfrequently places before them allurements stronger than either authority or duty. On this occasion, inducements were held out, than which nothing could have been more inviting to a licentious soldiery fresh from the horrid scenes enacted at the storming of St. Sebastian. The charms of the dark-eyed beauties of Spain were not represented to be more attractive, than were those of our fair country-women, who looked to the gallant little band assembled on the banks of the Mississippi, for safety and protection. The cupidity of the British soldiers was excited by the hope of plunder, and the most lawless passions of their natures were aroused to desperation, by the promised triumph over female innocence and purity. This fact has often been questioned, and in some instances positively denied; but the circumstances presented at the time of the transaction, leave no doubt of its truth. The books of two of the orderly sergeants taken in battle, and the voluntary statements of prisoners, show conclusively, that "*beauty* and *booty*," was the watchword of the day. These words, it is true, in and of themselves, might not, under certain circumstances, be regarded as of any weight; but when we consider the situation of the American army, and the defenceless condition of the city, if Jackson had been defeated, they assume an importance, which points irresistibly to the conclusion, that they were not idly adopted. It was fortunate for New Orleans, and its inhabitants, that the gallantry of the American general and the brave men who followed him to the battle-field, was sufficient to repel the attack of soldiers prompted to acts of courage and daring, by motives which disgrace and debase humanity.

The events of the 8th of January, afford abundant evidence of the generous kindness of the American soldiers, and exhibit a striking difference in the troops of the two nations. While those of one were incited to acts of bravery and duty, by the promised pillage and plunder of the inhabitants, and the commission of the most odious crimes; the other fought for their kindred and their country, and having repelled their assailants, instantly laid aside their enmity, and regarding their fallen foemen as brethren, hastened to relieve them, in several instances, at the hazard of their lives. The desperate courage of many of the British soldiers brought them close to the very ramparts, where they were shot down, and lay badly wounded. When the firing had ceased and the columns had retired, the Americans left their lines, to assist in bringing in their wounded enemies who were near the intrenchment; but while engaged in this commendable act of charity and kindness, they were fired upon by the British, from the ditch they had occupied, and several of them were seriously injured. Notwithstanding this dastardly attack, the American soldiers persevered in their laudable efforts to administer to the wants, and relieve the sufferings, of the wounded and dying.

Shortly after the British retired, a communication was received from Major-general Lambert, on whom the command devolved after the fall of Generals Packenham,

Gibbs, and Keane, acknowledging the kindness shown to his wounded men, and soliciting permission to bury the dead, and bring off those who were dangerously wounded. General Jackson refused to permit a near approach to his lines, but consented that the wounded who were at a greater distance than three hundred yards from the intrenchment should be relieved, and the dead buried: those nearer his lines, he agreed should be delivered over by his own men, to be interred by their countrymen. This precaution was taken, in order that the enemy might not have an opportunity to inspect, or learn any thing concerning his position, or the situation of the troops under his command. About noon, a proposition was made by General Lambert, for the cessation of hostilities until the same hour the next day. In the hope of being able to secure an important advantage which he had in contemplation, by his apparent willingness to comply with the proposal, General Jackson drew up an armistice and forwarded it to General Lambert, with directions for its immediate return, if approved. It contained a stipulation to this effect: that hostilities on the left bank of the river should be discontinued from its ratification, but that on the right bank, where Colonel Thornton had driven Morgan from his position, they should not cease; and that in the interim, under no circumstances were reinforcements to be sent across by either party. This was a bold stroke at stratagem; and although it succeeded even to the extent desired, was yet attended with considerable hazard. Reinforcements had been ordered over to retake the position lost by Morgan, in the morning, and the general presumed they had arrived at their point of destination; but at this time they had not passed the river, and it was not to be expected that it could be retaken by the same troops who had yielded it the day before, when possessed of advantages which gave them a decided superiority. The commanding general well knew this; yet, to spare the sacrifice of his men, which he foresaw must be considerable, in any attempt to regain it, he was disposed to venture upon a course which, he felt assured, could not fail to succeed. It was impossible that his object could be discovered, and he confidently believed the British commander would infer, from the prompt and ready manner in which his proposal had been met, that such additional troops were already thrown over as would be fully adequate to the purpose of attack, and greatly to endanger, if not wholly to cut off Colonel Thornton's retreat. General Lambert's construction was such as had been anticipated. Although the armistice contained a request that it should be immediately signed and returned, it was neglected to be acted upon until the next day; and Thornton and his command re-crossed the river, under cover of the night, and the ground they had occupied was peaceably left to the possession of the original holders.

The opportunity thus afforded, of regaining a position on which, in a great degree, depended the safety of those on the opposite shore, was accepted with an avidity its importance merited, and immediate measures were taken to increase its strength, and prepare it against any future attack that might be made. This delay of the British commander was evidently designed, in order that while the negotiation was pending, and before it was concluded, an opportunity might be had, either of throwing over reinforcements, or removing Colonel Thornton and his troops from a situation so extremely perilous. Early next morning, General Lambert returned his acceptance of what had been proposed, with an apology for having failed to reply sooner: he excused the omission, by pleading a press of business, which had occasioned the communication to be overlooked and neglected. Jackson was at no loss to attribute the delay to the correct motive; the apology, however, was as perfectly satisfactory to him as any thing that could have been offered; beyond the object intended to be effected, he felt unconcerned, and having secured this, he rested perfectly satisfied. The armistice was concluded on the 9th of January, and it was agreed that it should be continued until two o'clock in the evening. The dead and wounded were removed from the field; those within the line of demarcation, which the British were not permitted to cross, being delivered to them by the Americans, in accordance with the terms of the stipulation.

It has seldom happened, that officers have been more deceived, or atoned more severely for their error, than was the case with those commanding the British troops on this occasion. They seem to have taken it for granted that the militia would not maintain their ground when warmly assailed; and that at the approach of veteran troops, they would at once forsake the contest, and seek safety in flight. At what part of our line they were stationed, was ascertained by information derived through a deserter; and influenced by the belief that they wanted nerve and were deficient in bravery, the main assault was made at this point. They were indeed militia; but the enemy could have assailed no part of the American intrenchment where they would have met a warmer reception, or where they would have found greater strength; it was certainly the best defended part of the line. The Kentucky and Tennessee troops, under Generals Carroll, Thomas, and Adair, were there, and they had already won, on former occasions, a reputation that was too dear to be sacrificed. These divisions, alternately charging their pieces and mounting the platform, poured forth a constant fire, that was impossible to be withstood, repelled the advancing columns, and drove them from the field with prodigious slaughter. So enraged were the British officers at their repulse, and so firmly persuaded that the information given them by the deserter was false, that they called their informant before them, to account for the mischief he had done. It was in vain he urged his innocence, and with the most solemn protestations, declared he had stated the fact truly as it was. They could not be convinced—it was impossible that they had contended against any but the best disciplined troops; and without further ceremony, the poor fellow was suspended in view of the camp, and expiated his treachery, if not his misrepresentations, on the gibbet.

The gallant conduct of the American troops at the battle of New Orleans, has often been the subject of commendation. Their bravery and zeal were conspicuous during the continuance of the contest. It was impossible for men to serve under such a leader as Jackson, without becoming imbued with the same dauntless courage which he always exhibited. Bold without being rash, daring without being reckless, his own noble bearing was sufficient to arouse emotions of patriotism where none had existed. The 8th of January was a momentous day, not merely in his history, but also in that of the country. He felt the importance of the occasion, but nothing caused him to waver or hesitate. Those who were present at the battle, concur in saying, that there was a grandeur and sublimity about him, as he rode along the lines, that was absolutely irresistible. Every order was given with promptness and decision. Above the thunder of the artillery, and the roar of musketry, he was heard cheering and encouraging his men. Wherever his eagle-eye flashed, it excited the most intense enthusiasm; and when the shrill notes of his trumpet voice were heard amidst the din of battle, every heart beat with a stronger pulsation, and every arm was nerved with tenfold vigor.

After the battle, General Jackson could have easily captured every man belonging to the British force, on the land, if he had been supplied with arms, according to his repeated and urgent requests, and agreeably to the promises that were made to him. The want of these compelled him to remain stationary in his position, until the opportunity had passed. The British crossed the river, and embarked on board the vessels waiting to receive them, without further molestation. The account given by them of the battle, is so very different from what really took place, and there is such an evident attempt to conceal the extent of their defeat, that it is well worthy the perusal. The following official bulletin, professing to give a statement of the affair, was issued from the war office in London, on the reception of the intelligence:

"*War Department*, March 8, 1815.

"Captain Wylly arrived this morning, with despatches from Major-general Lambert, detailing the operations against the enemy in the neighborhood of New Orleans. It appears that the army, under the command of Major-general Keane, was landed at the head of the Bayonne, in the vicinity of New Orleans, on the morning of the 23d of December, without opposition; it was, however, attacked by the enemy in the course of the night succeeding the landing, when, after an obstinate contest, the enemy were repulsed at all points, with considerable loss. On the morning of the 25th, Sir E. Packenham arrived, and assumed the command of the army. On the 27th, at daylight, the troops moved forward, driving the enemy's pickets to within six miles of the town, when the main body of the enemy was discovered, posted behind a breastwork, extending about one thousand yards, with the right resting on the Mississippi, and the left on a thick wood. The interval between the 27th of December and the 8th of January, was employed in preparations for an attack upon the enemy's position. The attack which was intended to have been made on the night of the 7th, did not, owing to the difficulties experienced in the passage of the Mississippi, by a corps under Lieutenant-colonel Thornton, which was destined to act on the right bank of the river, take place till early on the morning of the 8th. The division to whom the storming of the enemy's work was intrusted, moved to the attack at that time, but being too soon discovered by the enemy, were received with a galling and severe fire from all parts of their line. Major-general Sir Edward Packenham, who had placed himself at the head of the troops, was unfortunately killed at the head of the glacis, and Major-generals Gibbs and Keane were nearly at the same moment wounded. The effect of this upon the troops caused a hesitation in their advance, and though order was restored by the advance of the reserve under Major-general Lambert, to whom the command of the army had devolved, and Colonel Thornton had succeeded in the operation assigned to him on the right bank of the river; yet the major-general, upon the consideration of the difficulties which yet remained to be surmounted, did not think himself justified in ordering a renewal of the attack. The troops, therefore, retired to the position which they had occupied previous to the attack. In that position they remained until the evening of the 18th, when, the whole of the wounded, with the exception of eighty, (whom it was considered dangerous to remove,) the field artillery, and all the stores of every description, having been embarked, the army retired to the head of the Bayonne, where the landing had been originally effected, and re-embarked without molestation."

CHAPTER X.

1815. Gratitude of the citizens of New Orleans to their deliverer—Jackson strengthens his position—Anonymous publications inciting his troops to revolt—The author placed in arrest—Judge Hall ordered into custody for his interference—The British retire to their shipping—Treaty of peace signed—Cessation of hostilities—Jackson submits to the fine imposed by the judge—Farewell address to his troops—Return to Nashville—Depredations committed by the Seminole Indians—Jackson ordered to take command of the southern army—Enters Florida with his army—Execution of Arbuthnot and Ambrister—Capture of St. Marks and Pensacola—Termination of hostilities—Jackson's conduct approved—Appointed governor of Florida—Administration of his judicial duties—Difficulty with the Ex-governor, Callava—Jackson's ill health compels him to return home. 1821.

The successful defence made by General Jackson against the attempt to storm his intrenchments, banished all the apprehensions of danger which the citizens of New Orleans had previously indulged. They eagerly hailed him as their deliverer and protector. No encomium could be too exalted to express the feelings of gratitude which they cherished towards him. In the midst of dangers and difficulties, he had perseveringly continued his defensive operations, until the result of the battle fully confirmed their efficiency. Obstacles that would have disheartened another commander, neither interfered with his plans, or daunted his spirit. Every thing was made to yield to the necessities of the crisis, and the bidding of his determined will. His influence was felt everywhere around and about him. What his feeble army lacked in numbers and in equipments, was more than made up, by the high-souled enthusiasm which he infused into their ranks. Treason shrunk abashed from his presence, and cowardice itself, at his side, became the most unflinching courage and the most devoted patriotism. The harsh and vigorous measures to which he was compelled to resort, led to frequent complaints; but when the danger was averted, and the city saved from plunder and rapine, even his arbitrary exercise of power was justified and approved. All classes and conditions united in the expression of their sincere and heartfelt thankfulness. Demonstrations of public respect succeeded each other daily; the congratulations of his fellow-countrymen, whose property and whose lives he had defended, flowed in upon him without stint; and the general sentiment of approbation which soon reached his ears was no more flattering to his pride, than it was just to his abilities and his services.

Although the defeat of the British on the 8th of January completely frustrated their plans, and put an end to their contemplated march upon the city, Jackson deemed it best to continue the same watchful discipline and care which had been attended with such satisfactory results. Had his men been properly supplied with arms, he would have completed the brilliant defence of the 8th of January, by the capture of the whole British force, but, situated as he was, it would have been rash in the extreme to have commenced any offensive operations. He confined himself, therefore, to perfecting his line of defences, and constructing new ones at assailable points, in order that the success already obtained might not be hazarded by remissness or neglect. While actively engaged in the discharge of his duty, the traitors and spies who had previously occasioned him so much trouble and vexation, were secretly at work in their efforts to counteract his plans. Having failed in one attempt to betray the country, they adopted a different mode of proceeding. Besides affording intelligence of his movements to the enemy, they caused anonymous articles, calculated to excite mutiny among his troops, to be inserted in one of the newspapers published in the city of New Orleans. So bold an act of treason was not to be overlooked, and with his characteristic energy and decision of character, Jackson promptly demanded of the publisher the name of the writer of the articles. The demand was complied with, and the traitor was discovered to be one of the members of the legislature. An order was forthwith issued by the general for his immediate arrest. An application was made to Judge Hall for a writ of *habeas corpus*, which was granted. As has been heretofore mentioned, the judge himself was at once arrested by command of Jackson, for interfering with his authority. At this time, the order proclaiming martial law had not been countermanded, in consequence of the proximity of the British army, and if the general had allowed one act of opposition to his authority to pass unnoticed, others might have followed in its train, which would have produced the most serious consequences.

The British forces retired to their shipping and took final leave of Louisiana, on the 18th of January, and early in the month of February the intelligence arrived, that a treaty of peace between Great Britain and the United States had been signed by the commissioners of the two governments, at Ghent, on the 24th of December previous. The cessation of hostilities was soon after officially announced. The appearance of the order releasing the city from the restraints of martial law, was followed by a rule of court granted by Judge Hall, commanding General Jackson to appear and show cause why an attachment should not issue against him for contempt, in refusing to obey a writ, and imprisoning the organ of the law. He did not hesitate to appear and submit a full and able answer justifying his proceedings. After argument before the court, the rule was made absolute; an attachment was sued out, and Jackson brought up to answer interrogatories. The proceedings were obviously unjust, but he preferred, like a good citizen, to submit quietly to the law. He therefore declined answering questions, and asked for the sentence, which the judge, who was exceedingly inimical towards him, then proceeded to pass. It was a fine of one thousand dollars. The spectators who crowded the hall evinced the strongest indignation. On entering his carriage, it was seized by the people and drawn to the coffee-house where he was residing. When he reached his head quarters, he put the amount of the fine into the hands of one of his aids, and caused it to be discharged without delay. He had scarcely anticipated the intentions of the citizens, as the full sum was raised among them by contribution, in a few moments. Jackson refused to accept the money, and at his request it was appropriated to a charitable institution. He enjoyed the consciousness that the powers which the exigency of the times forced him to assume, had been exercised exclusively for the public good, and were absolutely essential to the safety of the country. In addition to this, he was gratefully remembered by the people for whom he had sacrificed his ease and comfort, and endured so many hardships. In 1821, the corporation of New Orleans voted fifty thousand dollars for erecting a marble statue designed to commemorate his important military services; and the same body also gave one thousand dollars for his portrait painted by Mr. Earle. At the session of the United States Congress in 1844-5, complete though tardy justice was meted out to Jackson, by the passage of a law in effect approving of his conduct, and making provision for the restitution of the fine, with interest.

Notwithstanding the cessation of hostilities, General Jackson remained at New Orleans, with the troops under his command, until the month of March, at which time he was relieved by General Gaines. On taking leave of the brave volunteers who had cheerfully followed him through so many difficulties and dangers, previous to their final discharge, he issued the following address, thanking them for their fidelity to the country, and expressing his sincere wishes for their future happiness and prosperity:

" The major-general is at length enabled to perform the pleasing task of restoring to Tennessee, Kentucky, Louisiana, and the territory of the Mississippi, the brave troops who have acted such a distinguished part in the war which has just terminated. In restoring these brave men to their homes, much exertion is expected of, and great responsibility imposed on, the commanding officers of the different corps. It is required of Major-generals Carroll and Thomas, and Brigadier-general Coffee, to march their commands, without unnecessary delay, to their respective states. The troops from the Mississippi territory, and state of Louisiana, both militia and volunteers, will be immediately mustered out of service, paid, and discharged.

"The major-general has the satisfaction of announcing the approbation of the President of the United States to the conduct of the troops under his command, expressed in flattering terms, through the honorable the secretary of war.

"In parting with those brave men, whose destinies have been so long united with his own, and in whose labors and glories it is his happiness and his boast to have participated, the commanding general can neither suppress his feelings, nor give utterance to them as he ought. In what terms can he bestow suitable praise on merit so extraordinary, so unparalleled ? Let him, in one burst of joy, gratitude, and exultation, exclaim—' These are the saviors of their country—these the patriot soldiers, who triumphed over the invincibles of Wellington, and conquered the conquerors of Europe !' With what patience did you submit to privations—with what fortitude did you endure fatigue—what valor did you display in the day of battle ! You have secured to America a proud name among the nations of the earth—a glory which will never perish.

"Possessing those dispositions which equally adorn the citizen and the soldier, the expectations of your country will be met in peace, as her wishes have been gratified in war. Go, then, my brave companions, to your homes; to those tender connections, and blissful scenes, which render life so dear—full of honor, and crowned with laurels which will never fade. When participating, in the bosoms of your families, the enjoyment of peaceful life, with what happiness will you not look back to the toils you have borne—to the dangers you have encountered ? How will all your past exposures be converted into sources of inexpressible delight ! Who, that never experienced your sufferings, will be able to appreciate your joys ? The man who slumbered ingloriously at home, during your painful marches, your nights of watchfulness, and your days of toil, will envy you the happiness which these recollections will afford—still more will he envy the gratitude of that country, which you have so eminently contributed to save.

"Continue, fellow-soldiers, on your passage to your several destinations, to preserve that subordination, that dignified and manly deportment, which have so ennobled your character.

"While the commanding general is thus giving indulgence to his feelings towards those brave companions who accompanied him through difficulties and danger, he cannot permit the names of Blount, and Shelby, and Holmes, to pass unnoticed. With what generous ardor and patriotism have these distinguished governors contributed all their exertions to provide the means of victory! The recollection of their exertions, and of the success which has resulted, will be to them a reward more grateful than any which the pomp of title or the splendor of wealth can bestow.

"What happiness it is to the commanding general, that, while danger was before him, he was, on no occasion, compelled to use towards his companions in arms either severity or rebuke! If, after the enemy had retired, improper passions began their empire in a few unworthy bosoms, and rendered a resort to energetic measures necessary for their suppression, he has not confounded the innocent with the guilty—the seduced with the seducers. Towards you, fellow-soldiers, the most cheering recollections exist; blended, alas! with regret, that disease and war should have ravished from us so many worthy companions. But the memory of the cause in which they perished, and of the virtues which animated them while living, must occupy the place where sorrow would claim to dwell.

"Farewell, fellow-soldiers. The expression of your general's thanks is feeble, but the gratitude of a country of freemen is yours—yours the applause of an admiring world.   "ANDREW JACKSON,
        "*Major-general commanding.*"

On his route to Nashville, General Jackson saw, on every side, the certain evidences of exultation and delight. The reputation he had acquired during his campaigns in the Creek country, had extended from one section of the union to the other. All were familiar with the promptness and decision, the active intrepidity, and unyielding

RETURN HOME 161

firmness, he had evinced in his different engagements and marches through the Indian territory of the Hickory Ground, and in allusion to which the appellation of "Old Hickory" had been bestowed upon him; and the brilliant victory won at New Orleans threw the country into a complete fever of joy.

For two years afterwards, General Jackson, though still retaining his rank in the army, remained at home engaged in cultivating his farm, and busily occupied with rural pleasures and labors. In the winter of 1817, the hostile Creeks, or Seminoles, who had been driven into Florida, in connection with runaway negroes from the adjoining states, began to execute schemes of robbery and vengeance against the Americans living near the frontiers. Representations in regard to these outrages had been made to the American government, and General Gaines, the acting commander of the southern district, was ordered, in the summer of 1817, to occupy a position near the borders, with a considerable force, for the protection of the citizens. He was at first directed to keep within the territorial limits of the United States, and not to cross the Florida line; but to demand of the Indians the perpetrators of the crimes which had been committed, avoiding, if possible, a general rupture with the deluded Indians. General Gaines made the demand, in conformity with his orders. The savages, however, being deceived by the representations of certain foreign incendiaries and traders, who taught them to believe that they would receive assistance and encouragement from the British, not only refused to give up the murderers, but repeated their barbarities whenever an opportunity offered. Whilst matters remained in this condition, the intelligence was received that Lieutenant Scott, one of General Gaines' officers, with forty-seven persons, men, women and children, had been surprised by an ambuscade of Indians, when descending the Appalachicola river in a boat, about two miles below the junction of the Flint and Chattahoochie, and that the whole detachment had been killed or taken prisoners, except six men, who had made their escape. Those who were taken alive were wantonly butchered by the ferocious savages;

the little children were seized, and their brains dashed out against the side of the boat; and all the helpless females, with one exception, were murdered.

On the receipt of this intelligence, the government saw the necessity of adopting energetic measures. Orders were immediately issued to General Jackson to repair to Fort Scott and take command of the forces in that quarter, with authority, in case he should deem it necessary, to call upon the Executives of the adjoining states for additional troops. He was also authorized to cross the boundary line of Florida, which was still a Spanish territory, if necessary in the execution of his orders. The orders which had been issued to General Gaines, and to which he was referred for his own guidance, required him to adopt "measures necessary to terminate a conflict which had been avoided from considerations of humanity, but which had now become indispensable, from the settled hostility of the savage enemy." The Secretary of War also said, in a letter written to General Gaines in the month of January, 1818: "The honor of the United States requires that the war with the Seminoles should be terminated speedily, and with exemplary punishment for hostilities so unprovoked."

Having collected the Tennessee volunteers, with that zeal and promptness which ever marked his career, General Jackson repaired to the post assigned him, and assumed the command. The necessity of crossing the line into Florida was no longer a subject of doubt. A large body of Indians and negroes had made that territory their refuge, and the Spanish authorities were either too weak or too indifferent to restrain them. In order to comply with the orders issued to him, Jackson penetrated at once into the Seminole towns, reducing them to ashes, and driving the enemy before him. In the council-house of the Mickasukians, more than fifty fresh scalps, and in an adjacent house, upwards of three hundred scalps, of all ages and sexes, were found; and in the centre of the public square a red pole was erected, crowned with scalps, known by the hair to have belonged to the companions of Lieutenant Scott. To inflict merited punishment on the barbarians, and to prevent a repetition of the massacres, by bringing the war to a speedy and successful termination, he pursued his way to St. Marks. He there found, in conformity with previous information, that the Indians and negroes had demanded the surrender of the post to them ; and that the Spanish garrison, according to the commandant's own acknowledgment, was too weak to support it. He ascertained also that the enemy had been supplied with the means of carrying on the war, from the commandant of the post; that foreign incendiaries, who instigated the savages to cruelty, had free communication with the fort; and that councils of war were permitted by the commandant to be held by the chiefs and warriors, within his own quarters. The Spanish store-houses were appropriated to the use of the hostile party, and actually filled with goods belonging to them, though property known to have been plundered from American citizens was purchased from them by the commandant, while he professed friendship to the United States.

General Jackson, therefore, did not hesitate to demand of the officer commanding at St. Marks, the surrender of that post, that it might be garrisoned by an American force, and, when the Spaniard hesitated, he entered the fort by force, though without bloodshed ; the enemy having fled, and the garrison being too weak to offer any serious opposition. From this place he marched upon Suwanee, seized the stores of the enemy and burnt their villages.

A variety of circumstances now convinced General Jackson, that the savages had commenced the war and persisted in their barbarity. He therefore arrested at St. Marks several of the British incendiaries who had excited them to hostilities. One Alexander Arbuthnot, an Indian trader was taken at St. Marks, where he had been living as an inmate in the family of the commandant. He was tried by a court of inquiry, of thirteen respectable officers, and sentenced to be hung, which sentence was immediately carried into execution. Robert Ambrister, formerly a lieutenant in the British marine corps, was also tried ; and it having been proved that he had not only encouraged and assisted the hostile savages, but had also led them in their marauding excursions, he was sentenced by the court to receive fifty stripes and to be confined, with a ball and chain, at hard labor, for twelve calendar months. General Jackson, however, disapproved of this sentence, which he did not think sufficiently severe; and the case being reconsidered, Ambrister was sentenced to be shot, which sentence was forthwith executed.

It was now supposed by the commanding general that the war was at an end. St. Marks was garrisoned by an American force; the Indian towns of Mickasuky and Suwanee were destroyed; two prominent chiefs who had been the prime movers and leaders of the savages, had been killed; and the two foreign instigators taken and executed. The American commander, therefore, ordered the Georgia militia, who had joined him, to be discharged, and was about to return himself to Tennessee. While making his preparations, he was informed that the Indians were admitted freely by the governor at Pensacola; that they were collecting in large numbers, five hundred being in Pensacola on the 15th of April, many of whom were known to be hostile, and had just escaped from the pursuit of his troops; that the enemy were furnished with ammunition and supplies, and received intelligence of the movements of his forces, from that place; and that a number of them had sallied out and murdered eighteen American citizens, who had settled upon the Alabama, and were immediately received by the governor, and furnished with means of transportation across the lake, that they might escape pursuit.

These facts being ascertained by General Jackson, from reliable authority, he forthwith took up his line of march towards Pensacola, at the head of a detachment of about twelve hundred men, for the purpose of counteracting the views of the enemy. On the 18th of May, he crossed the Appalachicola at the Ocheese village, with the intention of scouring the country west of that river, and on the 23d of the month, he received a communication from the governor of West Florida, protesting against his entrance into that province, commanding him to retire from it, and declaring that he would repel force by force if he did not obey. This communication, together with other indications of the governor's hostility, were followed by prompt action on the part of the American general. He marched direct to Pensacola, and took possession of that place the following day. The governor himself fled to Fort Carlos de Barrancas, which post also surrendered, after a feeble resistance, on the 28th of May. This bold and energetic mode of carrying on the war soon put an end to the depredations of the Indians and negroes. Parties of them were scattered here and there through the country, and, to prevent them from attacking the frontier settlements, two of the volunteer companies were ordered to scour the country between the Mobile and the Appalachicola. Thus ended the Seminole campaign, which, though not distinguished by any heavy battles, was, nevertheless, a most arduous and harassing kind of warfare.

General Jackson returned to the Hermitage, in June, 1818. His promptness and decision in checking the incursions of the savages, and putting an end to their depredations, elicited new acknowledgments and new evidences of respect and admiration. The general government deemed it expedient ultimately to restore to Spain the posts of St. Marks and Pensacola: but the conduct of Jackson was approved, and President Monroe expressed the opinion in his annual message, at the commencement of the session of Congress in 1818, that the "misconduct of the Spanish officers," in affording countenance and protection to the savages, fully justified the course which had been pursued. The proceedings of the general in regard to Arbuthnot and Ambrister, were, in like manner, unequivocally confirmed. The British government even, though always prompt in protecting her citizens, could not but acknowledge the justice of their condemnation.

General Jackson returned home in the summer of 1818, and in the course of the following winter he visited Washington. The incidents of the Seminole campaign were then under consideration in Congress, and a report was made by a committee of the Senate extremely hostile to his character. It had not the concurrence of the ablest members of the committee, and on the appearance of an article in the National Intelligencer, written by General Jackson himself, triumphantly defending his conduct, all further action upon it was suspended. An attempt was also made in the House of Representatives, to pass a vote of censure, but it was rejected by a decisive majority. While at the east, the general visited Baltimore, Philadelphia, and New York, in each of which he was welcomed with distinguished honors. He received the freedom of the city of New York on the 19th of February, in a gold box; and there, as well as in Baltimore, the municipal council requested and obtained his portrait, to be placed in their hall.

On the 22d of February, 1819, a treaty was signed between Spain and the United States, by which the Floridas were ceded to the latter power. Upon the final ratification of the treaty, Congress passed a law, empowering the president to vest in such person or persons as he might select, all the military, civil, and judicial authority exercised by the officers of the Spanish government. Under this law, the president selected General Jackson to act as commissioner for receiving the provinces, and to assume the government of them. The intimate acquaintance of Jackson with the country, and the energy and decision of his character, specially recommended him for this position. The territory was completely overrun with smugglers, negro-stealers, and desperadoes of every description; and it required the exercise of no little firmness and rigor to restore quiet and good order. The general reluctantly accepted the office, and on the 1st of July, 1821, he issued his proclamation at Pensacola, announcing that he had taken possession of the territory in the name of the United States, and that all citizens were required to yield obedience to her authority. Prompt measures were adopted for enforcing the laws, and securing the due administration of justice. Courts were immediately organized, and a system of internal police instituted.

By the treaty with Spain it was expressly stipulated, that all the archives and documents relating to the property and sovereignty of the provinces should be delivered up to the American authorities. A case soon occurred under this clause of the treaty, which called out all General Jackson's well-known firmness and promptitude. On the 22d of August, he received a petition from certain individuals, setting forth that certain papers of great importance to the rights of several orphan females, whose inheritance was under litigation, had been feloniously retained by the Spanish Ex-governor, Callava, and that they were in the hands of a man named Sousa. Jackson forthwith ordered three officers to wait upon Sousa, and demand the documents. He exhibited them to the officers, but refused to give them up, as they had been intrusted to him by Callava. On being summoned to appear before Jackson with the papers, Sousa returned for answer that they had been sent to the house of the Ex-governor. Two officers were directed to repair thither and demand them; and if Callava refused to deliver them up, to arrest both him and his steward, who had received them, and bring them before the governor. After considerable parleying, Callava finally refused, in the most positive terms, to surrender the documents, whereupon he was conducted, under a guard, to the office of Jackson. Arrived there, he persisted in his refusal, and commenced protesting against the course pursued by the general, who instantly committed him to prison.

The box containing the papers was obtained the next morning, and opened by officers specially commissioned for that purpose. The papers sought for were found, together with decrees which Callava had made, in favor of the heirs, but corruptly suppressed. The object of his imprisonment having been gained, the Ex-governor was released from custody. Previous to his discharge, a writ of *habeas corpus* was issued to extricate him from his confinement, by Mr. Fromentin, who had been appointed judge by the United States government, with a jurisdiction expressly limited to cases arising under the revenue laws, and the acts of Congress prohibiting the introduction of slaves. At this time, the general judiciary act had not been extended to Florida, and General Jackson possessed, in his own person, by the terms of the law under which he was appointed, the supreme judicial power uniformly exercised by the Spanish governors, captains-general, and intendants. He, of course, refused to obey the writ, and reprimanded Mr. Fromentin, in severe terms, for his interference. Callava afterwards attempted to excite a prejudice against General Jackson, by an exposition which was published in some of the American papers; but the statements made by him were shown to be so grossly false, that he obtained little sympathy. The proceedings of Jackson underwent the rigid scrutiny of a committee of the House of Representatives, and the result was his complete justification. Although the measures he adopted appeared harsh, the American people were ready to approve his conduct, when it was ascertained that it originated in a desire to carry out his own noble sentiment, that "the great can protect themselves, but the poor and humble require the arm and shield of the law."

Several Spanish officers who had remained with Callava, published an article in a Pensacola paper, after his discharge, in which they accused the general of violence and tyranny. It was stipulated in the treaty that all Spanish officers should be withdrawn from the territories, within six months after its ratification. More than this term had elapsed. Jackson issued a proclamation without delay, commanding them, as trespassers and disturbers of the public peace, to depart in the course of a week. They wisely obeyed the order and left the territory. About the same time, the Ex-governor of East Florida attempted to retain a number of important documents which should have been delivered up. When the fact came to his knowledge, the general transmitted his orders to take them by force, if they were withheld. The order was carried into effect; the ex-governor protested against the act, but received little sympathy or encouragement.

The ill health of General Jackson compelled him to resign his position in a few months. On the 7th of October, he delegated his power to his secretaries, and returned to Nashville. In his valedictory address to the citizens of Florida, he informed them that he had completed the temporary organization of the two provinces, and justified and defended the acts of his administration. It was with great regret that the people of the territory saw him depart, and the spontaneous manifestations of esteem and gratitude which were exhibited towards him, were both creditable to him and to those whom he had so faithfully served.

CHAPTER XI.

1821. Jackson resigns his office in the army—Testimonials of public respect—A candidate for the Presidency—Defeated in the House of Representatives—Election of Mr. Adams—Course of Jackson's friends—His renomination—Warmth of the contest—Elected president—Death of his wife—Kindness to her relatives—His first message—Veto of the Maysville road bill—Dissolution of the cabinet—Opposition to the United States Bank—Veto message—Re-elected president—Difficulty with the nullifiers—Assaulted by Lieutenant Randolph—Removal of the deposits—Public excitement—Controversy with France—Retirement to private life. 1837.

THE hardships and privations which General Jackson had experienced in his different campaigns against the Indians, so far undermined his health, that he was compelled to resign his commission in the army of the United States, and retire to private life. But the gratitude of the nation followed him in his retirement, and only waited the opportunity to confer upon him the high reward which was due to his long and faithful services. The citizens of Tennessee were not only proud of the distinguished reputation which reflected so much honor on his adopted state, but they were eager to evince to the world the favorable estimation in which they regarded him. On the 4th day of July, 1822, the governor of the state, by order of the legislature, presented him with a sword, as a testimonial " of the high respect entertained for his public services ;" and on the 20th of August following, the same body recommended him to the union for the office of president. This recommendation was repeated by the legislature of Alabama, and various meetings of private citizens in different sections of the country. In 1823, the office of Minister Plenipotentiary to the Mexican government was tendered to him by President Monroe;

but he declined its acceptance. He was again elected to the Senate of the United States, in the autumn of that year, and remained in the office until 1825.

The canvass previous to the presidential election in 1824 commenced as early as the year 1822. A majority of the republican party, to which Jackson belonged, in the northern and middle states, were in favor of the nomination of John Quincy Adams, then secretary of state. The same party at the south and west, were divided between General Jackson, William H. Crawford, of Georgia, Henry Clay, of Kentucky, and John C. Calhoun, of South Carolina. During the congressional sessions in 1823 and 1824, the presidential question was constantly in agitation. The friends of Mr. Crawford were probably the most numerous in the two houses, but more than two-thirds of the members were in favor of some other candidate. It had usually been the custom to make the nominations in advance of the election, at a congressional caucus, and an effort was made at the session of 1824, to bring forward the name of Mr. Crawford in that way. A caucus was accordingly held, but it was not attended by a majority of the republican members. The consequence was, that each section of the country was left at liberty to support whichever of the candidates was preferred. The election was conducted with considerable spirit and animation, and the result was, that no candidate received a majority of the electoral votes. On counting the official returns, it appeared that Andrew Jackson had received ninety-nine votes; John Quincy Adams, eighty-four; William H. Crawford, forty-one, and Henry Clay, thirty-seven.

The constitution of the United States provides that where no candidate for the presidency receives a majority of the electoral votes, the election shall be made by the House of Representatives, from the three highest on the list; and that the members shall vote by states; each state being entitled to but one vote. No choice having been made by the people at the election in 1824, the matter was brought forward at the ensuing session of Congress, and John Quincy Adams was elected president, he having received the votes of thirteen states.

Soon after the result of this election, Mr. Crawford withdrew from public life, in consequence of a severe bodily affliction. Mr. Clay was appointed Secretary of State under Mr. Adams, and the friends of Jackson and Crawford subsequently united in opposition to the then administration. The manner in which Jackson had been defeated, notwithstanding his having received the greatest number of votes, encouraged his friends and supporters, who were quite numerous, and devotedly attached to him, to make renewed efforts for the next election. An attempt was made to bring forward De Witt Clinton of the state of New York, as a candidate; but he expressly refused to allow his name to be used in opposition to General Jackson. The friends of Mr. Adams, however, took prompt measures to procure his re-election. In September, 1827, the general republican committee of the city of New York, most of whom had previously been Crawford men, presented Jackson as their candidate for the presidency. At the November election in that year, a large majority of the electors of the state expressed their approbation of the movement, by the choice of a majority of members of the legislature friendly to his nomination. This satisfactory evidence of the feelings of the voters in so large and powerful a state, put an end to the idea of selecting any other candidate. His nomination was welcomed, with a feeling akin to enthusiasm, from one end of the union to the other, and the election, which took place in 1828, was one of the most animated and exciting which had been witnessed for several years.

During the canvass, the partizans on both sides became quite exasperated, and much was said and written concerning the candidates, which might have been wisely omitted. Among other things, the private character and public acts of General Jackson were subjected to a severe and rigid scrutiny. The circumstances attending his marriage, his conduct during the campaign against the Creeks, the attack on Pensacola, the arrest of Judge Hall, and the trial and merited punishment of Arbuthnot and Ambrister, were commented on in the harshest terms, and in many instances grossly misrepresented. These uncalled for attacks produced no effect on the public mind, except that of enlisting a warmer feeling of sympathy in his behalf, and animating his friends to renewed exertion. The result of the election was, that General Jackson received one hundred and seventy-eight of the electoral votes, and Mr. Adams eighty-three.

Not long after the result of the election was made known, General Jackson experienced a most afflicting bereavement, in the death of his amiable wife. To him the loss was irreparable. For many anxious years, when the duties of his position had called him from her side, by the lonely watch-fire, in the solitude of the forest, on the ramparts of his intrenchments at New Orleans, amid the leafy hammocks and everglades of the far south, had he looked forward to his retirement from his public duties, comforted by the cherished hope that the evening of his days would be gilded with the halo of that deep and earnest affection which had ever been the light and the joy of the Hermitage. It was hard for him to part with one to whom he was so devotedly attached, just as he was entering upon the enjoyment of the crowning reward of a brilliant and prosperous career. To the day of his death he continued to cherish her memory with a sincere and heart-felt reverence. Having no descendants of his own, he proved himself, if that were possible, even more than a father, to the younger branches of her family. He adopted them as his own, and always regarded them with marked favor and kindness.

General Jackson entered upon the duties of the chief magistracy of the Union, on the 4th day of March, 1829. In his inaugural address, he set forth, in general terms, his views in regard to the administration of the government, and expressed the diffidence he felt on assuming the high and responsible station to which he had been elevated. His first annual message to the two Houses of Congress, delivered on the 8th day of December, 1829, contained a more full exposition of his opinions in regard to questions of public policy. He averred his determination to bring the matters in dispute with Great Britain and France, growing out of the north-eastern boundary question and the claims of American citizens for depredations committed on their property, to a speedy settlement. He recommended the amendment of the constitution, so as to enable the electors of the country to vote directly for president and vice-president, the modification of the tariff, the apportionment of the surplus revenue among the several states, provided it was "warranted by the constitution," and the removal of the Indian tribes beyond the Mississippi. He also expressed his doubts as to the propriety of renewing the charter of the United States Bank, and his belief that if a similar institution was thought necessary for the purposes of the government, it should be exclusively a national one, founded upon the public revenues and credit. In the month of May, 1830, a bill passed the two Houses of Congress, proposing to authorize "a subscription of stock in the Maysville, Washington, Paris, and Lexington Turnpike Road Company." On the 27th of the month, the president returned the bill with his objections to its passage. Although friendly to works of internal improvement, he stated that he was opposed to the construction of any work involving a claim of jurisdiction to the territory necessary to be occupied for its preservation and use, paramount to the sovereignty of the state; and to the appropriation of money "from the national treasury, in aid of such works when undertaken by state authority, surrendering the claim of jurisdiction." Believing that the bill under consideration was liable to both objections, he withheld his official sanction.

The annual message of the president in December, 1830, contained no new recommendations of special importance. His views in regard to the amendment of the constitution, the distribution of the surplus revenue, and the recharter of the United States Bank, were again presented to the consideration of Congress. During the session, a resolution was presented by Colonel Benton in the Senate, declaring that the charter of the bank ought not to be renewed, which was lost by a vote of twenty to twenty-three.

At the time of General Jackson's election in 1828, it was thought that he might not be a candidate for re-election. Consequently, the question as to the selection of his

HIS FIRST MESSAGE 175

successor early attracted the attention of the politicians at the seat of government. In the winter of 1830, considerable ill feeling was produced in his cabinet, particularly on the part of the friends of the vice-president, Mr. Calhoun, growing out of what was said to be the especial favor shown to Mr. Van Buren, secretary of state. An unfortunate difficulty in regard to the family relations of several members of the cabinet, increased this ill-feeling to such an extent, that Mr. Van Buren, and Mr. Eaton, the secretary of war, tendered their resignations in April, 1831. On accepting the resignations, General Jackson signified to their associates his desire to reconstruct his cabinet, whereupon the other members resigned, and a new cabinet was formed which proved to be much more harmonious in its operations. It was always a prominent wish with General Jackson, to secure entire unanimity among his constitutional advisers; and this did not proceed from any desire to exact a slavish subserviency to his views; but it was the natural consequence of his remarkable energy and independence of character. Prepared at all times to assume every responsibility connected with his administration of the executive authority, he desired his cabinet to be a complete unit, and that it should adopt the plans and carry out the views approved by him whom the law and the constitution had recognised as its head.

The president announced to Congress, at the session commencing in December, 1831, the fact that a treaty had been signed with France providing for the payment of the claims for illegal seizures and confiscations during the war with the allied powers. This had long been a vexed question of difference between the two governments, and its adjustment was ardently desired on all hands. On the 4th day of July, 1832, the bill to recharter the United States Bank, which had been passed by the two Houses of Congress, was presented to General Jackson. His views in regard to that institution were well known. Previous to his election to the presidency, he had, on several occasions, avowed his hostility to a continuance of the charter. On the 10th day of July, he returned the bill to the Senate, in which it originated, accompanied with his reasons for declining to give the measure his approbation. This was a bold and decided step on the part of the president. Although many of his friends had long known what would be his decision, quite a number of them, and those among the most influential, were friendly to the bill, and indulged the hope that it would finally receive his sanction. When it became known that the veto-message was about to be sent in, he was beset with importunities to reconsider his determination. But the rock of Gibraltar could not have been more immovable. His opinions could not be changed, and the line of conduct he had marked out was fixed and unalterable.

Whatever may be the views entertained in regard to the positions laid down in the veto-message of General Jackson, no one can avoid admiring the unshrinking firmness and high moral courage displayed in his course on this question. The bank wielded an immense power. All classes, trades, and conditions, were more or less connected with its transactions. Its agents were scattered over the country, from one extremity to the other; and, as the sequel proved, those who controlled its affairs were not unwilling to enter into the arena of political strife, for the purpose of perpetuating its existence. General Jackson was renominated for the presidency, in 1832, in connection with Martin Van Buren, of New York, as the candidate for vice-president. The incidents of this important election are not yet forgotten. The sudden contractions and expansions of the currency produced by the bank were severely felt. The moneyed interests of the country were temporarily deranged. The storm was a severe one. No public man of his day but Andrew Jackson, possessed the fearlessness requisite to encounter it. No man save himself had that deep and abiding hold on the sympathies and affections of the American people, without which he would inevitably have been crushed. Nothing but his commanding influence and wide-spread popularity, connected with the unflinching resoluteness of his character, enabled him, like the proud oak, to set the whirlwind at defiance.

VETO OF THE UNITED STATES BANK 177

Henry Clay was selected as the candidate of the opponents of General Jackson's administration. The friends of Mr. Calhoun, in South Carolina, where the tariff question had already produced a most bitter feeling of hostility to the general government, remained almost entirely aloof from the contest. The anti-masonic party in the northern states, which had recently been formed, supported William Wirt of Maryland. A great deal of vindictiveness and animosity was engendered during the canvass, and much of the hostility evinced towards General Jackson during the remainder of his administration, may be traced to the veto and his subsequent re-election. The returns from the electoral colleges exhibited the following result: Andrew Jackson received two hundred and nineteen votes, and Henry Clay forty-nine; John Floyd received the eleven electoral votes of South Carolina; and seven were given for William Wirt in Vermont. The re-election of General Jackson, by so great a majority, in despite of the opposition arrayed against him, showed conclusively the extraordinary extent of his popularity and influence.

During the summer and fall of 1832, the state of South Carolina was agitated with the throes of an incipient revolution. It was claimed by Mr. Calhoun and his friends, who were known in the political parlance of the day, as nullifiers, that the operation of the revenue laws was so exceedingly unfair and unjust, that it released that state from all its obligations under the compact formed between the several members of the union. Arms were procured, and men organized into companies and regiments, under the orders of the state government, in order to resist the execution of the laws if an attempt were made to enforce them within her boundaries. Such proceedings could not be suffered to pass unnoticed. President Jackson immediately caused the fortifications of the United States in that quarter to be amply provided and garrisoned, and the attention of Congress was called to the subject in his annual message. Soon after the message was delivered, the information was received that a convention held in the state of South Carolina, had passed an ordinance declaring the several acts of Congress to which objections had been raised, to be unauthorized by the constitution and therefore null and void. The president forthwith issued his celebrated proclamation, which is deservedly regarded as one of the ablest state papers that ever came from his pen. It is remarkable alike for the nervous eloquence of its style, and the glowing and earnest patriotism which breathes forth in every line. On the 16th of January, 1833, the proceedings of the nullifiers were made the subject of a special communication to Congress. This exciting controversy was terminated, after considerable difficulty, by the passage of the Compromise Act, which contemplated an entire change in the tariff system of the country.

In the spring of 1833, a personal attack was made upon General Jackson, which shows how little age had dimmed the fire and intrepidity of his youth. On the 6th of May, he left Washington, in company with the members of his cabinet, and his private secretary, in compliance with the invitation of the " Monumental Committee" at Fredericksburg, to lay the corner-stone of the pillar, to be erected in honor of the mother of Washington. "The day," says the correspondent of a public paper, "was mild, and the air soft and refreshing. After the company had assembled on board, they paid their respects to the Executive, which that venerable patriot received with the ease and grace of the most finished gentleman of the old school. They then separated; some of the party went upon the upper deck, to admire the picturesque and beautiful scenery of the surrounding country, whence, from the north round to the south, lay a line of high grounds, forming within their interior an extensive amphitheatre. On the south, was the broad and peaceful Potomac, stretching as far as the eye could reach. On the eastern branch of the river was to be seen the navy yard, and several of the public armed vessels lying in the stream, with our flag floating on the breeze; and on the western branch, we had a distant but beautiful view of Georgetown, as it slopes from the high grounds to the river: and between that and the navy yard, was to be seen the city of Washington, whence we had just taken our departure; and from our situation we had, at one glance, a view of the bridge crossing the river, which exceeds a mile in extent, the chief magistrate's house, and the capitol, with its splendid dome, rearing its head over every other object. Among those who went upon the upper deck were the heads of departments. A group of ladies, with their attendants, were seated in the after part of the boat; and an excellent band of music was playing several national airs as the steamer glided on her way, and shortly arrived at the city of Alexandria. General Jackson had, just previous to the boat's reaching the wharf, retired to the cabin, and had taken his seat at a long table, which had been set preparatory for dinner. He was seated on the west side, and next to the berths, there being barely room enough left between the berths and table for a person to pass, by moving sidewise. Upon his left sat Mrs. Thruston, the wife of Judge Thruston, of Washington; and on the opposite side of the table sat Major Donelson, the general's private secretary; Mr. Potter, a clerk in one of the departments at Washington; and Captain Broome, of the marine corps. The president was reading a newspaper. While in this situation, (there being no other person in the cabin or near him,) a large number of citizens came on board, as it was supposed to pay their respects to him. Among the number was Randolph, late a lieutenant in the navy. He made his way into the cabin, and after speaking to Captain Broome, who had long been acquainted with him, he immediately advanced between the table and the berths towards the president, as if to address him. The president did not know him, and it seems that Captain Broome did not mention his name, because, he said, he believed that the object of his visit was to present a petition praying to be restored to the navy again; still, as the captain did not know that that was the object of his visit, and fearing, as he said, that he might intend to commit some act of violence, he stepped quickly to the same side of the table, and advanced up to and near Randolph, who had by this time come so near General Jackson as to be observed by him, who, supposing it was some person about to salute him, said that he was afflicted with a severe pain in his side, and begged to be excused for not rising; and seeing that Randolph had some difficulty in pulling off his glove, he stretched out his hand towards him, saying, at the same time, "Never mind your glove, sir." Upon this, Randolph thrust one hand violently into the president's face; but before he could make use of the other, or repeat his blow, Captain Broome seized and drew him off towards the door. A part of the table was broken down in the scuffle. Mr. Potter thrust his umbrella at Randolph across the table, at the moment Captain Broome seized him; whereupon, Randolph's friends clenched him, hurried him out of the cabin, and off from the boat, leaving his hat behind. This was done so quickly that the few persons who were near the president were not aware of it, as they had all turned round after pushing Randolph away, to inquire whether or not the chief magistrate was much hurt. He was so confined behind the table, that he could not rise with ease, nor could he seize his cane in time to defend himself. The news of this outrage was soon circulated around the boat, and at first it seemed so incredible that no one could be found to believe it; all, however, immediately repaired to the cabin, and heard the president relate the story himself.

"Had I been apprized," said he, "that Randolph stood before me, I should have been prepared for him, and I could have defended myself. No villain," said he, "has ever escaped me before; and he would not, had it not been for my confined situation."

Some blood was seen on his face, and he was asked whether he had been much injured.

"No," said he, "I am not much hurt; but in endeavoring to rise, I have wounded my side, which now pains me more than it did."

About this time, one of the citizens of Alexandria, who had heard of the outrage, addressed the general, and said: "Sir, if you will pardon me, in case I am tried and convicted, I will kill Randolph for this insult to you, in fifteen minutes!"

"No sir," said the president, "I cannot do that! I

want no man to stand between me and my assailants, and none to take revenge on my account. Had I been prepared for this *cowardly villain's* approach, I can assure you all, that he would never have the temerity to undertake such a thing again."

General Jackson had for some time been firmly impressed with the belief that the public deposits with the United States Bank were far from being safe, and in the summer of 1833 he decided to cause them to be removed. At tne close of the previous session of Congress, a resolution was adopted in the House of Representatives, declaring that they might be safely continued with the bank; but, in the vacation, circumstances transpired connected with the speculations of the bank, which, as the president thought, called for prompt action. Mr. Duane, the Secretary of the Treasury, refused to carry out the wishes of the president, and he was forthwith removed, to make room for Mr. Taney, then Attorney-General, and afterwards Chief Justice of the Supreme Court. The deposits were withdrawn from the bank in October, and the contest between the friends of that institution and the adherents of General Jackson was renewed with increased asperity and violence. At the next session of Congress the subject was brought up, and for weeks formed the principal topic of discussion. Several very able speeches were made by the leading politicians belonging to the two parties. On the 28th of March, a resolution was adopted in the Senate, which had been offered by Mr. Clay, expressing the opinion that the president, in his proceedings in relation to the public revenue, had "assumed upon himself authority and power not conferred by the constitution and laws, but in derogation of both." On the 15th of April following, the president sent a message to the Senate, respectfully protesting against their impeachment of his official acts, and requesting his communication to be entered on the journals. The controversy between the president and Senate was carried so far, that that body refused to confirm a large number of his appointments, in many instances solely upon political grounds. At several subsequent sessions, the removal of the deposits was discussed in Congress. Mr. Benton, of Missouri, at an early day, made a movement in favor of expunging the resolution of censure from the journals of the senate. After several ineffectual attempts, a vote to that effect was adopted in the Senate, in conformity with the expressions of several public meetings, and the instructions of the legislatures of different states. The resolution was ordered to be expunged, by drawing black lines across and around it.

In his annual message on the 3d of December, 1833, General Jackson informed Congress that the French government had failed to pay the instalment required by the stipulations of the convention concluded on the 4th of July, 1831. At the next session he again called their attention to the continued delay in the payment of the money, and recommended the passage of a law authorizing reprisals upon French property, in case provision should not be made for it at the approaching session of the Chamber of Deputies. The prompt and decisive tone of the president's message startled the chivalric feelings of the French nation. The passports of the American minister were tendered to him, and a serious rupture was confidently anticipated. The unyielding firmness of General Jackson, and the sense of justice which soon prevailed in the French Chamber, averted the danger, and restored the peace and harmony previously existing between the two nations.

Nothing of unusual interest occurred during the administration of General Jackson, after the amicable settlement of the difficulty with France. The severe panic which followed the derangement of the currency, consequent upon the efforts of the bank to procure a renewal of its charter, was followed by a season of unexampled prosperity. In 1835, the public debt was entirely liquidated; and on the final retirement of General Jackson to private life, in the spring of 1837, he issued a farewell address to the American people, setting forth the principles upon which he had conducted the affairs of government, and congratulating them on the peace and happiness which they enjoyed.

DEATH OF ANDREW JACKSON

CHAPTER XII.

1837. Ill health of General Jackson—Arrival at the Hermitage—Influence with his party—Friendly to the annexation of Texas—His occupations—Embarrassed in his pecuniary affairs—Refunding of the fine imposed by Judge Hall—Failure of his health—His last illness—His Christian resignation and death—Honors paid to his memory—Remarks of Reverdy Johnson—Speech of Daniel Webster—Character of Jackson—His qualifications as a soldier and statesman—Attachment to his friends—His personal appearance—His patriotism. 1845.

A SHORT time previous to the termination of his official career, General Jackson was attacked with a severe hemorrhage of the lungs, which for some days incapacitated him from attending to business. He recovered, however, sufficiently to be present at the inauguration of his successor, and take part in the ceremonies of the day. On his arrival at the Hermitage he was quite weak and infirm, but the relaxation from mental labor, and the kind attentions of his adopted children, soon restored him to comparative strength and health, though he still suffered much from the diseased state of his lungs. The various questions of public policy which afterwards agitated the country, and the movements of the two great political parties in the nation, did not fail to excite his attention. His influence was silently exerted and felt in our national politics up to the day of his death. He was still regarded as the leader of the party which had so long looked up to him as its head, and on all important occasions was consulted with as much veneration as were the oracles of olden time. He was, from the first, the warm and steadfast friend of the annexation of Texas to the Union. In the settlement of the Oregon boundary question he took a deep interest, though he did not live to see the boundary finally adjusted.

HIS LAST ILLNESS

Most of General Jackson's time, in his retirement, was spent in ministering to the comforts of those who were dependent on him, and in overseeing the labor performed on his estate. He was a sincere and devout communicant of the Presbyterian church, and he erected a house of worship in the immediate vicinity of the Hermitage, for the convenience of his family and servants. Towards the close of his life he became involved in his circumstances, on account of some endorsements for a friend. When his condition was made known, several offers were made to extend him such pecuniary assistance as he might need. At the session of 1844-5, a law was passed by Congress, providing for the reimbursement of the fine of one thousand dollars paid by General Jackson at New Orleans, with interest from the time of its original payment. This act of justice, tardy as it was, was peculiarly grateful to the feelings of the general, and it served to sweeten the closing reflections of his life.

For several months previous to his decease, the health of General Jackson began rapidly to fail. His constitution had been originally strong and vigorous, but exposure and privation during his Indian campaigns seriously impaired his physical vigor. A gentleman who visited him in the month of May, 1845, states that he had not, at that time, been in a condition to lie down for four months. His whole system was invaded with dropsy; he had not sufficient strength to stand; and his disease was attended with so much bodily pain, that he could obtain no sleep except by means of opiates. While in this dying condition, his portrait was taken by an artist employed for the purpose by Louis Phillippe, King of the French, who designed to place it by the side of Washington's in his gallery. He was constantly cheered by the visits of his old and attached personal friends; and the consolations of religion, to which he loved to resort, were a never-failing solace to his heart. On one occasion he remarked to a clergyman who called upon him, that he was "in the hands of a merciful God. I have full confidence," said he, " in his goodness and mercy. My lamp of life is nearly out, and the last glimmer is come. I am ready to depart when called. The

Bible is true. The principles and statutes of that holy book have been the rule of my life, and I have tried to conform to its spirit as near as possible. Upon that sacred volume I rest my hope of eternal salvation, through the merits and blood of our blessed Lord and Savior, Jesus Christ."

General Jackson continued to grow more feeble, until Sunday, the 8th day of June, 1845. Early in the morning of that day he swooned, and for some time was supposed to be dead. On reviving from the swoon, he became conscious that the spark of life was nearly extinguished, and, expecting to die before another sun would set, he sent for his family and domestics to come and receive his dying benediction. His remarks, it is said, were full of affection and Christian resignation. His mind retained its vigor to the last, and his dying moments, even more than his earlier years, exhibited its highest intellectual light. To his family and friends he said:—" Do not grieve that I am about to leave you, for I shall be better off. Although I am afflicted with pain and bodily suffering, they are as nothing compared with the sufferings of the Savior of the world, who was put to death on the accursed tree. I have fulfilled my destiny on earth, and it is better that this worn-out frame should go to rest, and my spirit take up its abode with the Redeemer."

He continued thus to address his relatives and friends, at intervals, during the forenoon, and, as the attending physician, Dr. Esleman, remarked, his confidence and faith in the great truths of religion seemed to be more firm and unwavering than any man he had ever seen die. He expressed a desire that Dr. Edgar, of the Presbyterian church, should preach his funeral sermon, and that no pomp or parade should be made over his grave. After years of patient suffering and endurance, the aged soldier and statesman thus quietly sunk into his last sleep. Calm and self-collected, though oppressed with pain, he yielded up his spirit with the resignation of a Christian. His death took place on the evening of the 8th of June, in the seventy-ninth year of his age.

The death of such a man, of one who had occupied so prominent a place in the affairs of the nation, and rendered so many signal services to his country, was not to be regarded as a thing of idle moment. Political opponents and friends met together like brethren, to offer the last tribute to his memory; and the rancorous hostility of the partisan was forgotten, as he bent over the grave of Andrew Jackson, and involuntarily bedewed it with his tears. Throughout the union, the respect paid to his memory was both solemn and impressive. All the courts and public bodies in session adjourned on receiving the intelligence. Funeral processions were formed, and addresses delivered in all the principal cities; and nothing was left undone to evince the sincere regard for his character which was universally entertained. Among the eloquent tributes which the occasion elicited, the annexed remarks of Reverdy Johnson, a senator in Congress from the state of Maryland, and a political opponent of General Jackson, before the Court of Appeals of that state, richly deserve a perusal:

"May it please the court—I rise to announce to the court the death of a great American, and to ask, in behalf of my brethren of the bar, as a respect justly due to his memory, that the court at once adjourn.

"ANDREW JACKSON is no more. A long and trying illness is at last terminated, and his spirit has winged its flight, I trust, to heaven. The life and character of the deceased have for many years filled a large space in the public eye; and perhaps no man has ever lived amongst us, whose popularity or influence with the American people was deeper seated, or more commanding.

"I need not inform the court, that the administration of the general government by this eminent citizen, during his presidency, in almost every particular of it, except his noble stand against the perilous and unconstitutional doctrine of nullification, did not receive the approval of a large political party of the country; but as a member of that party, I never doubted that he was in heart and soul a patriot, deeply attached to the free institutions under which we live, and ardently solicitous for the honor and prosperity of the nation.

"It is a redeeming trait in the character of our people, and greatly diminishes the mischiefs of mere party spirit, that we instinctively, when the nation is called upon to vindicate its honor, are found, to a man, united; and that on the death of a great and patriotic citizen, we are alike found, without regard to party, joining in a national lamentation at the afflictive event.

"In this instance, there were in the eventful life of the deceased, deeds of service rendered the country, by which we all feel that the national glory was eminently subserved.

"His military course seemed to know no disaster. With him, to go to battle was to go to victory. Whether warring at the head of American troops, with the cunning and daring of savage valor, or with the bravery and skill of the best disciplined army of the European world, the result was ever the same—a TRIUMPH. The crowning glory of his military life, the BATTLE OF NEW ORLEANS, whilst it immeasurably increases the fame of our arms, will, in all future time, serve as a beacon to protect our soil from hostile tread.

"In honor of such a man, it is fit that, in every portion of this great nation, due respect should be shown to his memory; and I therefore move the court to gratify the feelings of the bar, as I am sure they will their own, by adjourning for the day."

When the intelligence of the death of General Jackson reached New York, a special meeting of the New York Historical Society, of which the deceased was a member, was called, in order to express their regret at the national bereavement, and adopt measures for evincing their respect. Daniel Webster was present at the meeting, and made the following remarks, alike creditable to his head and his heart.

"Nothing could be more natural or proper, than that this society should take a respectful notice of the decease of so distinguished a member of its body. Accustomed occasionally to meet the society, and to enjoy the communications that are made to it, and proceed from it, illustrative of the history of the country and its government,

I have pleasure in being present at this time also, and on this occasion, in which an element so mournful mingles itself. General Andrew Jackson has been from an early period conspicuous in the service and in the councils of the country, though not without long intervals, so far as respects his connection with the general government. It is fifty years, I think, since he was a member of the Congress of the United States, and at the instant, sir, I do not know whether there be living an associate of General Jackson in the House of Representatives of the United States at that day, with the exception of the distinguished and venerable gentleman who is now president of this society. I recollect only of the Congress of '96, at this moment now living, but one—Mr. Gallatin—though I may be mistaken. General Jackson, Mr. President, while he lived, and his memory and character, now that he is deceased, are presented to his country and the world in different views and relations. He was a soldier—a general officer—and acted no unimportant part in that capacity. He was raised by repeated elections to the highest stations in the civil government of his country, and acted a part certainly not obscure or unimportant in that character and capacity.

"In regard to his military services, I participate in the general sentiment of the whole country, and I believe of the world. That he was a soldier of dauntless courage—great daring and perseverance—an officer of skill, and arrangement, and foresight, are truths universally admitted. During the period in which he administered the general government of the country, it was my fortune, during the whole period of it, to be a member of the Congress of the United States, and as it is well known, it was my misfortune not to be able to concur with many of the most important measures of his administration. Entertaining himself, his own views, and with a power of impressing them, to a remarkable degree, upon the conviction and approbation of others, he pursued such a course as he thought expedient in the circumstances in which he was placed. Entertaining on many questions of great importance, different opinions, it was of course my misfortune to differ from him, and that difference gave me great pain, because, in the whole course of my public life, it has been far more agreeable to me to support the measures of the government, than to be called upon by my judgment, and sense of what is to be done, to oppose them. I desire to see the government acting with a unity of spirit in all things relating to its foreign relations, especially, and generally in all great measures of domestic policy, as far as is consistent with the exercise of perfect independence among its members. But if it was my misfortune to differ from General Jackson on many, or most of the great measures of his administration, there were occasions, and those not unimportant, in which I felt it my duty, and according to the highest sense of that duty, to conform to his opinions, and support his measures. There were junctures in his administration—periods which I thought important and critical—in which the views he thought proper to adopt, corresponded entirely with my sentiments in regard to the protection of the best interests of the country, and the institutions under which we live; and it was my humble endeavor on these occasions to yield to his opinions and measures, the same cordial support as if I had not differed from him before, and expected never to differ from him again.

"That General Jackson was a marked character—that he had a very remarkable influence over other men's opinions—that he had great perseverance and resolution in civil as well as in military administration, all admit. Nor do I think that the candid among mankind will ever doubt that it was his desire—mingled with whatsoever portion of a disposition to be himself instrumental in that exaltation—to elevate his country to the highest prosperity and honor. There is one sentiment, to which I particularly recur, always with a feeling of approbation and gratitude. From an earlier period of his undertaking to administer the affairs of the government, he uttered a sentiment dear to me—expressive of a truth of which I am most profoundly convinced—a sentiment setting forth the necessity, the duty, and the patriotism of maintaining the union of these states. Mr. President, I am old enough

HIS CHARACTER

to recollect the deaths of all the presidents of the United States who have departed this life, from Washington down. There is no doubt that the death of an individual, who has been so much the favorite of his country, and partaken so largely of its regard as to fill that high office, always produces—has produced, hitherto, a strong impression upon the public mind. That is right. It is right that such should be the impression upon the whole community, embracing those who particularly approved, and those who did not particularly approve the political course of the deceased.

"All these distinguished men have been chosen of their country. They have fulfilled their station and duties upon the whole, in the series of years that have gone before us, in a manner reputable and distinguished. Under their administration, in the course of fifty or sixty years, the government, generally speaking, has prospered, and under the government, the people have prospered. It becomes, then, all to pay respect when men thus honored are called to another world. Mr. President, we may well indulge the hope and belief, that it was the feeling of the distinguished person who is the subject of these resolutions, in the solemn days and hours of closing life—that it was his wish, if he had committed few or more errors in the administration of the government, that their influence might cease with him; and that whatever of good he had done, might be perpetuated. Let us cherish the same sentiment. Let us act upon the same feeling; and whatever of true honor and glory he acquired, let us all hope that it will be his inheritance for ever! And whatever of good example, or good principle, or good administration, he has established, let us hope that the benefit of it may also be perpetual."

Andrew Jackson was, indeed, no ordinary man. The estimation in which he was held by his countrymen, the respect paid to his memory at home and abroad, are sufficient to confirm it, even if there could be a doubt. In many respects he was one of the most remarkable men that ever lived. As a soldier, he was prompt and resolute, stern and inflexible. With an intuitive sagacity, he foresaw danger, and was always prepared against it. His thoughts and perceptions were rapid, and his plans were often formed and executed before others had time for deliberation. It was this celerity in his movements that secured many of his laurels. His courage and fortitude were both unquestioned. The principle of fear did not enter into his composition. He certainly could not have understood the meaning of the word. The cheerfulness with which he shared the privations of his soldiers, shows that he possessed an entire indifference to hardship and suffering. But one of the most striking features in his character was his readiness in adapting himself to every position in which he was placed. There are many men who can do well, when the occasion does not overmatch them; but Jackson always rose with the occasion; and in the merest personal altercation, the same commanding traits were exhibited, which sustained themselves in a higher and nobler flight, on the field of battle, where the fate of nations depended on the issue of the day.

As a statesman, General Jackson was clear-headed and sagacious. When he had once determined upon a particular course, where any important principle was involved, he could not be swerved from what he conceived to be just and right. He never shrunk from the discharge of any public duty, and was always ready to avow any and every act of his administration, and unshrinkingly to abide the consequences. Never behind his party, but always in the advance, he eagerly sought for opportunities to carry out the principles by which he was guided. In private life, Jackson was kind-hearted, and generous in his disposition. His reputation was pure and unsullied. He abhorred every thing mean and grovelling, and cherished an instinctive hatred for what was dishonorable. He was irritable in his temperament, however, and easily excited. Yet, notwithstanding the impetuosity of his disposition frequently carried him beyond the limits of prudence and moderation, it was this trait in his character which saved New Orleans from plunder and devastation. His attachments were warm and sincere. He never forgot a favor, or failed to remember a friend. He was devotedly attached to his country, her interests, and her institutions. It may well be, that flattery, and there are few men who cannot be swerved by its seductions, sometimes induced him to commit an unintentional wrong, in the effort to favor the wishes of some active and influential partisan; but for all that, he was none the less a patriot.

In person, General Jackson was tall, and remarkably thin and erect. His weight bore no proportion to his height; and his frame did not appear fitted for such trials as he had encountered. His features were large; his eyes dark-blue, with a keen and strong glance; his eyebrows arched and prominent; and his complexion, that of the war-worn soldier.

It is hardly to be anticipated, perhaps, that full and complete justice will be rendered to Andrew Jackson during the present generation. Men may differ in regard to the propriety of his conduct, and the wisdom of his measures, and unintentionally do injustice to his many noble qualities. Still, it is not too much to hope that the valuable services rendered to his country, connected though they be with the stern and high-handed measures adopted by his iron will, may be cherished with gratitude and respect; and that the soldier, the statesman, the patriot, and the Christian, may be honored by a nation's blessing, and remembered in a nation's prayers.

CHAPTER XIII.

Eulogy on the Life and Character of General Jackson, delivered at Washington, June 27, 1845. By the Hon. George Bancroft.

THE men of the American Revolution are no more! That age of creative power has passed away. The last surviving signer of the Declaration of Independence has long since left the earth. Washington lies near his own Potomac, surrounded by his family and his servants. Adams, the Colossus of Independence, reposes in the modest grave-yard of his native region. Jefferson sleeps on the heights of his own Monticello, whence his eye overlooked his beloved Virginia. Madison, the last survivor of the men who made our constitution, lives only, in our hearts. But who shall say that the heroes, in whom the image of God shone most brightly, do not live forever? They were filled with the vast conceptions which called America into being; they lived for those conceptions, and their deeds praise them.

We are met to commemorate the virtues of one who shed his blood for our independence, took part in winning the territory and forming the early institutions of the West, and was imbued with all the great ideas which constitute the moral force of our country. On the spot where he gave his solemn fealty to the people—here, where he pledged himself before the world, to freedom, to the constitution, and to the laws—we meet to pay our tribute to the memory of the last great name, which gathers round itself all the associations that form the glory of America.

South Carolina gave a birthplace to Andrew Jackson. On its remote frontier, far up on the forest-clad banks of the Catawba, in a region where the settlers were just beginning to cluster, his eye first saw the light. There his infancy sported in the ancient forests, and his mind was nursed to freedom by their influence. He was the youngest son of an Irish emigrant of Scottish origin, who, two years after the great war of Frederic of Prussia, fled to America for relief from indigence and oppression. His birth was in 1767, at a time when the people of our land were but a body of dependent colonists, scarcely more than two millions in number, scattered along an immense coast, with no army, or navy, or union ; and exposed to the attempts of England to control America by the aid of military force. His boyhood grew up in the midst of the contest with Great Britain. The first great political truth that reached his heart was, that all men are free and equal ; the first great fact that beamed on his understanding was, his country's independence.

The strife, as it increased, came near the shades of his upland residence. As a boy of thirteen, he witnessed the scenes of horror that accompany civil war ; and when but a year older, with an elder brother, he shouldered his musket, and went forth to strike a blow for his country.

Joyous era for America and for humanity! But for him, the orphan boy the events were full of agony and grief. His father was no more. His oldest brother fell a victim to the war of the Revolution; another (his companion in arms) died of wounds received in their joint captivity: his mother went down to the grave a victim to grief and efforts to rescue her sons; and when peace came, he was alone in the world, with no kindred to cherish him, and little inheritance but his own untried powers.

The nation which emancipated itself from British rule organizes itself; the confederation gives way to the constitution; the perfecting of that constitution—that grand event of the thousand years of modern history—is accomplished! America exists as a people, gains unity as a government, and takes its place as a nation among the powers ef the earth.

The next great office to be performed by America is the taking possession of the wilderness. The magnificent western valley cried out to the civilization of popular power, that it must be occupied by cultivated man.

Behold, then, our orphan hero, sternly earnest, consecrated to humanity from childhood by sorrow, having neither father, nor mother, nor sister, nor surviving brother; so young, and yet so solitary, and therefore bound the more closely to collective man—behold him elect for his lot, to go forth and assist in laying the foundations of society in the great valley of the Mississippi.

At the very time when Washington was pledging his own and future generations to the support of the popular institutions which were to be the light of the human race—at the time when the institutions of the Old World were rocking to their centre, and the mighty fabric that had come down from the middle ages, was falling in—the adventurous Jackson, in the radiant glory and boundless hope and confident intrepidity of twenty-one, plunged into the wilderness, crossed the great mountain-barrier that divides the western waters from the Atlantic, followed the paths of the early hunters and fugitives, and, not content with the nearer neighborhood to his parent state, went still further and further to the west, till he found his home in the most beautiful region on the Cumberland. There, from the first, he was recognised as the great pioneer; under his courage, the coming emigrants were sure to find a shield.

The lovers of adventure began to pour themselves into the territory, whose delicious climate and fertile soil invited the presence of social man. The hunter, with his rifle and his axe, attended by his wife and children; the herdsman, driving the few cattle that were to multiply as they browsed; the cultivator of the soil—all came to the inviting region. Wherever the bending mountains opened a pass; wherever the buffaloes and the beasts of the forest had made a trace, these sons of nature, children of humanity, in the highest sentiment of personal freedom, came to occupy the beautiful wilderness whose prairies blossomed everywhere profusely with wild flowers; whose woods in spring put to shame, by their magnificence, the cultivated gardens of man.

And now that these unlettered fugitives, educated only by the spirit of freedom, destitute of dead letter erudition, but sharing the living ideas of the age, had made their homes in the west—what would follow? Would they degrade themselves to ignorance and infidelity? Would they make the solitudes of the desert excuses for licentiousness? Would the doctrines of freedom lead them to live in unorganized society, destitute of laws and fixed institutions?

At a time when European society was becoming broken in pieces, scattered, disunited, and resolved into its elements, a scene ensued in Tennessee, than which nothing more beautifully grand is recorded in the annals of the race.

These adventurers in the wilderness longed to come together in organized society. The overshadawing genius of their time inspired them with good designs, and filled them with the counsels of wisdom. Dwellers in the forest, freest of the free, bound in the spirit, they came up by their representatives, on foot, on horseback, through the forest, along the streams, by the buffalo traces, by the Indian paths, by the blazed forest avenues, to meet in convention among the mountains at Knoxville, and frame for themselves a constitution. Andrew Jackson was there, the greatest man of them all—modest, bold, determined, demanding nothing for himself, and shrinking from nothing that his heart approved.

The convention came together on the 11th day of January, 1796, and finished its work on the 6th day of February. How had the wisdom of the Old World vainly tasked itself to frame constitutions, that could, at least, be the subject of experiment! the men of Tennessee, in less than twenty-five days, perfected a fabric, which, in its essential forms, was to last for ever. They came together full of faith and reverence, of love to humanity, of confidence in truth. In the simplicity of wisdom, they framed their constitution, acting under higher influences than they were conscious of—

> They wrought in sad sincerity,
> Themselves from God they could not free;

> They builded better than they knew ;
> The conscious stones to beauty grew.

In the instrument which they framed, they embodied their faith in God, in the immortal nature of man. They gave the right of suffrage to every freeman; they vindicated the sanctity of reason, by giving freedom of speech and of the press; they reverenced the voice of God, as it speaks in the soul of man, by asserting the indefeasible right of man to worship the Infinite according to his conscience; they established the freedom and equality of elections; and they demanded from every future legislator a solemn oath "never to consent to any act or thing whatever, that shall have even a tendency to lessen the rights of the people."

These majestic lawgivers, wiser than the Solons and Lycurguses and Numas of the Old World—these prophetic founders of a state, who embodied in their constitution the sublimest truths of humanity, acted without reference to human praises.

They kept no special record of their proceedings; they took no pains to vaunt their deeds; and when their work was done, knew not that they had finished one of the sublimest acts ever performed among men. They left no record, as to whose agency was conspicuous, whose eloquence swayed, whose generous will predominated; nor should we know, but for tradition, confirmed by what followed among themselves.

The men of Tennessee were now a people, and they were to send forth a man to stand for them in the Congress of the United States—that avenue to glory—that home of eloquence—the citadel of popular power; and, with one consent, they united in selecting the foremost man among their lawgivers—Andrew Jackson.

The love of the people of Tennessee followed him to the American Congress, and he had served but a single term, when the state of Tennessee made him one of its representatives in the American Senate, where he sat under the auspices of Jefferson.

Thus, when he was scarcely more than thirty, he had

guided the settlement of the wilderness; swayed the deliberation of a people in establishing its fundamental laws; acted as the representative of that people, and again as the representative of his organized state, disciplined to a knowledge of the power of the people, and the power of the states; the associate of republican statesmen, the friend and companion of Jefferson.

The men who framed the constitution of the United States, many of them, did not know of the innate life and self-preserving energy of their work. They feared that freedom could not endure, and they planned a strong government for its protection.

During his short career in Congress, Jackson showed his quiet, deeply seated, innate, intuitive faith in human freedom, and in the institutions of freedom. He was ever, by his votes and opinions, found among those who had confidence in humanity; and in the great division of minds, this child of the woodlands, this representative of forest life in the west, was found modestly and firmly on the side of freedom. It did not occur to him to doubt the right of man to the free developement of his powers; it did not occur to him to seek to give durability to popular institutions, by giving to government a strength independent of popular will.

From the first, he was attached to the fundamental doctrines of popular power, and of the policy that favors it; and though his reverence for Washington surpassed his reverence for any human being, he voted against the address from the House of Representatives to Washington on his retirement, because its language appeared to sanction the financial policy which he believed hostile to republican freedom.

During his period of service in the Senate, Jackson was elected major-general by the brigadiers and field officers of the militia of Tennessee. Resigning his place in the Senate, he was made judge of the supreme court in law and equity; such was the confidence in his integrity of purpose, his clearness of judgment, and his vigor of will to deal justly among the turbulent who crowded into the new settlements of Tennessee.

Thus, in the short period of nine years, Andrew Jackson was signalized by as many evidences of public esteem as could fall to the lot of man. The pioneer of the wilderness, the defender of its stations, he was their lawgiver, the sole representative of a new people in Congress, the representative of the state in the Senate, the highest in judicial office. He seemed to be recognised as their first love of liberty, the first in the science of legislation, in judgment, and integrity.

Fond of private life, he would have resigned the judicial office; but the whole country demanded his service. "Nature," they cried, "never designed that your powers of thought and independence of mind should be lost in retirement." But after a few years, relieving himself from the cares of the bench, he gave himself to the activity and the independent life of a husbandman. He carried into retirement the fame of natural intelligence, and was cherished as "a prompt, frank, and ardent soul." His vigor of character constituted him first among all with whom he associated. A private man as he was, his name was familiarly spoken round every hearth-stone in Tennessee. Men loved to discuss his qualities. All discerned his power; and when the vehemence and impetuosity of his nature were observed upon, there were not wanting those who saw, beneath the blazing fires of his genius, the solidity of his judgment.

His hospitable roof sheltered the emigrant and the pioneer; and, as they made their way to their new homes, they filled the mountain-sides and the valleys with his praise.

Connecting himself, for a season, with a man of business, Jackson soon discerned the misconduct of his associate. It marked his character, that he insisted, himself, on paying every obligation that had been contracted; and rather than endure the vassalage of debt, he instantly parted with the rich domain which his early enterprise had acquired—with his own mansion—with his fields which he himself had first tamed to the ploughshare—with the forest whose trees were as familiar to him as his friends—and chose rather to dwell, for a time, in a rude log-cabin, in the pride of independence and integrity.

On all great occasions, Jackson's influence was deferred to. When Jefferson had acquired for the country the whole of Louisiana, and there seemed some hesitancy, on the part of Spain, to acknowledge our possession, the services of Jackson were solicited by the national administration, and were not called into full exercise, only from the peaceful termination of the incidents that occasioned the summons.

In the long series of aggressions on the freedom of the seas, and the rights of the American flag, Jackson was on the side of his country, and the new maritime code of republicanism. In his inland home, where the roar of the breakers was never heard, and the mariner was never seen, he resented the continued aggression on our commerce and on our sailors.

When the continuance of wrong compelled the nation to resort to arms, Jackson, led by the instinctive knowledge of his own greatness, yet with a modesty that would have honored the most sensitive delicacy of nature, confessed his willingness to be employed on the Canada frontier; and it is a fact, that he aspired to the command to which Winchester was appointed. We may ask, what would have been the result, if the command of the northwestern army had, at the opening of the war, been intrusted to a man who, in action, was ever so fortunate, that his vehement will seemed to have made destiny capitulate to his designs?

The path of duty led him in another direction. On the declaration of war, twenty-five hundred volunteers had risen at his word to follow his standard; but by countermanding orders from the seat of government, the movement was without effect.

A new and great danger hung over the West. The Indian tribes were to make one last effort to restore it to its solitude, and recover it for savage life. The brave, relentless Shawnees—who, from time immemorial, had strolled from the waters of the Ohio to the rivers of Alabama—were animated by Tecumseh and his brother the Prophet, who spoke to them as with the voice of the Great Spirit, and aroused the Creek nation to desperate massacres. Who has not heard of their terrible deeds, when their ruthless cruelty spared neither sex nor age? when the infant and its mother, the planter and his family, who had fled for refuge to the fortress, the garrison that capitulated—all were slain, and not a vestige of defence was left in the country? The cry of the West demanded Jackson for its defender; and though his arm was then fractured by a ball, and hung in a sling, he placed himself at the head of the volunteers of Tennessee, and resolved to terminate forever the hereditary struggle.

Who can tell the horrors of that campaign? Who can paint rightly the obstacles which Jackson overcame—mountains, the scarcity of untenanted forests; winter, the failure of supplies from the settlements, the insubordination of troops, mutiny, menaces of desertion? Who can measure the wonderful power over men, by which his personal prowess and attractive energy drew them in midwinter from their homes, across mountains and morasses, and through trackless deserts? Who can describe the personal heroism of Jackson, never sparing himself, beyond any of his men encountering toil and fatigue, sharing every labor of the camp and of the march, foremost in every danger; giving up his horse to the invalid soldier, while he himself waded through the swamps on foot? None equalled him in power of endurance; and the private soldiers, as they found him passing them on the march, exclaimed, "He is as tough as hickory." "Yes," they cried to one another, "There goes Old Hickory!"

Who cannot narrate the terrible events of the double battles of Emuckfaw, or the glorious victory of Tohopeka, where the anger of the general against the faltering was more appalling than the war-whoop and rifle of the savage? Who can rightly conceive the field of Enotochopoo, where the general, as he attempted to draw the sword to cut down a flying colonel who was leading a regiment from the field, broke again the arm which was but newly knit together; and quietly replacing it in the sling, with his commanding voice arrested the flight of the troops, and himself led them back to victory!

In six short months of vehement action, the most terrible Indian war in our annals was brought to a close; the prophets were silenced; the consecrated region of the Creek nation reduced. Through scenes of blood, the avenging hero sought only the path to peace. Thus, Alabama, a part of Mississippi, a part of his own Tennessee, and the highway to the Floridas, were his gifts to the Union. These were his trophies.

Genius as extraordinary as military events can call forth, was summoned into action in this rapid, efficient, and most fortunately conducted war.

Time would fail were I to track our hero down the watercourses of Alabama to the neighborhood of Pensacola. How he longed to plant the eagle of his country on its battlements!

Time would fail, and words be wanting, were I to dwell on the magical influence of his appearance in New Orleans. His presence dissipated gloom and dispelled alarm; at once he changed the aspect of despair into a confidence of security and a hope of acquiring glory. Every man knows the tale of the heroic, sudden, and yet deliberate daring which led him, on the night of the 23d of December, to precipitate his little army on his foes, in the thick darkness, before they grew familiar with their encampment, scattering dismay through veteran regiments of England, and defeating them, and arresting their progress by a far inferior force.

Who shall recount the counsels of prudence, the kindling words of eloquence that gushed from his lips to cheer his soldiers—his skirmishes and battles, till that eventful morning when the day at Bunker's Hill had its fulfilment in the glorious battle of New Orleans, and American independence stood before the world in the majesty of victorious power.

These were great deeds for the nation; for himself he did a greater. Had not Jackson been renowned for the vehement impetuosity of his passions, for his defiance of others' authority, and the unbending vigor of his self-will? Behold the saviour of Louisiana, all garlanded with victory, viewing around him the city he had preserved, the maidens and children whom his heroism had protected, stand in the presence of a petty judge, who gratifies his wounded vanity by an abuse of his judicial power. Every breast in the crowded audience heaves with indignation. He, the passionate, the impetuous—he whose power was to be humbled, whose honor questioned, whose laurels tarnished, alone stood sublimely serene; and when the craven judge trembled and faltered, and dared not proceed, himself, the arraigned one, bade him take courage, and stood by the law even in the moment when the law was made the instrument of insult and wrong on himself—at the moment of his most perfect claim to the highest civic honors.

His country, when it grew to hold many more millions, the generation that then was coming in, has risen up to do homage to the noble heroism of that hour. Woman, whose feeling is always right, did honor from the first to the purity of his heroism. The people of Louisiana, to the latest hour, will cherish his name as their greatest benefactor.

The culture of Jackson's mind had been much promoted by his services and associations in the war. His discipline of himself, as the chief in command; his intimate relations with men like Livingston; the wonderful deeds in which he bore a part; all matured his judgment and mellowed his character.

Peace came with its delights; once more the country rushed forward in the developement of its powers; once more the arts of industry healed the wounds that war had inflicted; and, from commerce and agriculture and manufactures, wealth gushed abundantly under the free activity of unrestrained enterprise.

And Jackson returned to his own fields and his own pursuits, to cherish his plantation, to care for his servants, to look after his stud, to enjoy the affection of the most kind and devoted wife, whom he respected with the gentlest deference, and loved with an almost miraculous tenderness.

And there he stood, like one of the mightiest forest trees of his own West, vigorous and colossal, sending its summit to the skies, and growing on its native soil in wild and inimitable magnificence, careless of beholders. From all parts of the country he received appeals to his political ambition, and the severe modesty of his well-balanced mind turned them all aside. He was happy in his farm, happy in seclusion, happy in his family, happy within himself.

But the passions of the southern Indians were not allayed by the peace with Great Britain; and foreign emissaries were still among them, to inflame and direct their malignity. Jackson was called forth by his country to restrain the cruelty of the treacherous and unsparing Seminoles. It was in the train of the events of this war that he placed the American eagle on St. Marks, and above the ancient towers of St. Augustine. His deeds in that war, of themselves, form a monument to human power, to the celerity of his genius, to the creative fertility of his resources, his intuitive sagacity. As Spain, in his judgment, had committed aggression, he would have emancipated her islands; of the Havana, he caused the reconnoissance to be made; and with an army of five thousand men, he stood ready to guaranty her redemption from colonial thraldom.

But when peace was restored, and his office was accomplished, his physical strength sunk under the pestilential influence of the climate, and, fast yielding to disease, he was borne in a litter across the swamps of Florida, towards his home. It was Jackson's character that he never solicited aid from any one; but he never forgot those who rendered him service in the hour of need. At a time when all around him believed him near his end, his wife hastened to his side, and, by her tenderness and nursing care, her patient assiduity, and the soothing influence of devoted love, withheld him from the grave.

He would have remained quietly at his home in repose, but that he was privately informed his good name was to be attainted by some intended congressional proceedings. He came, therefore, into the presence of the people's representatives at Washington, only to vindicate his name; and when that was achieved, he was once more communing with his own thoughts among the groves of the Hermitage.

It was not his own ambition which brought him again to the public view. The affection of Tennessee compelled him to resume a seat on the floor of the American Senate, and, after years of the intensest political strife, Andrew Jackson was elected President of the United States.

Far from advancing his own pretensions, he always kept them back, and had for years repressed the solicitations of his friends to become a candidate. He felt sensibly that he was devoid of scientific culture, and little familiar with letters; and he never obtruded his opinions, or preferred claims to place. But, whenever his opinion was demanded, he was always ready to pronounce it; and whenever his country invoked his services, he did not shrink even from the station which had been filled by the most cultivated men our nation had produced.

Behold, then, the unlettered man of the West, the nursling of the wilds, the farmer of the Hermitage, little versed in books, unconnected by science with the tradition of the past, raised by the will of the people to the highest pinnacle of honor, to the central post in the civilization of republican freedom, to the station where all the nations of the earth would watch his actions—where his words would vibrate through the civilized world, and his spirit be the moving-star to guide the nations. What policy will he pursue? What wisdom will he bring with him from the forest? What rules of duty will he evolve from the oracles of his own mind?

The man of the West came as the inspired prophet of the West: he came as one free from the bonds of hereditary or established custom; he came with no superior but conscience, no oracle but his native judgment; and, true to his origin and his education—true to the conditions and circumstances of his advancement, he valued right more than usage; he reverted from the pressure of established interests to the energy of first principles.

We tread on ashes, where the fire is not yet extinguished; yet not to dwell on his career as President, were to leave out of view the grandest illustrations of his magnanimity.

The legislation of the United States had followed the precedents of the legislation of European monarchies; it was the office of Jackson to lift the country out of the European forms of legislation, and to open to it a career resting on American sentiment and American freedom. He would have freedom everywhere—freedom under the restraints of right; freedom of industry, of commerce, of mind; of universal action; freedom, unshackled by restrictive privileges, unrestrained by the thraldom of monopolies.

The unity of his mind and his consistency were without a parallel. With natural dialectics, he developed the political doctrines that suited every emergency, with a precision and a harmony that no theorist could hope to equal. On every subject in politics—I speak but a fact— he was thoroughly and profoundly and immoveably radical; and would sit for hours, and in a continued flow of remark make the application of his principles to every question that could arise in legislation, or in the interpretation of the constitution.

His expression of himself was so clear, that his influence pervaded not our land only, but all America and all mankind. They say that, in the physical world, the magnetic fluid is so diffused, that its vibrations are discernible simultaneously in every part of the globe. So it is with the element of freedom. And as Jackson developed its doctrines from their source in the mind of humanity, the popular sympathy was moved and agitated throughout the world, till his name grew everywhere to be the symbol of popular power.

Himself the witness of the ruthlessness of savage life, he planned the removal of the Indian tribes beyond the limits of the organized states; and it is the result of his determined policy that the region east of the Mississippi has been transferred to the exclusive possession of cultivated man.

A pupil of the wilderness, his heart was with the pioneers of American life towards the setting sun. No American statesman has ever embraced within his affections a scheme so liberal for the emigrants as that of Jackson. He longed to secure to them, not pre-emption rights only, but more than pre-emption rights. He longed to invite labor to take possession of the unoccupied fields without money and without price; with no obligation except the perpetual devotion of itself by allegiance to its country. Under the beneficent influence of his opinions, the sons of misfortune, the children of adventure, find their way to the uncultivated West. There, in some wilderness glade, or in the thick forest of the fertile plain, or where the prairies most sparkle with flowers, they, like the wild bee which sets them the example of industry, may choose their home, mark the extent of their possessions, by driving stakes or blazing trees, shelter their log-cabin with the boughs and turf, and teach the virgin soil to yield itself to the ploughshare. Theirs shall be the soil, theirs the beautiful farms which they teach to be productive. Come, children of sorrow! you on whom the Old World frowns; crowd fearlessly to the forests; plant your homes in confidence, for the country watches over you; your children grow around you as hostages, and the wilderness, at your bidding, surrenders its grandeur of useless luxuriance to the beauty and loveliness of culture. Yet, beautiful and lovely as is this scene, it still by far falls short of the ideal which lived in the affections of Jackson. His heart was ever with the pioneer; his policy ever favored the diffusion of independent freeholds throughout the laboring classes of our land.

It would be a sin against the occasion, were I to omit to commemorate the deep devotedness of Jackson to the cause and to the rights of labor. It was for the welfare of the labouring classes that he defied all the storms of political hostility. He longed to secure to labor the fruits of its own industry; and he unceasingly opposed every system which tended to lessen their reward, or which exposed them to be defrauded of their dues. The laborers may bend over his grave with affectionate sorrow; for never, in the tide of time, did a statesman exist more heartily resolved to protect them in their rights, and to advance their happiness. For their benefit, he opposed partial legislation; for their benefit, he resisted all artificial methods of controlling labor, and subjecting it to capital.

It was for their benefit that he loved freedom in all its forms—freedom of the individual in personal independence, freedom of the states as separate sovereignties. He never would listen to counsels which tended to the centralization of power. The true American system presupposes the diffusion of freedom—organized life in all the parts of the American body politic, as there is organized life in every part of the human system. Jackson was deaf to every counsel which sought to subject general labor to a central will. His vindication of the just principles of the constitution derived its sublimity from his deep conviction that this strict construction is required by the lasting welfare of the great laboring classes of the United States.

To this end, Jackson revived the tribunicial power of the veto, and exerted it against the decisive action of both branches of Congress, against the votes, the wishes, the entreaties of personal and political friends. "Show me," was his reply to them, "show me an express clause in the constitution authorizing Congress to take the business of state legislatures out of their hands." "You will ruin us all," cried a firm partisan friend, "you will ruin your party and your own prospects." "Providence," answered Jackson, "will take care of me;" and he persevered.

In proceeding to discharge the debt of the United States—a measure thoroughly American—Jackson followed the example of his predecessors; but he followed it with the full consciousness that he was rescuing the country from the artificial system of finance which had prevailed throughout the world; and with him it formed a part of a system by which American legislation was to separate itself more and more effectually from European precedents, and develope itself more and more, according to the vital principles of our political existence.

The discharge of the debt brought with it, of necessity, a great reduction of the public burdens, and brought, of necessity, into view, the question, how far America should follow, of choice, the old restrictive system of high duties, under which Europe had oppressed America; or how far she should rely on her own freedom and enterprise and power, defying the competition, and seeking the markets, and receiving the products of the world.

The mind of Jackson, on this subject, reasoned clearly, and without passion. In the abuses of the system of revenue by excessive imposts, he saw evils which the public mind would remedy; and, inclining with the whole might of his energetic nature to the side of revenue duties, he made his earnest but tranquil appeal to the judgment of the people.

The portions of country that suffered most severely from a system of legislation, which, in its extreme character, as it then existed, is now universally acknowledged to have been unequal and unjust, were less tranquil; and rallying on the doctrines of freedom, which made our government a limited one, they saw in the oppressive acts an assumption of power which was nugatory, because it was exercised, as they held, without authority from the people.

The contest that ensued was the most momentous in our annals. The greatest minds of America engaged in the discussion. Eloquence never achieved sublimer triumphs in the American Senate, than on those occasions. The country became deeply divided; and the antagonist elements were arrayed against each other under forms of clashing authority, menacing civil war; the freedom of the several states was invoked against the power of the United States; and under the organization of a state in convention, the reserved rights of the people were summoned to display their energy, and balance the authority and neutralize the legislation of the central government. The states were agitated with prolonged excitement; the friends of freedom throughout the world looked on with divided sympathies, praying that the union of the states might be perpetual, and also that the commerce of the world might be free.

Fortunately for the country, and fortunately for mankind, Andrew Jackson was at the helm of state, the representative of the principles that were to allay excitement, and to restore the hopes of peace and freedom. By nature, by impulse, by education, by conviction, a friend to personal freedom—by education, political sympathies, and the fixed habit of his mind, a friend to the rights of the states—unwilling that the liberty of the states should be trampled under foot—unwilling that the constitution should lose its vigor or be impaired, he rallied for the constitution: and in its name he published to the world, "THE UNION: IT MUST BE PRESERVED." The words were a spell to hush evil passion, and to remove oppression. Under his guiding influence, the favored interests, which had struggled to perpetuate unjust legislation, yielded to the voice of moderation and reform; and every mind that had for a moment contemplated a rupture of the states, discarded it forever. The whole influence of the past was invoked in favor of the constitution; from the council chambers of the fathers who moulded our institutions—from the hall where American independence was declared, the clear, loud cry was uttered—"The Union: it must be preserved." From every battle-field of the Revolution—from Lexington and Bunker-Hill—from Saratoga and Yorktown—from the fields of Eutaw—from the cane-brakes that sheltered the men of Marion—the repeated, long-prolonged echoes came up—"The Union: it must be preserved." From every valley in our land—from every cabin on the pleasant mountain sides—from the ships at our wharves—from the tents of the hunter in our western-most prairies—from the living minds of the living millions of American freemen—from the thickly coming glories of futurity—the shout went up like the sound of many waters, "The Union: it must be preserved." The friends of the protective system, and they who had denounced the protective system—the statesmen of the north, that had wounded the constitution in their love of centralism—the statesmen of the south, whose minds had carried to its extreme the theory of state rights—all conspired together; all breathed prayers for the perpetuity of the Union. Under the prudent firmness of Jackson—under the mixture of justice and general regard for all interests, the greatest danger to our institutions was turned aside, and mankind was encouraged to believe that our Union, like our freedom, is imperishable.

The moral of the great events of those days is this: that the people can discern right, and will make their way to a knowledge of right; that the whole human mind, and therefore with it the mind of the nation, has a continuous, ever improving existence; that the appeal from the unjust legislation of to-day must be made quietly, earnestly, perseveringly, to the more enlightened collective reason of to-morrow; that submission is due to the popular will, in the confidence that the people, when in error, will amend their doings; that in a popular government, injustice is neither to be established by force, nor to be resisted by force; in a word, that the Union, which was constituted by consent, must be preserved by love.

It rarely falls to the happy lot of a statesman to receive such unanimous applause from the heart of a nation. Duty to the dead demands that, on this occasion, the course of measures should not pass unnoticed, in the progress of which his vigor of character most clearly appeared, and his conflict with opposing parties was most violent and protracted.

From his home in Tennessee, Jackson came to the presidency resolved to lift American legislation out of the forms of English legislation, and to place our laws on the currency in harmony with the principles of our government. He came to the presidency of the United States resolved to deliver the government from the Bank of the United States, and to restore the regulation of exchanges to the rightful depository of that power—the commerce of the country. He had designed to declare his views on this subject in his inaugural address, but was persuaded to relinquish that purpose, on the ground that it belonged rather to a legislative message. When the period for addressing Congress drew near, it was still urged that to attack the Bank would forfeit his popularity and secure his future defeat. "It is not," he answered, "it is not for myself that I care." It was urged that haste was unnecessary, as the Bank had still six unexpended years of chartered existence. "I may die," he replied, "before another Congress comes together, and I could not rest quietly in my grave, if I failed to do what I hold so essential to the liberty of my country." And his first annual message announced to the country that the Bank was neither constitutional nor expedient. In this he was in advance of the friends about him, in advance of Congress, and in advance of his party. This is no time for the analysis of measures, or the discussion of questions of political economy: on the present occasion, we have to contemplate the character of the man.

Never, from the first moment of his administration to the last, was there a calm in the strife of parties on the subject of the currency; and never, during the whole period, did he recede or falter. Always in advance of his party—always having near him friends who cowered before the hardihood of his courage, he himself, throughout all the contest, was unmoved, from the first suggestion of the unconstitutionality of the Bank, to the moment when he himself, first of all, reasoning from the certain tendency of its policy, with singular sagacity predicted to unbelieving friends, the coming insolvency of the institution.

The storm throughout the country rose with unexampled vehemence: his opponents were not satisfied with addressing the public or Congress, or his cabinet; they threw their whole force personally on him. From all parts men pressed around him, urging him, entreating him to bend. Congress was flexible; many of his personal friends faltered; the impetuous swelling wave rolled on, without one sufficient obstacle, till it reached his presence; but, as it dashed in its highest fury at his feet, it broke before his firmness. The commanding majesty of his will appalled his opponents and revived his friends. He, himself, had a proud consciousness that his will was indomitable. Standing over the rocks of the Rip Raps, and looking out upon the ocean, "Providence," said he to a friend, "Providence may change my determination; but man no more can do it, than he can remove these Rip Raps, which have resisted the rolling ocean from the beginning of time." And though a panic was spreading through the land, and the whole credit system, as it then existed, was crumbling to pieces and crashing around him, he stood erect, like a massive column, which the heaps of falling ruins could not break, nor bend, nor sway from its fixed foundation.

[At this point Mr. Bancroft turned to address the Mayor of the city of Washington; but, finding him not present, he proceeded.]

People of the District of Columbia,—I should fail of a duty on this occasion, if I did not give utterance to your sentiment of gratitude which followed General Jackson into retirement. Dwelling amongst you, he desired your prosperity. This beautiful city, surrounded by heights the most attractive, watered by a river so magnificent, the home of the gentle and the cultivated, not less than the seat of political power—this city, whose site Washington had selected, was dear to his affections; and if he won your grateful attachment by adorning it with monuments of useful architecture, by establishing its credit, and relieving its burdens, he regretted only that he had not the opportunity to have connected himself still more intimately with your prosperity.

As he prepared to take his final leave of the district, the mass of the population of this city, and the masses that had gathered from around, followed his carriage in crowds. All in silence stood near him, to wish him adieu; and as the cars started, and he displayed his grey hairs, as he lifted his hat in token of farewell, you stood around with heads uncovered, too full of emotion to speak, in solemn silence gazing on him as he departed, never more to be seen in your midst.

Behold the warrior and statesman, his work well done, retired to the Hermitage, to hold converse with his forests, to cultivate his farm, to gather around him hospitably his friends! Who was like HIM? He was still the loadstar of the American people. His fervid thoughts, frankly uttered, still spread the flame of patriotism through the American breast; his counsels were still listened to with reverence; and, almost alone among statesmen, he in his retirement was in harmony with every onward movement of his time. His prevailing influence assisted to sway a neighboring nation to desire to share our institutions, his ear heard the footsteps of the coming millions that are to gladden our western shores; and his eye discerned in the dim distance the whitening sails that are to enliven the waters of the Pacific with the social sounds of our successful commerce.

Age had whitened his locks and dimmed his eye, and spread around him the infirmities and venerable emblems of many years of toilsome service; but his heart beat as warmly as in his youth, and his courage was as firm as it had ever been in the day of battle. But while his affections were still for his friends and his country, his thoughts were already in a better world. That exalted mind, which in active life had always had unity of perception and will, which in action had never faltered from doubt, and which in council had always reverted to first principles and general laws, now gave itself up to communing with the Infinite. He was a believer: from feeling, from experience, from conviction. Not a shadow of scepticism ever dimmed the lustre of his mind. Proud philosopher! will you smile to know that Andrew Jackson perused reverently his Psalter and Prayer-book and Bible? Know that Andrew Jackson had faith in the eternity of truth, in the imperishable power of popular freedom, in the destinies of humanity, in the virtues and capacity of the people, in his country's institutions, in the being and overruling providence of a merciful and ever-living God.

The last moment of his life on earth is at hand. It is the Sabbath of the Lord: the brightness and beauty of summer clothe the fields around him: nature is in her glory; but the sublimest spectacle on that day, on earth, was the victory of his unblenching spirit over death itself.

When he first felt the hand of death upon him—"May my enemies," he cried, "find peace; may the liberties of my country endure for ever!"

When his exhausted system, under the excess of pain, sunk, for a moment, from debility, "Do not weep," said he to his adopted daughter; "my sufferings are less than those of Christ upon the cross;" for he, too, as a disciple of the cross, could have devoted himself, in sorrow, for mankind. Feeling his end near, he would see all his family once more; and he spoke to them, one by one, in words of tenderness and affection. His two little grandchildren were absent at Sunday-school. He asked for them; and as they came he prayed for them, and kissed them, and blessed them. His servants were then admitted: they gathered, some in his room, and some on the outside of the house, clinging to the windows, that they might gaze and hear. And that dying man, thus surrounded, in a gush of fervid eloquence, spoke with inspiration of God, of the Redeemer, of salvation through the atonement, of immortality, of heaven. For he ever thought that pure and undefiled religion was the foundation of private happiness, and the bulwark of republican institutions. Having spoken of immortality in perfect consciousness of his own approaching end, he bade them all farewell. "Dear children," such were his final words, "dear children, servants, and friends, I trust to meet you all in heaven, both white and black—all, both white and black." And having borne his testimony to immortality, he bowed his mighty head, and, without a groan, the spirit of the greatest man of his age escaped to the bosom of his God.

In life, his career had been like the blaze of the sun in the fierceness of its noon-day glory; his death was lovely as the mildest sunset of a summer's evening, when the sun goes down in tranquil beauty without a cloud. To the majestic energy of an indomitable will, he joined a heart capable of the purest and most devoted love, rich in the tenderest affections. On the bloody battle-field of Tohopeka, he saved an infant that clung to the breast of its dying mother: in the stormiest moment of his presidency, at the imminent moment of decision, he paused in his way to give good counsel to a poor suppliant that had come up to him for succor. Of the strifes in which he was engaged in his earlier life, not one sprung from himself, but in every case he became involved by standing forth as the champion of the weak, the poor, and the defenceless, to shelter the gentle against oppression, to protect the emigrant against the avarice of the speculator. His generous soul revolted at the barbarous practice of duels, and by no man in the land have so many been prevented.

The sorrows of those that were near to him went deeply into his soul; and at the anguish of the wife whom he loved, the orphans whom he adopted, he would melt into tears, and weep and sob like a child.

No man in private life so possessed the hearts of all around him: no public man of this century ever returned to private life with such an abiding mastery over the affections of the people. No man with truer instinct received American ideas: no man expressed them so completely, or so boldly, or so sincerely. He was as sincere a man as ever lived. He was wholly, always, and altogether sincere and true.

Up to the last, he dared do anything that it was right to do. He united personal courage and moral courage beyond any man of whom history keeps the record. Before the nation, before the world, before coming ages, he stands forth the representative, for his generation, of the American mind. And the secret of his greatness is this: By intuitive conception, he shared and possessed all the creative ideas of his country and his time. He expressed them with dauntless intrepidity; he enforced them with an immoveable will; he executed them with an electric power that attracted and swayed the American people. The nation, in his time, had not one great thought, of which he was not the boldest and clearest expositor.

History does not describe the man that equalled him in firmness of nerve. Not danger, not an army in battle array, not wounds, not wide-spread clamor, not age, not the anguish of disease, could impair in the least degree the vigor of his steadfast mind. The heroes of antiquity would have contemplated with awe the unmatched hardihood of his character; and Napoleon, had he possessed his disinterested will, could never have been vanquished. Jackson never was vanquished. He was always fortunate. He conquered the wilderness; he conquered the savage; he conquered the bravest veterans trained in the battlefields of Europe; he conquered everywhere in statesmanship; and, when death came to get the mastery over him, he turned that last enemy aside as tranquilly as he had done the feeblest of his adversaries, and escaped from earth in the triumphant consciousness of immortality.

His body has its fit resting-place in the great central

valley of the Mississippi; his spirit rests upon our whole territory; it hovers over the vales of Oregon, and guards, in advance, the frontier of the Del Norte. The fires of party spirit are quenched at his grave. His faults and frailties have perished. Whatever of good he has done lives, and will live forever.

INAUGURAL ADDRESS.

Delivered March 4th, 1829.

FELLOW-CITIZENS:—About to undertake the arduous duties that I have been appointed to perform by the choice of a free people, I avail myself of this customary and solemn occasion to express the gratitude which their confidence inspires, and to acknowledge the accountability which my situation enjoins. While the magnitude of their interests convinces me that no thanks can be adequate to the honor they have conferred, it admonishes me that the best return I can make, is the zealous dedication of my humble abilities to their service and their good.

As the instrument of the federal constitution, it will devolve upon me, for a stated period, to execute the laws of the United States; to superintend their foreign and confederate relations; to manage their revenue; to command their forces: and, by communications to the legislature, to watch over and to promote their interests generally. And the principles of action by which I shall endeavor to accomplish this circle of duties, it is now proper for me briefly to explain.

In administering the laws of Congress, I shall keep steadily in view the limitations as well as the extent of the executive power, trusting thereby to discharge the functions of my office without transcending its authority. With foreign nations it will be my study to preserve peace, and to cultivate friendship on fair and honorable terms; and in the adjustment of any differences that may exist or arise, to exhibit the forbearance becoming a powerful nation, rather than the sensibility belonging to a gallant people.

In such measures as I may be called on to pursue, in

regard to the rights of the separate states, I hope to be animated by a proper respect for those sovereign members of our Union; taking care not to confound the powers they have reserved to themselves with those they have granted to the confederacy.

The management of the public revenue—that searching operation in all governments—is among the most delicate and important trusts in ours; and it will, of course, demand no inconsiderable share of my official solicitude. Under every aspect in which it can be considered, it would appear that advantage must result from the observance of a strict and faithful economy. This I shall aim at the more anxiously, both because it will facilitate the extinguishment of the national debt, the unnecessary duration of which is incompatible with real independence, and because it will counteract that tendency to public and private profligacy which a profuse expenditure of money by the government is but too apt to engender.

Powerful auxiliaries to the attainment of this desirable end are to be found in the regulation provided by the wisdom of Congress for the specific appropriation of public money, and the prompt accountability of public officers.

With regard to a proper selection of the subjects of impost, with a view to revenue, it would seem to me that the spirit of equity, caution, and compromise, in which the constitution was formed, requires that the great interests of agriculture, commerce, and manufactures, should be equally favored; and that perhaps the only exception to this rule should consist in the peculiar encouragement of any products of either of them that may be found essential to our national independence.

Internal improvement, and the diffusion of knowledge, so far as they can be promoted by the constitutional acts of the federal government, are of high importance.

Considering standing armies as dangerous to free governments in time of peace, I shall not seek to enlarge our present establishment, nor to disregard that salutary lesson of political experience which teaches that the military should be held subordinate to the civil power. The gradual increase of our navy, whose flag has displayed in distant climes our skill in navigation and our fame in arms; the preservation of our forts, arsenals, and dock-yards; and the introduction of progressive improvements in the discipline and science of both branches of our military service, are so plainly prescribed by prudence, that I should be excused for omitting their mention, sooner than enlarging on their importance. But the bulwark of our defence is the national militia, which, in the present state of our intelligence and population, must render us invincible. As long as our government is administered for the good of the people, and is regulated by their will; as long as it secures to us the rights of person and property, liberty of conscience, and of the press, it will be worth defending; and so long as it is worth defending, a patriotic militia will cover it with an impenetrable *ægis*. Partial injuries and occasional mortification we may be subjected to; but a million of armed freemen, possessed of the means of war, can never be conquered by a foreign foe. To any just system, therefore, calculated to strengthen this natural safeguard of the country, I shall cheerfully lend all the aid in my power.

It will be my sincere and constant desire to observe toward the Indian tribes within our limits a just and liberal policy, and to give that humane and considerate attention to their rights and their wants which are consistent with the habits of our government and the feelings of our people.

The recent demonstration of public sentiment inscribes on the list of executive duties, in characters too legible to overlooked, the task of *reform;* which will require particularly the correction of those abuses that have brought the patronage of the federal government into conflict with the freedom of elections and the counteraction of those causes which have disturbed the rightful course of appointment, and have placed or continued power in unfaithful or incompetent hands.

In the performance of a task thus generally delineated, I shall endeavor to select men whose diligence and talents will insure, in their respective stations, able and faithful co-operation—depending for the advancement of the public service, more on the integrity and zeal of the public officers, than on their numbers.

A diffidence, perhaps too just, in my own qualification, will teach me to look with reverence to the examples of public vitrue left by my illustrious predecessors, and with veneration to the lights that flow from the mind that founded and the mind that reformed our system. The same diffidence induces me to hope for instruction and aid from the co-ordinate branches of the government, and for the indulgence and support of my fellow citizens generally. And a firm reliance on the goodness of that Power whose providence mercifully protected our national infancy, and has since upheld our liberties in various vicissitudes, encourages me to offer up my ardent supplication that he will continue to make our beloved country the object of his divine care and gracious benediction.

MAYSVILLE ROAD VETO.

Delivered, May 27th, 1830.

To the House of Representatives :—

GENTLEMEN: I have maturely considered the bill proposing to authorize "a subscription of stock in the Maysville, Washington, Paris, and Lexington Turnpike-road Company," and now return the same to the house of representatives, in which it originated, with my objections to its passage.

Sincerely friendly to the improvement of our country by means of roads and canals, I regret that any difference of opinion in the mode of contributing to it should exist between us; and if, in stating this difference, I go beyond what the occasion may be deemed to call for, I hope to find an apology in the great importance of the subject, an unfeigned respect for the high source from which this branch of it has emanated, and an anxious wish to be correctly understood by my constituents in the discharge of all my duties. Diversity of sentiment among public functionaries, actuated by the same general motives, on the character and tendency of particular measures, is an incident common to all governments, and the more to be expected in one which, like ours, owes its existence to the freedom of opinion, and must be upheld by the same influence. Controlled as we thus are by a higher tribunal, before which our respective acts will be canvassed with the indulgence due to the imperfections of our nature, and with that intelligence and unbiassed judgment which are the true correctives of error, all that our responsibility demands is that the public good should be the measure of our views, dictating alike their frank expression and honest maintenance.

In the message which was presented to Congress at

the opening of its present session, I endeavored to exhibit briefly my views upon the important and highly interesting subject to which our attention is now to be directed. I was desirous of presenting to the representatives of the several states in Congress assembled, the inquiry whether some mode could not be devised which would reconcile the diversity of opinion concerning the powers of this government over the subject of internal improvements, and the manner in which these powers, if conferred by the constitution, ought to be exercised. The act which I am called upon to consider has therefore been passed with a knowledge of my views on this question, as these are expressed in the message referred to. In that document the following suggestion will be found:—

"After the extinction of the public debt it is not probable that any adjustment of the tariff upon principles satisfactory to the people of the Union will, until a remote period, if ever, leave the government without a considerable surplus in the treasury beyond what may be required for its current service. As, then, the period approaches when the application of the revenue to the payment of debts will cease, the disposition of the surplus will present a subject for the serious deliberation of Congress; and it may be fortunate for the country that it is yet to be decided. Considered in connexion with the difficulties which have heretofore attended appropriations for purposes of internal improvement, and with those which this experience tells us will certainly arise, whenever power over such subjects may be exercised by the general government, it is hoped that it may lead to the adoption of some plan which will reconcile the diversified interests of the states, and strengthen the bonds which unite them. Every member of the Union, in peace and in war, will be benefited by the improvement of inland navigation, and the construction of highways in the several states. Let us then endeavor to obtain this benefit in a mode which will be satisfactory to all. That hitherto adopted has been deprecated as an infraction of the constitution by many of our fellow-citizens, while by others it has been viewed as inexpedient. All feel that it has been employed at the expense of harmony in the legislative councils." And adverting to the constitutional power of Congress to make what I consider a proper disposition of the surplus revenue, I subjoin the following remarks: "To avoid these evils it appears to me that the most safe, just, and federal disposition which could be made of the surplus revenue would be its apportionment among the several states according to their ratio of representation; and should this measure not be found warranted by the constitution, that it would be expedient to propose to the states an amendment authorizing it."

The constitutional power of the federal government to construct or promote works of internal improvement presents itself in two points of view: the first, as bearing upon the sovereignty of the states within whose limits their execution is contemplated, if jurisdiction of the territory which they may occupy be claimed as necessary to their preservation and use; the second, as asserting the simple right to appropriate money from the national treasury in aid of such works, when undertaken by state authority surrendering the claim of jurisdiction. In the first view, the question of power is an open one, and can be decided without the embarrassment attending the other, arising from the practice of the government. Although frequently and strenuously attempted, the power to this extent has never been exercised by the government in a single instance. It does not, in my opinion, possess it; and no bill, therefore, which admits it can receive my official sanction.

But in the other view of the power the question is differently situated. The ground taken at an early period of the government was, "that whenever money has been raised by the general authority, and is to be applied to a particular measure, a question arises whether the particular measure be within the enumerated authorities vested in Congress. If it be, the money requisite for it may be applied to it; if not, no such application can be made." The document in which this principle was first advanced is of deservedly high authority, and should be held in grateful remembrance for its immediate agency in rescuing the country from much existing abuse, and for its conservative effect upon some of the most valuable principles of the constitution. The symmetry and purity of the government would doubtless have been better preserved if this restriction of the power of appropriation could have been maintained without weakening its ability to fulfil the general objects of its institution—an effect so likely to attend its admission, notwithstanding its apparent fitness, that every subsequent administration of the government, embracing a period of thirty out of the forty-two years of its existence, has adopted a more enlarged construction of the power. It is not my purpose to detain you by a minute recital of the acts which sustain this assertion, but it is proper that I should notice some of the most prominent, in order that the reflections which they suggest to my mind may be better understood.

In the administration of Mr. Jefferson we have two examples of the exercise of the right of appropriation, which, in the considerations that led to their adoption, and in their effects upon the public mind, have had a greater agency in marking the character of the power, than any subsequent events. I allude to the payment of fifteen millions of dollars for the purchase of Louisiana, and to the original appropriation for the construction of the Cumberland road; the latter act deriving much weight from the acquiescence and approbation of three of the most powerful of the original members of the confederacy, expressed through their respective legislatures. Although the circumstances of the latter case may be such as to deprive so much of it as relates to the actual construction of the road of the force of an obligatory exposition of the constitution, it must nevertheless be admitted that so far as the mere appropriation of money is concerned, they present the principle in its most imposing aspect. No less than twenty-three different laws have been passed through all the forms of the constitution, appropriating upward of two millions and a half of dollars, out of the national treasury, in support of that improvement, with the approbation of every president of the United States, including my predecessor, since its commencement.

MAYSVILLE ROAD VETO 227

Independently of the sanction given to appropriations for the Cumberland and other roads and objects, under this power, the administration of Mr. Madison was characterized by an act which furnishes the strongest evidence of his opinion of its extent. A bill was passed through both houses of Congress and presented for his approval, "setting apart and pledging certain funds for constructing roads and canals, and improving the navigation of watercourses, in order to facilitate, promote, and give security to internal commerce among the several states, and to render more easy and less expensive the means and provisions for the common defence." Regarding the bill as asserting a power in the federal government to construct roads and canals within the limits of the states in which they were made, he objected to its passage on the ground of its unconstitutionality, declaring that the assent of the respective states, in the mode provided by the bill, could not confer the power in question; that the only cases in which the consent and cession of particular states can extend the power of Congress are those specified and provided for in the constitution; and superadding to these avowals his opinion that a restriction of the power "to provide for the common defence and general welfare" to cases which are to be provided for by the expenditure of money, would still leave within the legislative power of Congress all the great and most important measures of government, money being the ordinary and necessary means of carrying them into execution. I have not been able to consider these declarations in any other point of view than as a concession that the right of appropriation is not limited by the power to carry into effect the measure for which the money is asked, as was formerly contended.

The views of Mr. Monroe upon this subject were not left to inference. During his administration, a bill was passed through both houses of Congress, conferring the jurisdiction and prescribing the mode by which the federal government should exercise it in the case of the Cumberland road. He returned it with objections to its passage, and in assigning them took occasion to say, that in the early stages of the government he had inclined to the construction that it had no right to expend money, except in the performance of acts authorized by the other specific grants of power, according to a strict construction of them; but that on further reflection and observation, his mind had undergone a change; that his opinion then was: "that Congress have an unlimited power to raise money, and that in its appropriation they have a discretionary power, restricted only by the duty to appropriate it to purposes of common defence and of general, not local, national, not state, benefit;" and this was avowed to be the governing principle through the residue of his administration. The views of the last administration are of such recent date as to render a particular reference to them unnecessary. It is well known that the appropriating power, to the utmost extent which had been claimed for it in relation to internal improvements, was fully recognised and exercised by it.

This brief reference to known facts will be sufficient to show the difficulty, if not impracticability, of bringing back the operations of the government to the construction of the constitution set up in 1793, assuming that to be its true reading in relation to the power under consideration; thus giving an admonitory proof of the force of implication, and the necessity of guarding the constitution with sleepless vigilance against the authority of precedents which have not the sanction of its most plainly defined powers. For although it is the duty of all to look to that sacred instrument instead of the statute book; to repudiate at all times encroachments upon its spirit, which are too apt to be effected by the conjuncture of peculiar and facilitating circumstances; it is not less true that the public good and the nature of our political institutions require that individual differences should yield to a well-settled acquiescence of the people and confederate authorities in particular constructions of the constitution on doubtful points. Not to concede this much to the spirit of our institutions, would impair their stability and defeat the objects of the constitution itself.

The bill before me does not call for a more definite opinion upon the particular circumstances which will warrant appropriations of money by Congress to aid works of internal improvement; for although the extension of the power to apply money beyond that of carrying into effect the object for which it is appropriated has, as we have seen, been long claimed and exercised by the federal government, yet such grants have always been professedly under the control of the general principle, that the works which might be thus aided should be "of a general, not local, national, not state, character." A disregard of this distinction would, of necessity, lead to the subversion of the federal system. That even this is an unsafe one, arbitrary in its nature, and liable consequently to great abuses, is too obvious to require the confirmation of experience. It is, however, sufficiently definite and imperative to my mind to forbid my approbation of any bill having the character of the one under consideration. I have given to its provisions all the reflection demanded by a just regard for the interests of those of our fellow-citizens who have desired its passage, and by the respect which is due to a co-ordinate branch of the government; but I am not able to view it in any other light than as a measure of purely local character, or, if it can be considered national, that no further distinction between the appropriate duties of the general and state governments need be attempted, for there can be no local interest that may not with equal propriety be denominated national. It has no connexion with any established system of improvements; is exclusively within the limits of a state, starting at a point on the Ohio river, and running out sixty miles to an interior town; and, even as far as the state is interested, conferring partial instead of general advantages.

Considering the magnitude and importance of the power, and the embarrassments to which, from the very nature of the thing, its exercise must necessarily be subjected, the real friends of internal improvement ought not to be willing to confide it to accident and chance. What is properly *national* in its character or otherwise, is an inquiry which is of en extremely difficult of solution. The appropriations of one year, for an object which is considered national, may be rendered nugatory by the refusal of a succeeding Congress to continue the work, on the ground that it is local. No aid can be derived from the intervention of corporations. The question regards the character of the work, not that of those by whom it is to be accomplished. Notwithstanding the union of the government with the corporation, by whose immediate agency any work of internal improvement is carried on, the inquiry will still remain, is it national, and conducive to the benefit of the whole, or local, and operating only to the advantage of a portion of the Union?

But, although I might not feel it to be my official duty to interpose the executive veto to the passage of a bill appropriating money for the construction of such works as are authorized by the states, and are national in their character, I do not wish to be understood as expressing an opinion that it is expedient at this time for the general government to embark in a system of this kind; and, anxious that my constituents should be possessed of my views on this as well as on all other subjects which they have committed to my discretion, I shall state them frankly and briefly. Besides many minor considerations, there are two prominent views on the subject which have made a deep impression upon my mind, which I think are well entitled to your serious attention, and will, I hope, be maturely weighed by the people.

From the official communications submitted to you, it appears that if no adverse or unforeseen contingency happens in our foreign relations, and no unusual diversion be made of the funds set apart for the payment of the national debt, we may look with confidence to its entire extinguishment in the short period of four years. The extent to which this pleasing anticipation is dependent upon the policy which may be pursued in relation to measures of the character of the one now under consideration, must be obvious to all, and equally so that the events of the present session are well calculated to awaken public solicitude upon the subject. By the statement from the treasury department, and those from the clerks of the senate and house of representatives, herewith submitted, it appears that the bills which have passed into laws, and those which. in all probability, will pass before the adjournment of Congress, anticipate appropriations which, with the ordinary expenditures for the support of government, will exceed considerably the amount in the treasury for the year 1830. Thus, while we are diminishing the revenue by a reduction of the duties on tea, coffee, and cocoa, the appropriations for internal improvements are increasing beyond the available means of the treasury; and if to this calculation be added the amount contained in bills which are pending before the two houses, it may be safely affirmed that ten millions of dollars would not make up the excess over the treasury receipts, unless the payment of the national debt be postponed, and the means now pledged to that object applied to those enumerated in these bills. Without a well-regulated system of internal improvement, this exhausting mode of appropriation is not likely to be avoided, and the plain consequence must be, either a continuance of the national debt or a resort to additional taxes.

Although many of the states, with a laudable zeal, and under the influence of an enlightened policy, are successfully applying their separate efforts to works of this character, the desire to enlist the aid of the general government in the construction of such as, from their nature, ought to devolve upon it, and to which the means of the individual states are inadequate, is both rational and patriotic; and if that desire is not gratified now, it does not follow that it never will be. The general intelligence and public spirit of the American people furnish a sure guarantee that, at the proper time, this policy will be made to prevail under circumstances more auspicious to its successful prosecution than those which now exist. But, great as this object undoubtedly is, it is not the only one which demands the fostering care of the government. The preservation and success of the republican principle rest with us. To elevate its character and extend its influence rank amongst our most important duties, and the best means to accomplish this desirable end are those which will rivet the attachment of our citizens to the government of their choice, by the comparative lightness of their public burdens, and by the attraction which the superior success of its operations will present to the admiration and respect of the world. Through the favor of an overruling and indulgent Providence, our country is blessed with general prosperity, and our citizens exempted from the pressure of taxation which other less favored portions of the human family are obliged to bear; yet it is true that many of the taxes collected from our citizens, through the medium of imposts, have for a considerable period been onerous. In many particulars, those taxes have borne severely upon the laboring and less prosperous classes of the community, being imposed on the necessaries of life, and this, too, in cases where the burden was not relieved by the consciousness that it would ultimately contribute to make us independent of foreign nations for articles of prime necessity, by the encouragement of their growth and manufacture at home. They have been cheerfully borne, because they were thought to be necessary to the support of government, and the payment of the debts unavoidably incurred in the acquisition and maintenance of our national rights and privileges. But have we a right to calculate on the same cheerful acquiescence, when it is known that the necessity for their continuance would cease, were it not for the irregular, improvident, and unequal appropriations of the public funds? Will not the people demand, as they have a right to do, such a prudent system of expenditure as will pay the debts of the Union, and authorize the reduction of every tax to as low a point as the wise observance of the necessity to protect that portion of our manufactures and labor, whose prosperity is essential to our national safety and independence, will allow? When the national debt is paid, the duties upon those articles which we do not raise may be repealed with safety, and still leave, I trust, without oppression to any section of the country, an accumulating surplus fund, which may be beneficially applied to some well-digested system of improvement.

Under this view, the question, as to the manner in which the federal government can, or ought to embark in the construction of roads and canals, and the extent to which it may impose burdens on the people for these purposes, may be presented on its own merits, free of all disguise, and of every embarrassment except such as may arise from the constitution itself. Assuming these suggestions to be correct, will not our constituents require the observance of a course by which they can be effected? Ought they not to require it? With the best disposition to aid, as far as I can conscientiously, in the furtherance of works of internal improvement, my opinion is, that the soundest views of national policy, at this time, point to such a course. Besides the avoidance of an evil influence upon the local concerns of the country, how solid is the advantage which the government will reap from it in the elevation of its character! How gratifying the effect of presenting to the world the sublime spectacle of a republic, of more than twelve millions of happy people, in the forty-fourth year of her existence—after having passed through two protracted wars, the one for the acquisition, and the other for the maintenance of liberty—free from debt, and with all her immense resources unfettered! What a salutary influence would not such an exhibition exercise upon the cause of liberal principles and free government throughout the world. Would we not ourselves find, in its effect, an additional guarantee that our political institutions will be transmitted to the most remote posterity without decay? A course of policy destined to witness events like these, can not be benefited by a legislation which tolerates a scramble for appropriations that have no relation to any general system of improvement, and whose good effects must of necessity be very limited. In the best view of these appropriations, the abuses to which they lead far exceed the good which they are capable of promoting. They may be resorted to as artful expedients to shift upon the government the losses of unsuccessful private speculation, and thus, by ministering to personal ambition and self-aggrandizement, tend to sap the foundations of public virtue, and taint the administration of the government with a demoralizing influence.

In the other view of the subject, and the only remaining one which it is my intention to present at this time, is involved the expediency of embarking in a system of internal improvement without a previous amendment of the constitution, explaining and defining the precise powers of the federal government over it. Assuming the right to appropriate money to aid in the construction of national works, to be warranted by the contemporaneous and continued exposition of the constitution, its sufficiency for the successful prosecution of them must be admitted by all candid minds. If we look to usage to define the extent of the right, that will be found so variant, and embracing so much that has been overruled, as to involve the whole subject in great uncertainty, and to render the execution of our respective duties in relation to it replete with difficulty and embarrassment. It is in regard to such works, and the acquisition of additional territory, that the practice obtained its first footing. In most if not all other disputed questions of appropriation, the construction of the constitution may be regarded as unsettled, if the right to apply money, in the enumerated cases, is placed on the ground of usage.

This subject has been one of much, and, I may add, painful reflection to me. It has bearings that are well calculated to exert a powerful influence upon our hitherto prosperous system of government, and which, on some accounts, may even excite despondency in the breast of an American citizen. I will not detain you with professions of zeal in the cause of internal improvements. If to be their friend is a virtue which deserves commendation, our country is blest with an abundance of it; for I do not suppose there is an intelligent citizen who does not wish to see them flourish. But though all are their friends, but few, I trust, are unmindful of the means by which they should be promoted; none certainly are so degenerate as to desire their success at the cost of that sacred instrument, with the preservation of which is indissolubly bound our country's hopes. If different impressions are entertained in any quarter; if it is expected that the people of this country, reckless of their constitutional obligations, will prefer their local interest to the principles of the Union, such expectations will in the end be disappointed; or, if it be not so, then indeed has the world but little to hope from the example of free government. When an honest observance of constitutional compacts can not be obtained from communities like ours, it need not be anticipated elsewhere; and the cause in which there has been so much martyrdom, and from which so much was expected by the friends of liberty, may be abandoned, and the degrading truth, that man is unfit for self-government, admitted. And this will be the case, if *expediency* be made a rule of construction in interpreting the constitution. Power, in no government could desire a better shield for the insidious advances which it is ever ready to make upon the checks that are designed to restrain its action.

But I do not entertain such gloomy apprehensions. If it be the wish of the people that the construction of roads and canals should be conducted by the federal government, it is not only highly expedient, but indispensably necessary, that a previous amendment of the constitution, delegating the necessary power, and defining and restricting its exercise with reference to the sovereignty of the states, should be made. Without it, nothing extensively useful can be effected. The right to exercise as much jurisdiction as is necessary to preserve the works, and to raise funds by the collection of tolls to keep them in repair, can not be dispensed with. The Cumberland road should be an instructive admonition of the consequences of acting without this right. Year after year, contests are witnessed, growing out of efforts to obtain the necessary appropriations for completing and repairing this useful work. While one Congress may claim and exercise the power, a succeeding one may deny it; and this fluctuation of opinion must be unavoidably fatal to any scheme which, from its extent, would promote the interests and elevate the character of the country. The experience of the past has shown that the opinion of Congress is subject to such fluctuations.

If it be the desire of the people that the agency of the federal government should be confined to the appropriation of money in aid of such undertakings, in virtue of state authorities, then the occasion, the manner, and the extent of the appropriations, should be made the subject of constitutional regulation. This is the more necessary, in order that they may be equitable among the several states; promote harmony between different sections of the Union and their representatives; preserve other parts of the constitution from being undermined by the exercise of doubtful powers, or the too great extension of those which are not so; and protect the whole subject against the deleterious influence of combinations to carry, by concert, measures which, considered by themselves, might meet but little countenance. That a constitutional adjustment of this power upon equitable principles is in the highest degree desirable, can scarcely be doubted; nor can it fail to be promoted by every sincere friend to the success of our political institutions. In no government are appeals to the source of power in cases of real doubt more suitable than in ours. No good motive can be assigned for the exercise of power by the constituted authorities, while those for whose benefit it is to be exercised have not conferred it, and may not be willing to confer it. It would seem to me that an honest application of the conceded powers of the general government to the advancement of the common weal, presents a sufficient scope to satisfy a reasonable ambition. The difficulty and supposed impracticability of obtaining an amendment of the constitution in this respect is, I firmly believe, in a great degree unfounded. The time has never yet been when the patriotism and intelligence of the American people were not fully equal to the greatest exigency; and it never will, when the subject calling forth their interposition is plainly presented to them. To do so with the questions involved in this bill, and to urge them to an early, zealous, and full consideration of their deep importance, is, in my estimation, among the highest of our duties.

A supposed connexion between appropriations for internal improvement and the system of protecting duties, growing out of the anxieties of those more immediately interested in their success, has given rise to suggestions which it is proper I should notice on this occasion. My opinions on these subjects have never been concealed from those who had a right to know them. Those which I have entertained on the latter have frequently placed me in opposition to individuals as well as communities, whose claims upon my friendship and gratitude are of the strongest character; but I trust there has been nothing in my public life which has exposed me to the suspicion of being thought capable of sacrificing my views of duty to private considerations, however strong they may have been, or deep the regrets which they are capable of exciting.

As long as the encouragement of domestic manufactures is directed to national ends, it shall receive from me a temperate but steady support. There is no necessary connexion between it and the system of appropriations. On the contrary, it appears to me that the supposition of their dependence upon each other is calculated to excite the prejudices of the public against both. The former is sustained on the ground of its consistency with the letter and spirit of the constitution, of its origin being traced to the assent of all the parties to the original compact, and of its having the support and approbation of a majority of the people; on which account it is at least entitled to a fair experiment. The suggestions to which I have alluded refer to a forced continuance of the national debt, by means of large appropriations, as a substitute for the security which the system derives from the principles on which it has hitherto been sustained. Such a course would certainly indicate either an unreasonable distrust of the people, or a consciousness that the system does not possess sufficient soundness for its support, if left to their voluntary choice and its own merits. Those who suppose that any policy thus founded can be long upheld in this country, have looked upon its history with eyes very different from mine. This policy, like every other, must abide the will of the people, who will not be likely to allow any device, however specious, to conceal its character and tendency.

In presenting these opinions, I have spoken with the freedom and candor which I thought the occasion for their expression called for; and now respectfully return the bill which has been under consideration, for your further deliberation and judgment.

VETO OF THE BANK BILL

Message of President Jackson to the United States Senate, on returning the bank bill with his objections.—July 10, 1832.

To the Senate:

The bill " to modify and continue" the act entitled "An act to incorporate the subscribers to the Bank of the United States," was presented to me on the 4th of July instant. Having considered it with that solemn regard to the principles of the constitution which the day was calculated to inspire, and come to the conclusion that it ought not to become a law, I herewith return it to the Senate, in which it originated, with my objections.

A bank of the United States is, in many respects, convenient for the government, and useful to the people. Entertaining this opinion, and deeply impressed with the belief that some of the powers and privileges possessed by the existing bank are unauthorized by the constitution, subversive of the rights of the states, and dangerous to the liberties of the people, I felt it my duty, at an early period of my administration, to call the attention of Congress to the practicability of organizing an institution combining all its advantages, and obviating these objections. I sincerely regret that, in the act before me, I can perceive none of those modifications of the bank charter which are necessary, in my opinion, to make it compatible with justice, with sound policy, or with the constitution of our country.

The present corporate body, denominated the President, Directors, and Company of the Bank of the United States, will have existed, at the time this act is intended to take effect, twenty years. It enjoys an exclusive privilege of banking under the authority of the general government, a monopoly of its favor and support, and, as a necessary consequence, almost a monopoly of the foreign and domestic exchange. The powers, privileges, and favors bestowed upon it in the original charter, by increasing the value of the stock far above its par value, operated as a gratuity of many millions to the stockholders.

An apology may be found for the failure to guard against this result, in the consideration that the effect of the original act of incorporation could not be certainly foreseen at the time of its passage. The act before me proposes another gratuity to the holders of the same stock, and in many cases to the same men, of at least seven millions more. This donation finds no apology in any uncertainty as to the effect of the act. On all hands, it is conceded, that its passage will increase, at least twenty or thirty per cent. more, the market price of the stock, subject to the payment of the annuity of two hundred thousand dollars per year, secured by the act; thus adding, in a moment, one-fourth to its par value. It is not our own citizens only who are to receive the bounty of our government. More than eight millions of the stock of this bank are held by foreigners. By this act, the American republic proposes virtually to make them a present of some millions of dollars. For these gratuities to foreigners, and to some of our own opulent citizens, the act secures no equivalent whatever. They are the certain gains of the present stockholders, under the operation of this act, after making full allowance for the payment of the bonus.

Every monopoly, and all exclusive privileges, are granted at the expense of the public, which ought to receive a fair equivalent. The many millions which this act proposes to bestow on the stockholders of the existing bank, must come, directly or indirectly, out of the earnings of the American people. It is due to them, therefore, if their government sell monopolies and exclusive privileges, that they should at least exact for them as much as they are worth in open market. The value of the monopoly in this case may be correctly ascertained. The twenty-eight

VETO OF THE BANK BILL 241

millions of stock would probably be at an advance of fifty per cent., and command in market at least forty-two millions of dollars, subject to the payment of the present bonus. The present value of the monopoly, therefore, is seventeen millions of dollars, and this the act proposes to sell for three millions, payable in fifteen annual instalments, of two hundred thousand dollars each.

It is not conceivable how the present stockholders can have any claim to the special favor of the government. The present corporation has enjoyed its monopoly during the period stipulated in the original contract. If we must have such a corporation, why should not the government sell out the whole stock, and thus secure to the people the full market value of the privileges granted? Why should not Congress create and sell twenty-eight millions of stock, incorporating the purchasers with all the powers and privileges secured in this act, and putting the premium upon the sales into the treasury?

But this act does not permit competition in the purchase of this monopoly. It seems to be predicated on the erroneous idea, that the present stockholders have a prescriptive right, not only to the favor, but to the bounty of the government. It appears that more than a fourth part of the stock is held by foreigners, and the residue is held by a few hundred of our citizens, chiefly of the richest class; for their benefit does this act exclude the whole American people from competition in the purchase of this monopoly, and dispose of it for many millions less than it is worth. This seems the less excusable, because some of our citizens, not now stockholders, petitioned that the door of competition might be opened, and offered to take a charter on terms much more favorable to the government and country.

But this proposition, although made by men whose aggregate wealth is believed to be equal to all the private stock in the existing bank, has been set aside, and the bounty of our government is proposed to be again bestowed on the few who have been fortunate enough to secure the stock, and, at this moment, wield the power of the existing institution. I cannot perceive the justice or policy of this course. If our government must sell monopolies, it would seem to be its duty to take nothing less than their full value; and if gratuities must be made once in fifteen or twenty years, let them not be bestowed on the subjects of a foreign government, nor upon a designated or favorable class of men in our own country. It is but justice and good policy, as far as the nature of the case will admit, to confine our favors to our own fellow-citizens, and let each in his turn enjoy an opportunity to profit by our bounty. In the bearings of the act before me upon these points, I find ample reasons why it should not become a law.

It has been urged as an argument in favor of re-chartering the present bank, that calling in its loans will produce great embarrassment and distress. The time allowed to close its concerns is ample, and if it has been well managed its pressure will be light, and heavy only in case its management has been bad. If, therefore, it shall produce distress, the fault will be its own, and it would furnish a reason against renewing a power which has been so obviously abused. But will there ever be a time when this reason will be less powerful? To acknowledge its force is to admit that the bank ought to be perpetual, and as a consequence, the present stockholders, and those inheriting their rights, as successors, be established a privileged order, clothed both with great political power, and enjoying immense pecuniary advantages from their connection with the government.

The modifications of the existing charter, proposed by this act, are not such, in my view, as make it consistent with the rights of the states, or the liberties of the people. The qualification of the right of the bank to hold real estate, the limitation of its power to establish branches, and the power reserved to Congress to forbid the circulation of small notes, are restrictions comparatively of little value or importance. All the objectionable principles of the existing corporation, and most of its odious features, are retained without alleviation.

The fourth section provides "that the notes or bills of the said corporation, although the same be, on the faces thereof, respectively made payable at one place only, shall, nevertheless, be received by the said corporation at the bank, or at any of the offices of discount and deposit thereof, if tendered in liquidation or payment of any balance or balances due to said corporation, or to such office of discount and deposit from any other incorporated bank." This provision secures to the state banks a legal privilege in the Bank of the United States, which is withheld from all private citizens. If a state bank in Philadelphia owe the Bank of the United States, and have notes issued by the St. Louis Branch, it can pay the debt with those notes; but if a merchant, mechanic, or other private citizen, be in like circumstances, he cannot by law pay his debt with those notes, but must sell them at a discount, or send them to St. Louis to be cashed. This boon conceded to the state banks, though not unjust in itself, is most odious, because it does not measure out equal justice to the high and the low, the rich and the poor.

To the extent of its practical effect, it is a bond of union among the banking establishments of the nation, erecting them into an interest separate from that of the people, and its necessary tendency is to unite the Bank of the United States and the state banks, in any measure which may be thought conducive to their common interest.

The ninth section of the act recognises principles of worse tendency than any provision of the present charter.

It enacts that the "cashier of the bank shall annually report to the Secretary of the Treasury the names of all stockholders who are not resident citizens of the United States; and on the application of the treasurer of any state, shall make out, and transmit to such treasurer a list of stockholders residing in, or citizens of such state, with the amount owned by each."

Although this provision, taken in connection with a decision of the Supreme Court, surrenders, by its silence, the right of the states to tax the banking institutions created by this corporation, under the name of branches, throughout the Union, it is evidently intended to be construed as a concession of their right to tax that portion of the stock which may be held by their own citizens and residents. In this light, if the act becomes a law, it will be understood by the states, who will probably proceed to levy a tax equal to that paid upon the stock of banks incorporated by themselves. In some states that tax is now one per cent., either on the capital or on the shares; and that may be assumed as the amount which all citizens or resident stockholders would be taxed under the operation of this act. As it is only the stock held in the states, and not that employed within them, which would be subject to taxation, and as the names of foreign stockholders are not to be reported to the treasurers of the states, it is obvious that the stock held by them will be exempt from this burden. Their annual profits will, therefore, be increased one per cent. more than the citizen stockholders; and as the annual dividends of the bank may be safely estimated at seven per cent., the stock will be worth ten or fifteen per cent. more to foreigners than to citizens of the United States. To appreciate the effect which this state of things will produce, we must take a brief review of the operations and present condition of the Bank of the United States.

By documents submitted to Congress at the present session, it appears that on the 1st of January, 1832, of the 28,000,000 of private stock, in the corporation, 8,405,500 were held by foreigners, mostly of Great Britain. The amount of stock held in the nine Western States is 140,200 dollars; and in the four Southern States is 5,623,100 dollars; and in the Eastern and Middle States about 13,522,000 dollars. The profits of the bank in 1831, as shown in a statement of Congress, were about 3,455,598 dollars; of this there accrued in the nine Western States about 1,640,048 dollars; in the four Southern States about 352,507 dollars; and in the Middle and Eastern States about 1,463,041 dollars. As little stock is held in the West, it is obvious that the debt of the people in that section to the bank is principally a debt to the Eastern and foreign stockholders; that the interest they pay upon it is carried into the Eastern States and into Europe; and that it is a burden upon their industry, and a drain of their currency, which no country can bear without inconvenience and occasional distress. To meet this burden, and equalize the exchange operations of the bank, the amount of specie drawn from those states, through its branches, within the last two years, as shown by its official reports, was about 6,000,000 dollars. More than half a million of this amount does not stop in the Eastern States, but passes on to Europe, to pay the dividends to the foreign stockholders. In the principle of taxation recognised by this act, the western states find no adequate compensation for this perpetual burden on their industry, and drain of their currency. The Branch Bank at Mobile made last year, 95,140 dollars; yet, under the provisions of this act, the state of Alabama can raise no revenue from these profitable operations, because not a share of the stock is held by any of her citizens. Mississippi and Missouri are in the same condition in relation to the branches at Natchez and St. Louis, and such, in a greater or less degree, is the condition of every Western State. The tendency of the plan of taxation which this act proposes, will be to place the whole United States in the same relation to foreign countries which the Western States now bear the Eastern. When, by a tax on resident stockholders, the stock of this bank is made worth ten or fifteen per cent. more to foreigners than to residents, most of it will inevitably leave the country.

Thus will this provision, in its practical effect, deprive the Eastern as well as the Southern and Western states of the means of raising a revenue from the extension of business and great profits of this institution. It will make the American people debtors to aliens, in nearly the whole amount due to this bank, and send across the Atlantic from two to five millions of specie every year, to pay the bank dividends.

In another of its bearings, this provision is fraught with danger. Of the twenty-five directors of this bank, five are chosen by the government, and twenty by the citizen stockholders. From all voice in these elections, the foreign stockholders are excluded by the charter. In proportion, therefore, as the stock is transferred to foreign holders, the extent of suffrage in the choice of directors is curtailed. Already is almost a third of the stock in foreign hands, and not represented in elections. It is constantly passing out of the country, and this act will accelerate its departure. The entire control of the institution would necessarily fall into the hands of a few citizen stockholders, and the ease with which the object would be accomplished, would be a temptation to designing men, to secure that control in their own hands, by monopolizing the remaining stock. There is danger that a president and directors would then be able to elect themselves from year to year, and without responsibility or control, manage the whole concerns of the bank during the existence of the charter. It is easy to conceive that great evils to our country and its institutions might flow from such a concentration of power in the hands of a few men, irresponsible to the people.

Is there no danger to our liberty and independence in a bank, that, in its nature, has so little to bind it to our country? The president of the bank has told us that most of the state banks exist by its forbearance. Should its influence become concentred, as it may under the operation of such an act as this, in the hands of a self-elected directory, whose interests are identified with those of the foreign stockholder, will there not be cause to tremble for the purity of our elections in peace, and for the independence of our country in war? Their power would be great whenever they might choose to exert it; but if this monopoly were regularly renewed every fifteen or twenty years, on terms proposed by themselves, they might seldom in peace put forth their strength to influence elections or control the affairs of the nation; but if any private citizen or public functionary should interpose to curtail its powers, or prevent a renewal of its privileges, it cannot be doubted that he would be made to feel its influence.

Should the stock of the bank principally pass into the hands of the subjects of a foreign country, and we should unfortunately become involved in a war with that country, what would be our condition? Of the course which would be pursued by a bank almost wholly owned by the subjects of a foreign power, and managed by those whose interests, if not affections, would run in the same direction, there can be no doubt. All its operations within would be in aid of the hostile fleets and armies without. Controlling our currency, receiving our public moneys, and holding thousands of our citizens in dependence, it would be more formidable and dangerous than the naval and military power of the enemy.

If we must have a bank with private stockholders, every consideration of sound policy, and every impulse of American feeling, admonishes that it should be purely American. Its stockholders should be composed exclusively of our own citizens, who at least ought to be friendly to our government, and willing to support it in times of difficulty and danger. So abundant is domestic capital, that competition in subscribing for the stock of local banks has recently led almost to riots. To a bank exclusively of American stockholders, possessing the powers and privileges granted by this act, subscriptions for two hundred millions of dollars could be readily obtained. Instead of sending abroad the stock of the bank, in which the government must deposit its funds, and on which it must rely to sustain its credit in times of emergency, it would rather seem to be expedient to prohibit its sale to aliens, under penalty of absolute forfeiture.

It is maintained by the advocates of the bank, that its constitutionality in all its features ought to be considered as settled by precedent, and by the decision of the Supreme Court. To this conclusion I cannot assent. Mere precedent is a dangerous source of authority, and should not be regarded as deciding questions of constitutional power, except where the acquiescence of the people and the states can be considered as well settled. So far from this being the case on this subject, an argument against the bank might be based on precedent. One Congress, in 1791, decided in favor of a bank; another, in 1811, decided against it. One Congress, in 1815, decided against a bank; another, in 1816, decided in its favor. Prior to the present Congress, therefore, the precedents drawn from that source were equal. If we resort to the states, the expressions of legislative, judicial, and executive opinions against the bank have been probably, to those in its favor, as four to one. There is nothing in precedent, therefore, which, if its authority were admitted, ought to weigh in favor of the act before me.

If the opinion of the Supreme Court covered the whole ground of this act, it ought not to control the co-ordinate authorities of this government. The Congress, the Executive, and the Court, must each for itself be guided by its own opinion of the Constitution. Each public officer who takes an oath to support the Constitution, swears that he will support it as he understands it, and not as it is understood by others. It is as much the duty of the House of Representatives, of the Senate, and of the President, to decide upon the constitutionality of any bill or resolution which may be presented to them for passage or approval, as it is of the Supreme Judges, when it may be brought before them for judicial decision. The opinion of the Judges has no more authority over Congress than the opinion of Congress has over the Judges; and, on that point, the President is independent of both. The authority of the Supreme Court must not, therefore, be permitted to control the Congress or the Executive, when acting in their legislative capacities, but to have only such influence as the force of their reasoning may deserve.

But, in the case relied upon, the Supreme Court have not decided that all the features of this corporation are compatible with the Constitution. It is true that the Court have said that the law incorporating the bank is a constitutional exercise of power by Congress. But, taking into view the whole opinion of the Court, and the reasoning by which they have come to that conclusion, I understand them to have decided that, inasmuch as a bank is an appropriate means of carrying into effect the enumerated powers of the general government, therefore the law incorporating it is in accordance with that provision of the Constitution which declares that Congress shall have power " to make all laws which shall be necessary and proper for carrying those powers into execution." Having satisfied themselves that the word " necessary," in the Constitution, means " needful," " requisite," " essential," " conlucive to," and that " a bank" is a convenient, a useful,

VETO OF THE BANK BILL

and essential instrument in the prosecution of the government's "fiscal operations," they conclude that "to use one must be within the discretion of Congress;" and that "the act to incorporate the Bank of the United States, is a law made in pursuance of the Constitution." "But," say they, "where the law is not prohibited, and is really calculated to effect any of the objects intrusted to the government, to undertake here to inquire into the degree of its necessity, would be to pass the line which circumscribes the judicial department, and to tread on legislative ground."

The principle here affirmed is, that "the degree of its necessity," involving all the details of a banking institution, is a question exclusively for legislative consideration. A bank is constitutional; but it is the province of the legislature to determine whether this or that particular power, privilege, or exemption, is "necessary and proper" to enable the bank to discharge its duties to the government, and from their decision there is no appeal to the courts of justice. Under the decision of the Supreme Court, therefore, it is the exclusive province of Congress and the President to decide, whether the particular features of this act are "necessary and proper," in order to enable the bank to perform conveniently and efficiently the public duties assigned to it as a fiscal agent, and therefore constitutional; or *unnecessary* and *improper*, and therefore unconstitutional.

Without commenting on the general principle affirmed by the Supreme Court, let us examine the details of this act, in accordance with the rule of legislative action which they have laid down. It will be found that many of the powers and privileges conferred on it cannot be supposed necessary for the purpose for which it is proposed to be created, and are not, therefore, means necessary to attain the end in view, and consequently not justified by the Constitution.

The original act of corporation, section twenty-first, enacts "that no other bank shall be established by any future law of the United States, during the continuance of the corporation hereby created, for which the faith of the United States is hereby pledged *Provided*, Congress may renew existing charters for banks within the District of Columbia, not increasing the capital thereof, and may also establish any other bank or banks in said District, with capitals not exceeding, in the whole, six millions of dollars, if they shall deem it expedient." This provision is continued in force, by the act before me, fifteen years from the 3d of March, 1836.

If Congress possessed the power to establish one bank, they had power to establish more than one, if, in their opinion, two or more banks had been "necessary" to facilitate the execution of the powers delegated to them by the Constitution. If they possessed the power to establish a second bank, it was a power derived from the Constitution, to be exercised from time to time, and at any time when the interests of the country or the emergencies of the government might make it expedient. It was possessed by one Congress as well as another, and by all Congresses alike, and alike at every session. But the Congress of 1816 have taken it away from their successors for twenty years, and the Congress of 1832 proposed to abolish it for fifteen years more. It cannot be "necessary" or " proper" for Congress to barter away, or divest themselves of any of the powers vested in them by the Constitution, to be exercised for the public good. It is not "necessary" to the efficiency of the bank, nor is it " proper" in relation to themselves and their successors. They may properly use the discretion vested in them, but they may not limit the discretion of their successors. This restriction on themselves, and grant of a monopoly to the bank, is therefore unconstitutional.

In another point of view, this provision is a palpable attempt to amend the Constitution by an act of legislation. The Constitution declares that " the Congress shall have power" to exercise exclusive legislation, in all cases whatsoever, over the District of Columbia. Its constitutional power, therefore, to establish banks in the District of Columbia, and increase their capital at will, is unlimited and uncontrollable by any other power than that which gave authority to the Constitution. Yet this act declares that Congress shall not increase the capital of existing banks nor create other banks with capitals exceeding in the whole six millions of dollars. The Constitution declares that Congress *shall* have power to exercise exclusive legislation over this district, "*in all cases whatsoever;*" and this act declares they *shall not*. Which is the supreme law of the land? This provision cannot be "*necessary*," or "*proper*," or *constitutional*, unless the absurdity be admitted, that whenever it be " necessary and proper," on the opinion of Congress, they have a right to barter away one portion of the powers vested in them by the Constitution, as a means of executing the rest.

On two subjects only does the Constitution recognise in Congress the power to grant exclusive privileges or monopolies. It declares that "Congress shall have power to promote the progress of science and useful arts, by securing, for limited times, to authors and inventors, the exclusive right to their respective writings and discoveries." Out of this express delegation of power, have grown our laws of patents and copyrights. As the Constitution expressly delegates to Congress the power to grant exclusive privileges, in these cases, as the means of executing the substantive power " to promote the progress of science and useful arts," it is consistent with the fair rules of construction to conclude, that such a power was not intended to be granted as a means of accomplishing any other end. On every other subject which comes within the scope of congressional power, there is an ever-living discretion in the use of proper means, which cannot be restricted or abolished without an amendment of the Constitution. Every act of Congress, therefore, which attempts, by grants of monopolies, or sale of exclusive privileges for a limited time, or a time without limit, to restrict or extinguish its own discretion in the choice of means to execute its delegated powers, is equivalent to a legislative amendment of the Constitution, and palpably unconstitutional.

This act authorizes and encourages transfers of its stock to foreigners, and grants them an exemption from all state and national taxation. So far from being " necessary and proper" that the bank should possess this power, to make it a safe and efficient agent of the government in its fiscal operations, it is calculated to convert the Bank of the United States into a foreign bank, to impoverish our people in time of peace, to disseminate a foreign influence through every section of the republic, and, in war, to endanger our independence.

The several states reserved the power, at the formation of the Constitution, to regulate and control titles and transfers of real property; and most, if not all of them, have laws disqualifying aliens from acquiring or holding lands within their limits. But this act, in disregard of the undoubted right of the states to prescribe such disqualifications, gives to aliens, stockholders in this bank, an interest and title, as members of the corporation, to all the real property it may acquire within any of the states of this Union. This privilege granted to aliens is not "necessary" to enable the bank to perform its public duties, nor in any sense "proper," because it is virtually subversive of the rights of the states.

The government of the United States have no constitutional power to purchase lands within the states, except " for the erection of forts, magazines, arsenals, dock-yards, and other needful buildings," and even for these objects, only " by the consent of the legislature of the state in which the same shall be." By making themselves stockholders in the bank, and granting to the corporation the power to purchase lands for other purposes, they assume a power not granted in the Constitution, and grant to others what they do not themselves possess. It is not necessary to the receiving, safe-keeping, or transmission of the funds of government, that the bank should possess this power, and it is not proper that Congress should thus enlarge the powers delegated to them in the Constitution.

The old Bank of the United States possessed a capital of only eleven million of dollars, which was found fully sufficient to enable it, with despatch and safety, to perform all the functions required of it by the government The capital of the present bank is thirty-five millions of dollars, at least twenty-four more than experience has proved to be necessary to enable a bank to perform its public functions. The public debt which existed during the period of the old bank, and on the establishment of the new, has been nearly paid off, and our revenue will soon be reduced. This increase of capital is, therefore, not for public, but for private purposes.

The government is the only "proper" judge where its agents should reside and keep their offices, because it best knows where their presence will be "necessary." It cannot, therefore, be "necessary" or "proper" to authorize the bank to locate branches where it pleases, to perform the public service without consulting the government, and contrary to its will. The principle laid down by the Supreme Court, concedes that Congress cannot establish a bank for purposes of private speculation and gain, but only as a means of executing the delegated powers of the general government. By the same principle, a branch bank cannot constitutionally be established for other than public purposes. The power which this act gives to establish two branches in any state, without the injunction or request of the government, and for other than public purposes, is not "necessary" to the due execution of the powers delegated to Congress.

The bonus which is exacted from the bank, is a confession upon the face of the act, that the powers granted by it are greater than are "necessary" to its character of a fiscal agent. The government does not tax its officers and agents for the privilege of serving it. The bonus of a million and a half, required by the original charter, and that of three millions proposed by this act, are not exacted for the privilege of giving "the necessary facilities for transferring the public funds from place to place, within the United States or the territories thereof, and for distributing the same in payment of the public creditors, without charging commission, or claiming allowance on account of the difference of exchange," as required by the act of incorporation, but for something more beneficial to the stockholders. The original act declares, that it (the bonus) is granted "in consideration of the exclusive privileges and benefits conferred by this act upon the said bank;" and the act before me declares it to be "in consideration of the exclusive benefits and privileges continued by this act to the said corporation for fifteen years as aforesaid." It is, therefore, for "exclusive privileges and benefits," conferred for their own use and emolument, and not for the advantage of the government, that a bonus is exacted. These surplus powers, for which the bank is required to pay, cannot surely be "necessary," to make it the fiscal agent of the treasury. If they were, the exaction of a bonus for them would not be "proper."

It is maintained by some, that the bank is a means of executing the constitutional power "to coin money, and regulate the value thereof." Congress have established a mint to coin money, and passed laws to regulate the value thereof. The money so coined, with its value so regulated, and such foreign coins as Congress may adopt, are the only currency known to the Constitution. But if they have other power to regulate the currency, it was conferred to be exercised by themselves, and not to be transferred to a corporation. If the bank be established for that purpose, with a charter unalterable without its consent, Congress have parted with their power for a term of years, during which the Constitution is a dead letter. It is neither necessary nor proper to transfer its legislative powers to such a bank, and therefore unconstitutional.

By its silence, considered in connection with the decision of the Supreme Court, in the case of McCulloch against the State of Maryland, this act takes from the states the power to tax a portion of the banking business carried on within their limits, in subversion of one of the strongest barriers which secured them against federal encroachments. Banking, like farming, manufacturing, or any other occupation or profession, is a business, the right to follow which is not originally derived from the laws. Every citizen, and every company of citizens, in all of our states, possessed the right, until the state legislatures deemed it good policy to prohibit private banking by law. If the prohibitory state laws were now repealed, every citizen would again possess the right. The state banks are a qualified restoration of the right which has been taken away by the laws against banking, guarded by such provisions and limitations as, in the opinion of the state legislatures, the public interest requires. These corporations, unless there be an exemption in their charter, are, like private bankers and banking companies, subject to state taxation. The manner in which these taxes shall be laid, depends wholly on legislative discretion. It may be upon the bank, upon the stock, upon the profits, or in any other mode which the sovereign power shall will.

Upon the formation of the Constitution, the states guarded their taxing power with peculiar jealousy. They surrendered it only as it regards imports and exports. In relation to every other subject within their jurisdiction, whether persons, property, business, or professions, it was secured in as ample a manner as it was before possessed. All persons, though United States' officers, are liable to a poll tax by the states within which they reside. The lands of the United States are liable to the usual land tax, except in the new states, from whom agreements, that they will not tax unsold lands, are exacted when they are admitted into the Union: horses, wagons, any beasts or vehicles, tools or property, belonging to private citizens, though employed in the service of the United States, are subject to state taxation. Every private business, whether carried on by an officer of the general government or not, whether it be mixed with public concerns or not, even if it be carried on by the government of the United States itself, separately or in partnership, falls within the scope of the taxing power of the state. Nothing comes more fully within it than banks, and the business of banking, by whomsoever instituted and carried on. Over this whole subject-matter, it is just as absolute, unlimited, and uncontrollable, as if the Constitution had never been adopted, because, in the formation of that instrument, it was reserved without qualification.

The principle is conceded, that the states cannot rightfully tax the operations of the general government. They cannot tax the money of the government deposited in the state banks, nor the agency of those banks in remitting it; but will any man maintain that their mere selection to perform this public service for the general government, would exempt the state banks, and their ordinary business, from state taxation? Had the United States, instead of establishing a bank at Philadelphia, employed a private banker to keep and transmit their funds, would it have deprived Pennsylvania of the right to tax his bank and his usual banking operations? It will not be pretended. Upon what principle, then, are the banking establishments of the Bank of the United States, and their usual banking operations, to be exempted from taxation? It is not their public agency, or the deposits of the government, which the states claim a right to tax, but their banks and their banking powers, instituted and exercised within state jurisdiction for their private emolument—those powers and privileges for which they pay a bonus, and which the states tax in their own banks. The exercise of these powers within a state, no matter by whom or under what authority, whether by private citizens in their original right, by corporate bodies created by the states, by foreigners, or the agents of foreign governments located within their limits, forms a legitimate object of state taxation. From this, and like sources, from the persons, property, and business, that are found residing, located, or carried on, under their jurisdiction, must the states, since the surrender of their right to raise a revenue from imports and exports, draw all the money necessary for the support of their governments, and the maintenance of their independence. There is no more appropriate subject of taxation than banks, banking, and bank stock, and none to which the states ought more pertinaciously to cling.

It cannot be necessary to the character of the bank, as a fiscal agent of the government, that its private business should be exempted from that taxation to which all the state banks are liable ; nor can I conceive it " proper" that the substantive and most essential powers reserved by the states shall be thus attacked and annihilated as a means of executing the powers delegated to the general government. It may be safely assumed that none of those sages who had an agency in forming or adopting our Constitution, ever imagined that any portion of the taxing power

VETO OF THE BANK BILL

of the states, not prohibited to them, nor delegated to Congress, was to be swept away and annihilated, as a means of executing certain powers delegated to Congress.

If our power over means is so absolute, that the Supreme Court will not call in question the constitutionality of an act of Congress, the subject of which is "not prohibited, and is really calculated to effect any of the objects intrusted to the government," although, as in the case before me, it takes away powers expressly granted to Congress, and rights scrupulously reserved to the states, it becomes us to proceed in our legislation with the utmost caution. Though not directly, our own powers and the rights of the states may be indirectly legislated away in the use of means to execute substantive powers. We may not enact that Congress shall not have the power of exclusive legislation over the District of Columbia; but we may pledge the faith of the United States, that, as a means of executing other powers, it shall not be exercised for twenty years, or for ever! We may not pass an act prohibiting the states to tax the banking business carried on within their limits; but we may, as a means of executing our powers over other objects, place that business in the hands of our agents, and then declare it exempt from state taxation in their hands! Thus may our own powers, and the rights of the states, which we cannot directly curtail or invade, be frittered away and extinguished in the use of means employed by us to execute other powers. That a Bank of the United States, competent to all the duties which may be required by the government, might be so organized as not to infringe on our own delegated powers, or the reserved rights of the states, I do not entertain a doubt. Had the Executive been called upon to furnish the project of such an institution, the duty would have been cheerfully performed. In the absence of such a call, it was obviously proper that he should confine himself to pointing out those prominent features in the act presented, which, in his opinion, make it incompatible with the Constitution and sound policy. A general discussion will now take place, eliciting new light, and settling important principles; and a new Congress, elected in the midst of such discussion, and furnishing an equal representation of the people, according to the last census, will bear to the Capitol the verdict of public opinion, and, I doubt not, bring this important question to a satisfactory result.

Under such circumstances, the bank comes forward and asks a renewal of its charter for a term of fifteen years, upon conditions which not only operate as a gratuity to the stockholders, of many millions of dollars, but will sanction any abuses, and legalize any encroachments.

Suspicions are entertained, and charges are made, of gross abuse and violation of its charter. An investigation, unwillingly conceded, and so restricted in time as necessarily to make it incomplete and unsatisfactory, disclosed enough to excite suspicion and alarm. In the practices of the principal bank, partially unveiled in the absence of important witnesses, and in numerous charges confidently made, and as yet wholly uninvestigated, there was enough to induce a majority of the committee of investigation, a committee which was selected from the most able and honorable members of the House of Representatives, to recommend a suspension of farther action upon the bill, and a prosecution of the inquiry. As the charter had yet four years to run, and as a renewal now was not necessary to the successful prosecution of its business, it was to have been expected that the bank itself, conscious of its purity, and proud of its character, would have withdrawn its application for the present, and demanded the severest scrutiny into all its transactions. In their declining to do so, there seems to be an additional reason why the functionaries of the government should proceed with less haste, and more caution, in the renewal of their monopoly.

The bank is professedly established as an agent of the executive branches of the government, and its constitutionality is maintained on that ground. Neither upon the propriety of present action, nor upon the provisions of this act, was the Executive consulted. It has had no opportunity to say, that it neither needs nor wants an agent clothed with such powers, and favored by such exemptions. There is nothing in its legitimate functions which makes it necessary or proper. Whatever interest or influence, whether public or private, has given birth to this act, it cannot be found either in the wishes or necessities of the Executive Department, by which present action is deemed premature, and the powers conferred upon its agent not only unnecessary, but dangerous to the government and country.

It is to be regretted that the rich and powerful too often bend the acts of government to their selfish purposes. Distinctions in society will always exist under every just government. Equality of talents, of education, or of wealth, cannot be produced by human institutions. In the full enjoyment of the gifts of Heaven, and the fruits of superior industry, economy, and virtue, every man is equally entitled to protection by law. But when the laws undertake to add to these natural and just advantages artificial distinctions—to grant titles, gratuities, and exclusive privileges—to make the rich richer, and the potent more powerful—the humble members of society, the farmers, mechanics, and laborers, who have neither the time nor the means of securing like favors to themselves, have a right to complain of the injustice of their government. There are no necessary evils in government. Its evils exist only in its abuses. If it would confine itself to equal protection, and, as Heaven does its rains, shower its favors alike on the high and the low, the rich and the poor, it would be an unqualified blessing. In the act before me, there seems to be a wide and unnecessary departure from these just principles.

Nor is our government to be maintained, or our Union preserved, by invasions of the rights and powers of the several states. In thus attempting to make our general government strong, we make it weak. Its true strength consists in leaving individuals and states, as much as possible, to themselves; in making itself felt, not in its power, but in its beneficence—not in its control, but in its protection—not in binding the states more closely to the centre, but leaving each to move, unobstructed, in its proper orbit.

Experience should teach us wisdom. Most of the difficulties our government now encounters, and most of the dangers which impend over our Union, have sprung from an abandonment of the legitimate objects of government by our national legislation, and the adoption of such principles as are imbodied in this act. Many of our rich men have not been content with equal protection and equal benefits, but have besought us to make them richer by acts of Congress. By attempting to gratify their desires, we have, in the results of our legislation, arrayed section against section, interest against interest, and man against man, in a fearful commotion, which threatens to shake the foundations of our Union. It is time to pause in our career, to review our principles, and, if possible, revive that devoted patriotism, and spirit of compromise, which distinguished the sages of the Revolution and the fathers of our Union. If we cannot, at once, in justice to interests vested under improvident legislation, make our government what it ought to be, we can, at least, take a stand against all new grants of monopolies and exclusive privileges, against any prostitution of our government to the advancement of the few at the expense of the many, and in favor of compromise and gradual reform in our code of laws and system of political economy.

I have now done my duty to my country. If sustained by my fellow-citizens, I shall be grateful and happy : if not, I shall find in the motives which impel me, ample grounds for contentment and peace. In the difficulties which surround us, and the dangers which threaten our institutions, there is cause for neither dismay or alarm. For relief and deliverance, let us firmly rely on that kind Providence which, I am sure, watches with peculiar care over the destinies of our republic, and on the intelligence and wisdom of our countrymen. Through *His* abundant goodness, and *their* patriotic devotion, our liberty and Union will be preserved.

Proclamation on the Nullification Question.—December 11, 1832.

WHEREAS, a Convention assembled in the State of South Carolina, having passed an ordinance by which they declare, "That the several acts and parts of acts of the Congress of the United States, purporting to be laws for the imposing of duties and imposts on the importation of foreign commodities, and now having actual operation and effect within the United States, and more especially," two acts for the same purpose, passed on the 29th of May, 1828, and on the 14th of July, 1832, "are unauthorized by the Constitution of the United States, and violate the true meaning and intent thereof, and are null and void, and no law," nor binding on the citizens of that state or its officers: and by the said ordinance, it is further declared to be unlawful for any of the constituted authorities of the state, or of the United States, to enforce the payment of the duties imposed by the said acts within the same state, and that it is the duty of the legislature to pass such laws as may be necessary to give full effect to the said ordinance:

And whereas, by the said ordinance, it is further ordained, that in no case, of law or equity, decided in the courts of said state, wherein shall be drawn in question the validity of the said ordinance, or of the acts of the legislature that may be passed to give it effect, or of the said laws of the United States, no appeal shall be allowed to the Supreme Court of the United States, nor shall any copy of the record be permitted or allowed for that purpose, and that any person attempting to take such appeal shall be punished as for a contempt of court:

And, finally, the said ordinance declares, that the people of South Carolina will maintain the said ordinance at every hazard; and that they will consider the passage of any act by Congress, abolishing or closing the ports of the said state, or otherwise obstructing the free ingress or egress of vessels to and from the said ports, or any other act of the federal government to coerce the state, shut up her ports, destroy or harass her commerce, or to enforce the said acts otherwise than through the civil tribunals of the country, as inconsistent with the longer continuance of South Carolina in the Union; and that the people of the said state will thenceforth hold themselves absolved from all further obligation to maintain or preserve their political connection with the people of the other states, and will forthwith proceed to organize a separate government, and do all other acts and things which sovereign and independent states may of right do:

And whereas, the said ordinance prescribes to the people of South Carolina a course of conduct, in direct violation of their duty as citizens of the United States, contrary to the laws of their country, subversive of its Constitution, and having for its object the destruction of the Union—that Union, which, coeval with our political existence, led our fathers, without any other ties to unite them than those of patriotism and a common cause, through a sanguinary struggle to a glorious independence—that sacred Union, hitherto inviolate, which, perfected by our happy Constitution, has brought us, by the favor of Heaven, to a state of prosperity at home, and high consideration abroad, rarely, if ever, equalled in the history of nations: To preserve this bond of our political existence from destruction, to maintain inviolate this state of national honor and prosperity, and to justify the confidence my fellow-citizens have reposed in me, I, ANDREW JACKSON, President of the United States, have thought proper to issue this my *Proclamation*, stating my views of the Constitution and laws applicable to the measures adopted by the Convention of South Carolina, and to the reasons they have put forth to sustain them, declaring the course which duty will require me to pursue, and, appealing to the understanding and patriotism of the people, warn them of the consequences that must inevitably result from an observance of the dictates of the Convention.

Strict duty would require of me nothing more than the exercise of those powers with which I am now, or may hereafter be invested, for preserving the peace of the Union, and for the execution of the laws. But the imposing aspect which opposition has assumed in this case, by clothing itself with state authority, and the deep interest which the people of the United States must all feel in preventing a resort to stronger measures, while there is a hope that any thing will be yielded to reasoning and remonstrance, perhaps demand, and will certainly justify, a full exposition to South Carolina and the nation, of the views I entertain of this important question, as well as a distinct enunciation of the course which my sense of duty will require me to pursue.

The ordinance is founded, not on the indefeasible right of resisting acts which are plainly unconstitutional and too oppressive to be endured; but on the strange position that any one state may not only declare an act of Congress void, but prohibit its execution; that they may do this consistently with the Constitution; that the true construction of that instrument permits a state to retain its place in the Union, and yet be bound by no other of its laws than it may choose to consider constitutional. It is true, they add, that to justify this abrogation of a law, it must be palpably contrary to the Constitution; but it is evident, that to give the right of resisting laws of that description, coupled with the uncontrolled right to decide what laws deserve that character, is to give the power of resisting all laws. For, as by the theory, there is no appeal, the reasons alleged by the state, good or bad, must prevail. If it should be said that public opinion is a sufficient check against the abuse of this power, it may be asked why it is not deemed a sufficient guard against the passage of an unconstitutional act by Congress. There is, however, a restraint in this last case, which makes the assumed power of a state more indefensible, and which does not exist in the other. There are two appeals from an unconstitutional act passed by Congress—one to the judiciary, the other to the people and the states. There is no appeal from the state decision in theory, and the practical illustration shows that the courts are closed against an application to review it, both judge and jurors being sworn to decide in its favor. But reasoning on this subject is superfluous, when our social compact in express terms declares, that the laws of the United States, its Constitution and treaties made under it, are the supreme law of the land—and for greater caution adds, "that the judges in every state shall be bound thereby, any thing in the Constitution or laws of any state to the contrary notwithstanding." And it may be asserted without fear of refutation, that no federative government could exist without a similar provision. Look for a moment to the consequences. If South Carolina considers the revenue laws unconstitutional, and has a right to prevent their execution in the port of Charleston, there would be a clear constitutional objection to their collection in every other port, and no revenue could be collected anywhere; for all imposts must be equal. It is no answer to repeat, that an unconstitutional law is no law, so long as the question of its legality is to be decided by the state itself; for every law operating injuriously upon any local interest, will be perhaps thought, and certainly represented, as unconstitutional, and, as has been shown, there is no appeal.

If this doctrine had been established at an earlier day, the Union would have been dissolved in its infancy. The excise law in Pennsylvania, the embargo and non-intercourse law in the Eastern States, the carriage tax in Virginia, were all deemed unconstitutional, and were more unequal in their operation than any of the laws now complained of; but fortunately none of those states discovered that they had the right now claimed by South Carolina. The war into which we were forced, to support the dignity of the nation and the rights of our citizens, might have ended in defeat and disgrace, instead of victory and honor, if the states who supposed it a ruinous and unconstitutional measure, had thought they possessed the right of nullifying the act by which it was declared, and denying supplies for its prosecution. Hardly and unequally as those measures bore upon several members of the Union, to the legislatures of none did this efficient and peaceable remedy, as it is called, suggest itself. The discovery of this important feature in our Constitution was reserved for the present day. To the statesmen of South Carolina belongs the invention, and upon the citizens of that state will unfortunately fall the evil of reducing it to practice.

If the doctrine of a state veto upon the laws of the Union carries with it internal evidence of its impracticable absurdity, our constitutional history will also afford abundant proof that it would have been repudiated with indignation, had it been proposed to form a feature in our government.

In our colonial state, although dependent on another power, we very early considered ourselves as connected by common interest with each other. Leagues were formed for common defence, and before the Declaration of Independence we were known in our aggregate character as the UNITED COLONIES OF AMERICA. That decisive and important step was taken jointly. We declared ourselves a nation, by a joint, not by several acts, and when the terms of confederation were reduced to form, it was in that of a solemn league of several states by which they agreed, that they would collectively form one nation for the purpose of conducting some certain domestic concerns and all foreign relations. In the instrument forming that union is found an article which declares that, "every state shall abide by the determination of Congress on all questions which by that confederation should be submitted to them."

Under the Confederation, then, no state could legally annul a decision of the Congress, or refuse to submit to its execution; but no provision was made to enforce these decisions. Congress made requisitions, but they were not complied with. The government could not operate on individuals. They had no judiciary, no means of collecting revenue.

But the defects of the Confederation need not be detailed. Under its operation we could scarcely be called a nation. We had neither prosperity at home, nor consideration abroad. This state of things could not be endured, and our present happy Constitution was formed, but formed in vain if this fatal doctrine prevails. It was formed for important objects that are announced in the preamble, made in the name and by the authored of the people of the United States, whose delegates framed and whose conventions approved it. The most important among these objects, that which is placed first in rank, on which all others rest, is "TO FORM A MORE PERFECT UNION." Now, is it possible that even if there were no express provisions giving supremacy to the Constitution and Laws of the United States over those of the states—can it be conceived that an instrument made for the purpose of "FORMING A MORE PERFECT UNION" than that of the Confederation, could be so constructed by the assembled wisdom of our country as to substitute for that confederation a form of government dependent for its existence on the local interest, the party spirit of a state, or of a prevailing faction in a state? Every man of plain, unsophisticated understanding, who hears the question, will give such an answer as will preserve the Union. Metaphysical subtlety, in pursuit of an impracticable theory, could alone have devised one that is calculated to destroy it.

I consider then the power to annul a law of the United States, assumed by one state, INCOMPATIBLE WITH THE EXISTENCE OF THE UNION, CONTRADICTED EXPRESSLY BY THE LETTER OF THE CONSTITUTION, UNAUTHORIZED BY ITS SPIRIT, INCONSISTENT WITH EVERY PRINCIPLE ON WHICH IT WAS FOUNDED, AND DESTRUCTIVE OF THE GREAT OBJECT FOR WHICH IT WAS FORMED.

After this general view of the leading principle, we must examine the particular application of it which is made in the ordinance.

The preamble rests its justification on these grounds: It assumes as a fact, that the obnoxious laws, although they purport to be laws for raising revenue, were in reality intended for the protection of manufactures, which purpose it asserts to be unconstitutional; that the operation of these laws is unequal; that the amount raised by them is greater than is required by the wants of the government: and finally, that the proceeds are to be applied to objects un-

PROCLAMATION

authorized by the Constitution. These are the only causes alleged to justify an open opposition to the laws of the country, and a threat of seceding from the Union, if any attempt should be made to enforce them. The first virtually acknowledges, that the law in question was passed under a power expressly given by the Constitution, to lay and collect imposts: but its constitutionality is drawn in question from the motives of those who passed it. However apparent this purpose may be in the present case, nothing can be more dangerous than to admit the position that an unconstitutional purpose, entertained by the members who assent to a law enacted under a constitutional power, shall make that law void; for how is that purpose to be ascertained? Who is to make the scrutiny? How often may bad purposes be falsely imputed—in how many cases are they concealed by false professions—in how many is no declaration of motives made? Admit this doctrine, and you give to the states an uncontrolled right to decide, and every law may be annulled under this pretext. If, therefore, the absurd and dangerous doctrine should be admitted, that a state may annul an unconstitutional law, or one that it deems such, it will not apply to the present case.

The next objection is, that the laws in question operate unequally. This objection may be made with truth, to every law that has been or can be passed. The wisdom of man never yet contrived a system of taxation that would operate with perfect equality. If the unequal operation of a law makes it unconstitutional, and if all laws of that description may be abrogated by any state for that cause, then indeed is the Federal Constitution unworthy of the slightest effort for its preservation. We have hitherto relied on it as the perpetual bond of our union. We have received it as the work of the assembled wisdom of the nation. We have trusted to it as to the sheet anchor of our safety in the stormy times of conflict with a foreign or domestic foe. We have looked to it with sacred awe as the palladium of our liberties, and with all the solemnities of religion have pledged to each other our lives and fortunes here, and our hopes of happiness hereafter, in its defence and support. Were we mistaken, my countrymen, in attaching this importance to the Constitution of our country? Was our devotion paid to the wretched, inefficient, clumsy contrivance which this new doctrine would make it? Did we pledge ourselves to the support of an airy nothing, a bubble that must be blown away by the first breath of disaffection? Was this self-destroying, visionary theory, the work of the profound statesmen, the exalted patriots, to whom the task of constitutional reform was intrusted? Did the name of Washington sanction, did the states ratify, such an anomaly in the history of fundamental legislation? No. We were not mistaken. The letter of this great instrument is free from this radical fault: its language directly contradicts the imputation: its spirit—its evident intent, contradicts it. No; we do not err! Our Constitution does not contain the absurdity of giving power to make laws, and another power to resist them. The sages whose memory will always be reverenced, have given us a practical, and, as they hoped, a permanent constitutional compact. The father of his country did not affix his revered name to so palpable an absurdity. Nor did the states, when they severally ratified it, do so under the impression that a veto on the laws of the United States was reserved to them, or that they could exercise it by implication. Search the debates in all their conventions—examine the speeches of the most zealous opposers of federal authority—look at the amendments that were proposed—they are all silent —not a syllable uttered, not a vote given, not a motion made, to correct the explicit supremacy given to the laws of the Union over those of the states—or to show that implication, as is now contended, could defeat it. No; we have not erred! The Constitution is still the object of our reverence, the bond of our union, our defence in danger, the source of our prosperity in peace. It shall descend, as we have received it, uncorrupted by sophistical construction, to our posterity; and the sacrifices of local interest, of state prejudices, of personal animosities, that were made to bring it into existence, will again be patriotically offered for its support.

The two remaining objections made by the ordinance to these laws are, that the sums intended to be raised by them are greater than required, and that the proceeds will be unconstitutionally employed.

The Constitution has given expressly to Congress the right of raising revenue, and of determining the sum the public exigencies will require. The states have no control over the exercise of this right, other than that which results from the power of changing the representatives who abuse it; and thus procure redress. Congress may undoubtedly abuse this discretionary power, but the same may be said of others with which they are vested. Yet the discretion must exist somewhere. The Constitution has given it to the representatives of all the people, checked by the representatives of the states and by the executive power. The South Carolina construction gives it to the legislature, or the convention of a single state, where neither the people of the different states, nor the states in their separate capacity, nor the chief magistrate elected by the people, have any representation. Which is the most discreet disposition of the power? I do not ask you, fellow-citizens, which is the constitutional disposition—that instrument speaks a language not to be misunderstood. But if you were assembled in general convention, which would you think the safest depository of this discretionary power in the last resort? Would you add a clause giving it to each of the states, or would you sanction the wise provisions already made by your Constitution? If this should be the result of your deliberations when providing for the future, are you, can you be ready, to risk all that we hold dear, to establish, for a temporary and a local purpose, that which you must acknowledge to be destructive, and even absurd, as a general provision? Carry out the consequences of this right vested in the different states, and you must perceive that the crisis your conduct presents at this day would recur whenever any law of the United States displeased any of the states, and that we should soon cease to be a nation.

The ordinance, with the same knowledge of the future that characterizes a former objection, tells you that the proceeds of the tax will be unconstitutionally applied. If this could be ascertained with certainty, the objection would, with more propriety, be reserved for the laws so applying the proceeds, but surely cannot be urged against the law levying the duty.

These are the allegations contained in the ordinance. Examine them seriously, my fellow-citizens.—judge for yourselves. I appeal to you to determine whether they are so clear, so convincing, as to leave no doubt of their correctness; and even if you should come to this conclusion, how far they justify the reckless, destructive course which you are directed to pursue. Review these objections, and the conclusions drawn from them, once more. What are they? Every law, then, for raising revenue, according to the South Carolina ordinance, may be rightfully annulled, unless it be so framed as no law ever will or can be framed. Congress have a right to pass laws for raising revenue, and each state has a right to oppose their execution—two rights directly opposed to each other—and yet is this absurdity supposed to be contained in an instrument drawn for the express purpose of avoiding collisions between the states and the general government, by an assembly of the most enlightened statesmen and purest patriots ever imbodied for a similar purpose.

In vain have these sages declared that Congress shall have power to lay and collect taxes, duties, imposts, and excises—in vain have they provided that they shall have power to pass laws which shall be necessary and proper to carry those powers into execution; that those laws and that Constitution shall be the "supreme law of the land, and that the judges in every state shall be bound thereby, any thing in the constitution or laws of any state to the contrary, notwithstanding." In vain have the people of the several states solemnly sanctioned these provisions made them their paramount law, and individually sworn to support them whenever they were called on to execute any office. Vain provisions! ineffectual restrictions! vile profanation of oaths! miserable mockery of legislation! if a bare majority of the voters in any one state may, on a real or supposed knowledge of the intent in which a law has been passed, declare themselves free from its operations—say here it gives too little, there too much, and operates unequally—here it suffers articles to be free that ought to be taxed—there it taxes those that ought to be free—in this case the proceeds are intended to be applied to purposes which we do not approve—in that, the amount raised is more than is wanted. Congress, it is true, are invested by the Constitution with the right of deciding these questions according to their sound discretion; Congress is composed of the representatives of all the states and of all the people of all the states; but, WE, part of the people of one state, to whom the Constitution has given no power on the subject, from whom it has expressly taken it away—WE, who have solemnly agreed that this Constitution shall be our law—WE, most of whom have sworn to support it—WE now abrogate this law and swear, and force others to swear, that it shall not be obeyed! And we do this, not because Congress have no right to pass such laws; this we do not allege; but because they have passed them with improper views. They are unconstitutional from the motives of those who passed them, which we can never with certainty know—from their unequal operation, although it is impossible from the nature of things that they should be equal—and from the disposition which we presume may be made of their proceeds, although that disposition has not been declared. This is the plain meaning of the ordinance in relation to laws which it abrogates for alleged unconstitutionality. But it does not stop there. It repeals, in express terms, an important part of the Constitution itself, and of laws passed to give it effect, which have never been alleged to be unconstitutional. The Constitution declares that the judicial powers of the United States extend to cases arising under the laws of the United States, and that such laws, the Constitution and treaties, shall be paramount to the state constitutions and laws. The judiciary act prescribes the mode by which the case may be brought before a court of the United States, by appeal, when a state tribunal shall decide against this provision of the Constitution. The ordinance declares there shall be no appeal

—makes the state law paramount to the Constitution and laws of the United States—forces judges and jurors to swear that they will disregard their provisions; and even makes it penal in a suitor to attempt relief by appeal. It further declares that it shall not be lawful for the authorities of the United States, or of that state, to enforce the payment of duties imposed by the revenue laws within its limits.

Here is a law of the United States not even pretended to be unconstitutional, repealed by the authority of a small majority of the voters of a single state. Here is a provision of the Constitution which is solemnly abrogated by the same authority.

On such expositions and reasonings the ordinance grounds not only an assertion of the right to annul the laws of which it complains, but to enforce it by a threat of seceding from the Union if any attempt is made to execute them.

This right to secede is deduced from the nature of the Constitution, which they say is a compact between sovereign states, who have preserved their whole sovereignty, and, therefore, are subject to no superior; that because they made the compact, they can break it, when, in their opinion, it has been departed from by the other states. Fallacious as this course of reasoning is, it enlists state pride, and finds advocates in the honest prejudices of those who have not studied the nature of our government sufficiently to see the radical error on which it rests.

The people of the United States formed the Constitution, acting through the state legislatures in making the compact, to meet and discuss its provisions, and acting in separate conventions when they ratified those provisions; but the terms used in its construction, show it to be a government in which the people of all the states collectively are represented. We are one people in the choice of a President and Vice-President. Here the states have no other agency than to direct the mode in which the votes shall be given. The candidates having the majority of all the votes are chosen. The electors of a majority of the states may have given their votes for one candidate, and yet another may be chosen. The people, then, and not the states, are represented in the executive branch.

In the House of Representatives there is this difference, that the people of one state do not, as in the case of President and Vice-President, all vote for the same officers. The people of all the states do not vote for all the members, each state electing only its own representatives. But this creates no material distinction. When chosen, they are all representatives of the United States, not representatives of the particular state from which they come. They are paid by the United States, not by the state; nor are they accountable to it for any act done in the performance of their legislative functions; and however they may, in practice, as it is their duty to do, consult and prefer the interests of their particular constituents when they come in conflict with any other partial or local interest, yet it is their first and highest duty, as Representatives of the United States, to promote the general good.

The Constitution of the United States then forms a government, not a league, and whether it be formed by compact between the states, or in any other manner, its character is the same. It is a government in which all the people are represented, which operates directly on the people individually, not upon the state—they retained all the power they did not grant. But each state having expressly parted with so many powers, as to constitute jointly with the other states a single nation, cannot from that period possess any right to secede, because such secession does not break a league, but destroys the unity of a nation, and any injury to that unity is not only a breach which would result from the contravention of a compact, but it is an offence against the whole Union. To say that any state may at pleasure secede from the Union, is to say that the United States are not a nation, because it would be a solecism to contend that any part of a nation might dissolve its connection with the other parts, to their injury or ruin, without committing any offence. Secession, like any other revolutionary act, may be morally justified by the extremity of oppression; but to call it a constitutional right, is confounding the meaning of terms, and can only be done through gross error, or to deceive those who are willing to assert a right, but would pause before they made a revolution, or incur the penalties consequent on a failure.

Because the Union was formed by compact, it is said the parties to that compact may, when they feel themselves aggrieved, depart from it, but it is precisely because it is a compact that they cannot. A compact is an agreement or binding obligation. It may by its terms have a sanction or penalty for its breach, or it may not. If it contains no sanction, it may be broken with no other consequence than moral guilt; if it have a sanction, then the breach incurs the designated or implied penalty. A league between independent nations, generally, has no sanction other than a moral one; or if it should contain a penalty, as there is no common superior, it cannot be enforced. A government, on the contrary, always has a sanction express or implied, and in our case, it is both necessarily implied and expressly given. An attempt by force of arms to destroy a government, is an offence, by whatever means the constitutional compact may have been formed; and such government has the right, by the law of self-defence, to pass acts for punishing the offender, unless that right is modified, restrained, or resumed by the constitutional act. In our system, although it is modified in the case of treason, yet authority is expressly given to pass all laws necessary to carry its powers into effect, and under this grant, provision has been made for punishing acts which obstruct the due administration of the laws.

It would seem superfluous to add any thing to show the nature of that union which connects us; but as erroneous opinions on this subject are the foundation of doctrines the most destructive to our peace, I must give some further development to my views on this subject. No one, fellow-citizens, has a higher reverence for the reserved rights of the states than the magistrate who now addresses you. No one would make greater personal sacrifices, or official exertions, to defend them from violation, but equal care must be taken to prevent on their part an improper interference with, or resumption of the rights they have vested in the nation. The line has not been so distinctly drawn as to avoid doubts in some cases of the exercise of power. Men of the best intentions and soundest views may differ in the construction of some parts of the Constitution; but there are others on which dispassionate reflection can leave no doubt. Of this nature appears to be the assumed right of secession. It rests, as we have seen, on the alleged undivided sovereignty of the states, and on their having formed in this sovereign capacity a compact which is called the Constitution, from which, because they made it, they have the right to secede. Both of these positions are erroneous, and some of the arguments to prove them so have been anticipated.

The states severally have not retained their entire sovereignty. It has been shown that in becoming parts of a nation, not members of a league, they surrendered many of their essential parts of sovereignty. The right to make treaties, declare war, levy taxes, exercise exclusive judicial and legislative powers, were all of them functions of sovereign power. The states, then, for all these important purposes, were no longer sovereign. The allegiance with their citizens was transferred in the first instance to the government of the United States; they became American citizens, and owed obedience to the Constitution of the United States, and to laws made in conformity with powers it vested in Congress. This last position has not been, and cannot be denied. How then can that state be said to be sovereign and independent whose citizens owe obedience to laws not made by it, and whose magistrates are sworn to disregard those laws, when they come in conflict with those passed by another? What shows conclusively that the states cannot be said to have reserved an undivided sovereignty, is that they expressly ceded the right to punish treason, not treason against their separate power, but treason against the United States. Treason is an offence against SOVEREIGNTY, and sovereignty must reside with the power to punish it. But the reserved rights of the states are not the less sacred because they have for the common interest made the general government the depository of these powers. The unity of our political character (as has been shown for another purpose) commenced with its very existence. Under the royal government, we had no separate character; our opposition to its oppressions began as UNITED COLONIES. We were the UNITED STATES under the Confederation, and the name was perpetuated and the Union rendered more perfect by the Federal Constitution. In none of these stages did we consider ourselves in any other light than as forming one nation. Treaties and alliances were made in the name of all. Troops were raised for the joint defence. How, then, with all these proofs, that under all changes of our position we had, for designated purposes, and with defined powers, created national governments; how is it that the most perfect of those several modes of union should now be considered as a mere league that may be dissolved at pleasure? It is from an abuse of terms. Compact is used as synonymous with league, although the true term is not employed, because it would at once show the fallacy of the reasoning. It would not do to say that our Constitution was only a league, but, it is labored to prove it a compact, (which in one sense it is,) and then to argue that as a league is a compact, every compact between nations must of course be a league, and that from such an engagement every sovereign power has a right to recede. But it has been shown, that in this sense the states are not sovereign, and that even if they were, and the National Constitution had been formed by compact, there would be no right in any one state to exonerate itself from its obligations.

So obvious are the reasons which forbid this secession, that it is necessary only to allude to them. The Union was formed for the benefit of all. It was produced by mutual sacrifices of interests and opinion. Can those sacrifices be recalled? Can the states, who magnanimously surrendered their title to the territories of the west, recall the grant? Will the inhabitants of the inland states agree to pay the duties that may be imposed without their assent by those on the Atlantic or the gulf, for their own benefit? Shall there be a free port in one state and onerous duties in another? No one believes that any right exists in a single state to involve all the others in these and countless other evils, contrary to engagements solemnly made. Every one must see that the other states, in self-defence, must oppose it at all hazards.

These are the alternatives that are presented by the Convention; a repeal of all the acts for raising revenue, leaving the government without the means of support; or an acquiescence in the dissolution of our Union by the secession of one of its members. When the first was proposed, it was known that it could not be listened to for a moment. It was known if force was applied to oppose the execution of the laws, that it must be repelled by force —that Congress could not, without involving itself in disgrace and the country in ruin, accede to the proposition; and yet if this is done on a given day, or if any attempt is made to execute the laws, the state is, by the ordinance, declared to be out of the Union.

The majority of a Convention assembled for the purpose, have dictated these terms, or rather its rejection of all terms, in the name of the people of South Carolina. It is true that the Governor of the state speaks of submission of their grievances to a Convention of all the states; which he says they "sincerely and anxiously seek and desire." Yet this obvious and constitutional mode of obtaining the sense of the other states on the construction of the federal compact, and amending it, if necessary, has never been attempted by those who have urged the state on to this destructive measure. The state might have proposed the call for a general Convention to the other states; and Congress, if a sufficient number of them concurred, must have called it.

But the first magistrate of South Carolina, when he expressed a hope that, "on a review by Congress and the functionaries of the general government of the merits of the controversy," such a Convention will be accorded to them, must have known that neither Congress nor any functionary of the general government has authority to call such a Convention, unless it be demanded by two-thirds of the states. This suggestion, then, is another instance of a reckless inattention to the provisions of the Constitution with which this crisis has been madly hurried on; or of the attempt to persuade the people that a constitutional remedy had been sought and refused. If the legislature of South Carolina "anxiously desire" a general Convention to consider their complaints, why have they not made application for it in the way the Constitution points out? The assertion that they "earnestly seek it" is completely negatived by the omission.

This, then, is the position in which we stand. A small majority of the citizens of one state in the Union have elected delegates to a State Convention; that Convention has ordained that all the revenue laws of the United States must be repealed, or that they are no longer a member of the Union. The Governor of that state has recommended to the legislature the raising of an army to carry the secession into effect, and that he may be empowered to give clearances to vessels in the name of the state. No act of violent opposition to the laws has yet been committed, but such a state of things is hourly apprehended, and it is the intent of this instrument to PROCLAIM not only the duty imposed on me by the Constitution " to take care that the laws be faithfully executed," shall be performed to the extent of the powers already vested in me by law, or of such others as the wisdom of Congress shall devise and intrust to me for that purpose; but to warn the citizens of South Carolina, who have been deluded into an opposition to the laws, of the danger they will incur by obedience to the illegal and disorganizing ordinance of the Convention—to exhort those who have refused to support it, to persevere in their determination to uphold the Constitution and laws of their country—and to point out to all, the perilous situation into which the good people of that state have been led—and that the course they are urged to pursue is one of ruin and disgrace to the very state whose rights they affect to support.

Fellow-citizens of my native state!—let me not only admonish you, as the first Magistrate of our common country, not to incur the penalty of its laws, but use the influence that a father would over his children, whom he saw rushing to certain ruin. In that paternal language, with that paternal feeling, let me tell you, my countrymen, that you are deluded by men who are either deceived themselves, or wish to deceive you. Mark under what pretences you have been led on to the brink of insurrection and treason, on which you stand! First, a diminution of the value of your staple commodity lowered by over production in other quarters, and the consequent diminution in the value of your lands, were the sole effect of the tariff laws. The effect of those laws was confessedly injurious, but the evil was greatly exaggerated by the unfounded theory you were taught to believe, that its burdens were in proportion to your exports, not to your consumption of imported articles. Your pride was roused by the assertion that a submission to those laws was a state of vassalage, and that resistance to them was equal, in patriotic merit, to the opposition our fathers offered to the oppressive laws of Great Britain. You were told that this opposition might be peaceably—might be constitutionally made—that you might enjoy all the advantages of the Union and bear none of its burdens. Eloquent appeals to your passions, to your state pride, to your native courage, to your sense of real injury, were used to prepare you for the period when the mask which concealed the hideous features of DISUNION should be taken off. It fell, and you were made to look with complacency on objects which not long since you would have regarded with horror. Look back at the arts which have brought you to this state; look forward to the consequences to which it must inevitably lead! Look back to what was first told you as an inducement to enter into this dangerous course. The great political truth was repeated to you, that you had the revolutionary right of resisting all laws that were palpably unconstitutional and intolerably oppressive—it was added that the right to nullify a law rested on the same principle, but that it was a peaceable remedy! This character which was given to it, made you receive with too much confidence the assertions that were made of the unconstitutionality of the law and its oppressive effects.

Mark, my fellow-citizens, that by the admission of your leaders, the unconstitutionality must be palpable, or it will not justify either resistance or nullification! What is the meaning of the word *palpable* in the sense in which it is here used?—that which is apparent to every one, that which no man of ordinary intellect will fail to perceive. Is the unconstitutionality of these laws of that description? Let those among your leaders who once approved and advocated the principle of protective duties answer the question; and let them choose whether they will be considered as incapable, then, of perceiving that which must have been apparent to every man of common understanding, or as imposing upon your confidence and endeavoring to mislead you now. In either case they are unsafe guides in the perilous paths they urge you to tread. Ponder well on this circumstance, and you will know how to appreciate the exaggerated language they addressed to you. They are not champions of liberty, emulating the fame of our Revolutionary Fathers, nor are you an oppressed people, contending, as they repeat to you, against worse than colonial vassalage. You are free members of a flourishing and happy Union. There is no settled design to oppress you. You have indeed felt the unequal operations of laws which may have been unwisely, not unconstitutionally passed; but that inequality must necessarily be removed.

At the very moment when you were madly urged on to the unfortunate course you have begun, a change in public opinion had commenced. The nearly approaching payment of the public debt, and the consequent necessity of a diminution of duties, had already produced a considerable reduction, and that too on some articles of general consumption in your state. The importance of this change was understood, and you were authoritatively told that no further alleviation of your burdens was to be expected at the very time when the condition of the country imperiously demanded such a modification of the duties as should reduce them to a just and equitable scale. But, as if apprehensive of the effect of this change in allaying your discontents, you were precipitated into the fearful state in which you now find yourselves.

I have urged you to look back to the means that were

used to hurry you on to the position you have now assumed, and forward to the consequences it will produce. Something more is necessary. Contemplate the condition of that country of which you still form an important part! consider its government uniting in one bond of common interest and general protection so many different states—giving to all their inhabitants the proud title of *American citizens*—protecting their commerce—securing their literature and their arts—facilitating their intercommunication—defending the frontiers—and making their names respected in the remotest parts of the earth! Consider the extent of its territory, its increasing and happy population, its advance in arts which render life agreeable, and the sciences which elevate the mind: see education spreading the lights of religion, humanity, and general information into every cottage in this wide extent of our territories and states! Behold it as the asylum where the wretched and the oppressed find a refuge and support! Look on this picture of happiness and honor, and say, WE, TOO, ARE CITIZENS OF AMERICA! Carolina is one of these proud states; her arms have defended, her best blood has cemented this happy Union! And then add, if you can, without horror and remorse, this happy Union we will dissolve—this picture of peace and prosperity we will deface—this free intercourse we will interrupt—these fertile fields we will deluge with blood—the protection of that glorious flag we will renounce—the very name of Americans we discard. And for what, mistaken men! for what do you throw away these inestimable blessings—for what would you exchange your share in the advantage and honor of the Union? For the dream of a separate independence—a dream interrupted by bloody conflicts with your neighbors, and a vile dependence on a foreign power. If your leaders could succeed in establishing a separation, what would be your situation? Are you united at home—are you free from the apprehension of civil discord, with all its fearful consequences? Do our neighboring republics, every day suffering some new revolution or contending with some new insurrection—do they excite your envy?

But the dictates of a high duty oblige me solemnly to announce that you cannot succeed.

The laws of the United States must be executed. I have no discretionary power on the subject; my duty is emphatically pronounced in the Constitution. Those who told you that you might peaceably prevent their execution, deceived you—they could not have been deceived themselves. They know that a forcible opposition could alone prevent the execution of the laws, and they know that such opposition must be repelled. Their object is disunion: but be not deceived by names; disunion, by armed force, is TREASON. Are you really ready to incur its guilt? If you are, on the heads of the instigators of the act be the dreadful consequences—on their heads be the dishonor, but on yours may fall the punishment—on your unhappy state will inevitably fall all the evils of the conflict you force upon the government of your country. It cannot accede to the mad project of disunion, of which you would be the first victims—its first magistrate cannot, if he would, avoid the performance of his duty—the consequence must be fearful for you, distressing to your fellow-citizens here, and to the friends of good government throughout the world. Its enemies have beheld our prosperity with a vexation they could not conceal—it was a standing refutation of their slavish doctrines, and they will point to our discord with the triumph of malignant joy. It is yet in your power to disappoint them. There is yet time to show that the descendants of the Pinckneys, the Sumpters, the Rutledges, and of the thousand other names which adorn the pages of your Revolutionary history, will not abandon that Union, to support which, so many of them fought, and bled, and died. I adjure you, as you honor their memory—as you love the cause of freedom, to which they dedicated their lives—as you prize the peace of your country, the lives of its best citizens, and your own fair fame, to retrace your steps. Snatch from the archives of your state the disorganizing edict of its convention—bid its members to re-assemble and promulgate the decided expressions of your will to remain in the path which alone can conduct you to safety, prosperity, and honor—tell them that, compared to disunion, all other evils are light, because that brings with it an accumulation of all—declare that you will never take the field unless the star-spangled banner of your country shall float over you—that you will not be stigmatized when dead, and dishonored and scorned while you live, as the authors of the first attack on the Constitution of your country!—Its destroyers you cannot be. You may disturb its peace—you may interrupt the course of its prosperity—you may cloud its reputation for stability—but its tranquillity will be restored, its prosperity will return, and the stain upon its national character will be transferred, and remain an eternal blot on the memory of those who caused the disorder.

Fellow-citizens of the United States! The threat of unhallowed disunion—the names of those, once respected, by whom it was uttered—the array of military force to support it—denote the approach of a crisis in our affairs, on which the continuance of our unexampled prosperity, our political existence, and perhaps that of all free governments, may depend. The conjuncture demanded a free, a full and explicit enunciation, not only of my intentions, but of my principles of action; and as the claim was asserted of a right by a state to annul the laws of the Union, and even to secede from it at pleasure, a frank exposition of my opinions in relation to the origin and form of our government, and the construction I give to the instrument by which it was created, seemed to be proper. Having the fullest confidence in the justness of the legal and constitutional opinion of my duties, which has been expressed, I rely with equal confidence on your undivided support in my determination to execute the laws—to preserve the Union by all constitutional means—to arrest, if possible, by moderate but firm measures, the necessity of a recourse to force; and if it be the will of Heaven that the recurrence of its primeval curse on man for the shedding of a brother's blood should fall upon our land, that it be not called down by any offensive act on the part of the United States.

Fellow-citizens! The momentous case is before you.

On your undivided support of your government depends the decision of the great question it involves, whether your sacred Union will be preserved, and the blessing it secures to us as one people shall be perpetuated. No one can doubt that the unanimity with which that decision will be expressed, will be such as to inspire new confidence in republican institutions, and that the prudence, the wisdom, and the courage which it will bring to their defence, will transmit them unimpaired and invigorated to our children.

May the Great Ruler of nations grant that the signal blessings with which He has favored ours, may not, by the madness of party or personal ambition, be disregarded and lost; and may His wise Providence bring those who have produced this crisis, to see the folly, before they feel the misery of civil strife; and inspire a returning veneration for that Union, which, if we may dare to penetrate His designs, he has chosen as the only means of attaining the high destinies to which we may reasonably aspire.

Extracts from President Jackson's Protest against the Action of the United States Senate,—April 15, 1834.

REASONS FOR THE PROTEST.

It appears by the published journal of the Senate, that on the 26th of December last, a resolution was offered by a member of the Senate, which, after a protracted debate, was on the 28th day of March last modified by the mover, and passed by the votes of twenty-six senators out of forty-six, who were present and voted, in the following words, viz.:

"*Resolved*, That the President, in the late executive proceeding in relation to the public revenue, has assumed upon himself authority and power not conferred by the Constitution and laws, but in derogation of both."

Having had the honor, through the voluntary suffrages of the American people, to fill the office of President of the United States, during the period which may be presumed to have been referred to in this resolution, it is sufficiently evident, that the censure it inflicts was intended for myself. Without notice, unheard and untried, I thus find myself charged on the records of the Senate, and in a form hitherto unknown in our history, with the high crime of violating the laws and Constitution of my country.

It can seldom be necessary for any department of the government, when assailed in conversation, or debate, or by the strictures of the press or of popular assemblies, to step out of its ordinary path for the purpose of vindicating its conduct, or of pointing out any irregularity or injustice in the manner of the attack. But when the Chief Executive Magistrate is, by one of the most important branches of the government, in its official capacity, in a public manner, and by its recorded sentence, but without precedent, competent authority, or just cause, declared guilty of the breach of the laws and Constitution, it is due to his station, to public opinion, and to proper self-respect, that the officer thus denounced should promptly expose the wrong which has been done.

In the present case, moreover, there is even a stronger necessity for such a vindication. By an express provision of the Constitution, before the President of the United States can enter on the execution of his office, he is required to take an oath or affirmation, in the following words :

"I do solemnly swear (or affirm) that I will faithfully execute the office of President of the United States ; and will, to the best of my ability, preserve, protect, and defend the Constitution of the United States."

The duty of defending, so far as in him lies, the integrity of the Constitution, would indeed have resulted from the very nature of his office ; but, by thus expressing it in the official oath or affirmation, which, in this respect, differs from that of every other functionary, the founders of our republic have attested their sense of its importance, and have given to it a peculiar solemnity and force. Bound to the performance of this duty by the oath I have taken, by the strongest obligations of gratitude to the American people, and by the ties which unite my every earthly interest with the welfare and glory of my country ; and perfectly convinced that the discussion and passage of the above-mentioned resolution were not only unauthorized by the Constitution, but in many respects repugnant to its provisions, and subversive of the rights secured by it to other co-ordinate departments, I deem it an imperative duty to maintain the supremacy of that sacred instrument, and the immunities of the department intrusted to my care, by all means consistent with my own lawful powers, with the rights of others, and with the genius of our civil institutions. To this end, I have caused this, my *solemn protest* against the aforesaid proceedings, to be placed on the files of the Executive Department, and to be transmitted to the Senate.

PROTEST

POWERS OF THE SENATE IN CASES OF IMPEACHMENT.

Under the Constitution of the United States, the powers and functions of the various departments of the federal government, and their responsibilities for violation or neglect of duty, are clearly defined, or result by necessary inference. The legislative power, subject to the qualified negative of the President, is vested in the Congress of the United States composed of the Senate and House of Representatives. The executive power is vested exclusively in the President, except that in the conclusion of treaties, and in certain appointments to office, he is to act with the advice and consent of the Senate. The judicial power is vested exclusively in the Supreme and other Courts of the United States, except in cases of impeachment, for which purpose the accusatory power is vested in the House of Representatives, and that of hearing and determining in the Senate. But although, for the special purposes which have been mentioned, there is an occasional intermixture of the powers of the different departments, yet, with these exceptions, each of the three great departments is independent of the others in its sphere of action; and when it deviates from that sphere, is not responsible to the others, further than it is expressly made so in the Constitution. In every other respect, each of them is the coequal of the other two, and all are the servants of the American people, without power or right to control or censure each other in the service of their common superior, save only in the manner and to the degree which that superior has prescribed.

The responsibilities of the President are numerous and weighty. He is liable to impeachment for high crimes and misdemeanors, and, on due conviction, to removal from office, and perpetual disqualification; and notwithstanding such conviction, he may also be indicted and punished according to law. He is also liable to the private action of any party, who may have been injured by his illegal mandates or instructions, in the same manner and to the same extent as the humblest functionary. In addition to the responsibilities which may thus be enforced by impeachment, criminal prosecution, or suit at law, he is also accountable at the bar of public opinion, for every act of his administration. Subject only to the restraints of truth and justice, the free people of the United States have the undoubted right, as individuals or collectively, orally or in writing, at such times, and in such language and form as they may think proper, to discuss his official conduct, and to express and promulgate their opinions concerning it. Indirectly, also, his conduct may come under review in either branch of the legislature, or in the Senate when acting in its executive capacity, and so far as the executive or legislative proceedings of these bodies may require it, it may be examined by them. These are believed to be the proper and only modes in which the President of the United States is to be held accountable for his official conduct.

Tested by these principles, the resolution of the Senate is wholly unauthorized by the Constitution, and in derogation of its entire spirit. It assumes that a single branch of the legislative department may, for the purposes of a public censure, and without any view to legislation or impeachment, take up, consider, and decide upon the official acts of the Executive. But in no part of the Constitution is the President subjected to any such responsibility; and in no part of that instrument is any such power conferred on either branch of the legislature.

The justice of these conclusions will be illustrated and confirmed by a brief analysis of the powers of the Senate, and a comparison of their recent proceedings with those powers.

The high functions assigned by the Constitution to the Senate, are in their nature either legislative, executive, or judicial. It is only in the exercise of its judicial powers, when sitting as a court for the trial of impeachments, that the Senate is expressly authorized and necessarily required to consider and decide upon the conduct of the President or any other public officer. Indirectly, however, as has been already suggested, it may frequently be called on to perform that office. Cases may occur in the course of its legislative or executive proceedings, in which it may be indispensable to the proper exercise of its powers, that it should inquire into, and decide upon, the conduct of the President or other public officers; and in every such case, its constitutional right to do so is cheerfully conceded. But to authorize the Senate to enter on such a task, in its legislative or executive capacity, the inquiry must actually grow out of and tend to some legislative or executive action; and the decision, when expressed, must take the form of some appropriate legislative or executive act.

The resolution in question was introduced, discussed, and passed, not as a joint, but as a separate resolution. It asserts no legislative power; proposes no legislative action; and neither possesses the form nor any of the attributes of a legislative measure. It does not appear to have been entertained or passed with any view or expectation of its issuing in a law or joint resolution, or in the repeal of any law or joint resolution, or in any other legislative action.

While wanting both the form and substance of a legislative measure, it is equally manifest that the resolution was not justified by any of the executive powers conferred on the Senate. These powers relate exclusively to the consideration of treaties and nominations to office, and they are exercised in secret session, and with closed doors. This resolution does not apply to any treaty or nomination, and was passed in a public session.

Nor does this proceeding in any way belong to that class of incidental resolutions which relate to the officers of the Senate, to their chamber, and other appurtenances, or to subjects of order, and other matters of the like nature —in all which either House may lawfully proceed, without any co-operation with the other, or with the President.

On the contrary, the whole phraseology and sense of the resolution seem to be judicial. Its essence, true character, and only practical effect, are to be found in the conduct which it charges upon the President, and in the judgment which it pronounces upon that conduct. The resolution, therefore, though discussed and adopted by the Senate in its legislative capacity, is, in its office, and in all its characteristics, essentially judicial.

That the Senate possesses a high judicial power, and

that instances may occur in which the President of the United States will be amenable to it, is undeniable. But under the provisions of the Constitution, it would seem to be equally plain, that neither the President, nor any other officer, can be rightfully subjected to the operation of the judicial power of the Senate, except in the cases and under the forms prescribed by the Constitution.

The Constitution declares that "the President, Vice-president, and all civil officers of the United States, shall be removed from office, on impeachment for and conviction of treason, bribery, or other high crimes and misdemeanors;" that the House of Representatives "shall have the sole power of impeachment;" that the Senate "shall have the sole power to try all impeachments;" that "when sitting for that purpose, they shall be on oath or affirmation:" that "when the President of the United States is tried, the Chief Justice shall preside;" that "no person shall be convicted without the concurrence of two-thirds of the members present;" and that judgment shall not extend farther than "to removal from office, and disqualification to hold and enjoy any office of honor, trust, or profit, under the United States."

The resolution above quoted, charges, in substance, that in certain proceedings relating to the public revenue, the President has usurped authority and power not conferred upon him by the Constitution and laws, and that in doing so, he violated both. Any such act constitutes a high crime—one of the highest, indeed, which the President can commit—a crime which justly exposes him to impeachment by the House of Representatives, and, upon due conviction, to removal from office, and to the complete and immutable disfranchisement prescribed by the Constitution.

The resolution, then, was in substance an impeachment of the President; and in its passage, amounts to a declaration by a majority of the Senate, that he is guilty of an impeachable offence. As such, it is spread upon the journals of the Senate—published to the nation and to the world—made part of our enduring archives—and incorporated in the history of the age. The punishment of removal from office and future disqualification, does not, it is true, follow this decision; nor would it have followed the like decision, if the regular forms of proceeding had been pursued, because the requisite number did not concur in the result. But the moral influence of a solemn declaration, by a majority of the Senate, that the accused is guilty of the offence charged upon him, has been as effectually secured, as if the like declaration had been made upon an impeachment expressed in the same terms. Indeed, a greater practical effect has been gained, because the votes given for the resolution, though not sufficient to authorize a judgment of guilty on an impeachment, were numerous enough to carry that resolution.

That the resolution does not expressly allege that the assumption of power and authority, which it condemns, was intentional and corrupt, is no answer to the preceding view of its character and effect.

The act thus condemned, necessarily implies violation and design in the individual to whom it is imputed, and being unlawful in its character, the legal conclusion is, that it was prompted by improper motives, and committed with an unlawful intent. The charge is not of a mistake in the exercise of supposed powers, but of the assumption of powers not conferred by the Constitution and laws, and in derogation of both; and nothing is suggested to excuse or palliate the turpitude of the act. In the absence of any such excuse or palliation, there is only room for one inference; and that is, that the intent was unlawful and corrupt. Besides, the resolution not only contains no mitigating suggestion, but, on the contrary, it holds up the act complained of as justly obnoxious to censure and reprobation; and thus as distinctly stamps it with impurity of motive, as if the strongest epithets had been used.

The President of the United States, therefore, has been, by a majority of his constitutional triers, accused and found guilty of an impeachable offence; but in no part of this proceeding have the directions of the Constitution been observed.

The impeachment, instead of being preferred and prosecuted by the House of Representatives, originated in the Senate, and was prosecuted without the aid or concurrence of the other house. The oath or affirmation prescribed by the Constitution, was not taken by the senators ; the Chief Justice did not preside ; no notice of the charge was given to the accused ; and no opportunity afforded him to respond to the accusation, to meet his accusers face to face, to cross-examine the witnesses, to procure counteracting testimony, or to be heard in his defence. The safeguards and formalities which the Constitution has connected with the power of impeachment, were doubtless supposed, by the framers of that instrument, to be essential to the protection of the public servant, to the attainment of justice, and to the order, impartiality, and dignity of the procedure. These safeguards and formalities were not only practically disregarded, in the commencement and conduct of these proceedings, but, in their result, I find myself convicted by less than two-thirds of the members present, of an impeachable offence.

In vain it may be alleged in defence of this proceeding, that the form of the resolution is not that of an impeachment or a judgment thereupon—that the punishment prescribed in the Constitution does not follow its adoption, or that in this case no impeachment is to be expected from the House of Representatives. It is because it did not assume the form of an impeachment, that it is more palpably repugnant to the Constitution ; for it is through that form only that the President is judicially responsible to the Senate ; and though neither removal from office, nor future disqualification ensues, yet it is not to be presumed that the framers of the Constitution considered either or both of those results as constituting the whole of the punishment they prescribed. The judgment of guilty by the highest tribunal in the Union ; the stigma it would inflict on the offender, his family and fame ; and the perpetual record on the journal, handing down to future generations the story of his disgrace, were doubtless regarded by them as the bitterest portions, if not the very essence of that punishment. So far, therefore, as some of its most material parts are concerned, the passage, recording, and promulgation of the resolution, are

PROTEST

an attempt to bring them on the President, in a manner unauthorized by the Constitution. To shield him and other officers who are liable to impeachment, from consequences so momentous, except when really merited by official delinquencies, the Constitution has most carefully guarded the whole process of impeachment. A majority of the House of Representatives must think the officer guilty before he can be charged. Two-thirds of the Senate must pronounce him guilty, or he is deemed to be innocent. Forty-six senators appear by the journal to have been present when the vote on the resolution was taken. If, after all the solemnities of an impeachment, thirty of those senators had voted that the President was guilty, yet would he have been acquitted; but by the mode of proceeding adopted in the present case, a lasting record of conviction has been entered up by the votes of twenty-six senators, without an impeachment or trial; whilst the Constitution expressly declares, that to the entry of such a judgment on accusation by the House of Representatives, a trial by the Senate, and a concurrence of two-thirds in the vote of guilty, shall be indispensable prerequisites.

Whether or not an impeachment was to be expected from the House of Representatives, was a point on which the Senate had no constitutional right to speculate, and in respect to which, even had it possessed the spirit of prophecy, its anticipations would have furnished no just grounds for this procedure. Admitting that there was reason to believe that a violation of the Constitution and laws had been actually committed by the President, still it was the duty of the Senate, as his sole constitutional judges, to wait for an impeachment until the other house should think proper to prefer it. The members of the Senate could have no right to infer that no impeachment was intended. On the contrary, every legal and rational presumption on their part ought to have been, that if there was good reason to believe him guilty of an impeachable offence, the House of Representatives would perform its constitutional duty by arraigning the offender before the justice of his country. The contrary presumption would involve an implication derogatory to the integrity and honor of the representatives of the people. But suppose the suspicion thus implied were actually entertained, and for good cause, how can it justify the assumption by the Senate, of powers not conferred by the Constitution?

It is only necessary to look at the condition in which the Senate and the President have been placed by this proceeding, to perceive its utter incompatibility with the provisions and spirit of the Constitution, and with the plainest dictates of humanity and justice.

If the House of Representatives shall be of opinion that there is just ground for the censure pronounced upon the President, then will it be the solemn duty of that House to prefer the proper accusation, and to cause him to be brought to trial by the constitutional tribunal. But in what condition would he find that tribunal? A majority of its members have already considered the case, and have not only formed, but expressed a deliberate judgment upon its merits. It is the policy of our benign system of jurisprudence, to secure in all criminal proceedings, and even in the most trivial litigations, a fair, unprejudiced, and impartial trial. And surely it cannot be less important, that such a trial should be secured to the highest officer of the government.

The Constitution makes the House of Representatives the exclusive judges, in the first instance, of the question, whether the President has committed an impeachable offence. A majority of the Senate, whose interference with this preliminary question has, for the best of all reasons, been studiously excluded, anticipate the action of the House of Representatives, assume not only the function which belongs exclusively to that body, but convert themselves into accusers, witnesses, counsel, and judges, and pre-judge the whole case. Thus presenting the appalling spectacle, in a free state, of judges going through a labored preparation for an impartial hearing and decision, by a previous *ex parte* investigation and sentence against the supposed offender.

There is no more settled axiom in that government whence we derive the model of this part of our Constitution, than "that the lords cannot impeach any to themselves, nor join in the accusation, *because they are judges.*" Independently of the general reason on which this rule is founded, its propriety and importance are greatly increased by the nature of the impeaching power. The power of arraigning the high officers of government, before a tribunal whose sentence may expel them from their seats, and brand them as infamous, is eminently a popular remedy—a remedy designed to be employed for the protection of private right and public liberty, against the abuses of injustice, and the encroachments of arbitrary power. But the framers of the Constitution were also undoubtedly aware that this formidable instrument had been and might be abused; and that from its very nature, an impeachment for high crimes and misdemeanors, whatever might be its result, would in most cases be accompanied by so much of dishonor and reproach, solicitude and suffering, as to make the power of preferring it, one of the highest solemnity and importance. It was due to both these considerations that the impeaching power should be lodged in the hands of those who, from the mode of their election and the tenure of their offices, would most accurately express the popular will, and at the same time be most directly and speedily amenable to the people. The theory of these wise and benignant intentions is, in the present case, effectually defeated by the proceedings of the Senate. The members of that body represent not the people, but the states; and though they are undoubtedly responsible to the states, yet, from their extended term of service, the effect of that responsibility, during the whole period of that term, must very much depend upon their own impressions of its obligatory force. When a body, thus constituted, expresses beforehand its opinion in a particular case, and thus indirectly invites a prosecution, it not only assumes a power intended for wise reasons to be confined to others, but it shields the latter from that exclusive and personal responsibility under which it was intended to be exercised, and reverses the whole scheme of this part of the Constitution.

Such would be some of the objections to this procedure

even if it were admitted that there is just ground for imputing to the President the offences charged in the resolution. But if, on the other hand, the House of Representatives shall be of opinion that there is no reason for charging them upon him, and shall therefore deem it improper to prefer an impeachment, then will the violation of privilege, as it respects that House, of justice, as it regards the President, and of the Constitution as it relates to both, be only the more conspicuous and impressive.

RIGHT OF THE PRESIDENT TO REMOVE THE SECRETARY OF THE TREASURY.

By the Constitution, the executive power is vested in the President of the United States. Among the duties imposed upon him, and which he is sworn to perform, is that of " taking care that the laws be faithfully executed." Being thus made responsible for the entire action of the executive department, it was but reasonable that the power of appointing, overseeing, and controlling those who execute the laws—a power in its nature executive—should remain in his hands. It is therefore not only his right, but the Constitution makes it his duty to " nominate, and by and with the advice and consent of the Senate, appoint" all " officers of the United States, whose appointments are not in the Constitution otherwise provided for," with the proviso that the appointment of inferior officers may be vested in the President alone, in the courts of justice, or in the heads of departments.

The executive power vested in the Senate is neither that of " nominating" nor " appointing." It is merely a check upon the executive power of appointment. If individuals are proposed for appointment by the President, by them deemed incompetent or unworthy, they may withhold their consent, and the appointment cannot be made. They check the action of the Executive, but cannot, in relation to these very subjects, act themselves, nor direct him. Selections are still made by the President; and the negative given to the Senate, without diminishing his responsibility, furnishes an additional guarantee to the country that the subordinate executive, as well as the judicial offices, shall be filled with worthy and competent men.

The whole executive power being vested in the President, who is responsible for its exercise, it is a necessary consequence that he should have a right to employ agents of his own choice to aid him in the performance of his duties, and to discharge them when he is no longer willing to be responsible for their acts. In strict accordance with this principle, the power of removal, which, like that of appointment, is an original executive power, is left unchecked by the Constitution in relation to all executive officers, for whose conduct the President is responsible, while it is taken from him in relation to judicial officers, for whose acts he is not responsible. In the government from which many of the fundamental principles of our system are derived, the head of the executive department originally had power to appoint and remove at will all officers, executive and judicial. It was to take the judges out of this general power of removal, and thus make them independent of the Executive, that the tenure of their offices was changed to good behavior. Nor is it conceivable why they are placed in our Constitution upon a tenure different from that of all other officers appointed by the Executive, unless it be for the same purpose.

But if there were any just ground for doubt, on the face of the Constitution, whether all executive officers are removable at the will of the President, it is obviated by the cotemporaneous construction of the instrument and the uniform practice under it.

The power of removal was a topic of solemn debate in the Congress of 1789, while organizing the administrative departments of the government, and it was finally decided, that the President derived from the Constitution the power of removal, so far as it regards that department for whose acts he is responsible. Although the debate covered the whole ground, embracing the treasury as well as all the other executive departments, it arose on a motion to strike out of the bill to establish a department of foreign affairs, since called the department of state, a clause declaring the secretary "to be removable from office by the President of the United States." After that motion had been decided in the negative, it was perceived that these words did not convey the sense of the House of Representatives in relation to the true source of the power of removal. With the avowed object of preventing any future inference, that this power was exercised by the President in virtue of a grant from Congress, when in fact that body considered it as derived from the Constitution, the words which had been the subject of debate, were struck out and in lieu thereof a clause was inserted in a provision concerning the chief clerk of the department, which declared that "whenever the said principal officer shall be *removed* from office by the President of the United States, or in any other case of vacancy," the chief clerk should during such vacancy have charge of the papers of the office. This change having been made for the express purpose of declaring the sense of Congress, that the President derived the power of removal from the Constitution, the act, as it passed, has always been considered as a full expression of the sense of the legislature on this important part of the American Constitution.

Here, then, we have the concurrent authority of President Washington, of the Senate, and House of Representatives, numbers of whom had taken an active part in the Convention which framed the Constitution, and in the state Convention which adopted it, that the President derived an unqualified power of removal from that instrument itself, which is "beyond the reach of legislative authority." Upon this principle the government has now been steadily administered for about forty-five years, during which there have been numerous removals made by the President, or by his direction, embracing every grade of executive officers, from the heads of departments to the messengers of bureaus.

The treasury department, in the discussions of 1789, was considered on the same footing as the other executive departments, and in the act establishing it, the precise words were incorporated indicative of the sense of Congress, that the President derives his power to remove the secretary from the Constitution, which appear in the act establishing the department of foreign affairs. An assistant secretary of the treasury was created, and it was provided that he should take charge of the books and papers of the department, "whenever the secretary shall be *removed* from office by the President of the United States." The secretary of the treasury being appointed by the President, and being considered as constitutionally removable by him, it appears never to have occurred to any one in the Congress of 1789, or since, until very recently, that he was other than an executive officer, the mere instrument of the Chief Magistrate in the execution of the laws, subject, like all other heads of departments, to his supervision and control. No such idea, as an officer of the Congress, can be found in the Constitution, or appears to have suggested itself to those who organized the government.

CONCLUSION.

The honest differences of opinion which occasionally exist between the Senate and the President, in regard to matters in which both are obliged to participate, are sufficiently embarrassing. But if the course recently adopted by the Senate shall hereafter be frequently pursued, it is not only obvious that the harmony of the relations between the President and the Senate will be destroyed, but that other and graver effects will ultimately ensue. If the censures of the Senate be submitted to by the President, the confidence of the people in his ability and virtue, and the character and usefulness of his administration, will soon be at an end, and the real power of the government will fall into the hands of a body, holding their offices for long terms, not elected by the people, and not to them directly responsible. If, on the other hand, the illegal censures of the Senate should be resisted by the President, collisions and angry controversies might ensue, discreditable in their progress, and in the end compelling the people to adopt the conclusion, either that their Chief Magistrate was unworthy of their respect, or that the Senate was chargeable with calumny and injustice. Either of these results would impair public confidence in the perfection of the system, and lead to serious alterations of its framework, or to the practical abandonment of some of its provisions.

The influence of such proceedings on the other departments of the government, and more especially on the states, could not fail to be extensively pernicious. When the judges, in the last resort, of official misconduct, themselves overleaped the bounds of their authority, as prescribed by the Constitution, what general disregard of its provisions might not their example be expected to produce? And who does not perceive that such contempt of the federal Constitution, by one of its most important departments, would hold out the strongest temptations to resistance on the part of the state sovereignties, whenever they shall suppose their just rights to have been invaded? Thus all the independent departments of the government, and the states which compose our confederated union, instead of attending to their appropriate duties, and leaving those who may offend to be reclaimed or punished in the manner pointed out in the Constitution, would fall to mutual crimination and recrimination, and give to the people confusion and anarchy, instead of order and law; until at length some form of aristocratic power would be established on the ruins of the Constitution, or the states be broken into separate communities.

Far be it from me to charge, or to insinuate, that the present Senate of the United States intended, in the most distant way, to encourage such a result. It is not of their motives or designs, but only of the tendency of their acts, that it is my duty to speak. It is, if possible, to make senators themselves sensible of the danger which lurks under the precedent set in their resolution; and at any rate to perform my duty, as the responsible head of one of the co-equal departments of the government, that I have been compelled to point out the consequences to which the discussion and passage of the resolution may lead, if the tendency of the measure be not checked in its inception. It is due to the high trust with which I have been charged; to those who may be called to succeed me in it; to the representatives of the people, whose constitutional prerogative has been unlawfully assumed; to the people of the states; and to the Constitution they have established; that I shall not permit its provisions to be broken down, by such an attack on the executive department, without at least some effort "to preserve, protect, and defend them." With this view, and for the reasons which have been stated, I do hereby SOLEMNLY PROTEST against the aforementioned proceedings of the Senate, as unauthorized by the Constitution; contrary to its spirit and to several of its express provisions; subversive of that distribution of the powers of government which it has ordained and established; destructive of the checks and safeguards by which those powers were intended, on the one hand to be controlled, and on the other to be protected; and calculated by their immediate and collateral effects, by their character and tendency, to concentrate in the hands of a body not directly amenable to the people, a degree of influence and power dangerous to their liberties, and fatal to the Constitution of their choice.

The resolution of the Senate contains an imputation upon my private as well as upon my public character; and as it must stand for ever on their journals, I cannot close this substitute for that defence which I have not been allowed to present in the ordinary form, without remarking, that I have lived in vain, if it be necessary to enter into a formal vindication of my character and motives from such an imputation. In vain do I bear upon my person, enduring memorials of that contest in which American liberty was purchased—in vain have I since perilled property, fame, and life, in defence of the rights and privileges so dearly bought—in vain am I now, without a personal aspiration, or the hope of individual advantage, encountering responsibilities and dangers, from which, by mere inactivity in relation to a single point, I might have been exempt—if any serious doubts can be entertained as to the purity of my purposes and motives. If I had been ambitious, I should have sought an alliance with that powerful institution, which even now aspires to no divided empire. If I had been venal, I should have sold myself to its designs. Had I preferred personal comfort and official ease to the performance of my arduous duty, I should have ceased to molest it. In the history of conquerors and usurpers, never, in the fire of youth, nor in the vigor of manhood, could I find an attraction to lure me from the path of duty; and now, I shall scarcely find an inducement to commence their career of ambition, when gray hairs and a decaying frame, instead of inviting to toil and battle, call me to the contemplation of other worlds, where conquerors cease to be honored, and usurpers expiate their crimes.

The only ambition I can feel is, to acquit myself to Him to whom I must soon render an account of my stewardship, to serve my fellow-men, and live respected and honored in the history of my country. No! the ambition which leads me on, is an anxious desire and a fixed determination, to return to the people, unimpaired, the sacred trust they have confided to my charge; to heal the wounds of the Constitution and preserve it from further violation; to persuade my countrymen, so far as I may, that it is not in a splendid government, supported by powerful monopolies and aristocratical establishments, that they will find happiness, or their liberties protection; but in a plain system, void of pomp—protecting all, and granting favors to none—dispensing its blessings like the dews of Heaven, unseen and unfelt, save in the freshness and beauty they contribute to produce. It is such a government that the genius of our people requires— such an one only under which our states may remain for ages to come, united, prosperous, and free. If the Almighty Being who has hitherto sustained and protected me, will but vouchsafe to make my feeble powers instrumental to such a result, I shall anticipate with pleasure the place to be assigned me in the history of my country, and die contented with the belief, that I have contributed, in some small degree, to increase the value and prolong the duration of American liberty.

To the end that the resolution of the Senate may not

be hereafter drawn into precedent, with the authority of silent acquiescence on the part of the executive department, and to the end, also, that my motives and views in the executive proceedings denounced in that resolution, may be known to my fellow-citizens, to the world, and to all posterity, I respectfully request that this message and protest may be entered at length on the journals of the Senate.

SIXTH ANNUAL MESSAGE.

Delivered, Decmber 2d, 1834.

Fellow-Citizens of the Senate and House of Representatives:—

In performing my duty at the opening of your present session, it gives me pleasure to congratulate you again upon the prosperous condition of our beloved country. Divine Providence has favored us with general health, with rich rewards in the fields of agriculture and in every branch of labor, and with peace to cultivate and extend the various resources which employ the virtue and enterprise of our citizens. Let us trust that in surveying a scene so flattering to our free institutions, our joint deliberations to preserve them may be crowned with success.

Our foreign relations continue, with but few exceptions, to maintain the favorable aspect which they bore in my last annual message, and promise to extend those advantages which the principles that regulate our intercourse with other nations are so well calculated to secure.

The question of the northeastern boundary is still pending with Great Britain, and the proposition made in accordance with the resolution of the senate for the establishment of a line according to the treaty of 1783, has not been accepted by that government. Believing that every disposition is felt on both sides to adjust this perplexing question to the satisfaction of all the parties interested in it, the hope is yet indulged that it may be effected on the basis of that proposition.

With the governments of Austria, Russia, Prussia, Holland, Sweden, and Denmark, the best understanding exists. Commerce with all is fostered and protected by reciprocal good will, under the sanction of liberal conventional or legal provisions.

SIXTH ANNUAL MESSAGE 305

In the midst of her internal difficulties, the queen of Spain has ratified the convention for the payment of the claims of our citizens arising since 1819. It is in the course of execution on her part, and a copy of it is now laid before you for such legislation as may be found necessary to enable those interested to derive the benefits of it.

Yielding to the force of circumstances, and to the wise councils of time and experience, that power has finally resolved no longer to occupy the unnatural position in which she stood to the new governments established on this hemisphere. I have the great satisfaction of stating to you that, in preparing the way for the restoration of harmony between those who have sprung from the same ancestors, who are allied by common interests, profess the same religion, and speak the same language, the United States have been actively instrumental. Our efforts to effect this good work will be persevered in while they are deemed useful to the parties, and our entire disinterestedness continues to be felt and understood. The act of Congress to countervail the discriminating duties levied to the prejudice of our navigation, in Cuba and Porto Rico, has been transmitted to the minister of the United States at Madrid, to be communicated to the government of the queen. No intelligence of its receipt has yet reached the department of state. If the present condition of the country permits the government to make a careful and enlarged examination of the true interests of these important portions of its dominions, no doubt is entertained that their future intercourse with the United States will be placed upon a more just and liberal basis.

The Florida archives have not yet been selected and delivered. Recent orders have been sent to the agent of the United States at Havana, to return with all that he can obtain, so that they may be in Washington before the session of the supreme court, to be used in the legal questions there pending, to which the government is a party.

Internal tranquility is happily restored to Portugal. The distracted state of the country rendered unavoidable the postponement of a final payment of the just claims of our citizens. Our diplomatic relations will be soon resumed, and the long subsisting friendship with that power affords the strongest guarantee that the balance due will receive prompt attention.

The first instalment due under the convention of indemnity with the king of the Two Sicilies has been duly received, and an offer has been made to extinguish the whole by a prompt payment; an offer I did not consider myself authorized to accept, as the indemnification provided is the exclusive property of individual citizens of the United States. The original adjustment of our claims, and the anxiety displayed to fulfil at once the stipulations made for the payment of them, are highly honorable to the government of the Two Sicilies. When it is recollected that they were the result of the injustice of an intrusive power, temporarily dominant in its territory, a repugnance to acknowledge and to pay which would have been neither unnatural or unexpected, the circumstances can not fail to exalt its character for justice and good faith in the eyes of all nations.

The treaty of amity and commerce between the United States and Belgium, brought to your notice in my last annual message, as sanctioned by the senate, but the ratifications of which had not been exchanged, owing to a delay in its reception at Brussels, and a subsequent absence of the Belgian minister of foreign affairs, has been, after mature deliberation, finally disavowed by that government as inconsistent with the powers and instructions given to their minister who negotiated it. This disavowal was entirely unexpected, as the liberal principles embodied in the convention, and which form the groundwork of the objections to it, were perfectly satisfactory to the Belgian representative, and were supposed to be not only within the powers granted, but expressly conformable to the instructions given to him. An offer, not yet accepted, has been made by Belgium to renew negotiations for a treaty less liberal in its provisions, on questions of general maritime law.

Our newly established relations with the Sublime Porte promise to be useful to our commerce, and satisfactory in every respect to this government. Our intercourse with the Barbary powers continues without important change, except that the present political state of Algiers has induced me to terminate the residence there of a salaried consul, and to substitute an ordinary consulate, to remain so long as the place continues in the possession of France. Our first treaty with one of these powers, the emperor of Morocco, was formed in 1786, and was limited to fifty years. That period has almost expired. I shall take measures to renew it with the greater satisfaction, as its stipulations are just and liberal, and have been, with mutual fidelity and reciprocal advantage, scrupulously fulfilled.

Intestine dissensions have too frequently occurred to mar the prosperity, interrupt the commerce, and distract the governments of most of the nations of this hemisphere, which have separated themselves from Spain. When a firm and permanent understanding with the parent country shall have produced a formal acknowledgment of their independence, and the idea of danger from that quarter can be no longer entertained, the friends of freedom expect that those countries, so favored by nature, will be distinguished for their love of justice, and their devotion to those peaceful arts, the assiduous cultivation of which confers honor upon nations, and gives value to human life. In the meantime, I confidently hope that the apprehensions entertained that some of the people of these luxuriant regions may be tempted, in a moment of unworthy distrust of their own capacity for enjoyment of liberty, to commit the too common error of purchasing present repose by bestowing on some favorite leaders the fatal gift of irresponsible power, will not be realized. With all these governments, and with that of Brazil, no unexpected changes in our relations have occurred during the present year. Frequent causes of just complaint have arisen upon the part of the citizens of the United States—sometimes from the irregular action of the constituted subordinate authorities of the maritime regions, and sometimes from the leaders or partisans of those in arms against the established governments. In all cases, representations have been or will be made; and as soon as their political affairs are in a settled position, it is expected that our friendly remonstrances will be followed by adequate redress.

The government of Mexico made known in December last, the appointment of commissioners and surveyors on its part, to run, in conjunction with ours, the boundary line between its territories and the United States, and excused the delay for the reasons anticipated—the prevalence of civil war. The commissioners and surveyors not having met within the time stipulated by the treaty, a new arrangement became necessary, and our charge d'affaires was instructed in January last, to negotiate in Mexico an article addtional to the pre-existing treaty. This instruction was acknowledged, and no difficulty was apprehended in the accomplishment of that object. By information just received, that additional article to the treaty will be obtained and transmitted to this country, as soon as it can receive the ratification of the Mexican Congress.

The reunion of the three states of New Grenada, Venezuela, and Equador, forming the republic of Columbia, seems every day to become more improbable. The commissionnrs of the first two are understood to be now negotiating a just division of the obligations contracted by when united under one government. The civil war in Equador, it is believed, has prevented even the appointment of a commissioner on its part.

I propose, at an early day, to submit, in the proper form, the appointment of a diplomatic agent to Venezuela; the importance of the commerce of that country to the United States, and the large claims of our citizens upon the government, arising before and since the division of Colombia, rendering it, in my judgment, improper longer to delay the step.

Our representatives to Central America, Peru, and Brazil, are either at, or on their way, to their respective posts.

From the Argentine republic, from which a minister was expected to this government, nothing further has been heard. Occasion has been taken, on the departure

SIXTH ANNUAL MESSAGE

of a new consul to Buenos Ayres, to remind that government that its long-delayed minister, whose appointment has been made known to us, had not arrived.

It becomes my unpleasant duty to inform you that this specific and highly gratifying picture of our foreign relations, does not include those with France at this time. It is not possible that any government and people could be more sincerely desirous of conciliating a just and friendly intercourse with another nation, than are those of the United States, with their ancient ally and friend. This disposition is founded, as well on the most grateful and honorable recollections associated with our struggle for independence, as upon a well-grounded conviction that it is consonant with the true policy of both. The people of the United States could not, therefore, see, without the deepest regret, even a temporary interruption of the friendly relations between the two countries—a regret which would, I am sure, be greatly aggravated, if there should turn out to be any reasonable ground for attributing such a result to any act of omission or commission on our part. I derive, therefore, the highest satisfaction from being able to assure you that the whole course of this government has been characterized by a spirit so conciliatory and forbearing, as to make it impossible that our justice and moderation should be questioned, whatever may be the consequences of a longer perseverance, on the part of the French government, in her omission to satisfy the conceded claims of our citizens.

The history of the accumulated and unprovoked aggressions upon our commerce, committed by authority of the existing governments of France, between the years 1800 and 1817, has been rendered too painfully familiar to Americans to make its repetition either necessary or desirable. It will be sufficient here to remark that there has for many years been scarcely a single administration of the French government by whom the justice and legality of the claims of our citizens to indemnity were not, to a very considerable extent, admitted; and yet near a quarter of a century has been wasted in ineffectual negotiations to secure it.

Deeply sensible of the injurious effects resulting from this state of things upon the interests and character of both nations, I regarded it as among my first duties to cause one more effort to be made to satisfy France that a just and liberal settlement of our claims was as well due to her own honor as to their incontestable validity. The negotiation for this purpose was commenced with the late government of France, and was prosecuted with such success as to leave no reasonable ground to doubt that a settlement of a character quite as liberal as that which was subsequently made, would have been effected, had not the revolution, by which the negotiation was cut off, taken place. The discussions were resumed with the present government, and the result showed that we were not wrong in supposing that an event by which the two governments were made to approach each other so much nearer in their political principles, and by which the motives for the most liberal and friendly intercourse were so greatly multiplied, could exercise no other than a salutary influence upon the negotiation. After the most deliberate and thorough examination of the whole subject, a treaty between the two governments was concluded and signed at Paris on the 4th of July, 1831, by which it was stipulated that " the French government, in order to liberate itself from all the reclamations preferred against it by citizens of the United States for unlawful seizures, captures, sequestrations, confiscations, or destruction of their vessels, cargoes, or other property, engages to pay a sum of twenty-five millions of francs to the United States, who shall distribute it among those entitled, in the manner and according to the rules it shall determine;" and it was also stipulated, on the part of the French government, that this twenty-five millions of francs should " be paid at Paris in six annual instalments of four millions, one hundred and sixty-six thousand, six hundred and sixty-six francs, and sixty-six centimes each, into the hands of such person or persons as shall be authorized by the government of the United States to receive it." The first instalment to be paid " at the expiration of one year next following the exchange of the ratifications of this convention, and the others at successive intervals of a year, one after another, till the whole shall be paid. To the amount of each of the said instalments shall be added interest at four per cent thereupon, as upon the other instalments then remaining unpaid, the said interest to be computed from the day of the exchange of the present convention."

It was also stipulated, on the part of the United States, for the purpose of being completely liberated from all the reclamations presented by France on behalf of its citizens, that the sum of one million five hundred thousand francs should be paid to the government of France, in six annual instalments, to be deducted out of the annual sums which France had agreed to pay, interest thereupon being in like manner computed from the day of the exchange of the ratifications. In addition to this stipulation, important advantages were secured to France by the following articles, viz: "The wines of France, from and after the exchange of the ratifications of the present convention, shall be admitted to consumption in the states of the Union, at duties which shall not exceed the following rates by the gallon (such as is used at present for wines in the United States), to wit: six cents for red wines in casks, ten cents for white wines in casks; and twenty-two cents for wines of all sorts in bottles. The proportions existing between the duties on French wines thus reduced, and the general rates of the tariff which went into operation the first of January, 1829, shall be maintained in case the government of the United States should think proper to diminish those general rates in a new tariff.

"In consideration of this stipulation, which shall be binding on the United States for ten years, the French government abandons the reclamations which it had formed in relation to the eighth article of the treaty of cession of Louisiana. It engages, moreover, to establish on the *long staple* cottons of the United States, which, after the exchange of the ratifications of the present convention, shall be brought directly thence to France by the vessels of the United States, or by French vessels, the same duties as on *short staple* cottons."

This treaty was duly ratified in the manner prescribed

by the constitutions of both countries, and the ratifications were exchanged at the city of Washington on the 2d of February, 1832. On account of its commercial stipulations, it was, within five days thereafter, laid before the Congress of the United States, which proceeded to enact such laws favorable to the commerce of France as were necessary to carry it into full execution; and France has, from that period to the present, been in the unrestricted enjoyment of the valuable privileges that were thus secured to her. The faith of the French nation having been thus solemnly pledged, through its constitutional organ, for the liquidation and ultimate payment of the long-deferred claims of our citizens, as also for the adjustment of other points of great and reciprocal benefits to both countries, and the United States having, with a fidelity and promptitude by which their conduct will, I trust, be always characterized, done everything that was necessary to carry the treaty into full and fair effect on their part, counted, with the most perfect confidence, on equal fidelity and promptitude on the part of the French government. In this reasonable expectation we have been, I regret to inform you, wholly disappointed. No legislative provision has been made by France for the execution of the treaty, either as it respects the indemnities to be paid, or the commercial benefits to be secured to the United States, and the relations between the United States and that power, in consequence thereof, are placed in a situation threatening to interrupt the good understanding which has so long and so happily existed between the two nations.

Not only has the French government been thus wanting in the performance of the stipulations it has so solemnly entered into with the United States, but its omissions have been marked by circumstances which would seem to leave us without satisfactory evidences that such performance will certainly take place at a future period. Advice of the exchange of ratifications reached Paris prior to the 8th of April, 1832. The French chambers were then sitting, and continued in session until the 21st of that month; and although one instalment of the indemnity was payable on the 2d of February, 1833, one year after the exchange of ratifications, no application was made to the chambers for the required appropriation, and, in consequence of no appropriation having then been made, the draft of the United States government for that instalment was dishonored by the minister of finance, and the United States thereby involved in much controversy. The next session of the chambers commenced on the 19th of November, 1832, and continued until the 25th of April, 1833. Notwithstanding the omission to pay the first instalment had been made the subject of earnest remonstrance on our part, the treaty with the United States, and a bill making the necessary appropriations to execute it, were not laid before the chamber of deputies until the 6th of April, nearly five months after its meeting, and only nineteen days before the close of the session. The bill was read and referred to a committee, but there was no further action upon it. The next session of the chambers commenced on the 26th of April 1833, and continued until the 25th of June following. A new bill was introduced on the 11th of June, but nothing important was done in relation to it during the session. In the month of April, 1834, nearly three years after the signature of the treaty, the final action of the French chambers upon the bill to carry the treaty into effect was obtained, and resulted in a refusal of the necessary appropriations. The avowed grounds upon which the bill was rejected, are to be found in the published debates of that body, and no observations of mine can be necessary to satisfy Congress of their utter insufficiency. Although the gross amount of the claims of our citizens, is probably greater than will be ultimately allowed by the commissioners, sufficient is, nevertheless, shown, to render it absolutely certain that the indemnity falls far short of the actual amount of our just claims, independently of the question of damages and interest for the detention. That the settlement involved a sacrifice in this respect was well known at the time—a sacrifice which was cheerfully acquiesced in by the different branches of the federal government, whose action upon the treaty was required, from a sincere desire to avoid further collision upon this old and disturbed subject, and in the confident expectation that the general relations between the two countries would be improved thereby.

The refusal to vote the appropriation, the news of which was received from our minister in Paris, about the 15th day of May last, might have been considered the final determination of the French government not to execute the stipulations of the treaty, and would have justified an immediate communication of the facts to Congress, with a recommendation of such ultimate measures as the interest and honor of the United States might seem to require. But with the news of the refusal of the chambers to make the appropriation, were conveyed the regrets of the king, and a declaration that a national vessel should be forthwith sent out, with instructions to the French minister to give the most ample explanations of the past, and the strongest assurances for the future. After a long passage, the promised despatch vessel arrived. The pledges given by the French minister, upon receipt of his instructions, were, that as soon after the election of the new members as the charter would permit, the legislative chambers of France should be called together, and the proposition for an appropriation laid before them; that all the constitutional powers of the king and his cabinet should be exerted to accomplish the object; and that the result should be made known early enough to be communicated to Congress at the commencement of the present session. Relying upon these pledges, and not doubting that the acknowledged justice of our claims, the promised exertions of the king and his cabinet, and above all, that sacred regard for the national faith and honor for which the French character has been so distinguished, would secure an early execution of the treaty in all its parts, I did not deem it necessary to call the attention of Congress to the subject at the last session.

I regret to say that the pledges made through the minister of France have not been redeemed. The new chambers met on the 31st of July last, and although the subject of fulfilling treaties was alluded to in the speech from the throne, no attempt was made by the king or his cabinet to procure an appropriation to carry it into execution. The reasons given for this omission, although they might be considered sufficient in an ordinary case, are not consistent with the expectations founded upon the assurances given here, for there is no constitutional obstacle to entering into legislative business at the first meeting of the chambers. This point, however, might have been overlooked, had not the chambers, instead of being called to meet at so early a day that the result of their deliberations might be communicated to me before the meeting of Congress, been prorogued to the 29th of the present month—a period so late that their decision can scarcely be made known to the present Congress prior to its dissolution. To avoid this delay, our minister in Paris, in virtue of the assurance given by the French minister in the United States, strongly urged the convocation of the chambers at an earlier day, but without success. It is proper to remark, however, that this refusal has been accompanied with the most positive assurances, on the part of the executive government of France, of their intention to press the appropriation at the ensuing session of the chambers.

The executive branch of this government has, as matters stand, exhausted all the authority upon the subject with which it is invested, and which it had any reason to believe could be beneficially employed.

The idea of acquiescing in the refusal to execute the treaty will not, I am confident, be for a moment entertained by any branch of this government; and further negotiation upon the subject is equally out of the question.

If it shall be the pleasure of Congress to await the further action of the French chambers, no further consideration of the subject will, at this session, probably be required at your hands. But if, from the original delay in asking for an appropriation; from the refusal of the chambers to grant it when asked; from the omission to bring the subject before the chambers at their last session; from the fact that, including that session, there have been five different occasions when the appropriation might have been made; and from the delay in convoking the chambers until some weeks after the meeting of Congress, when it was well known that a communication of the whole subject to Congress at the last session was prevented by assurances that it should be disposed of before its present meeting, you should feel yourselves constrained to doubt whether it be the intention of the French government, in all its branches, to carry the treaty into effect, and think that such measures as the occasion may be deemed to call for, should be now adopted, the important question arises, what those measures shall be.

Our institutions are essentially pacific. Peace and friendly intercourse with all nations are as much the desire of our government as they are the interest of our people. But these objects are not to be permanently secured, by surrendering the rights of our citizens, or permitting solemn treaties for their indemnity, in cases of flagrant wrong, to be abrogated or set aside.

It is undoubtedly in the power of Congress seriously to affect the agricultural and manufacturing interests of France, by the passage of laws relating to her trade with the United States. Her products, manufactures, and tonnage, may be subjected to heavy duties in our ports, or all commercial intercourse with her may be suspended. But there are powerful, and to my mind conclusive objections to this mode of proceeding. We can not embarrass or cut off the trade of France, without at the same time, in some degree, embarrassing or cutting off our own trade. The injury of such a warfare must fall, though unequally, upon our own citizens, and could not but impair the means of the government, and weaken that united sentiment in support of the rights and honor of the nation which must now pervade every bosom. Nor is it impossible that such a course of legislation would introduce once more into our national councils those disturbing questions in relation to the tariff of duties which have been so recently put to rest. Besides, by every measure adopted by the government of the United States, with the view of injuring France, the clear perception of right which will induce our own people, and the rulers and people of all other nations, even of France herself, to pronounce our quarrel just, will be obscured, and the support rendered to us, in a final resort to more decisive measures, will be more limited and equivocal. There is but one point in the controversy, and upon that, the whole civilized world must pronounce France to be in the wrong. We insist that she shall pay us a sum of money, which she has acknowledged to be due; and of the justice of this demand there can be but one opinion among mankind. True policy would seem to dictate the question at issue should be kept thus disencumbered, and that not the slightest pretence should be given to France to persist in her refusal to make payment, by any act on our part affecting the interests of her people. The question should be left as it is now, in such an attitude that, when France fulfils her treaty stipulations, all controversy will be at an end.

It is my conviction that the United States ought to insist on a prompt execution of the treaty, and in case it be refused, or longer delayed, take redress into their own hands. After the delay on the part of France, of a quarter of a century, in acknowledging these claims by treaty, it is not to be tolerated that another quarter of a century is to be wasted in negotiating about the payment. The laws of nations provide a remedy for such occasions. It is a well-settled principle of the international code, that where one nation owes another a liquidated debt, which it refuses or neglects to pay, the aggrieved party may seize on the property belonging to the other, its citizens or subjects, sufficient to pay the debt, without giving just cause of war. This remedy has been repeatedly resorted to, and recently by France herself toward Portugal, under circumstances less unquestionable.

The time at which resort should be had to this, or any other mode of redress, is a point to be decided by Congress. If an appropriation shall not be made by the French chambers at their next session, it may justly be concluded that the government of France has finally determined to disregard its own solemn undertaking, and refuse to pay an acknowledged debt. In that event, every day's delay on our part will be a stain upon our national honor, as well as a denial of justice to our injured citizens. Prompt measures, when the refusal of France shall be complete, will not only be most honorable and just, but will have the best effect upon our national character.

Since France, in violation of the pledges given through her minister here, has delayed her final action so long that her decision will not probably be known in time to be communicated to this Congress, I recommend that a law be passed authorizing reprisals upon French property, in case provision shall not be made for the payment of the debt at the approaching session of the French chambers. Such a measure ought not to be considered by France as a menace. Her pride and power are too well known to expect any thing from her fears, and preclude the necessity of a declaration that nothing partaking of the character of intimidation is intended by us. She ought to look upon it only as the evidence of an inflexible determination on the part of the United States to insist on their rights. That government, by doing only what it has itself acknowledged to be just, will be able to spare the United States the necessity of taking redress into their own hands, and save the property of French citizens from that seizure and sequestration which American citizens so long endured without retaliation or redress. If she should continue to refuse that acknowledged justice, and, in violation of the law of nations, make reprisals on our part the occasion of hostilities against the United States, she would but add violence to injustice, and could not fail to expose herself to the just censure of civilized nations, and to the retributive judgments of Heaven.

Collision with France is the more to be regretted, on account of the position she occupies in Europe in relation to liberal institutions. But, in maintaining our national rights and honor, all governments are alike to us. If, by a collision, in a case where she is clearly in the wrong, the march of liberal principles shall be impeded, the responsibility for that result, as well as every other, will rest on her own head.

SIXTH ANNUAL MESSAGE

Having submitted these considerations, it belongs to Congress to decide whether, after what has taken place, it will still await the further action of the French chambers, or now adopt such provisional measures as it may deem necessary, and best adapted to protect the rights and maintain the honor of the country. Whatever that decision may be, it will be faithfully enforced by the executive, as far as he is authorized so to do.

According to the estimates of the treasury department, the revenue accruing from all sources, during the present year, will amount to twenty millions six hundred and twenty-four thousand seven hundred and seventeen dollars, which, with the balance remaining in the treasury on the 1st of January last, eleven millions seven hundred and two thousand nine hundred and five dollars, produces an aggregate of thirty-two millions three hundred and twenty-seven thousand six hundred and twenty-three dollars. The total expenditure during the year for all objects, including the public debt, is estimated at twenty-five millions five hundred and ninety-one thousand three hundred and ninety dollars, which will leave a balance in the treasury on the 1st of January, 1835, of six millions seven hundred and thirty-six thousand two hundred and thirty-two dollars. In this balance, however, will be included about one million one hundred and fifty thousand dollars of what was heretofore reported by the department as not effective.

Of former appropriations it is estimated that there will remain unexpended at the close of the year, eight millions and two thousand nine hundred and twenty-five dollars, and that of this sum there will not be required more than five millions one hundred and forty-one thousand nine hundred and sixty-four dollars, to accomplish the objects of all the current appropriations. Thus it appears that, after satisfying all those appropriations, and after discharging the last item of our public debt, which will be done on the 1st of January next, there will remain unexpended in the treasury an effective balance of about four hundred and forty thousand dollars. That such should be the aspect of our finances, is highly flattering to the industry and enterprise of our population, and auspicious of the wealth and prosperity which await the future cultivation of their growing resources. It is not deemed prudent, however, to recommend any change for the present in our impost rates, the effect of the gradual reduction now in progress in many of them not being sufficiently tested to guide us in determining the precise amount of revenue which they will produce.

Free from public debt, at peace with all the world, and with no complicated interest to consult in our intercourse with foreign powers, the present may be hailed as that epoch in our history the most favorable for the settlement of those principles in our domestic policy which shall be best calculated to give stability to our republic, and secure the blessings of freedom to our citizens. Among these principles, from our past experience it can not be doubted that simplicity in the character of the federal government, and a rigid economy in its administration, should be regarded as fundamental and sacred. All must be sensible that the existence of the public debt, by rendering taxation necessary for its extinguishment, has increased the difficulties which are inseparable from every exercise of the taxing power; and that it was, in this respect, a remote agent in producing those disturbing questions which grew out of the discussions relating to the tariff. If such has been the tendency of a debt incurred in the acquisition and maintenance of our national rights and liberties, the obligations of which all portions of the Union cheerfully acknowledged, it must be obvious that whatever is calculated to increase the burdens of government without necessity, must be fatal to all our hopes of preserving its true character. While we are felicitating ourselves, therefore, upon the extinguishment of the national debt, and the prosperous state of our finances, let us not be tempted to depart from those sound maxims of public policy, which enjoin a just adaptation of the revenue to the expenditures that are consistent with a rigid economy, and an entire abstinence from all topics of legislation that are not clearly within the constitutional powers of the government, and suggested by the wants of the country. Properly regarded under such a policy, every diminution of the public burdens, arising from taxation, gives to individual enterprise increased power, and furnishes to all the members of our happy confederacy new motives for patriotic affection and support. But, above all, its most important effect will be found in its influence upon the character of the government, by confining its action to those objects which will be sure to secure to it the attachment and support of our fellow-citizens.

Circumstances make it my duty to call the attention of Congress to the bank of the United States. Created for the convenience of the government, that institution has become the scourge of the people. Its interference to postpone the payment of a portion of the national debt, that it might retain the public money appropriated for that purpose, to strengthen it in a political contest; the extraordinary extension and contraction of its accommodations to the community; its corrupt and partisan loans; its exclusion of the public directors from a knowledge of its most important proceedings; the unlimited authority conferred on the president to expend its funds in hiring writers, and procuring the execution of printing, and the use made of that authority; the retention of the pension money and books after the selection of new agents; the groundless claim to heavy damages, in consequence of the protest of the bill drawn on the French government, have, through various channels, been laid before Congress. Immediately after the close of the last session, the bank, through its president, announced its ability and readiness to abandon the system of unparalleled curtailment, and the interruption of domestic exchanges, which it had practised upon from the 1st of August 1833, to the 30th of June, 1834, and to extend its accommodations to the community. The grounds assumed in this renunciation amounted to an acknowledgment that the curtailment, in the extent to which it had been carried, was not necessary to the safety of the bank, and had been persisted in merely to induce Congress to grant the prayer of the bank in its memorial relative to the removal of the deposites, and to give it a new charter. They were substantially a confession that all the real distresses which individuals and the country had endured for the preceding six or eight months had been needlessly produced by it, with the view of affecting, through the sufferings of the people, the legislative action of Congress. It is a subject of congratulation that Congress and the country had the virtue and firmness to bear the affliction; that the energies of our people soon found relief from this wanton tyrranny, in vast importations of the precious metals from almost every part of the world: and that, at the close of this tremendous effort to control our government, the bank found itself powerless, and no longer able to loan out its surplus means. The community had learned to manage its affairs without its assistance, and trade had already found new auxiliaries; so that, on the 1st of October last, the extraordinary spectacle was presented of a national bank, more than one half of whose capital was either lying unproductive in its vaults, or in the hands of foreign bankers.

To the needless distresses brought on the country during the last session of Congress has since been added the open seizure of the dividends on the public stock, to the amount of one hundred and seventy thousand and forty-one dollars, under pretence of paying damages, cost, and interest, upon the protested French bill. This sum constituted a portion of the estimated revenues for the year 1834, upon which the appropriations made by Congress were based. It would as soon have been expected that our collectors would seize on the customs, or the receivers of our land offices on the moneys arising from the sale of public lands, under pretences of claims against the United States, as that the bank would have retained the dividends. Indeed, if the principle be established that any one who chooses to set up a claim against the United States may, without authority of law, seize on the public property or money wherever he can find it, to pay the claim, there will remain no assurance that our revenue will reach the treasury, or that it will be applied after the appropriation to the purposes designated in the law. The paymasters of our army and the pursers of our navy, may, under like pretences, apply to their own use moneys appropriated to set in motion the public force, and in time of war leave the country without defence. This measure resorted to by the bank is disorganizing and revolutionary, and, if generally resorted to by private citizens in like cases, would fill the land with anarchy and violence.

It is a constitutional provision, that " no money shall be drawn from the treasury but in consequence of appropriations made by law." The palpable object of this provision is to prevent the expenditure of the public money for any purpose whatsoever, which shall not have been first approved by the representatives of the people and the states in Congress assembled. It vests the power of declaring for what purpose the public money shall be expended in the legislative department of the government, to the exclusion of the executive and judicial, and it is not within the constitutional authority of either of those departments to pay it away without law, or to sanction its payment. According to this plain constitutional provision, the claim of the bank can never be paid without an appropriation by act of Congress. But the bank has never asked for an appropriation. It attempts to defeat the provisions of the constitution, and obtain payment without an act of Congress. Instead of awaiting an appropriation passed by both houses, and approved by the president, it makes an appropriation for itself, and invites an appeal to the judiciary to sanction it. That the money has not technically been paid into the treasury, does not affect the principle intended to be established by the constitution. The executive and judiciary have as little right to appropriate and expend the public money without authority or law, before it is placed to the credit of the treasurer, as to take it from the treasury. In the annual report of the secretary of the treasury, and in his correspondence with the president of the bank, and the opinion of the attorney-general accompanying it, you will find a further examination of the claim of the bank, and the course it has pursued.

It seems due to the safety of the public funds remaining in that bank, and to the honor of the American people, that measures be taken to separate the government entirely from an institution so mischievous to the public prosperity, and so regardless of the constitution and laws. By transferring the public deposites, by appointing other pension agents, as far as it had the power, by ordering the discontinuance of the receipt of bank checks in payment of the public dues after the first day of January next, the executive has exerted all its lawful authority to sever the connexion between the government and this faithless corporation.

The high-handed career of this institution imposes upon the constitutional functionaries of this government, duties of the gravest and most imperative character—duties which they can not avoid, and from which I trust there will be no inclination on the part of any of them to shrink. My own sense of them is most clear, as is also my readiness to discharge those which may rightfully fall on me. To continue any business relations with the bank of the United States, that may be avoided without a violation of the national faith, after that institution has set at open defiance the conceded right of the government to examine its affairs; after it has done all in its power to deride the public authority in other respects, and to bring it into disrepute at home and abroad; after it has attempted to defeat the clearly expressed will of the people, by turning against them the immense power intrusted to its hands, and by involving a country otherwise peaceful, flourishing, and happy, in dissension, embarrassment, and distress; would make the nation itself a party to the degradation so sedulously prepared for its public agents, and do much to destroy the confidence of mankind in popular governments, and to bring into contempt their authority and efficiency. In guarding against an evil of such magnitude, considerations of temporary convenience should be thrown out of the question, and we should be influenced by such motives only as look to the honor and preservation of the republican system. Deeply and solemnly impressed with the justice of these views, I feel it to be my duty to recommend to you that a law be passed authorizing the sale of the public stock; that the provisions of the charter requiring the receipt of notes of the bank in payment of public dues, shall, in accordance with the power reserved to Congress in the 14th section of the charter, be suspended until the bank pays to the treasury the dividends withheld; and that all laws, connecting the government or its officers with the bank, directly or indirectly, be repealed; and that the institution be left hereafter to its own resources and means.

Events have satisfied my mind, and I think the minds of the American people, that the mischiefs and dangers which flow from a national bank far overbalance all its advantages. The bold effort the present bank has made to control the government, the distresses it has wantonly produced, the violence of which it has been the occasion in one of our cities famed for the observance of law and order, are but premonitions of the fate which awaits the American people, should they be deluded into a perpetuation of this institution, or the establishment of another like it. It is fervently hoped that, thus admonished, those who have heretofore favored the establishment of a substitute for the present bank, will be induced to abandon it, as it is evidently better to incur any inconvenience that may be reasonably expected, than to concentrate the whole moneyed power of the republic, in any form whatsoever, under any restrictions.

Happily, it is already illustrated that the agency of such an institution is not necessary to the fiscal operations of the government. The state banks are found fully adequate to the performance of all services which were required of the bank of the United States, quite as promptly and with the same cheapness. They have maintained themselves, and discharged all these duties, while the bank of the United States was still powerful, and in the field as an open enemy; and it is not possible to perceive that they will find greater difficulties in their operations when that enemy shall cease to exist.

The attention of Congress is earnestly invited to the regulation of the deposites in the state banks by law. Although the power now exercised by the executive department in this behalf, is only such as was uniformly exerted through every administration, from the origin of the government up to the establishment of the present bank, yet it is one which is susceptible of regulation by law, and therefore ought so to be regulated. The power of Congress to direct in what places the treasurer shall keep the moneys in the treasury, and to impose restrictions upon the executive authority in relation to their custody and removal, is unlimited, and its exercise will rather be courted than discouraged by those public officers and agents on whom rests the responsibility for their safety. It is desirable that as little power as possible should be left to the president or secretary of the treasury over those institutions which, being thus freed from executive influence, and without a common head to direct their operations, would have neither the temptation nor the ability to interfere in the political conflicts of the country. Not deriving their charters from the national authorities, they would never have those inducements to meddle in general elections which have led the bank of the United States to agitate and convulse the country for upward of two years.

The progress of our gold coinage is creditable to the officers of the mint, and promises in a short period to furnish the country with a sound and portable currency, which will much diminish the inconvenience to travellers of the want of a general paper currency, should the state banks be incapable of furnishing it. Those institutions have already shown themselves competent to purchase and furnish domestic exchange for the convenience of trade, at reasonable rates, and not a doubt is entertained that in a short period, all the wants of the country, in bank accommodations and in exchange, will be supplied as promptly and cheaply as they have heretofore been by the bank of the United States. If the several states shall be induced gradually to reform their banking systems, and prohibit the issue of all small notes, we shall, in a few years, have a currency as sound, and as little liable to fluctuations, as any other commercial country.

The report of the secretary of war, together with accompanying documents from the several bureaus of that department will exhibit the situation of the various objects committed to its administration.

No event has occurred since your last session, rendering necessary any movements of the army, with the exception of the expedition of the regiment of dragoons into the territory of the wandering and predatory tribes inhabiting the western frontier, and living adjacent to the Mexican boundary. These tribes have been heretofore known to us principally by their attacks upon our own citizens, and upon other Indians entitled to the protection of the United States. It became necessary for the peace of the frontiers, to check these habitual inroads, and I am happy to inform you that the object has been effected without the commission of any act of hostility. Colonel Dodge, and the troops under his command, have acted with equal firmness and humanity, and an arrangement has been made with those Indians, which it is hoped will insure their permanent pacific relations with the United States, and the other tribes of Indians upon that border.

It is to be regretted that the prevalence of sickness in that quarter has deprived the country of a number of valuable lives, and particularly that of General Leavenworth, an officer well known and esteemed for his gallant services during the late war, and for subsequent good conduct, who has fallen a victim to his zeal and exertions in the discharge of his duty.

The army is in a high state of discipline. Its moral condition, so far as that is known here, is good, and the various branches of the public service are carefully attended to. It is amply sufficient, under its present organization, for providing the necessary garrisons for the seaboard, and for the defence of the internal frontier, and also for preserving the elements of military knowledge, and for keeping pace with those improvements which modern experience is continually making. And these objects appear to me to embrace all the legitimate purposes for which a permanent military force should be maintained in our country. The lessons of history teach us its danger, and the tendency which exists to an increase.

This can be best met and averted by a just caution on the part of the public itself, and of those who represent them in Congress.

From the duties which devolve on the engineer department, and upon the topographical engineers, a different organization seems to be demanded by the public interest, and I recommend the subject to your consideration.

No important change has, during this season, taken place in the condition of the Indians. Arrangements are in progress for the removal of the Creeks, and will soon be for the removal of the Seminoles. I regret that the Cherokees east of the Mississippi have not yet determined as a community to remove. How long the personal causes which have hitherto retarded that ultimately inevitable measure will continue to operate, I am unable to conjecture. It is certain, however, that delay will bring with it accumulated evils, which will render their condition more and more unpleasant. The experience of every year adds to the conviction that emigration, and that alone, can preserve from destruction the remnant of tribes yet living among us. The facility with which the necessaries of life are procured, and the treaty stipulations providing aid for the emigrant Indians in their agricultural pursuits and in the important concern of education, and their removal from those causes which have heretofore depressed all, and destroyed many of the tribes, can not fail to stimulate their exertions, and to reward their industry.

The two laws passed at the last session of Congress on the subject of Indian affairs, have been carried into effect, and detailed instructions for their administration have been given. It will be seen by the estimates for the present session, that a great reduction will take place in the expenditures of the department in consequence of these laws, and there is reason to believe that their operation will be salutary, and that the colonization of the Indian on the western frontier, together with a judicious system of administration, will still further reduce the expenses of this branch of the public service, and at the same time promote its usefulness and efficiency.

Circumstances have been recently developed, showing the existence of extensive frauds under the various laws granting pensions and gratuities for revolutionary services.

It is impossible to estimate the amount which may have been thus fraudulently obtained from the national treasury. I am satisfied, however, that it has been such as to justify a re-examination of the system, and the adoption of the necessary checks in its administration. All will agree that the services and sufferings of the remnant of our revolutionary band should be fully compensated; but while this is done, every proper precaution should be taken to prevent the admission of fabricated and fraudulent claims. In the present mode of proceeding, the attestations and certificates of judicial officers of the various states form a considerable portion of the checks which are interposed against the commission of frauds. These, however, have been and may be fabricated, and in such a way as to elude detection at the examining offices; and independently of this practical difficulty, it is ascertained that these documents are often loosely granted; sometimes even blank certificates have been issued; sometimes prepared papers have been signed without inquiry; and in one instance, at least, the seal of the court has been within reach of a person most interested in its improper application. It is obvious that under such circumstances, no severity of administration can check the abuse of the law; and information has from time to time been communicated to the pension office, questioning or denying the right of persons placed upon the pension list to the bounty of the country. Such cautions are always attended to, and examined, but a far more general investigation is called for; and I therefore recommend, in conformity with the suggestion of the secretary of war, that an actual inspection should be made in each state, into the circumstances and claims of every person now drawing a pension. The honest veteran has nothing to fear from such a scrutiny, while the fraudulent claimant will be detected, and the public treasury relieved to an amount, I have reason to believe, far greater than has heretofore been suspected. The details of such a plan could be so regulated as to interpose the necessary checks without any burdensome operation upon the pensioners. The object should be twofold:—

1. To look into the original justice of the claims, so far as this can be done under a proper system of regulations, by an examination of the claimants themselves, and by inquiring in the vicinity of their residence into their history, and into the opinion entertained of their revolutionary services;

2. To ascertain, in all cases, whether the original claimant is living, and this by actual personal inspection.

This measure will, if adopted, be productive, I think, of the desired results, and I therefore recommend it to your consideration, with the further suggestion, that all payments should be suspended till the necessary reports are received.

It will be seen by a tabular statement annexed to the documents transmitted to Congress, that the appropriations for objects connected with the war department made at the last session, for the service of the year 1834, excluding the permanent appropriation for the payment of military gratuities under the act of June 7, 1832, the appropriation of two hundred thousand dollars for arming and equipping the militia, and the appropriation of ten thousand dollars for the civilization of the Indians, which are not annually renewed, amounted to the sum of nine millions three thousand two hundred and sixty-one dollars, and that the estimates of appropriations necessary for the same branches of service for the year 1835, amount to the sum of five millions seven hundred and seventy-eight thousand nine hundred and sixty-four dollars, making a difference in the appropriations of the current year over the estimates of the appropriations for the next, of three millions two hundred and twenty-four thousand two hundred and ninety-seven dollars.

The principal causes which have operated at this time to produce this great difference, are shown in the reports and documents, and in the detailed estimates. Some of these causes are accidental and temporary, while others are permanent, and, aided by a just course of adminstration, may continue to operate beneficially upon the public expenditures.

A just economy, expending where the public service requires, and withholding where it does not, is among the indispensable duties of the government.

I refer you to the accompanying report of the secretary of the navy, and to the documents with it, for a full view of the operations of that important branch of our service during the present year. It will be seen that the wisdom and liberality with which Congress have provided for the gradual increase of our navy material, have been seconded by a corresponding zeal and fidelity on the part of those to whom has been confided the execution of the laws on the subject; and that but a short period would be now required to put in commission a force large enough for any exigency into which the country may be thrown.

When we reflect upon our position in relation to other nations, it must be apparent that, in the event of conflicts with them, we must look chiefly to our navy for the protection of our national rights. The wide seas which separate us from other governments, must of necessity be the theatre on which an enemy will aim to assail us, and, unless we are prepared to meet him on this element, we can not be said to possess the power requisite to repel or prevent aggressions. We can not, therefore, watch with too much attention this arm of our defence, or cherish with too much care the means by which it can possess the necessary efficiency and extension. To this end our policy has been heretofore wisely directed to the constant employment of a force sufficient to guard our commerce, and to the rapid accumulation of the materials which are necessary to repair our vessels, and construct with ease such new ones as may be required in a state of war.

In accordance with this policy, I recommend to your consideration the erection of the additional dry-dock described by the secretary of the navy, and also the construction of the steam-batteries to which he has referred, for the purpose of testing their efficiency as auxiliaries to the system of defence now in use.

The report of the postmaster-general, herewith submitted, exhibits the condition and prospects of that department. From that document it appears that there was a deficit in the funds of the department, at the commencement of the present year, beyond its available means, of three hundred and fifteen thousand five hundred and ninety-nine dollars and ninety-eight cents, which, on the first of July last, had been reduced to two hundred and sixty-eight thousand and ninety-two dollars and seventy-four cents. It appears, also, that the revenues for the coming year will exceed the expenditures about two hundred and seventy thousand dollars, which, with the excess of the revenue which will result from the operations of the current half-year, may be expected, independently of any increase in the gross amount of postages, to supply the entire deficit before the end of 1835. But as this calculation is based on the gross amount of postages which have accrued within the period embraced by the times of striking the balances, it is obvious that, without a progressive increase in the amount of postages, the existing retrenchments must be persevered in through the year 1836, that the department may accumulate a surplus fund sufficient to place it in a condition of perfect ease.

It will be observed that the revenues of the postoffice department, though they have increased, and their amount is above that of any former year, have yet fallen short of the estimates more than a hundred thousand dollars. This is attributed, in a great degree, to the increase of free letters, growing out of the extension and abuse of the franking privilege. There has been a gradual increase in the number of executive officers to which it has been granted; and by an act passed in March, 1833, it was extended to members of Congress throughout the whole year. It is believed that a revision of the laws relative to the franking privilege, with some enactments to enforce more rigidly the restrictions under which it is granted, would operate beneficially to the country, by enabling the department at an early period to restore the mail facilities which have been withdrawn, and to extend them more widely, as the growing settlement of the country may require.

To a measure so important to the government, and so just to our constituents, who ask no exclusive privileges for themselves, and are not willing to concede them to others, I earnestly recommend the serious attention of Congress.

The importance of the postoffice department, and the magnitude to which it has grown, both in its revenues and in its operations, seem to demand its reorganization by law. The whole of its receipts and disbursements have hitherto been left entirely to executive control and individual discretion. The principle is as sound in relation to this as to any other department of the government, that as little discretion should be confided to the executive officer who controls it, as is compatible with its efficiency. It is therefore earnestly recommended that it be organized with an auditor and treasury of its own, appointed by the president and senate, who shall be branches of the treasury department.

Your attention is again respectfully invited to the defect which exists in the judicial system of the United States. Nothing can be more desirable than the uniform operation of the federal judiciary throughout the several states, all of which, standing on the same footing as members of the Union, have equal rights to the advantages and benefits resulting from its laws. This object is not attained by the judicial acts now in force, because they leave one-fourth of the states without circuit courts.

It is undoubtedly the duty of Congress to place all the states on the same footing in this respect, either by the creation of an additional number of associate judges, or by an enlargement of the circuits assigned to those already appointed, so as to include the new states. Whatever may be the difficulty in a proper organization of the judicial system, so as to secure its efficiency and uniformity in all parts of the Union, and at the same time to avoid such an increase of judges as would encumber the supreme appellate tribunal, it should not be allowed to weigh against the great injustice which the present operation of the system produces.

I trust that I may be also pardoned for renewing the

recommendations I have so often submitted to your attention, in regard to the mode of electing the president and vice-president of the United States. All the reflection I have been able to bestow upon the subject increases my conviction that the best interests of the country will be promoted by the adoption of some plan which will secure, in all contingencies, that important right of sovereignty to the direct control of the people. Could this be attained, and the terms of those officers be limited to a single period of either four or six years, I think our liberties would possess an additional safeguard.

At your last session I called the attention of Congress to the destruction of the public building occupied by the treasury department. As the public interest requires that another building should be erected with as little delay as possible, it is hoped that the means will be seasonably provided, and that they will be ample enough to authorize such an enlargement and improvement in the plan of the building as will more effectually accommodate the public officers, and secure the public documents deposited in it from the casualties of fire.

I have not been able to satisfy myself that the bill entitled, "An act to improve the navigation of the Wabash river," which was sent to me at the close of your last session, ought to pass, and I have therefore withheld from it my approval, and now return it to the senate, the body in which it originated.

There can be no question connected with the administration of public affairs, more important, or more difficult to be satisfactorily dealt with, than that which relates to the rightful authority and proper action of the federal government upon the subject of internal improvements. To inherent embarrassments have been added others resulting from the course of our legislation concerning it.

I have heretofore communicated freely with Congress upon this subject, and, in adverting to it again, I can not refrain from expressing my increased conviction of its extreme importance, as well in regard to its bearing upon the maintenance of the constitution, and the prudent management of the public revenue, as on account of its disturbing effect upon the harmony of the Union.

We are in no danger from violations of the constitution, by which encroachments are made upon the personal rights of the citizens. The sentence of condemnation long since pronounced by the American people upon acts of that character, will, I doubt not, continue to prove as salutary in its effects as it is irreversible in its nature. But against the dangers of unconstitutional acts which, instead of menacing the vengeance of offended authority, proffer local advantages, and bring in their train the patronage of the government, we are, I fear, not so safe. To suppose that, because our government has been instituted for the benefit of the people, it must therefore have the power to do whatever may seem to conduce to the public good, is an error into which even honest minds are too apt to fall. In yielding themselves to this fallacy, they overlook the great considerations in which the federal constitution was founded. They forget that, in consequence of the conceded diversities in the interest and condition of the different states, it was foreseen, at the period of its adoption, that, although a particular measure of the government might be beneficial and proper in one state, it might be the reverse in another—that it was for this reason the states would not consent to make a grant to the federal government of the general and usual powers of government, but of such only as were specifically enumerated, and the probable effects of which they could, as they thought, safely anticipate; and they forget also the paramount obligation upon all to abide by the compact, then so solemnly, and as it was hoped, so firmly established. In addition to the dangers to the constitution springing from the sources I have stated, there has been one which was perhaps greater than all. I allude to the materials which this subject has afforded for sinister appeals to selfish feelings, and the opinion heretofore so extensively entertained of its adaptation to the purposes of personal ambition. With such stimulants, it is not surprising that the acts and pretensions of the federal government, in this behalf, should sometimes have been carried to an alarming extent. The questions which have arisen upon this subject have related—

1. To the power of making internal improvements within the limits of a state, with the right of territorial jurisdiction, sufficient at least for their preservation and use;

2. To the right of appropriating money in aid of such works when carried on by a state, or by a company in virtue of state authority, surrendering the claim of jurisdiction; and,

3. To the propriety of appropriations for improvements of a particular class, viz., for lighthouses, beacons, buoys, public piers, and for the removal of sandbars, sawyers, and other temporary and partial impediments in our navigable rivers and harbors.

The claims of power for the general government upon each of these points certainly present matter of the deepest interest. The first is, however, of much the greatest importance, inasmuch as, in addition to the dangers of unequal and improvident expenditures of public moneys, common to all, there is superadded to that the conflicting jurisdictions of the respective governments. Federal jurisdiction, at least to the extent I have stated, has been regarded by its advocates as necessarily appurtenant to the power in question, if that exists by the constitution. That the most injurious conflicts would unavoidably arise between the respective jurisdictions of the state and federal governments, in the absence of a constitutional provision marking out their respective boundaries, can not be doubted. The local advantages to be obtained would induce the states to overlook in the beginning the dangers and difficulties to which they might ultimately be exposed. The powers exercised by the federal government would soon be regarded with jealousy by the state authorities, and originating, as they must, from implication or assumption, it would be impossible to affix to them certain and safe limits. Opportunities and temptations to the assumption of power incompatible with state sovereignty, would be increased, and those barriers which resist the tendency of our system toward consolidation, greatly weakened. The officers and agents of the general government might not always have the discretion to abstain from intermeddling with state concerns; and if they did, they would not always escape the suspicion of having done so. Collisions and consequent irritations would spring up; that harmony which should ever exist between the general government and each member of the confederacy, would be frequently interrupted; a spirit of contention would be engendered; and the dangers of division greatly multiplied.

Yet we all know that, notwithstanding these grave objections, this dangerous doctrine was at one time, apparently, proceeding to its final establishment with fearful rapidity. The desire to embark the federal government in works of internal improvement, prevailed in the highest degree during the first session of the first Congress that I had the honor to meet in my present situation. When the bill authorizing a subscription on the part of the United States for stock in the Maysville and Lexington turnpike company, passed the two houses, there had been reported by the committees on internal improvements, bills containing appropriations for such objects, exclusive of those for the Cumberland road, and for harbors and lighthouses, to the amount of about one hundred and six millions of dollars. In this amount was included authority to the secretary of the treasury to subscribe for the stock of different companies to a great extent, and the residue was principally for the direct construction of roads by this government. In addition to these projects, which have been presented to the two houses under the sanction and recommendation of their respective committees on internal improvements, there were then still pending before the committees, and in memorials to Congress, presented, but not referred, different projects for works of a similar character, the expense of which can not be estimated with certainty, but must have exceeded one hundred millions of dollars.

Regarding the bill authorizing a subscription to the stock of the Maysville and Lexington turnpike company as the entering wedge of a system which, however weak at first, might soon become strong enough to rive the bands of the Union asunder; and believing that, if its passage was acquiesced in by the executive and the people, there would no longer be any limitation upon the authority of the general government in respect to the appropriation of money for such objects, I deemed it an imperative duty to withhold from it the executive approval. Although, from the obviously local character of that work, I might well have contented myself with a refusal to approve the bill upon that ground, yet, sensible of the vital importance of the subject, and anxious that my views and opinions in regard to the whole matter should be fully understood by Congress, and by my constituents, I felt it my duty to go further. I therefore embraced that early occasion to apprize Congress that, in my opinion, the constitution did not confer upon it the power to authorize the construction of ordinary roads and canals within the limits of a state, and to say, respectfully, that no bill admitting such a power could receive my official sanction. I did so in the confident expectation that the speedy settlement of the public mind upon the whole subject would be greatly facilitated by the difference between the two houses and myself, and that the harmonious action of the several departments of the federal government in regard to it would be ultimately secured.

So far, at least, as it regards this branch of the subject, my best hopes have been realized. Nearly four years have elapsed, and several sessions of Congress have intervened, and no attempt within my recollection has been made to induce Congress to exercise this power. The applications for the construction of roads and canals, which were formerly multiplied upon your files, are no longer presented; and we have good reason to infer that the current of public sentiment has become so decided against the pretension as effectually to discourage its reassertion. So thinking, I derive the greatest satisfaction from the conviction that thus much at least has been secured upon this important and embarrassing subject.

From attempts to appropriate the national funds to objects which are confessedly of a local character, we can not, I trust, have anything further to apprehend. My views in regard to the expediency of making appropriations for works which are claimed to be of a national character, and prosecuted under state authority, assuming that Congress have the right to do so, were stated in my annual message to Congress in 1830, and also in that containing my objections to the Maysville road bill.

So thoroughly convinced am I that no such appropriations ought to be made by Congress, until a suitable constitutional provision is made upon the subject, and so essential do I regard the point to the highest interests of our country, that I could not consider myself as discharging my duty to my constituents in giving the executive sanction to any bill containing such an appropriation. If the people of the United States desire that the public treasury shall be resorted to for the means to prosecute such works, they will concur in an amendment of the constitution, prescribing a rule by which the national character of the works is to be tested, and by which the greatest practicable equality of benefits may be secured to each member of the confederacy. The effects of such a regulation would be most salutary in preventing unprofitable expenditures, in securing our legislation from the pernicious consequences of a scramble for the favors of government, and in repressing the spirit of discontent which must inevitably arise from an unequal distribution of treasures which belong alike to all.

There is another class of appropriations for what may be called, without impropriety, internal improvements, which have always been regarded as standing upon different grounds from those to which I have referred. I allude to such as have for their object the improvement of our harbors, the removal of partial and temporary obstructions in our navigable rivers, for the facility and security of our foreign commerce. The grounds upon which I distinguished appropriations of this character from others have already been stated to Congress. I will now only add that, at the first session of Congress under the new constitution, it was provided by law, that all expenses which should accrue from and after the 15th day of August, 1789, in the necessary support and maintenance and repairs of all light-houses, beacons, buoys, and public piers, erected, placed, or sunk, before the passage of the act, within any bay, inlet, harbor, or port of the United States, for rendering the navigation thereof easy and safe, should be defrayed out of the treasury of the United States; and further, that it be the duty of the secretary of the treasury to provide by contracts, with the approbation of the President, for rebuilding when necessary and keeping in good repair the lighthouses, beacons, buoys, and public piers, in the several states and for furnishing them with supplies. Appropriations for similar objects have been continued from that time to the present without interruption or dispute. As a natural consequence of the increase and extension of our foreign commerce, ports of entry and delivery have been multiplied and established, not only upon our seaboard, but in the interior of the country, upon our lakes and navigable rivers. The convenience and safety of this commerce have led to the gradual extension of these expenditures; to the erection of lighthouses, the placing, planting and sinking of buoys, beacons, and piers, and to the removal of partial and temporary obstructions in our navigable rivers, and the harbors upon our great lakes, as well as on the seaboard. Although I expressed to Congress my apprehension that these expenditures have sometimes been extravagant and disproportionate to the advantages to be derived from them, I have not felt it to be my duty to refuse my assent to bills containing them, and have contented myself to follow, in this respect, in the footsteps of all my predecessors. Sensible, however, from experience and observation, of the great abuses to which the unrestricted exercise of this authority by Congress was exposed, I have prescribed a limitation for the government of my own conduct, by which expenditures of this character are confined to places below the ports of entry or delivery established by law. I am very sensible that this restriction is not as satisfactory as could be desired, and that much embarrassment may be caused to the executive department in its execution, by appropriations for remote and not well-understood objects. But as neither my own reflections, nor the lights which I may properly derive from other sources, have supplied me with a better, I shall continue to apply my best exertions to a faithful application of the rule upon which it is founded. I sincerely regret that I could not give my assent to the bill entitled, "An act to improve the navigation of the Wabash river;" but I could not have done so without receding from the ground which I have, upon the fullest consideration, taken upon this subject, and of which Congress has been heretofore apprized, and without throwing the subject again open to abuses which no good citizen, entertaining my opinions, could desire.

I rely upon the intelligence and candor of my fellow-citizens, in whose liberal indulgence I have already so largely participated, for a correct appreciation of my motives in interposing, as I have done, on this, and other occasions, checks to a course of legislation which, without, in the slightest degree, calling in question the motives of others, I consider as sanctioning improper and unconstitutional expenditures of public treasure.

I am not hostile to internal improvements, and wish to see them extended to every part of the country. But I am fully persuaded, if they are not commenced in a proper manner, confined to proper objects, and conducted under an authority generally conceded to be rightful, that a successful prosecution of them can not be reasonably expected. The attempt will meet with resistance where it might otherwise receive support; and instead of strengthening the bonds of our confederacy, it will only multiply and aggravate the causes of disunion.

MESSAGE IN RELATION TO TEXAS.

Delivered December 21st, 1836.

To the Senate of the United States:—

DURING the last session, information was given to Congress by the executive, that measures had been taken to ascertain "the political, military, and civil condition of Texas." I now submit for your consideration, extracts from the report of the agent who had been appointed to collect it, relative to the condition of that country.

No steps have been taken by the executive toward the acknowledgment of the independence of Texas; and the whole subject would have been left without further remark on the information now given to Congress, were it not that the two houses at their last session, acting separately, passed resolutions "that the independence of Texas ought to be acknowledged by the United States, whenever satisfactory information should be received that it had in successful operation a civil government, capable of performing the duties, and fulfilling the obligations of an independent power." This mark of interest in the question of the independence of Texas, and indication of the views of Congress, make it proper that I should, somewhat in detail, present the considerations that have governed the executive in continuing to occupy the ground previously taken in the contest between Mexico and Texas.

The acknowledgment of a new state as independent, and entitled to a place in the family of nations, is at all times an act of great delicacy and responsibility; but more especially so when such state has forcibly separated itself from another, of which it had formed an integral part, and which still claims dominion over it. A premature recognition under these circumstances, if not looked upon as

MESSAGE IN RELATION TO TEXAS 343

justifiable cause of war, is always liable to be regarded as a proof of an unfriendly spirit to one of the contending parties. All questions relative to the government of foreign nations, whether of the old or new world, have been treated by the United States as questions of fact only, and our predecessors have cautiously abstained from deciding upon them until the clearest evidence was in their possession, to enable them, not only to decide correctly, but to shield their decisions from every unworthy imputation. In all the contests that have arisen out of the revolutions of France, out of the disputes relating to the crowns of Portugal and Spain, out of the separation of the American possessions of both from the European governments, and out of the numerous and constantly occurring struggles for dominion in Spanish America, so wisely consistent with our just principles has been the action of our government, that we have, under the most critical circumstances, avoided all censure, and encountered no other evil than that produced by a transient estrangement of good will in those against whom we have been by force of evidence compelled to decide.

It has thus made known to the world, that the uniform policy and practice of the United States is to avoid all interference in disputes which merely relate to the internal government of other nations, and eventually to recognise the authority of the prevailing party without reference to our particular interests and views, or to the merits of the original controversy. Public opinion here is so firmly established and well understood in favor of this policy, that no serious disagreement has ever risen among ourselves in relation to it, although brought under view in a variety of forms, and at periods when the minds of the people were greatly excited by the agitation of topics purely domestic in their character. Nor has any deliberate inquiry ever been instituted in Congress, or in any of our legislative bodies, as to whom belonged the power of originally recognising a new state—a power, the exercise of which is equivalent, under some circumstances, to a declaration of war—a power nowhere expressly delegated, and only granted in the constitution, as it is necessarily involved in some of the great powers given to Congress; in that given to the president and senate to form treaties with foreign powers, and to appoint ambassadors and other public ministers; and in that conferred upon the president to receive ministers from foreign nations.

In the preamble to the resolution of the house of representatives, it is distinctly intimated that the expediency of recognising the independence of Texas should be left to the decision of Congress. In this view, on the ground of expediency, I am disposed to concur; and do not, therefore, consider it necessary to express any opinion as to the strict constitutional right of the executive, either apart from, or in conjunction with the senate, over the subject. It is to be presumed that on no future occasion will a dispute arise, as none has heretofore occurred, between the executive and the legislature in the exercise of the power of recognition. It will always be considered consistent with the spirit of the constitution, and most safe, that it should be exercised, when probably leading to war, with a previous understanding with that body by whom war can alone be declared, and by whom all the provisions for sustaining its perils must be furnished. Its submission to Congress, which represents in one of its branches the states of the Union, and, in the other, the people of the United States, where there may be reasonable ground to apprehend so grave a consequence, would certainly afford the fullest satisfaction to our own country, and a perfect guarantee to all other nations, of the justice and prudence of the measures which might be adopted.

In making these suggestions, it is not my purpose to relieve myself from the responsibility of expressing my own opinions of the course the interests of our country prescribe, and its honor permits us to follow.

It is scarcely to be imagined that a question of this character could be presented, in relation to which it would be more difficult for the United States to avoid exciting the suspicion and jealousy of other powers, and maintain their established character for fair and impartial dealing. But on this, as on every other trying occasion, safety is to be found in a rigid adherence to principle.

MESSAGE IN RELATION TO TEXAS

In the contest between Spain and her revolted colonies we stood aloof, and waited not only until the ability of the new states to protect themselves was fully established, but until the danger of their being again subjugated had entirely passed away. Then, and not until then, were they recognised. Such was our course in regard to Mexico herself. The same policy was observed in all the disputes growing out of the separation into distinct governments of those Spanish American states, who began, or carried on the contest with the parent country, united under one form of government. We acknowledged the separate independence of New Grenada, of Venezuela, and of Ecuador, only after their independent existence was no longer a subject of dispute, or was actually acquiesced in by those with whom they had been previously united. It is true that, with regard to Texas, the civil authority of Mexico has been expelled, its invading army defeated, the chief of the republic himself captured, and all present power to control the newly organized government of Texas annihilated within its confines. But, on the other hand, there is, in appearance at least, an immense disparity of physical force on the side of Texas. The Mexican republic, under another executive, is rallying its forces under a new leader, and menacing a fresh invasion to recover its lost dominion.

Upon the issue of this threatened invasion, the independence of Texas may be considered as suspended; and were there nothing peculiar in the relative situation of the United States and Texas, our acknowledgment of its independence at such a crisis could scarcely be regarded as consistent with that prudent reserve with which we have heretofore held ourselves bound to treat all similar questions. But there are circumstances in the relations of the two countries, which require us to act on this occasion, with even more than our wonted caution. Texas was once claimed as a part of our property, and there are those among our citizens who, always reluctant to abandon that claim, can not but regard with solicitude the prospect of the reunion of the territory to this country. A large portion of its civilized inhabitants are emigrants from the United States; speak the same language with ourselves; cherish the same principles, political and religious, and are bound to many of our citizens by ties of friendship and kindred blood; and more than all, it is known that the people of that country have instituted the same form of government with our own; and have, since the close of your last session, openly resolved, on the acknowledgment by us of their independence, to seek admission into the Union as one of the federal states. This last circumstance is a matter of peculiar delicacy, and forces upon us considerations of the gravest character. The title of Texas to the territory she claims is identified with her independence; she asks us to acknowledge that title to the territory, with an avowed design to treat immediately of its transfer to the United States. It becomes us to beware of a too early movement, as it might subject us, however unjustly, to the imputation of seeking to establish the claim of our neighbors to a territory, with a view to its subsequent acquisition by ourselves. Prudence, therefore, seems to dictate that we should still stand aloof, and maintain our present attitude, if not until Mexico itself, or one of the great foreign powers, shall recognise the independence of the new government, at least until the lapse of time, or the course of events shall have proved, beyond cavil or dispute, the ability of the people of that country to maintain their separate sovereignty, and to uphold the government constituted by them. Neither of the contending parties can justly complain of this course. By pursuing it, we are but carrying out the long-established policy of our government—a policy which has secured to us respect and influence abroad, and inspired confidence at home.

Having thus discharged my duty, by presenting with simplicity and directness the views which, after much reflection, I have been led to take of this important subject, I have only to add the expression of my confidence, that if Congress shall differ with me upon it, their judgment will be the result of dispassionate, prudent, and wise deliberation; with the assurance that, during the short time I shall continue connected with the government, I shall promptly and cordially unite with you in such measures as may be deemed best fitted to increase the prosperity and perpetuate the peace of our favored country.

Farewell Address of President Jackson.

FELLOW-CITIZENS: Being about to retire finally from public life, I beg leave to offer you my grateful thanks for the many proofs of kindness and confidence which I have received at your hands. It has been my fortune, in the discharge of public duties, civil and military, frequently to have found myself in difficult and trying situations, where prompt decision and energetic action were necessary, and where the interests of the country required that high responsibilities should be fearlessly encountered; and it is with the deepest emotions of gratitude that I acknowledge the continued and unbroken confidence with which you have sustained me in every trial. My public life has been a long one, and I cannot hope that it has at all times been free from errors. But I have the consolation of knowing, that if mistakes have been committed, they have not seriously injured the country I so anxiously endeavored to serve; and at the moment when I surrender my last public trust, I leave this great people prosperous and happy; in the full enjoyment of liberty and peace; and honored and respected by every nation in the world.

If my humble efforts have, in any degree, contributed to preserve to you these blessings, I have been more than rewarded by the honors you have heaped upon me; and, above all, by the generous confidence with which you have supported me in every peril, and with which you have continued to animate and cheer my path to the closing hour of my political life. The time has now come, when advanced age and a broken frame warn me to retire from public concerns; but the recollection of the many favors you have bestowed upon me is engraven upon my heart, and I have felt that I could not part from your service without making this public acknowledgment of the gratitude I owe you. And if I use the occasion to offer to you the counsels of age and experience, you will, I trust, receive them with the same indulgent kindness which you have so often extended to me; and will, at least, see in them an earnest desire to perpetuate, in this favored land, the blessings of liberty and equal laws.

We have now lived almost fifty years under the Constitution framed by the sages and patriots of the Revolution. The conflicts in which the nations of Europe were engaged during a great part of this period; the spirit in which they waged war with each other; and our intimate commercial connections with every part of the civilized world, rendered it a time of much difficulty for the government of the United States. We have had our seasons of peace and of war, with all the evils which precede or follow a state of hostility with powerful nations. We encountered these trials, with our Constitution yet in its infancy, and under the disadvantages which a new and untried government must always feel, when it is called upon to put forth its whole strength, without the lights of experience to guide it, or the weight of precedents to justify its measures. But we have passed triumphantly through all these difficulties. Our Constitution is no longer a doubtful experiment; and at the end of nearly half a century, we find that it has preserved, unimpaired, the liberties of the people, and secured the rights of property, and that our country has improved, and is flourishing beyond any former example in the history of nations.

In our domestic concerns, there is every thing to encourage us; and if you are true to yourselves, nothing can impede your march to the highest point of national prosperity. The states which had so long been retarded in their improvements by the Indian tribes residing in the midst of them, are at length relieved from the evil; and this unhappy race—the original dwellers in our land—are now placed in a situation where we may well hope that they will share in the blessings of civilization, and be saved from that degradation and destruction to which they were rapidly hastening, while they remained in the states; and while the safety and comfort of our own citizens have been greatly promoted by their removal, the philanthropist will rejoice that the remnant of this ill-fated race has been at length placed beyond the reach of injury or oppression, and that the paternal care of the general government will hereafter watch over them and protect them.

If we turn to our relations with foreign powers, we find our condition equally gratifying. Actuated by the sincere desire to do justice to every nation, and to preserve the blessings of peace, our intercourse with them has been conducted on the part of this government in the spirit of frankness, and I take pleasure in saying that it has generally been met in a corresponding temper. Difficulties of old standing have been surmounted by friendly discussion, and the mutual desire to be just; and the claims of our citizens, which had been long withheld, have at length been acknowledged and adjusted, and satisfactory arrangements made for their final payment; and with a limited, and I trust a temporary exception, our relations with every foreign power are now of the most friendly character—our commerce continually expanding, and our flag respected in every quarter of the world.

These cheering and grateful prospects, and these multiplied favors, we owe, under Providence, to the adoption of the Federal Constitution. It is no longer a question whether this great country can remain happily united, and flourish under our present form of government. Experience, the unerring test of all human undertakings, has shown the wisdom and foresight of those who formed it; and has proved, that in the union of these states there is a sure foundation for the brightest hopes of freedom, and for the happiness of the people. At every hazard, and by every sacrifice, this Union must be preserved.

The necessity of watching with jealous anxiety, for the preservation of the Union, was earnestly pressed upon his fellow-citizens by the Father of his country, in his farewell address. He has there told us, that "while experience shall not have demonstrated its impracticability, there will always be reason to distrust the patriotism of those who, in any quarter, may endeavor to weaken its bonds;" and he has cautioned us, in the strongest terms, against the formation of parties on geographical discriminations, as one of the means which might disturb our Union, and to which designing men would be likely to resort.

The lessons contained in this invaluable legacy of Washington to his countrymen, should be cherished in the heart of every citizen to the latest generation; and, perhaps, at no period of time could they be more usefully remembered than at the present moment. For when we look upon the scenes that are passing around us, and dwell upon the pages of his parting address, his paternal counsels would seem to be not merely the offspring of wisdom and foresight, but the voice of prophecy foretelling events and warning us of the evil to come. Forty years have passed since this imperishable document was given to his countrymen. The Federal Constitution was then regarded by him as an experiment, and he so speaks of it in his address; but an experiment upon the success of which the best hopes of his country depended, and we all know that he was prepared to lay down his life, if necessary, to secure to it a full and fair trial. The trial has been made. It has succeeded beyond the proudest hopes of those who framed it. Every quarter of this widely extended nation has felt its blessings, and shared in the general prosperity produced by its adoption. But amid this general prosperity and splendid success, the dangers of which he warned us are becoming every day more evident, and the signs of evil are sufficiently apparent to awaken the deepest anxiety in the bosom of the patriot. We hold systematic efforts publicly made to sow the seeds of discord between different parts of the United States, and to place party divisions directly upon geographical distinctions; to excite the *South* against the *North*, and the *North* against the *South*, and to force into the controversy the most delicate and exciting topics upon which it is impossible that a large portion of the Union can ever speak without strong emotions. Appeals, too, are constantly made to sectional interests, in order to influence the election of the Chief Magistrate, as if it were desired that he should favor a particular quarter of the country, instead of fulfilling the duties of his station with impartial justice to all;

and the possible dissolution of the Union has at length become an ordinary and familiar subject of discussion. Has the warning voice of Washington been forgotten? or have designs already been formed to sever the Union? Let it not be supposed that I impute to all of those who have taken an active part in these unwise and unprofitable discussions, a want of patriotism or of public virtue. The honorable feeling of state pride, and local attachments, find a place in the bosoms of the most enlightened and pure. But while such men are conscious of their own integrity and honesty of purpose, they ought never to forget that the citizens of other states are their political brethren; and that, however mistaken they may be in their views, the great body of them are equally honest and upright with themselves. Mutual suspicions and reproaches may in time create mutual hostility, and artful and designing men will always be found, who are ready to foment these fatal divisions, and to inflame the natural jealousies of different sections of the country. The history of the world is full of such examples, and especially the history of republics.

What have you to gain by division and dissension? Delude not yourselves with the belief that a breach once made, may be afterwards repaired. If the Union is once severed, the line of separation will grow wider and wider, and the controversies which are now debated and settled in the halls of legislation, will then be tried in fields of battle, and be determined by the sword. Neither should you deceive yourselves with the hope, that the first line of separation would be the permanent one, and that nothing but harmony and concord would be found in the new associations, formed upon the dissolution of this Union. Local interests would still be found there, and unchastened ambition. And if the recollection of common dangers, in which the people of these United States stood side by side against the common foe; the memory of victories won by their united valor; the prosperity and happiness they have enjoyed under the present Constitution; the proud name they bear as citizens of this great republic, if all these recollections and proofs of common interest are not strong enough to bind us together as one people, what tie will hold united the new divisions of empire, when these bonds have been broken and this Union dissevered? The first line of separation would not last for a single generation; new fragments would be torn off; new leaders would spring up; and this great and glorious republic would soon be broken into a multitude of petty states; without commerce, without credit; jealous of one another; armed for mutual aggression; loaded with taxes to pay armies and leaders; seeking aid against each other from foreign powers; insulted and trampled upon by the nations of Europe, until, harassed with conflicts, and humbled and debased in spirit, they would be ready to submit to the absolute dominion of any military adventurer, and to surrender their liberty for the sake of repose. It is impossible to look on the consequences that would inevitably follow the destruction of this government, and not feel indignant when we hear cold calculations about the value of the Union, and have so constantly before us a line of conduct so well calculated to weaken its ties.

There is too much at stake to allow pride or passion to influence your decision. Never for a moment believe that the great body of the citizens of any state or states can deliberately intend to do wrong. They may, under the influence of temporary excitement or misguided opinions, commit mistakes; they may be misled for a time by the suggestions of self-interest; but in a community so enlightened and patriotic as the people of the United States, argument will soon make them sensible of their errors; and when convinced, they will be ready to repair them. If they have no higher or better motives to govern them, they will at least perceive that their own interest requires them to be just to others, as they hope to receive justice at their hands.

But in order to maintain the Union unimpaired, it is absolutely necessary that the laws passed by the constituted authorities, should be faithfully executed in every part of the country, and that every good citizen should, at all times, stand ready to put down, with the combined force of the nation, every attempt at unlawful resistance, under whatever pretext it may be made, or whatever shape it may assume. Unconstitutional or oppressive laws may no doubt be passed by Congress, either from erroneous views, or the want of due consideration; if they are within reach of judicial authority, the remedy is easy and peaceful; and if, from the character of the law, it is an abuse of power not within the control of the judiciary, then free discussion and calm appeals to reason and to the justice of the people, will not fail to redress the wrong. But until the law shall be declared void by the courts, or repealed by Congress, no individual or combination of individuals, can be justified in forcibly resisting its execution. It is impossible that any government can continue to exist upon any other principles. It would cease to be a government, and be unworthy of the name, if it had not the power to enforce the execution of its own laws within its own sphere of action.

It is true that cases may be imagined, disclosing such a settled purpose of usurpation and oppression, on the part of the government, as would justify an appeal to arms. These, however, are extreme cases, which we have no reason to apprehend in a government where the power is in the hands of a patriotic people; and no citizen who loves his country would, in any case whatever, resort to forcible resistance, unless he clearly saw that the time had come when a freeman should prefer death to submission; for if such a struggle is once begun, and the citizens of one section of the country arrayed in arms against those of another, in doubtful conflict, let the battle result as it may, there will be an end of the Union, and with it an end of the hopes of freedom. The victory of the injured would not secure to them the blessings of liberty; it would avenge their wrongs, but they would themselves share in the common ruin.

But the Constitution cannot be maintained, nor the Union preserved in opposition to public feeling, by the mere exertion of the coercive powers confided to the general government. The foundations must be laid in the affections of the people; in the security it gives to life, liberty, character and property, in every quarter of the country; and in the fraternal attachments which the citizens of the several states bear to one another, as members of one political family, naturally contributing to promote the happiness of each other. Hence, the citizens of every state should studiously avoid every thing calculated to wound the sensibility or offend the just pride of the people of other states; and they should frown upon any proceedings within their own borders likely to disturb the tranquillity of their political brethren in other portions of the Union. In a country so extensive as the United States, and with pursuits so varied, the internal regulations of the several states must frequently differ from one another in important particulars; and this difference is unavoidably increased by the varying principles upon which the American colonies were originally planted; principles which had taken deep root in their social relations before the Revolution, and therefore, of necessity, influencing their policy since they became free and independent states. But each state has the unquestionable right to regulate its own internal concerns according to its own pleasure; and while it does not interfere with the rights of the people of other states, or the rights of the Union, every state must be the sole judge of the measures proper to secure the safety of its citizens and promote their happiness; and all efforts on the part of the people of other states to cast odium upon their institutions, and all measures calculated to disturb their rights of property, or to put in jeopardy their peace and internal tranquillity, are in direct opposition to the spirit in which the Union was formed, and must endanger its safety. Motives of philanthropy may be assigned for this unwarrantable interference; and weak men may persuade themselves for a moment that they are laboring in the cause of humanity, and asserting the rights of the human race; but every one, upon sober reflection, will see that nothing but mischief can come from these improper assaults upon the feelings and rights of others. Rest assured, that the men found busy in this work of discord are not worthy of your confidence, and deserve your strongest reprobation.

In the legislation of Congress, also, and in every measure of the general government, justice to every portion of the United States should be faithfully observed. No free government can stand without virtue in the people, and a lofty spirit of patriotism; and if the sordid feelings of mere selfishness shall usurp the place which ought to be filled by public spirit, the legislation of Congress will soon be converted into a scramble for personal and sectional advantages. Under our free institutions, the citizens of every quarter of our country are capable of attaining a high degree of prosperity and happiness, without seeking to profit themselves at the expense of others; and every such attempt must, in the end, fail to succeed; for the people in every part of the United States are too enlightened not to understand their own rights and interests, and to detect and defeat every effort to gain undue advantages over them; and when such designs are discovered, it naturally provokes resentments which cannot always be allayed. Justice, full and ample justice, to every portion of the United States, should be the ruling principle of every freeman, and should guide the deliberations of every public body, whether it be state or national.

It is well known that there have always been those among us who wish to enlarge the powers of the general government; and experience would seem to indicate that there is a tendency on the part of this government to overstep the boundaries marked out for it by the Constitution. Its legitimate authority is abundantly sufficient for all the purposes for which it was created: and its powers being expressly enumerated, there can be no justification for claiming any thing beyond them. Every attempt to exercise power beyond these limits should be promptly and firmly opposed. For one evil example will lead to other measures still more mischievous; and if the principle of constructive powers, or supposed advantages, or temporary circumstances, shall ever be permitted to justify the assumption of a power not given by the Constitution, the general government will before long absorb all the powers of legislation, and you will have, in effect, but one consolidated government. From the extent of our country, its diversified interests, different pursuits, and different habits, it is too obvious for argument that a single

FAREWELL ADDRESS

consolidated government would be wholly inadequate to watch over and protect its interests; and every friend of our free institutions should be always prepared to maintain unimpaired and in full vigor the rights and sovereignty of the states, and to confine the action of the general government strictly to the sphere of its appropriate duties.

There is, perhaps, no one of the powers conferred on the federal government so liable to abuse as the taxing power. The most productive and convenient sources of revenue were necessarily given to it, that it might be able to perform the important duties imposed upon it; and the taxes which it lays upon commerce being concealed from the real payer in the price of the article, they do not so readily attract the attention of the people as smaller sums demanded from them directly by the tax-gatherer. But the tax imposed on goods, enhances by so much the price of the commodity to the consumer; and as many of these duties are imposed on articles of necessity which are daily used by the great body of the people, the money raised by these imposts is drawn from their pockets. Congress has no right under the Constitution to take money from the people, unless it is required to execute some one of the specific powers intrusted to the government; and if they raise more than is necessary for such purposes, it is an abuse of the power of taxation, and unjust and oppressive. It may indeed happen that the revenue will sometimes exceed the amount anticipated when the taxes were laid. When, however, this is ascertained, it is easy to reduce them; and, in such a case, it is unquestionably the duty of the government to reduce them, for no circumstances can justify it in assuming a power not given to it by the Constitution, nor in taking away the money of the people when it is not needed for the legitimate wants of the government.

Plain as these principles appear to be, you will yet find that there is a constant effort to induce the general government to go beyond the limits of its taxing power, and to impose unnecessary burdens upon the people. Many powerful interests are continually at work to procure heavy duties on commerce, and to swell the revenue beyond the real necessities of the public service ; and the country has already felt the injurious effects of their combined influence. They succeeded in obtaining a tariff of duties bearing most oppressively on the agricultural and laboring classes of society, and producing a revenue that could not be usefully employed within the range of the powers conferred upon Congress ; and in order to fasten upon the people this unjust and unequal system of taxation, extravagant schemes of internal improvement were got up, in various quarters, to squander the money and to purchase support. Thus, one unconstitutional measure was intended to be upheld by another, and the abuse of the power of taxation was to be maintained by usurping the power of expending the money in internal improvements. You cannot have forgotten the severe and doubtful struggle through which we passed, when the executive department of the government, by its veto, endeavored to arrest the prodigal scheme of injustice, and to bring back the legislation of Congress to the boundaries prescribed by the Constitution. The good sense and practical judgment of the people, when the subject was brought before them, sustained the course of the Executive, and this plan of unconstitutional expenditure for the purposes of corrupt influence is, I trust, finally overthrown.

The result of this decision has been felt in the rapid extinguishment of the public debt, and the large accumulation of a surplus in the treasury, notwithstanding the tariff was reduced, and is now far below the amount originally contemplated by its advocates. But, rely upon it, the design to collect an extravagant revenue, and to burden you with taxes beyond the economical wants of the government, is not yet abandoned. The various interests which have combined together to impose a heavy tariff, and to produce an overflowing treasury, are too strong, and have too much at stake, to surrender the contest. The corporations and wealthy individuals who are engaged in large manufacturing establihsments, desire a high tariff to increase their gains. Designing politicians will support it to conciliate their favor, and to obtain the means of profuse

FAREWELL ADDRESS

expenditure, for the purpose of purchasing influence in other quarters; and since the people have decided that the federal government cannot be permitted to employ its income in internal improvements, efforts will be made to seduce and mislead the citizens of the several states, by holding out to them the deceitful prospect of benefits to be derived from a surplus revenue collected by the general government, and annually divided among the states. And if, encouraged by these fallacious hopes, the states should disregard the principles of economy which ought to characterize every republican government, and should indulge in lavish expenditures exceeding their resources, they will, before long, find themselves oppressed with debts which they are unable to pay, and the temptation will become irresistible to support a high tariff, in order to obtain a surplus distribution. Do not allow yourselves, my fellow-citizens, to be misled on this subject. The federal government cannot collect a surplus for such purposes, without violating the principles of the Constitution, and assuming powers which have not been granted. It is, moreover, a system of injustice, and, if persisted in, will inevitably lead to corruption, and must end in ruin. The surplus revenue will be drawn from the pockets of the people—from the farmer, the mechanic, and the laboring classes of society; but who will receive it when distributed among the states, where it is to be disposed of by leading state politicians who have friends to favor, and political partisans to gratify? It will certainly not be returned to those who paid it, and who have most need of it, and are honestly entitled to it. There is but one safe rule, and that is, to confine the general government rigidly within the sphere of its appropriate duties. It has no power to raise a revenue, or impose taxes, except for the purposes enumerated in the Constitution; and if its income is found to exceed these wants, it should be forthwith reduced, and the burdens of the people so far lightened.

In reviewing the conflicts which have taken place between different interests in the United States, and the policy pursued since the adoption of our present form of government, we find nothing that has produced such deep-seated evil as the course of legislation in relation to the currency. The Constitution of the United States unquestionably intended to secure the people a circulating medium of gold and silver. But the establishment of a national bank by Congress, with the privilege of issuing paper money receivable in payment of the public dues, and the unfortunate course of legislation in the several states, upon the same subject, drove from general circulation the constitutional currency, and substituted one of paper in its place.

It was not easy for men engaged in the ordinary pursuits of business, whose attention had not been particularly drawn to the subject, to foresee all the consequences of a currency exclusively of paper; and we ought not, on that account, to be surprised at the facility with which laws were obtained to carry into effect the paper system. Honest, and even enlightened men, are sometimes misled by the specious and plausible statements of the designing. But experience has now proved the mischiefs and dangers of a paper currency, and it rests with you to determine whether the proper remedy shall be applied.

The paper system being founded on public confidence, and having of itself no intrinsic value, it is liable to great and sudden fluctuations, thereby rendering property insecure, and the wages of labor unsteady and uncertain. The corporations which create the paper money cannot be relied upon to keep the circulating medium uniform in amount. In times of prosperity, when confidence is high, they are tempted by the prospect of gain, or by the influence of those who hope to profit by it, to extend their issues of paper beyond the bounds of discretion and the reasonable demands of business. And when these issues have been pushed on, from day to day, until public confidence is at length shaken, then a reaction takes place, and they immediately withdraw the credits they have given; suddenly curtail their issues, and produce an unexpected and ruinous contraction of the circulating medium, which is felt by the whole community. The banks by this means save themselves, and the mischievous consequences of their imprudence or cupidity are visited upon the public. Nor does the evil stop here. These ebbs and flows of the currency, and these indiscreet extensions of credit, naturally engender a spirit of speculation injurious to the habits and character of the people. We have already seen its effects in the wild spirit of speculation in the public lands, and various kinds of stocks, which, within the last year or two, seized upon such a multitude of our citizens, and threatened to pervade all classes of society, and to withdraw their attention from the sober pursuits of honest industry. It is not by encouraging this spirit that we shall best preserve public virtue, and promote the true interests of our country. But if your currency continues as exclusively paper as it now is, it will foster this eager desire to amass wealth without labor; it will multiply the number of dependents on bank accommodations and bank favors; the temptation to obtain money at any sacrifice, will become stronger and stronger, and inevitably lead to corruption, which will find its way into your public councils, and destroy, at no distant day, the purity of your government. Some of the evils which arise from this system of paper, press with peculiar hardship upon the class of society least able to bear it. A portion of this currency frequently becomes depreciated or worthless, and all of it is easily counterfeited, in such a manner as to require peculiar skill and much experience to distinguish the counterfeit from the genuine notes.

These frauds are most generally perpetrated in the smaller notes, which are used in the daily transactions of ordinary business; and the losses occasioned by them are commonly thrown upon the laboring classes of society, whose situation and pursuits put it out of their power to guard themselves from these impositions, and whose daily wages are necessary for their subsistence. It is the duty of every government, so to regulate its currency as to protect this numerous class, as far as practicable, from the impositions of avarice and fraud. It is more especially the duty of the United States, where the government is emphatically the government of the people, and where this respectable portion of our citizens are so proudly distinguished from the laboring classes of all other nations, by their independent spirit, their love of liberty, their intelligence, and their high tone of moral character. Their industry in peace is the source of our wealth; their bravery in war has covered us with glory; and the government of the United States will but ill discharge its duties, if it leaves them a prey to such dishonest impositions. Yet it is evident that their interests cannot be effectually protected, unless silver and gold are restored to circulation.

These views, alone, of the paper currency, are sufficient to call for immediate reform; but there is another consideration which should still more strongly press it upon your attention.

Recent events have proved that the paper money system of this country may be used as an engine to undermine your free institutions; and that those who desire to engross all power in the hands of a few, and to govern by corruption or force, are aware of its power, and prepared to employ it. Your banks now furnish your only circulating medium, and money is plenty or scarce, according to the quantity of notes issued by them. While they have capitals not greatly disproportionate to each other, they are competitors in business, and no one of them can exercise dominion over the rest; and although, in the present state of the currency, these banks may and do operate injuriously upon the habits of business, the pecuniary concerns, and the moral tone of society; yet, from their number and dispersed situation, they cannot combine for the purposes of political influence; and whatever may be the dispositions of some of them, their power of mischief must necessarily be confined to a narrow space, and felt only in their immediate neighborhoods.

But when the charter for the Bank of the United States was obtained from Congress, it perfected the schemes of the paper system, and gave to its advocates the position they have struggled to obtain from the commencement of the federal government down to the present hour. The immense capital and peculiar privileges bestowed upon it, enabled it to exercise despotic sway over the other banks in every part of the country. From its superior strength, it could seriously injure, if not destroy, the business of

FAREWELL ADDRESS

any one of them which might incur its resentment; and it openly claimed for itself the power of regulating the currency throughout the United States. In other words, it asserted (and undoubtedly possessed) the power to make money plenty or scarce, at its pleasure, at any time, and in any quarter of the Union, by controlling the issues of other banks, and permitting an expansion, or compelling a general contraction, of the circulating medium, according to its own will. The other banking institutions were sensible of its strength, and they soon generally became its obedient instruments, ready at all times to execute its mandates; and with the banks necessarily went also that numerous class of persons in our commercial cities who depend altogether on bank credits for their solvency and means of business, and who are therefore obliged, for their own safety, to propitiate the favor of the money power by distinguished zeal and devotion in its service. The result of the ill-advised legislation which established this great monopoly, was to concentrate the whole moneyed power of the Union, with its boundless means of corruption, and its numerous dependents, under the direction and command of one acknowledged head; thus organizing this particular interest as one body, and securing to it unity and concert of action throughout the United States, and enabling it to bring forward, upon any occasion, its entire and undivided strength to support or defeat any measure of the government. In the hands of this formidable power, thus perfectly organized, was also placed unlimited dominion over the amount of the circulating medium, giving it the power to regulate the value of property and the fruits of labor in every quarter of the Union; and to bestow prosperity, or bring ruin upon any city or section of the country, as might best comport with its own interest or policy.

We are not left to conjecture how the moneyed power, thus organized, and with such a weapon in its hands, would be likely to use it. The distress and alarm which pervaded and agitated the whole country, when the Bank of the United States waged war upon the people in order to compel them to submit to its demands, cannot yet be forgotten. The ruthless and unsparing temper with which whole cities and communities were oppressed, individuals impoverished and ruined, and a scene of cheerful prosperity suddenly changed into one of gloom and despondency, ought to be indelibly impressed on the memory of the people of the United States. If such was its power in a time of peace, what would it not have been in a season of war, with an enemy at your doors? No nation but the freemen of the United States could have come out victorious from such a contest; yet, if you had not conquered, the government would have passed from the hands of the many to the hands of the few; and this organized money power, from its secret conclave, would have dictated the choice of your highest officers, and compelled you to make peace or war, as best suited their own wishes. The forms of your government might for a time have remained, but its living spirit would have departed from it.

The distress and sufferings inflicted on the people by the bank are some of the fruits of that system of policy which is continually striving to enlarge the authority of the federal government beyond the limits fixed by the Constitution. The powers enumerated in that instrument do not confer on Congress the right to establish such a corporation as the Bank of the United States: and the evil consequences which followed may warn us of the danger of departing from the true rule of construction, and of permitting temporary circumstances, or the hope of better promoting the public welfare, to influence in any degree our decisions upon the extent of the authority of the general government. Let us abide by the Constitution as it is written, or amend it in the constitutional mode, if it is found to be defective.

The severe lessons of experience will, I doubt not, be sufficient to prevent Congress from again chartering such a monopoly, even if the Constitution did not present an insuperable objection to it. But you must remember, my fellow-citizens, that eternal vigilance by the people is the price of liberty; and that you must pay the price if you wish to secure the blessing. It behooves you, therefore, to be watchful in your states, as well as in the federal government. The power which the moneyed interest can exercise, when concentrated under a single head and with our present system of currency, was sufficiently demonstrated in the struggle made by the Bank of the United States. Defeated in the general government, the same class of intriguers and politicians will now resort to the states, and endeavor to obtain there the same organization, which they failed to perpetuate in the Union; and with specious and deceitful plans of public advantages, and state interests, and state pride, they will endeavor to establish, in the different states, one moneyed institution with overgrown capital, and exclusive privileges, sufficient to enable it to control the operations of the other banks. Such an institution will be pregnant with the same evils produced by the Bank of the United States, although its sphere of action is more confined; and in the state in which it is chartered, the money power will be able to embody its whole strength, and to move together with undivided force, to accomplish any object it may wish to attain. You have already had abundant evidence of its power to inflict injury upon the agricultural, mechanical and laboring classes of society; and over those whose engagements in trade or speculation render them dependent on bank facilities, the dominion of the state monopoly will be absolute, and their obedience unlimited. With such a bank, and a paper currency, the money power would in a few years govern the state and control its measures; and if a sufficient number of states can be induced to create such establishments, the time will soon come when it will again take the field against the United States, and succeed in perfecting and perpetuating its organization by a charter from Congress.

It is one of the serious evils of our present system of banking, that it enables one class of society—and that by no means a numerous one—by its control over the currency, to act injuriously upon the interests of all the others, and to exercise more than its just proportion of influence in political affairs. The agricultural, the mechanical, and the laboring classes, have little or no share in the direction of the great moneyed corporations; and from their habits and the nature of their pursuits, they are incapable of forming extensive combinations to act together with united force. Such concert of action may sometimes be produced in a single city, or in a small dist ict of country, by means of personal communications with each other; but they have no regular or active correspondence with those who are engaged in similar pursuits in distant places; they have but little patronage to give to the press, and exercise but a small share of influence over it; they have no crowd of dependents about them, who hope to grow rich without labor, by their countenance and favor, and who are, therefore, always ready to execute their wishes. The planter, the farmer, the mechanic, and the laborer, all know that their success depends upon their own industry and economy, and that they must not expect to become suddenly rich by the fruits of their toil. Yet these classes of society form the great body of the people of the United States; they are the bone and sinew of the country; men who love liberty, and desire nothing but equal rights and equal laws, and who, moreover, hold the great mass of our national wealth, although it is distributed in moderate amounts among the millions of freemen who possess it. But with overwhelming numbers and wealth on their side, they are in constant danger of losing their fair influence in the government, and with difficulty maintain their just rights against the incessant efforts daily made to encroach upon them. .

The mischief springs from the power which the moneyed interest derives from a paper currency, which they are able to control, from the multitude of corporations with exclusive privileges, which they have succeeded in obtaining in the different states, and which are employed altogether for their benefit; and unless you become more watchful in your states, and check this spirit of monopoly and thirst for exclusive privileges, you will, in the end, find that the most important powers of government have been given or bartered away, and the control over your dearest interests have passed into the hands of these corporations.

The paper-money system, and its natural associates, monopoly and exclusive privileges, have already struck their roots deep in the soil; and it will require all your efforts to check its farther growth, and to eradicate the evil. The men who profit by the abuses, and desire to perpetuate them, will continue to besiege the halls of legislation in the general government, as well as in the states, and will seek, by every artifice, to mislead and deceive the public servants. It is to yourselves that you must look for safety and the means of guarding and perpetuating your free institutions. In your hands is rightfully placed the sovereignty of the country, and to you every one placed in authority is ultimately responsible. It is always in your power to see that the wishes of the people are carried into faithful execution, and their will, when once made known, must sooner or later be obeyed. And while the people remain, as I trust they ever will, uncorrupted and incorruptible, and continue watchful and jealous of their rights, the government is safe, and the cause of freedom will continue to triumph over all its enemies. But it will require steady and persevering exertions on your part to rid yourselves of the iniquities and mischiefs of the paper system, and to check the spirit of monopoly and other abuses, which have sprung up with it, and of which it is the main support. So many interests are united to resist all reform on this subject, that you must not hope the conflict will be a short one, nor success easy. My humble efforts have not been spared, during my administration of the government, to restore the constitutional currency of gold and silver; and something, I trust, has been done towards the accomplishment of this most desirable object. But enough yet remains to require all your nergy and perseverance. The power, however, is in your hands, and the remedy must and will be applied if you determine upon it.

While I am thus endeavoring to press upon your attention the principles which I deem of vital importance to the domestic concerns of the country, I ought not to pass over without notice the important considerations which should govern your policy towards foreign powers. It is unquestionably our true interest to cultivate the most friendly understanding with every nation, and to avoid, by every honorable means, the calamities of war; and we shall best attain this object by frankness and sincerity in our foreign intercourse, by the prompt and faithful execution of treaties, and by justice and impartiality in our conduct to all. But no nation, however desirous of peace, can hope to escape collisions with other powers; and the soundest dictates of policy require that we should place ourselves in a condition to assert our rights, if a resort to force should ever become necessary. Our local situation, our long line of sea-coast, indented by numerous bays, with deep rivers opening into the interior, as well as our extended and still increasing commerce, point to the navy as our natural means of defence. It will, in the end, be found to be the cheapest and most effectual; and now is the time, in the season of peace, and with an overflowing revenue, that we can year after year add to its strength, without increasing the burdens of the people. It is your true policy. For your navy will not only protect your rich and flourishing commerce in distant seas, but enable you to reach and annoy the enemy, and will give to defence its greatest efficiency by meeting danger at a distance from home. It is impossible by any line of fortifications to guard every point from attack against a hostile force advancing from the ocean and selecting its object; but they are indispensable to protect cities from bombardment; dock-yards and navy arsenals from destruction; to give shelter to merchant vessels in time of war, and to single ships or weaker squadrons when pressed by superior force. Fortifications of this description cannot be too soon completed and armed, and placed in a condition of the most perfect preparation. The abundant means we now possess cannot be applied in any manner more useful to the country; and when this is done, and our naval force sufficiently strengthened, and our militia armed, we need not fear that any nation will wantonly insult us, or needlessly provoke hostilities. We shall more certainly preserve peace, when it is well understood that we are prepared for war.

In presenting to you, my fellow-citizens, these parting counsels, I have brought before you the leading principles upon which I endeavored to administer the government in the high office with which you twice honored me. Knowing that the path of freedom is continually beset by enemies, who often assume the disguise of friends, I have devoted the last hours of my public life to warn you of the dangers. The progress of the United States, under our free and happy institutions, has surpassed the most sanguine hopes of the founders of the Republic. Our growth has been rapid beyond all former example, in numbers, in wealth, in knowledge, and all the useful arts which contribute to the comforts and convenience of man; and from the earliest ages of history to the present day, there never have been thirteen millions of people associated together in one political body, who enjoyed so much freedom and happiness as the people of these United States. You have no longer any cause to fear danger from abroad; your strength and power are well known throughout the civilized world, as well as the high and gallant bearing of your sons. It is from within, among yourselves, from cupidity, from corruption, from disappointed ambition, and inordinate thirst for power, that factions will be formed and liberty endangered. It is against such designs, whatever disguise the actors may assume, that you have especially to guard yourselves. You have the highest of human trusts committed to your care. Providence has showered on this favored land blessings without number, and has chosen you as the guardians of freedom, to preserve it for the benefit of the human race. May He, who holds in his hands the destinies of nations, make you worthy of the favors he has bestowed, and enable you, with pure hearts, and pure hands, and sleepless vigilance, to guard and defend to the end of time the great charge he has committed to your keeping.

My own race is nearly run; advanced age and failing

health warn me that before long I must pass beyond the reach of human events, and cease to feel the vicissitudes of human affairs. I thank God that my life has been spent in a land of liberty, and that he has given me a heart to love my country with the affection of a son. And filled with gratitude for your constant and unwavering kindness, I bid you a last and affectionate farewell.

General Jackson's Letter to Commodore Elliott, declining a Sarcophagus.

Hermitage, March 27, 1845.

DEAR SIR: Your letter of the 18th instant, together with a copy of the proceedings of the National Institute, furnished me by their corresponding secretary, on the presentation, by you, of the Sarcophagus for their acceptance, on condition it shall be preserved, and in honor of my memory, have been received, and are now before me.

Although laboring under great debility and affliction, from a severe attack from which I may not recover, I raise my pen and endeavor to reply. The steadiness of my nerves may perhaps lead you to conclude my prostration of strength is not so great as here expressed. Strange as it may appear, my nerves are as steady as they were forty years gone by; whilst, from debility and affliction, I am gasping for breath.

I have read the whole proceedings of the presentation, by you, of the Sarcophagus, and the resolutions passed by the Board of Directors, so honorable to my fame, with sensations and feelings more easily to be conjectured, than by me expressed. The whole proceedings call for my most grateful thanks, which are hereby tendered to you, and through you to the President and Directors of the National Institute. But with the warmest sensations that can inspire a grateful heart, I must decline accepting the honor intended to be bestowed. I cannot consent that my mortal body shall be laid in a repository prepared for an emperor or a king. My republican feelings and principles forbid it; the simplicity of our system of government forbids it. Every monument erected to perpetuate the memory of our heroes and statesmen ought to bear evidence of the economy and simplicity of our republican institutions, and the plainness of our republican citizens, who are the sovereigns of our glorious Union, and whose virtue is to perpetuate it. True virtue cannot exist where pomp and parade are the governing passions: it can only dwell with the people—the great laboring and producing classes that form the bone and sinew of our confederacy.

For these reasons I cannot accept the honor you and the President and Directors of the National Institute intended to bestow. I cannot permit my remains to be the first in these United States to be deposited in a sarcophagus made for an emperor or king. I again repeat, please accept for yourself, and convey to the President and Directors of the National Institute, my most profound respects for the honor you and they intend to bestow. I have prepared an humble depository for my mortal body beside that wherein lies my beloved wife, where, without any pomp or parade, I have requested, when my God calls me to sleep with my fathers, to be laid; for both of us there to remain until the last trumpet sounds to call the dead to judgment, when we, I hope, shall rise together, clothed with that heavenly body promised to all who believe in our glorious Redeemer, who died for us that we might live, and by whose atonement I hope for a blessed immortality.

I am, with great respect,
your friend and fellow-citizen,
ANDREW JACKSON.

To Commodore J. D. ELLIOTT, United States Navy.

LAST WILL AND TESTAMENT.

Hermitage, June 7th, 1843.

IN THE NAME OF GOD, AMEN:—I, Andrew Jackson, Sen'r., being of sound mind, memory, and understanding, and impressed with the great uncertainty of life and the certainty of death, and being desirous to dispose of my temporal affairs so that after my death no contention may arise relative to the same—And whereas, since executing my will of the 30th of September, 1833, my estate has become greatly involved by my liabilities for the debts of my well-beloved and adopted son Andrew Jackson, Jun., which makes it necessary to alter the same: Therefore I, Andrew Jackson, Sen'r., of the county of Davidson, and state of Tennessee, do make, ordain, publish, and declare this my last will and testament, revoking all other wills by me heretofore made.

First, I bequeath my body to the dust whence it comes, and my soul to God who gave it, hoping for a happy immortality through the atoning merits of our Lord Jesus Christ, the Saviour of the world. My desire is, that my body be buried by the side of my dear departed wife, in the garden at the Hermitage, in the vault prepared in the garden, and all expenses paid by my executor hereafter named.

Secondly, That all my just debts to be paid out of my personal and real estate by my executor; for which purpose to meet the debt my good friends Gen'l J. B. Planchin & Co. of New Orleans, for the sum of six thousand dollars, with the interest accruing thereon loaned to me to meet the debt due by A. Jackson, Jun., for the purchase of the plantation from Hiram G. Runnels, lying on the east bank of the river Mississippi, in the state of Mississippi. Also, a debt due by me of ten thousand dollars, borrowed of my friends Blair and Rives, of the city of Washington and District of Columbia, with the interest accruing thereon; being applied to the payment of the lands bought of Hiram G. Runnels as aforesaid, and for the faithful payment of the aforesaid recited debts, I hereby bequeath all my real and personal estate. After these debts are fully paid—

Thirdly, I give and bequeath to my adopted son, Andrew Jackson, Junior, the tract of land whereon I now live, known by the Hermitage tract, with its butts and boundaries, with all its appendages of the three lots of land bought of Samuel Donelson, Thomas J. Donelson, and Alexander Donelson, sons and heirs of Sovern Donelson, deceased, all adjoining the Hermitage tract, agreeable to their butts and boundaries, with all the appurtenances thereto belonging or in any wise appertaining, with all my negroes that I may die possessed of, with the exception hereafter named, with all their increase after the before recited debts are fully paid, with all the household furniture, farming tools, stock of all kind, both on the Hermitage tract farms, as well as those on the Mississippi plantation, to him and his heirs for ever.—The true intent and meaning of this my last will and testament is, that all my estate, real, personal, and mixed, is hereby first pledged for the payment of the above recited debts and interest; and when they are fully paid, the residue of all my estate, real, personal and mixed, is hereby bequeathed to my adopted son A. Jackson, Jun., with the exceptions hereafter named, to him and his heirs for ever.

Fourth, Whereas I have heretofore by conveyance, deposited with my beloved daughter Sarah Jackson, wife of my adopted son A. Jackson, Jun., given to my beloved granddaughter, Rachel Jackson, daughter of A. Jackson, Jun. and Sarah his wife, several negroes therein described, which I hereby confirm.—I give and bequeath to my beloved grandson Andrew Jackson, son of A. Jackson, Jun. and Sarah his wife, a negro boy named Ned, son of Blacksmith Aaron and Hannah his wife, to him and his heirs for ever.

Fifth, I give and bequeath to my beloved little grandson, Samuel Jackson, son of A. Jackson, Jun. and his much beloved wife Sarah, one negro boy named Davy or George, son of Squire and his wife Giney, to him and his heirs for ever.

Sixth, To my beloved and affectionate daughter, Sarah Jackson, wife of my adopted and well beloved son, A. Jackson, Jun., I hereby recognise, by this bequest, the gift I made her on her marriage, of the negro girl Gracy, which I bought for her, and gave her to my daughter Sarah as her maid and seamstress, with her increase, with my house-servant Hannah and her two daughters, namely, Charlotte and Mary, to her and her heirs for ever. This gift and bequest is made for my great affection for her—as a memento of her uniform attention to me and kindness on all occasions, and particularly when worn down with sickness, pain, and debility—she has been more than a daughter to me, and I hope she never will be disturbed in the enjoyment of this gift and bequest by any one.

Seventh, I bequeath to my well beloved nephew, Andrew J. Donelson, son of Samuel Donelson, deceased, the elegant sword presented to me by the state of Tennessee, with this injunction, that he fail not to use it when necessary in support and protection of our glorious union, and for the protection of the constitutional rights of our beloved country, should they be assailed by foreign enemies or domestic traitors. This, from the great change in my worldly affairs of late. is, with my blessing, all I can bequeath him, doing justice to those creditors to whom I am responsible. This bequest is made as a memento of my high regard, affection, and esteem I bear for him as a high-minded, honest, and honorable man.

Eighth, To my grand-nephew Andrew Jackson Coffee, I bequeath the elegant sword presented to me by the Rifle Company of New Orleans, commanded by Capt. Beal, as a memento of my regard, and to bring to his recollection the gallant services of his deceased father Gen'l John Coffee, in the late Indian and British war, under my command, and his gallant conduct in defence of New Orleans in 1814 and 1815; with this injunction, that he wield it in the protection of the rights secured to the American citizen under our glorious constitution, against all invaders, whether foreign foes, or intestine traitors.

I bequeath to my beloved grandson Andrew Jackson, son of A. Jackson, Jun. and Sarah his wife, the sword presented to me by the citizens of Philadelphia, with this injunction, that he will always use it in defence of the constitution and our glorious union, and the perpetuation of our republican system: remembering the motto—" Draw me not without occasion, nor sheath me without honour."

The pistols of Gen'l Lafayette, which were presented by him to Gen'l George Washington, and by Col. Wm. Robertson presented to me, I bequeath to George Washington Lafayette, as a memento of the illustrious personages through whose hands they have passed—*his father, and the father of his country.*

The gold box presented to me by the corporation of the City of New York, the large silver vase presented to me by the ladies of Charleston, South Carolina, my native state, with the large picture representing the unfurling of the American banner, presented to me by the citizens of South Carolina when it was refused to be accepted by the United States Senate, I leave in trust to my son A. Jackson, Jun., with directions that should our happy country not be blessed with peace, an event not always to be expected, he will at the close of the war or end of the conflict, present each of said articles of inestimable value, to that patriot residing in the city or state from which they were preented, who shall be adjudged by his countrymen or the ladies to have been the most valiant in defence of his country and our country's rights.

The pocket spyglass which was used by Gen'l Washington during the revolutionary war, and presented to me by Mr. Custis, having been burned with my dwellinghouse, the Hermitage, with many other invaluable relics, I can make no dispositon of them. As a memento of my high regard for Gen'l Robert Armstrong as a gentleman, patriot and soldier, as well as for his meritorious military services under my command during the late British and Indian war, and remembering the gallant bearing of him and his gallant little band at Enotochopco creek, when, falling desperately wounded, he called out—"My brave fellows, some may fall, but save the cannon"—as a memento of all these things, I give and bequeath to him my case of pistols and sword worn by me throughout my military career, well satisfied that in his hands they will never be disgraced—that they will never be used or drawn without occasion, nor sheathed but with honour.

Lastly, I leave to my beloved son all my walking-canes and other relics, to be distributed amongst my young relatives—namesakes—first, to my much esteemed namesake, Andrew J. Donelson, son of my esteemed nephew A. J. Donelson, his first choice, and then to be distributed as A. Jackson, Jun. may think proper.

Lastly, I appoint my adopted son Andrew Jackson, Jun., my whole and sole executor to this my last will and testament, and direct that no security be required of him for the faithful execution and discharge of the trusts hereby reposed in him.

In testimony whereof I have this 7th day of June, one thousand eight hundred and forty-three, hereunto set my hand, and affixed my seal, hereby revoking all wills heretofore made by me, and in the presence of

MARION ADAMS,
ELIZABETH D. LOVE,
THOS. J. DONELSON,
RICHARD SMITH,
R. ARMSTRONG.

ANDREW JACKSON. (*Seal.*)

State of Tennessee, Davidson County Court,
July Term, 1845.

A paper writing, purporting to be the last will and testament of Andrew Jackson, Sen., dec'd., was produced in open court for probate, and proved thus:—Marion Adams, Elizabeth D. Love, and Richard Smith, three of the subscribing witnesses thereto, being first duly sworn, depose and say, that they became such in the presence of the said Andrew Jackson, Sr., dec'd., and at his request and in the presence of each other; and that they verily believe he was of sound and disposing mind and memory at the time of executing the same.

Ordered, That said paper writing be admitted to record as such will and testament of the said Audrew Jackson, Sr., dec'd. Whereupon Andrew Jackson, Jun., the executor named in said will, came into court and gave bond in the sum of two hundred thousand dollars, (there being no security required by said will,) and qualified according to law.

Ordered, That he have letters testamentary granted to him.

State of Tennessee, Davidson County:

I, Robert B. Castleman, Clerk of the County Court, of said county, do certify that the foregoing is a true and perfect copy of the original will of Andrew Jackson, Sr., dec'd., together with the probate of the same, as proven at the July term, 1845, of said court, as the same remains of record in my office. In testimony whereof I have hereunto set my hand and affixed the seal of said court at my office, this the 15th day of August, in the year of our Lord one thousand eight hundred and forty-five.

Ro. B. CASTLEMAN
By his deputy,
PHINEAS GARRETT.

DR. BETHUNE'S DISCOURSE,

Pronounced July 6th, 1845.

"For he established a testimony in Jacob, and appointed a law in Israel, which he commanded our fathers that they should make them known to their children; that the generation to come might know them, even the children which should be born, who should arise and declare them to their children, that they might set their hope in God, and not forget the works of God, but keep his commandments."—Psalm lxxviii. 5, 6, 7.

Among our many national sins, there is none more likely to provoke divine chastisement, yet less considered or repented of, even by Christians, than ingratitude for political blessings. That there are evils among us, no one will deny; that changes might be made for the better, it were unreasonable to doubt; and, concerning methods of removing evil, or working good, we may differ widely, yet honestly. Evil is inseparable from human nature, the best human schemes are capable of improvement, and human opinions must be various, because they are fallible. It is a narrow, unthankful spirit, which, brooding over imperfections, or sighing after greater advantages, or bitterly condemning all who think not the same way, refuses to perceive and acknowledge the vast benefits we actually enjoy. Never was there a revolution at once so just and so successful as that which won our country's independence: never, except in the Bible, have the rights of man been so clearly and truly defined as in our constitution; never did greater success attend a social experiment than has followed ours. Since the establishment of our confederacy, tumults, insurrections, and violent changes, have been busy in all the civilized world besides. Throne after throne has fallen, and dynasties have been built up on the bloody ruins of dynasties. In some nations the people have wrung, by force, partial concessions from hereditary rule; in others, after convulsive, misdirected efforts, they have been crushed again by the iron hoof of despotism; nor is the voice of a prophet needed to foretell a long, desperate struggle of uprising humanity with the powers of political darkness; while the bloody discords and constant confusion of other republics on the same continent with ourselves, demonstrate the incompatibility of freedom with ignorance and superstition. Ours is now, with the exception of the Russian and British (if, indeed, the passage of the Reform Bill was not an organic change), older than any monarchical government in christendom. The increase of our population from less than three millions to twenty, in seventy years, multiplies many times any former example; yet, notwithstanding the enormous migration to us from various countries, where free principles are unknown, our wide land has more than enough room for all: growth in numbers has been a chief cause of our growth in wealth, and our laws, strong as they are liberal, have proved themselves sufficient to compose, maintain and rule all in concord, prosperity and power. You will search in vain for another example of a vast nation governed, without troops or armed police, by their own will. It is not five years since, that our people, spread out over an immense territory, after a contest in which the utmost enthusiasm excited both parties, changed their rulers. Yet not a bayonet was fixed, nor a cannon pointed, nor a barricade raised, to guard the place of suffrage. The ballot, falling noiselessly as snow upon the rock, achieved the result. Within the last twelvemonth, the stupendous process has been repeated as peaceably and safely. Each of the great political sects, which divide the popular vote, has triumphed and been beaten. Much there has been to censure in the harsh recrimination and unfraternal bigotry on either side; but when the decision was reached, though the long-rolling swells which succeed the storm did not at once subside, and here and there some violent partisan may have betrayed his vexation, the surface became calm, and the noise soon died away Every true patriot, submissive to the oracle of the polls, whether wisdom or error, said in his heart, GOD BLESS THE PEOPLE!

Our difficulties, real or supposed, have arisen out of our advantages, for good and evil are mixed with all human affairs. The freedom of those institutions under which we live, has its price, which must be paid, so long as man is prone to abuse, by impatience and excess, those favours of Almighty God which yield happiness only when they are used moderately and religiously. Elated by prosperity, we have forced our growth too fast. We have attempted by plausible inventions to transcend the laws of trade and production. We have complicated the machinery of our interests until our clear, simple constitution, has become, in the hands of sophisticating politicians, a riddle of mysteries. The limits of habitation have been enlarged beyond the blessings of church and school-house. Vices and faults, peculiar to new settlements, have reached the heart of our legislation. To carry on our far grasping schemes, we have strained our credit till it broke. Freedom of speech and of the press, has been abused to licentiousness by prejudice, rashness, and selfish ambition. Acknowledging as we do the rights of conscience in their broadest meaning, even the holy name of religion has been dragged upon the arena of party.

Our republic is not a paradise: our countrymen, like ourselves, are not angels, but frail, erring men. Our history has been an experiment. Mistakes have been and will be made. It is thus that we are to learn. Shall we, in coward skepticism, overlook our immense advantages to hang our fears upon a few faults, or prognosticate the failure of a system which has accomplished so much, because it shares with others the imperfections of humanity? Is there a sober-minded man among us, who would be willing to encounter the oppressions of what are called strong governments, that he might escape from under our present system. Our faults are our own, and our misfortunes are consequences of our faults; but our political advantages are God's rich gifts, which it becomes us thankfully to receive and piously improve. All our evils have their legitimate remedies, and there is no danger which may not be avoided by a wise care. Instead, therefore, of querulous fears and ungrateful discontent, the Christian patriot should zealously inquire what he can do to secure and advance the best welfare of our beloved land. Our holy text is full of instruction to this end.

The psalmist is describing the policy of God with Israel, the people whom he wished to know no king but himself, and therefore, the only safe policy for any people who would preserve their liberties from the encroachment of despotic rule.

"He established a testimony in Jacob, and appointed a law in Israel, which he commanded our fathers that they should make them known to their children; that the generation to come might know them, even the children which should be born; who should arise and declare them to their children, that they might set their hopes in God, and not forget the works of God, but keep his commandments."

We see here,

FIRST: THE CHARACTER OF A SAFE AND HAPPY PEOPLE.

"They set their hopes in God; they forget not the works of God; they keep his commandments."

SECONDLY: THE MEANS WHICH GOD HAS APPOINTED FOR CULTIVATING THIS CHARACTER.

"He established a law in Jacob, and appointed a testimony in Israel."

THIRDLY: THE OBLIGATION UPON A CHRISTIAN PATRIOT ARISING FROM THIS PROVIDENCE OF JEHOVAH.

"He commanded our fathers that they should make them known to their children; that the generation to come might know them, even the children which might be born; who should arise and declare them to their children."

FIRST: THE CHARACTER OF A SAFE AND HAPPY PEOPLE.

They "set their hopes in God." The man who looks to God as the source of his welfare, is lifted above temptation within and without. Conscious of a holy, heart-searching eye, upon him, his virtue will not be an outward semblance, cloaking from human sight, secret crime or selfish purposes. The opinions, fashions, or rewards of the world, will neither shape his principles nor modify his practice. He will fear to do evil, lest he should offend against God. He will do justice and love mercy, because he walks humbly with God.

His expectations of eternity will guard and sustain him in honesty. He knows himself to be immortal and God eternal; that vice, which no human scrutiny can detect and no human laws can punish, will meet a terrible vengeance, while good acts and purposes will be rewarded openly by Him, who seeth in secret, at the judgment day. The pains of virtue and the pleasures of vice, being alike transitory, are of little account in his estimation, who sets his hope in God, his Saviour, and his judge. He relies upon God, because He is merciful, and knows that he is safe, because God is Almighty.

Were our nation composed of such believers, how untroubled would be our peace! how entire our mutual confidence! how free our affairs from intrigue, corruption and wrong! The key would never be turned in the lock, the gibbet seen no more, and the prison doors stand open. No man would fear, but every man would love his neighbour, and the true interests of all be acknowledged by each as his own.

They "forget not the works of God." When God is the treasury of a man's hopes, he loves to trace the workings of God's wisdom and power, that he may know the sources upon which he can draw. He considers creation, and in its minuteness as well as its vastness, he reads certain proof of the same Power which made, ruling so perfectly, that nothing is overlooked, and so absolutely, that nothing is beyond his presiding will. He considers redemption, that God so loved the world as to give his only begotten Son as the deliverer of all who believe upon his name, and that all power is in the hands of our Elder Brother, the incarnate God. Therefore is he sure, that God rules in mercy as well as justice, that he will listen to the prayer of his people, and that, however mysterious his methods, all things are working together by the Holy Spirit for the universal triumph of truth, and righteousness, and peace.

With such convictions, how cheering to him must be the study of Providence! With what confidence, remembering the faithfulness of God in the past, will he confide in him amidst the difficulties of the present, and for the developements of the future! and how steadfastly reject for himself and for his country, any policy which crosses the unchangeable laws of God, the everliving Lord!

How strong would this nation be in hope and virtue, did our people thus remember the works of God! For never, since the world began, has the providence of God been more remarkable, kind, and instructive, than towards us. Jehovah did not lead Israel forth from Egypt to the inheritance of Canaan with a more mighty hand or manifest care, than has been seen in our history since the first prayer of the pilgrim from the tyrrany of the old world to this better country, rose through its virgin forests, until our present day of unexampled prosperity.

They " keep his commandments." The believer's obedience to the directions of God is the necessary result of such trust and study. Gratitude will make him loyal to a sovereign so kind and faithful: a sense of his own weakness and short-sightedness will incline him to follow landmarks so certain, and the approbation of an honest conscience reward and incite him to persevere.

" Happy is the people that are in such a case! Yea, happy is that people whose God is the Lord!"

SECONDLY: THE MEANS WHICH GOD HAS APPOINTED FOR CULTIVATING SUCH A CHARACTER.

" He established a testimony in Jacob, and appointed a law in Israel:" or as an admirable critic translates it, "He established an oracle in Jacob, and deposited a revelation with Israel."

The Psalmist, doubtless, here refers not only to the law given on the Mount, in which God defined human duties and prescribed religious worship, but to all the communications which he had made or might yet make to man.

The value of the word of God is seen in the fact, that it is the word of God. What almighty mercy and wisdom saw fit to reveal, must be of the last importance. We are sure of nothing but that which God has made known. Never could we have discovered his will concerning us, or known how to walk in safety, had he not said, "This is the way." Never could we have been assured of a Providence over us, or looked within the tremendous realities of eternity, had not he manifested himself by his own declarations, and brought immortality to light by Jesus Christ, the man whom he has ordained as saviour and judge. Without the word of God, we should be without God, ignorant, hopeless, lost in perplexity, the sport of conjecture, of passion, appetite, and dread. Truth would have no definition, oaths no confirmation, laws no sanction, and the grave no promise; the past would teach us nothing but our ruin, and the future would be black with despair. When we have that word, how glorious is the reverse to the pious believer! We stand by the side of God when he laid the foundation of the earth, and we look beyond the catastrophe of created things to the fixed results of justice and love. We trace back our lineage to a brotherhood with every human soul; and we learn the will of our common father concerning the relations which bind us to him and his family on earth. We see the path of righteousness marked for our feet, and one walking by our side, "whose form is like to that of the Son of God," sustaining our weakness and assuring our faithful obedience of eternal reward, after the shadows and the labours of time shall have passed away and ceased for ever. Nay, in the rest of the Sabbath, the worship of the sanctuary, the communion of saints, and the witnessing sacraments, we have the foretaste, sign, and confirmation of an eternal rest, love, and satisfaction in the house of God, eternal and undefiled.

Need I ask you to consider the blessedness, here and hereafter, of a nation who know and obey that word, and who cultivate and delight in that worship! Where is the suicidal, traitor hand, that would dare pluck this cornerstone from the foundation of our hopes, and, extinguishing the light which heaven has kindled, give our country back to the gloom, the licentiousness, and cruelties of those nations which have forgotten God!

THIRDLY: THE OBLIGATIONS UPON THE CHRISTIAN PATRIOT ARISING FROM THIS PROVIDENCE OF GOD.

"He commanded our fathers to make them known to their children; that the generation to come might know them, even the children which should be born, who should arise and declare them unto their children."

The first duty laid upon us is, to study and practise the word of God ourselves. It is by the light of Christian example, that the saving power of the gospel is made manifest to the world. The believer of the word of God, therefore, owes a profession and practice of Christiainty not only to God, to himself, and the church, but to his country, because its welfare can be secured only by religion.

Then, it is our duty, to the utmost of our means, to give the advantage of the same religion to those who neglect, or cannot, of themselves, obtain the means of grace, especially in the new settlements of that immense valley, the power of which already overbalances the older states. Wherever a fellow citizen is without the knowledge of God, there is an element of danger mingling with the aggregate of the national will. We can never control crime, nor refute error, but by truth; and in withholding the truth of God, we consent to all the mischief that may be done by those, to whom we might teach the right, but do not.

But, especially, are we to strive that the Bible should be in the hands, and by the blessing of God upon our labours, in the hearts of the rising generation. Upon their shoulders the burthens of society, our country, and the cause of God, are soon to rest. From them their children are to learn good or evil. Neglect a child, and you have neglected the man, the woman, the father, the mother, generations yet unborn. The truth of God in our hands belongs to them, as much as to ourselves. It is deposited with us for their benefit. By omitting to give it, we rob them of God's best gift, and our land, in future years, of its best defence and glory. The means of education, so far as the arts of reading and writing go, are not enough. Educate with all your energies. Do nothing that may by any possibility interfere with, and everything to increase such instruction; but let us be ever ready to set the Bible before the opened eye and the craving mind. Better that a child should learn to read without the Bible, than to know not how to read the Bible. Thank God! Christians need not contend for debateable ground in this matter. With our Bible, and Tract, and Sunday School Societies, if we be only faithful in supporting them, we are more than a match, by God's help, for all the infidelity and superstition among us. We lose time and waste our strength, by petty squabblings with evil on its own dunghill. Let us rather devote all our power and zeal to those ready and open methods of disseminating truth, which no force in this land can forbid us to use. When the true church of God consecrates the talents she has from Him, to the spread of the gospel through our country, every wall that the enmity or idolatry of men can build against it shall fall like those of Jericho at the trumpeting of the Levites; when she walks forth, the light of her presence shall dissipate every shadow, and, "terrible as an army with banners," her peaceful triumphs will crown our whole people with the glory of the Lord, a joy and a defence.

Blessed be God, there are those who have felt the necessity of these religious efforts for the good of our country, and the immortal well-being of our countrymen. They are, indeed, but too few, and their zeal has not always been equal to their opportunities and responsibility.

Yet in them, their examples of Christian conduct, their testimony to the power of religion, and their benevolent labours for the illumination of the ignorant, we see the providence of God blessing our nation with moral life, and confirming our government, founded upon the will of the people, by the only sufficient buttresses, knowledge, virtue, and the fear of God. The faithful Christian is the only faithful patriot, and he is not a faithful Christian who serves not his country in the name of Christ, and in the spirit of his gospel.

These thoughts, as you know, have been suggested by

the recent anniversary of our national independence, a day which should be dear and sacred to us all, thongh often miserably polluted by intemperance, and profaned by party assemblages. Surely we might devote one day of the year to the charities of patriotic brotherhood, and lose all minor distinctions in our common citizenship; nor should we forget before the altar of our father's God, the Author of all mercies, his mighty doings for us in the past; the good, the great, the wise, the valiant, whom he has raised up to serve, guide, and defend us; and the blessing which he has caused to rest upon their counsels, their arms, their zeal, and their sacrifices. Such recollections are due to Him, to our country, and to humanity. Children should hear the story, and the best genius contribute to its illustration. Fresh laurels should be plucked and wreathed upon the graves of the beloved for their country's sake, and eloquence pay its richest tribute to their heaven-sent worth, that the living may hear and follow their example.

While I thus speak, the spell of a great name comes upon our hearts, compelling us to utter their thoughts and emotions. When the sun of that morning rose, it gilded the fresh tomb of one whose ear, for the first time since the 4th of July, 1776, failed to vibrate with the thunderings of his country's birth-day joy; and a voice, for the first time, answered not its cheers, which, since its boyish shout was heard through the Revolutionary strife, had never been wanting in the annual conclamation. The iron will, whose upright strength never quivered amidst the lightning storms that crashed around it in battle or controversy; the adamantine judgment, against which adverse opinions dashed themselves to break into scattered foam; the far-reaching faith, that flashed light upon dangers hidden from the prudence of all beside; the earnest affection, that yearned in a child's simplicity, the purpose of a sage, a parent's tenderness, and the humble fidelity of a sworn servant over the people who gave it rule and elevation, have ceased among us: Andrew Jackson is with God. He, who confessed no authority on earth but the welfare of his country and his own convictions of right;

who never turned to rest while a duty remained to be done, and who never asked the support of any human arm in his hour of utmost difficulty; bowed his head meekly to the command of the Highest, and walked calmly down into the grave, leaning upon the strength of Jesus; paused on the threshold of immortality to forgive his enemies, to pray for our liberties, to bless his weeping household, and to leave the testimony of his trust in the gospel of the Crucified; and then, at the fall of a Sabbath evening, passed into the rest which is eternal. His last enemy to be destroyed was death. Thanks be to God, who gave him the victory through our Lord Jesus Christ!

To say that he had faults, is to say that he was human; the errors of a mind so energetic, in a career so eventful, must have been striking; nor could a character be subjected to censure more merciless, than he provoked by a policy original and unhesitating, at open war with long-established usages, and dogmas that had grown into unquestioned axioms. Bereft in his early youth of parental guidance and restraint, educated in the camp and the forest bivouac, and forced to push his own fortunes through the rough trials of a border life, we can scarcely wonder that, until age had schooled his spirit and tempered his blood, he was impetuous, sensitive to insult, and prone to use the strong hand. Warm in his attachments, he was slow to discover frailty in those he loved, or to accord confidence where once he had doubted. Grasping, by his untutored genius, conclusions which other men reach by philosophical detail, he made, while sure of just ends, some mistakes in his methods, for the time disastrous. Called to act at a crisis when the good and evil in our national growth had become vigorous enough for conflict, and wealth and labour, like the twins of Rebecca, were struggling for the right of the elder born, his decisions in great but sudden emergencies were denounced by that after criticism, which can look back to condemn, but is blind to lead. Compelled to resolve stupendous, unprecedented questions of government and political economy, he roused the hostility of opposite schools in those difficult sciences. Never shrinking from any responsibility, personal or official, he sternly fulfilled his interpretations of duty, as a co-ordinate branch of the national legislature, leaving his course to the verdict of his constituents; nor did he hesitate to avail himself of all the means he could extract from the letter of the constitution, to achieve what he thought was the intent of its spirit. His was a stern, prompt, and energetic surgery, and though the body politic writhed under the operation, none can tell, though some may conjecture, the more fatal consequences his severity averted. If he were wrong, public opinion has since adopted the chief of his heresies, and there is no hand strong enough or daring enough to lay one stone upon another of that which he threw down into ruins. But in all this, his heart was with the people, his faith firm in the sufficiency of free principles; and regardless alike of deprecating friends and denouncing opponents, he held on throughout to one only purpose, the permanent good of the whole, unchecked by particular privileges, and unfettered by artificial restrictions. To use his own lofty language, "In vain did he bear upon his person enduring memorials of that contest in which American liberty was purchased; * * * in vain did he since peril property, fame, and life, in defence of the rights and privileges so dearly bought, if any doubts can be entertained of the purity of his purposes and motives. * *

Nor could he have found an inducement to commence a career of ambition, when gray hairs and a decaying frame, instead of inviting to toil and battle, called him to contemplate other worlds, where conquerors cease to be honoured, and usurpers expatiate their crimes."

But though there are passages in his life, about which the most honest have held, and may yet hold, contrary opinions, there are services of his demanding the gratitude of all, and virtues all must delight to honour. Can we forget that victory, in which his ready strategy and consummate skill turned back, by the valour of scarcely disciplined men, the superior numbers and veteran determination of a foreign foe from the spoil and dishonour of a rich and populous territory? or the entire success, with which he delivered from the scalping-knife and torture of wily and ferocious savages, the Florida settlements, an achievement, which in subsequent trials far less arduous, no other leader has been able to imitate? Or the triumph of simple firmness over diplomatic, procrastinating subtleties, when, planting his foot upon what was clearly right, in a determination to suffer nothing that was clearly wrong, he swung round a mighty European empire to pay its long-withheld indemnity for injuries done to American commerce? And in that darkest hour of our country's history, when a narrow sectionalism counterfeited the colour of patriotic zeal, and discord shook her gorgon locks, and men shuddered as they saw, yawning wide in the midst of our confederacy, a gulf which threatened to demand the devotion of many a life before it would close again, how sublimely did he proclaim over the land that doctrine sacred as the name of Washington, *The Union must be preserved!* and the storm died away with impotent mutterings. Nor is his glory in this the less, that he shared it with another, and that other, one whose name the applauses of his countrymen have taught the mountains and the valleys to echo down for far generations, as the gallant, the frank, the brilliant statesman, to whose fame the highest office could add no decoration, nor disappointment rob of just claims to the people's love. It was a lofty spectacle, full of rebuke to party jealousy and of instruction to their countrymen, when Henry Clay offered the compromise of his darling theory, and Andrew Jackson endorsed the new bond that made the Union again, and, as we trust, indissolubly firm.

Remarkable as the contrast is, there were traits in the temper of the indomitable old man, tender, simple, and touching. With what faithful affection he honoured her while living, whose dear dust made the hope of his last resting-place more sweet, that he might sleep again at her side! And, if his heart seemed sometimes steeled against the weakness of mercy, when crime was to be punished, or mutiny controlled, or danger annihilated; he could also stoop in his career of bloody conquest, to take a wailing, new-made orphan to his pitying heart; with the same hand, that had just struck down invading foes, he steadied the judgment-seat shaken with the tremors of him who sat upon it, to pronounce sentence against him for law violated in martial necessity; and at the height of authority, the poor man found him a brother and a friend.

But, O how surpassingly beautiful was his closing scene, when, as the glories of his earthly honour were fading in the brightness of his eternal anticipations, and his head humbly rested upon the bosom of Him who was crucified for our sins, his latest breath departed in the praises of that religion which had become his only boast, and in earnest counsel that all who loved him might obtain the like faith, and meet him in heaven! There was no doubt in his death; he had prepared to meet his God; and when his giant heart fainted, and his iron frame failed, God was the strength of his heart, and his portion for ever. Little would all his achievements have won for him, had he gained the whole world, yet lost his soul; but now his fame will survive until time shall be no more, and his spirit is immortal among the redeemed. The angels bore him from us, no longer the hero, the statesman, the guide of millions, and the master mind of his country; but a sinner saved by grace, to the feet of the Lamb that was slain, a little child of God to the bosom of his Father. My hearers, have you been his friends? Obey his parting counsel, and by faith in Jesus, follow him to heaven, whom you have delighted to follow on earth. Have you been in opposition to his life? Refuse not the profit of his death, but find in that blood, which cleansed him from all his sins, atonement for your own. O that his last testimony had the same power over men's souls, as his cheer in battle, and his proclamations of political doctrine! Then would he shine bright among the brightest in the constellation of those who turn many to righteousness.

My brethren, I have spoken much longer than I meant to have done, but you would not have withheld from me the privilege. If I have dwelt upon the best traits in the notable character of one, who has not been suffered to escape the earnest crimination of many, it has been because he is dead. You, who listened to me with so much candour, when I paid, four years since, an humble tribute to the merits of him who reached the height of authority to sink into a grave watered by a nation's tears, will not condemn my utterance of similar emotions now. The jackal hate, that howls over the lifeless body, is far removed from your Christian charity and generous judgment.

> "Vile is the vengeance on the ashes cold,
> And envy base to bark at sleeping mould."

Let us rather pray as Christians, that the memory of good deeds may live, and the example of a Christian's death be sanctified. Let us, as Christian patriots, take new courage in setting forth, by word and practice, the paramount virtue of the religion we profess, to save our country, as it saves the soul; and, while we mourn the conflicts of evil passion, not forget the actual good which, by the Divine favour, is working out health from the mysterious fermentation.

There is, notwithstanding occasional agitation, a calm good sense among our people, sufficient to recover and maintain the equilibrium. It is not seen blustering around the polls; it is not heard vociferating and applauding in party meetings; nor, unhappily, does it often appear on the arena, where misnomered statesmen struggle rather for personal advancement than their country's good; but it lives with those, who, in honest toil, are too independent to be bought, or, in honest competence, too content to desire the doubtful distinctions of popular favor. It is nurtured by the lessons of holy religion. It is breathed in the prayer of God's true worshippers. It deliberates around the domestic hearth, where the father thinks of the posterity who are to live after him; in the philosophic retirement of the man of letters; in the workshop where the freeman feels proud of his sweat; and in the cultured field, from which the farmer knows that his bread is sure by the bounty of heaven. It is felt in the practice of common duties, the example of daily virtues, and the results of observant experience. It is like oil on the waves of noisy strife. The man in power trembles as he hears its still small voice; the secret conspirator finds its clear eye upon him, and quails beneath the searching scrutiny; and, like the angel of Israel, it meets the demagogue on his way to curse the land which God has blest, and, if he be not turned back, it alarms and forewarns the beast on which he rides.

It may be said, that the party of the honest and intelligent is small, far smaller than, with my respect for my country, I believe it to be; but, if it be, it has still the controlling voice from the divisions of the rest. Each disastrous experiment teaches them new prudence, each well-sustained trial new courage. They have not looked for immediate perfection, and, therefore, are willing yet to learn. They are the men who hold the country together, and their influence is the salt which saves the mass from utter corruption. I look upward above the dust which is raised by scuffling partisans, to the throne of our fathers' God; I look backward on all the threatening events through which he has brought us; and I can commit my country to the care of Him who "maketh even the wrath of man to praise him," and believe that it is safe. Under providence, I rely with an unshaken faith on the intelligent will of the American people. If my faith be a delusion, may it go with me to my grave. When its warrant proves false, I could pray God, if it be his will, to let me die; for the brightest hope that ever dawned on political freedom shall have been lost in darkness, the fairest column ever reared by the hands of men cast down, and the beacon light of the world gone out.

My hearers, we must soon appear before God to answer for all our conduct here. Then, what will avail all our busy, anxious, most successful pursuit of this world, if, through neglect of a timely faith and repentance, we are lost for ever? Let me entreat you, therefore, to seek first the kingdom of God and his righteousness, that the Holy Spirit may be your guide, Christ your intercessor, and the Father receive you among the children of his love. Until we have obtained this grace for ourselves, we shall seek in vain to do any real good; there is no promise of an answer to our prayers, or of a blessing upon our zeal.

We cannot be faithful to others, while we remain unfaithful to God and our own souls. May the voice of Providence, confirming the testimony of the Scriptures, prevail with us all to prepare for eternity, that in our wise preparation, we may secure our own best happiness, by rendering the best service to God, our country, and our race! Amen.

THE END.

A Controversial Leader and Visionary Man of God!

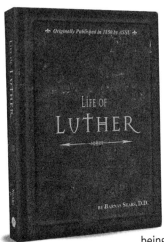

Martin Luther is one of early Christianity's most pivotal figures, and now in this detailed biography reproduced from an 1850 American Sunday School Union original, you can learn more about this influential and enigmatic man. From his early years, to his religious education, to the events leading up to the Protestant Reformation, you will discover the views and experiences that led to his excommunication by the Pope in 1520. The book recounts detailed correspondence and accounts that shed further light on Luther's dispute with the Catholic Church over indulgences being purchased to avoid punishment from sin and why he chose to defiantly translate the Bible from Latin to the language of the common man so they could read the biblical truth for themselves.

The book is a comprehensive presentation of Martin Luther's life and contributions to the faith that impact our lives even today. Often controversial, sometimes visionary, and defiantly confident of his actions, *the Life of Luther* is a fascinating and important historical account you won't want to miss!

5 x 7 • 496 pages • Case Bound
Retail: $17.99
ISBN 13: 978-0-89051-599-0

Available where fine books are sold or go to www.nlpg.com.

The Faith of Our First Founding Father!

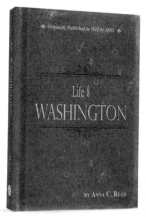

As modern revisionists seek to minimize or erase all traces of America's Christian heritage, a very rare vintage biography sheds a remarkable light of truth on the life of our first president, George Washington!

Originally published by the American Sunday School Union (ASSU), *The Life of Washington* is a fascinating read.

Anna C. Reed, the niece of a signer of the Declaration of Independence, authored this amazing work for ASSU prior to 1850. Originally translated into over 20 languages within a few years, the book was among the most widely-read biographies of Washington at the time.

For over two hundred years, the American Sunday School Union provided quality books and Christian education titles for young people through their missions to start Sunday School programs, and eventually began church planting, church camps, and numerous other programs. ASSU missionaries carried books in saddlebags to leave with these fledgling schools, promoting literacy, education, and the very best in Christan moral values.

5 x 7 • 290 pages • Case Bound
Retail: $16.99
ISBN 13: 978-0-89051-578-5

Available where fine books are sold or go to www.nlpg.com.

The Protestant Reformation's Fiercest Defender!

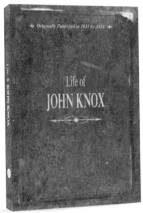

Forced to flee his enemies on many occasions, John Knox (c. 1505-1572) had a life of exciting adventure, harsh imprisonment, and brilliant scholarship. Fighting battles both political and religious, Knox bravely defied royalty, nobility, and the established power of the Papacy to speak the truth. A fiery and inspirational preacher, he fiercely upheld the authority of Scripture and salvation through Christ's sacrifice. In perilous times, Knox risked his life daily in a fearless and tireless defense of the faith!

In this fine reproduction of the 1833 original about John Knox, discover rare vignettes featuring the Protestant Reformation's fiercest defender.

5 x 7 • 144 pages • Case Bound
Retail: $14.99
Release Date: February 2011
ISBN 13: 978-0-89051-602-7

Available where fine books are sold or go to www.nlpg.com.